The Investment Industry for
IT Practitioners

The Securities & Investment Institute

Mission Statement:

> *To set standards of professional excellence and integrity for the investment and securities industry, providing qualifications and promoting the highest level of competence to our members, other individuals and firms.*

The Securities and Investment Institute is the UK's leading professional and membership body for practitioners in the securities and investment industry, with more than 21 000 members with an increasing number working outside the UK. It is also the major examining body for the industry, with a full range of qualifications aimed at people entering and working in it. More than 40 000 examinations are taken annually in more than 30 countries.

You can contact us through our website *www.sii.org.uk*

Our membership believes that keeping up to date is central to professional development. We are delighted to endorse the Wiley/SII publishing partnership and recommend this series of books to our members and all those who work in the industry.

As part of the SII CPD Scheme, reading relevant financial publications earns members of the Securities & Investment Institute the appropriate number of CPD hours under the Self-Directed learning category. For further information, please visit *www.sii.org.uk/cpdscheme*

Ruth Martin
Managing Director

The Investment Industry for IT Practitioners

An Introductory Guide

Andrew Bradford

John Wiley & Sons, Ltd

Copyright © 2008 Andrew Bradford

Published by   John Wiley & Sons Ltd, The Atrium, Southern Gate, Chichester,
West Sussex PO19 8SQ, England

Telephone   (+44) 1243 779777

Email (for orders and customer service enquiries): cs-books@wiley.co.uk
Visit our Home Page on www.wiley.com

Other Wiley Editorial Offices

John Wiley & Sons Inc., 111 River Street, Hoboken, NJ 07030, USA

Jossey-Bass, 989 Market Street, San Francisco, CA 94103-1741, USA

Wiley-VCH Verlag GmbH, Boschstr. 12, D-69469 Weinheim, Germany

John Wiley & Sons Australia Ltd, 42 McDougall Street, Milton, Queensland 4064, Australia

John Wiley & Sons (Asia) Pte Ltd, 2 Clementi Loop #02-01, Jin Xing Distripark, Singapore 129809

John Wiley & Sons Canada Ltd, 6045 Freemont Blvd, Mississauga, ONT, L5R 4J3, Canada

Wiley also publishes its books in a variety of electronic formats. Some content that appears in print may not be
available in electronic books.

Library of Congress Cataloging-in-Publication Data

Bradford, Andrew.
The investment industry for IT practitioners: an introductory guide / Andrew Bradford.
      p.   cm.   – (Financial services operations)
   Includes bibliographical references and index.
   ISBN 978-0-470-99780-2 (cloth)
  1. Financial services industry–Information technology.   2. Investments–Data processing.
   3. Investment analysis–Data processing.   4. Business–Data processing.
   5. Information technology–Management.   I. Title.   II. Title: Guide to the investment
     industry for IT practitioners.
   HG173.B673 2008
   332.6–dc22   2008031719

British Library Cataloguing in Publication Data

A catalogue record for this book is available from the British Library

ISBN 978-0-470-99780-2 (H/B)

Typeset in 10/12pt Times by Aptara Inc., New Delhi, India
Printed and bound in Great Britain by CPI Antony Rowe, Chippenham, Wiltshire

To Marilyn, Victoria and Charlotte

Contents

Introduction

A high proportion of information technology graduates find themselves working for investment firms such as investment banks, fund managers, custodians and wealth managers. In their new jobs they very often feel overwhelmed by the complexity of what it is that their new employers are trying to do; the jargon that is used and the complexity of the application configurations that are involved in processing the transactions.

This book is aimed at information technologists who are employed in the investment industry in roles such as developers, business analysts and quality assurance analysts.

The book fulfils two functions. Part One provides the reader with an understanding of the financial instruments and transactions that their employer is concerned with. It introduces the concept of straight-through-processing (STP), explains the lifecycle of the common transactions in the relevant instruments and also deals with the events and actions that are the consequences of holding positions in the instruments concerned. It does not deal in detail with the valuation and analytical tools that are required to value and price complex instruments and transactions, as these topics are well covered by a number of other publications.

The instruments and transaction types that are included in the book's scope are equities, debt instruments (including fixed rate bonds and floating rate notes), currencies (including money market loans and deposits and foreign exchange), listed futures and options, OTC derivatives such as swaps and hybrid transactions (including stock lending and repo transactions).

Because many financial institutions – including those with little or no historical connection with Islamic countries – now trade Sharia compliant products such as Sukuks, the book also provides an introduction to these instruments.

This book also explains how investment firms are regulated and the impact of financial regulation on the business applications that are used to process transactions and manage positions; as well as outlining the financial accounting requirements of investment firms.

As each of the above topics is explained, the book goes on to examine the necessary content of the business applications. It explains what static data these applications need to hold and why; what messages they need to send and receive and why; and what accounting entries they need to pass for both cash and stock for each of the instruments within the book's scope.

There are many different kinds of "players" in the financial markets, including investment banks, institutional fund managers, private client fund managers and stockbrokers, money brokers, custodians and investment exchanges to name but a few. The IT infrastructures of each type of market player are different. This book is written from the perspective of a bank or broker that processes trades in and holds positions in all the instruments and transaction types that are within the book's scope.

Chapter by Chapter, Part One is structured as follows.

Chapters 1 to 5 introduce the reader to five classes of financial instrument that are used as investments – equities, debt instruments, cash, listed derivatives and OTC derivatives. It explains the basic characteristics of each instrument, and introduces the reader to the basic calculations involved in trades in these instruments. Chapter 6 then summarises the common elements of all these different instruments.

Chapter 7 describes the roles of the various types of companies that operate in the investment industry, including investment banks, fund managers, hedge funds, investment exchanges, clearing houses, custodians, central securities depositaries and private client stockbrokers, and examines how these firms interact with each other when the various financial instruments are bought or sold, or borrowed and lent.

Chapter 8 describes how investment firms are regulated, with particular emphasis on the UK and the European Economic Area.

Chapter 9 introduces the reader to the concept of straight-through-processing, and Chapter 10 examines the importance of accurate static data to achieve this goal.

Chapter 11 examines how messages are exchanged between the different types of market practitioners in the process of placing orders, executing them, agreeing that the resulting trades are correct and then settling the trades. This chapter covers all the instruments described in Chapters 1 to 6. It also describes the role of SWIFT and the FIX Protocol in standardising and carrying messages between different companies that are active in investment.

Chapter 12 describes the processes of trade agreement and the contents of settlement instruction messages for all the instruments that were covered in Chapters 1 to 5; and Chapter 13 examines the consequences of failed or late settlement of transactions.

Chapter 14 examines the concepts involved in investment accounting and book-keeping, both for cash amounts and the business content requirements of the general ledger applications; while Chapter 15 examines the function and business content of the stock record application, which fulfils the same function for security quantity book-keeping.

Chapters 16 to 20 provide example STP flows from the order being placed through to the trade being executed, confirmed and settled for each of the instruments that were described in Chapters 1 to 5.

Chapter 21 examines securities lending and borrowing and repo transactions and the business content requirements of applications that are used to process these transactions.

Chapter 22 examines the impact of the growing market for financial instruments that meet the requirements of Sharia law, and how these Sharia compliant instruments and transactions differ from the standard instruments and transactions that were described in earlier chapters.

Chapter 23 examines the activities involved in and the business application content requirements for the management of an investment portfolio, including dividend, coupon and corporate actions processing, marking to market, accrual of interest and reconciliation.

Chapter 24 outlines how risk is measured and managed in an investment firm and the business applications that are involved in the process.

Part Two of the book looks at the role of the information technology department of the investment firm. The activities covered in Part Two are common to all types of organisations, not just investment industry firms.

Chapter 25 examines how the IT department manages day-to-day activities such as application support, helpdesk management, data retention requirements, change control procedures and business continuity planning.

Chapter 26 examines how the department manages change. It looks at software development lifecycles, project management standards, requirement gathering techniques and application testing strategies and techniques.

Chapter 27 examines the processes of software vendor and package selection, and outsourcing and offshoring of activities.

HOW TO USE THIS BOOK

I have attempted to gradually build up the reader's knowledge of instruments, transactions and events within transactions as the book progresses. As a consequence, the later chapters of Part One often make reference to points covered in earlier chapters, and there are also forward references within the earlier chapters. I therefore recommend reading the book chapter by chapter, rather than reading individual chapters in isolation.

Words and terms that are included in the Glossary of Terms are highlighted in bold the first time that they appear in the text.

I have made every effort to avoid errors in the text, but any that remain are my responsibility and I apologise for them. I would welcome opportunities to correct errors in any future editions, and would appreciate being informed of them by email to acbradford@btinternet.com.

Acknowledgements

I would like to thank the following individuals who have assisted with this book:

Andy Mead of National Grid plc
Ashley Rayfield of Cable and Wireless plc
David Flinders and Marcus Dutton of City Networks Limited
John Silver of Atlassian Software Systems Pty Limited
Kim Arnold and Christian Galligher of Omgeo llc
Jenny McCall, Viv Wickham and Hana Bellova of John Wiley, and Elaine Andrews for her helpful comments on the first draft of this book.

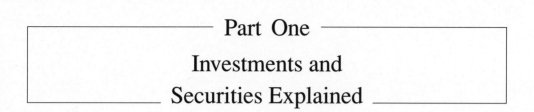

Part One

Investments and
Securities Explained

1
An Introduction to Financial Instruments

1.1 INTRODUCTION

The investment industry exists to serve its customers. There are two main groups of customers – investors and security issuers. Investors may be private individuals, charities, companies, banks, collective investment schemes such as pension funds and insurance funds, central and local governments or "supranational institutions" such as the World Bank.

Investors in turn have investment objectives, which may be to increase wealth (capital growth) or to provide income. Some investors will have only one of these objectives, some will have both. For example, a high earning private individual probably has all the income that he or she needs from employment, and wishes to invest surplus cash to provide capital growth. A charity, however, may need the maximum possible income that it can get from its investments in order to fund its activities.

There are four main classes of financial instrument that investors make use of to achieve either income or capital growth. These are:

- Equities, also known as *stocks* or *shares*
- Debt instruments, also known as *bonds* or *bills*
- Cash
- Derivatives.

Equities and debt instruments are collectively known as **securities**. In order for there to be any securities for the investor to invest in, then some organisation, such as a company, a bank, a government or a supranational institution, has to issue securities. Securities issuers are the other main customer group, and the reason that securities are issued is to provide capital for a business or (if the issuer of the security is a government) to fund government expenditure.

The next four chapters provide the basic details of each instrument type, and Chapter 6 summarises the features that are common to them all.

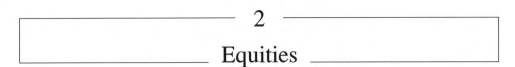

2

Equities

Companies issue equities to provide them with a permanent stock of capital to fund their business activities. The investors in that company are known as shareholders, as each investor holds a share in the ownership of the business. The investor expects to be rewarded in two ways. If the company does well then the market value of each share will increase over time, providing the investor with capital growth. In addition, the investor expects that the company will also provide a source of income in the form of regular **dividends**. Dividends are a way of distributing the profits of the company to its shareholders.

There are no guarantees that the investor will in fact benefit from either capital growth or from dividend income. For example, a young company with an exciting new product which it is bringing to market for the first time may not have any income to distribute yet, but because other investors take a very positive view of its long-term prospects, there may be considerable scope for capital growth. At the other end of the spectrum, an old established company that produces low technology products that do not require lots of investment may have a high income, but very limited prospects for capital growth.

Case study: Amazon.com

Amazon.com was founded in 1994 and issued its shares to the public for the first time in 1997, at US$18.00 per share. It made losses until 2002 when it produced a profit of US$5 million, just 1¢ per share, on revenues of over US$1 billion. In 2006 it made a profit of US$190 million, but it has never distributed any profits to investors in the form of dividends. However, as a result of three **stock splits**[1] in 1999 each investor who purchased one share now owns 12 shares, which at the time of writing in 2007 were trading at US$82.70 each. This means that the original investment of US$18 is now worth US$992, and there has been capital growth of US$974 over 10 years.

A third possibility is that a company continues to make either very low profits or actual losses and investors take a negative view of its long-term prospects. In such a case income distribution in the form of dividends is likely to be very low or non-existent, and the prospects for capital growth are negative. In other words the investors are more likely to lose capital than to increase it.

2.1 LISTED AND UNLISTED EQUITIES

In this book we are concerned with equities that are regularly bought and sold by professional investment firms. Usually, such equities are listed on one or more **stock exchanges**. However,

---

[1] A stock split is a form of **corporate action** where the total number of shares in issue is increased, and the additional shares are given to existing shareholders in proportion to their existing shareholding free of cost.

not all equities are listed on a stock exchange. Private companies are often owned by their founding families and do not have stock exchange listing. Companies that do have their shares listed are known as public companies; and most medium-sized public companies list their shares on a single stock exchange in the country in which they are incorporated.

2.2   MULTI-LISTED SECURITIES

Many large multinational companies, however, list their shares on a number of exchanges in different countries. For example, Sony Corporation shares are listed on the Tokyo Stock Exchange (where Sony shares are priced in Japanese yen), the **London Stock Exchange** (where prices are quoted both in yen and sterling); the New York Stock Exchange (prices quoted in US dollars); and on the Deutsche Borse (prices quoted in euros).

2.3   THE ISSUANCE OF LISTED EQUITIES – THE PRIMARY MARKET

When a company that was previously privately owned lists its shares on a stock exchange, it will almost invariably look to issue additional new shares in order to raise extra capital at the same time. The money paid by investors for the newly issued shares goes directly to the company. The sale of shares by the company for the first time is known as the **primary market** for that company's shares. It is also known as an **initial public offering (IPO)**, or just **public offering**, of those shares.

The IPO introduces the company to a wide pool of stock market investors to provide it with capital for future growth. The existing shareholders will see their shareholdings diluted as a proportion of the company's shares. However, they hope that the capital investment will make their shareholdings more valuable in absolute terms.

In addition, once a company is listed, it will be able to issue further shares to the new and existing shareholders via **rights issues**. Rights issues enable existing shareholders to buy further stock at a discounted price, and also provide the issuer with further capital for expansion. This regular ability to raise large amounts of capital from the general market, rather than having to seek and negotiate with individual investors, is a key incentive for many companies seeking to list their shares.

IPOs generally involve one or more investment banks as "underwriters". The company offering its shares, called the "issuer", enters a contract with a lead underwriter to sell its shares to the public. The underwriter then approaches investors with offers to sell them these new shares.

2.4   THE SECONDARY MARKET IN EQUITIES

Equity capital is permanent; the issuer does not as a rule return it to the investor[2] and therefore there has to be a means by which the investor can realise its capital gain, or sell its holding to prevent further losses. For this reason, stock exchanges provide a marketplace for investors to buy and sell shares in the companies in which they are interested. This marketplace is known as the **secondary market**, to distinguish it from the initial distribution of shares by the company,

---

[2] There are exceptions to this rule; some companies that have surplus capital do engage in share buyback programmes.

which is known as the primary market. The role of investment exchanges is discussed more fully in Chapter 7.

When shares are bought and sold on the secondary market, each purchase and sale is known as a **trade.** When one investor (the seller) sells all or part of a holding to another investor (the buyer), then:

1. The buyer needs to pay the sale proceeds to the seller
2. The seller needs to deliver the equities to the buyer.

The process of organising the exchange of stock and cash is known as **trade settlement**. Settlement can occur on the same day that the trade was done, but more usually occurs a few days after the date of the trade. In most securities markets, settlement normally takes place three business days after the trade date.

2.4.1   Trade prices in the secondary market

The price at which equities are bought and sold in the secondary market depends upon supply and demand, and prices of an individual company's shares fluctuate according to market participants' views as to the prospects of:

- Individual companies
- Industry sectors in which these companies operate
- The economies of the countries in which they operate
- The perceived probability of another company paying a premium to acquire this company.

2.4.2   Secondary market terminology

When equities are traded on the secondary market there are a number of terms used to describe the features of that trade. Table 2.1 examines *some* of these terms before proceeding – others will be introduced later in the book.

On most exchanges, equity prices are quoted as units of currency, e.g. US$10.00 per share. The notable exception to this rule is the London Stock Exchange, where equity prices are more often quoted in pennies than in whole pound units.

2.4.3   Forms of securities

Securities (both equities and debt instruments in this context) may be issued in one of the following forms:

- **Registered securities** are where the name and address of the owner are recorded on a register maintained by a firm is known in some countries as a registrar and in others as a **transfer agent**. The register contains the holder's name, address, quantity of shares or bonds owned, and the dates on which they were acquired. Registered shares may, in turn, exist in one or other of the following forms:
  - Certificated form – the evidence of ownership is represented by a **share certificate** which is printed and sent to the holder shortly after purchase. If the holder wishes to sell some or all of its holding, then it has to deliver the certificates as part of the settlement process.
  - **Dematerialised** form – no certificates are issued, the share register itself is the evidence of ownership.

Table 2.1   Equity trade terminology

Term	Explanation
Bid price	This is the price that a professional dealer is prepared to buy a given quantity of the security concerned from an investor
Commission	The amount that an agent will charge the investor for executing the trade
Consideration	Principal value + Commission + Fees
Fees	Any other charges levied on this trade other than commission
Mid price	The average of bid price and offer price
Nominal amount	The quantity of securities being purchased or sold
Offer price	This is the price that a professional dealer is prepared to sell a given quantity of the security concerned to an investor
Principal value	Nominal amount ∗ The price of the trade
Settlement	The process where the buyer pays the proceeds of the trade and receives legal title to the item it has purchased; while the seller receives the proceeds of the trade and has to deliver the item it has sold to the buyer
Trade	When one investor sells some or all of its holding in a financial instrument, or another investor buys a holding in a financial instrument, then the resulting transaction between the two investors is known as a trade. The terms deal and bargain are also often used to describe this activity
Trade date	The date that the two parties agreed to carry out the trade
Trade price	The price of this particular trade
Value date	The date that the seller will deliver the securities to the buyer and the buyer will pay the consideration to the seller. Also the date that the legal ownership of the securities changes from the buyer to the seller

- **Bearer securities** are issued where there is no register or registrar. When the security is first issued on the primary market, the issuer prints certificates representing the entire amount of shares or bonds issued, and these are posted to the investors who have purchased the shares in the primary market. If an investor wishes to sell all or part of its holding then it has to deliver the bearer certificates as part of the settlement process.

Prior to 1990, most securities were issued in either registered certificated form, or in bearer form. However, as securities trading became more global, the need to move large amounts of physical paper around the world whenever bonds or equities were traded in the secondary market became a major obstacle to efficient settlement. Financial regulators encouraged issuers to issue securities in dematerialised form, and investment exchanges set up the necessary market infrastructure to handle the trading and settlement of dematerialised securities.

3

Debt Instruments

Companies, banks, central governments (such as the United Kingdom, Republic of France, etc.); local governments (such as the city of Manchester, province of Quebec, State of California, etc.) and supranational institutions (such as the World Bank, European Union, etc.) also raise cash by issuing debt instruments, also known as bonds and bills.

A debt instrument is effectively an "IOU" – a promise to pay the investor periodic amounts of interest (known as the **coupon**) on a loan and also the promise to return the amount borrowed to the investor at a date in the future. Unlike equities, debt instruments are usually (but not exclusively) issued for a defined period of time, after which they are said to mature. Upon maturity date the amount borrowed is returned to the investors together with the final coupon payment. As with equities, debt instruments are traded on a secondary market so that investors may buy and sell them without the involvement of the issuer.

The main differences between debt and equity finance are as follows:

- Only companies can issue equity shares, as companies can be owned by others. Central and local governments belong to society as a whole; by definition they cannot be owned by others, so when governments need to raise capital they have to use the debt markets.
- Debt instruments provide a predictable, guaranteed form of income – the interest on the bond – which is known as the coupon. The coupon is paid at regular intervals at a guaranteed rate of return; unlike dividends which are dependent upon the fortunes of the company that issued the shares. For this reason, debt instruments are also known as fixed income securities.
- Debt instruments provide very restricted opportunities for capital growth compared with equities.

Like listed equities, bonds are issued on the primary market and may be bought and sold by investors in the secondary market. They are sometimes listed on stock exchanges, but more often they are traded by investment banks outside of the stock exchange, on what is known at the **over-the-counter** market, or OTC market. An investor that wishes to buy or sell a particular bond contacts a number of investment banks to ask them at what price they are willing to buy or sell a given quantity of a given bond. As with equities, secondary market bond prices vary according to supply and demand, and the factors that affect those prices are discussed in section 3.4.

3.1   TYPES OF DEBT INSTRUMENTS

3.1.1   Straight bonds

Straight bonds, also known as "plain vanilla" bonds, are the simplest type of debt instrument, because the amount of the coupon to be paid by the borrower is fixed for the entire life of the bond. Consider the following example:

National Grid plc   EUR 500 million 4.375% fixed rate instruments due 2020

On 10 March 2006 the UK utility National Grid plc issued bonds with a total value of EUR 500 million (the **principal amount** or **face value** of the bond), which pay an annual coupon of 4.375% on 10 March each year (the coupon date), until 10 March 2020 (the **maturity date**) when National Grid will repay the proceeds of the bond to the investors.

When the bond was issued it was sold on the primary market at an issue price of 98.935% of face value to a large number of investors in smaller quantities, who may then sell all or part of their holding on the secondary market in the future.

From the bond issuer's perspective:

1. Because the issue price was 98.935% National Grid therefore raised EUR 494 675 000 – 98.395% of face value.
2. The total cost to National Grid of issuing this bond is therefore EUR 21 875 000 per annum (4.375% of EUR 500 million) each year for 14 years, plus EUR 5 325 000 (the difference between the issue price of 98.935% and the face value).

From the investor's perspective

1. The total annual coupon income that an investor who has purchased bonds with a face value of EUR 1 000 000 is EUR 43 750.
2. In addition, an investor who purchased face value of EUR 1 000 000 bonds on issue date would earn a capital gain of EUR 16 050.00 (the difference between the issue price of 98.935% and the face value).

3.1.2   Floating rate notes (FRNs)

FRNs are more complicated than straight bonds because the amount of the coupon to be paid by the borrower will vary during the life of the bond. Consider the following example:

National Grid plc   EUR 750 million floating rate instruments due 2012

On 18 September 2006 the UK utility National Grid plc issued bonds with a total value of EUR 750 million (the principal amount of the bond), which pay quarterly coupons of EURIBOR + 35 basis points (one basis point is 1/100 of 1%) on 18 January, 18 April, 18 July and 18 October) each year (the coupon dates), until 18 January 2012 (the maturity date) when National Grid will repay the proceeds of the bond to the investors. On the primary market the bond was sold to a large number of investors in smaller quantities at an issue price of 99.853% of face value.

The difference between this bond and the fixed rate bond is that the interest rate that is payable by the borrower, and therefore received by the investor, is not a fixed percentage of the principal amount. Instead, its coupon rate is usually linked to a specified **benchmark interest rate** (in this case EURIBOR, the European InterBank Offered Rate).[1]

---

[1] EURIBOR (Euro Interbank Offered Rate) is the benchmark rate at which Euro Interbank term deposits within the Eurozone are offered by one prime bank to another prime bank. It is one of the two benchmarks for the money and capital markets in the Eurozone (the other one being Eonia). EURIBOR is sponsored by the European Banking Federation (FBE), which represents the interests of

Two working days before the end of each **coupon period** (the interval between the two semi-annual coupon dates) the coupon rate of the bond is reset according to the current value of EURIBOR. For example, if EURIBOR is 5.0% on 16 January then the interest rate for the coupon period starting 18 January will be 5.35%. If six months later the value of LIBOR is 5.5% then the coupon rate of this bond will increase to 5.85%.

From the bond issuer's perspective

Because the bond was sold to investors at an issue price of 99.853% of face value, National Grid raised EUR 748 897 500.00. They will have to repay EUR 750 000.00 in January 2012.

There is less certainty regarding the interest amounts payable or receivable, the annual interest cost will be whatever EURIBOR is at the time +0.35%. FRNs are often issued with guaranteed minimum and/or maximum interest rates. The total cost to National Grid of issuing this bond is the annual coupon payment of EURIBOR +35 basis points each year for six years, plus EUR 1 102 500.00 (the difference between the issue price of 99.835% and the face value of the bond).

From the investor's perspective

Like the issuer, the investor has no certainty as to the value of future coupon payments. An investor who purchased face value 1 000 000 of the bond on the primary market will receive coupon payments of EURIBOR +35 basis points each year for six years, and will earn a capital gain of EUR 1470.00 (the difference between the issue price of 99.853% and face value).

Other features of FRNs

Some FRNs are issued with guaranteed minimum and/or maximum coupon rates. The minimum rate is known as a **floor**, and the maximum rate is known as a **cap**. Where there is both a floor and a cap, then this is known as a **collar**. Some issuers have also issued perpetual floating rate notes which have no maturity date.

3.1.3   Zero coupon bonds

As the name implies, these bonds do not pay a regular coupon to the investors. Instead, the investors purchase the bonds on the primary market at a discount to their face value, and will be rewarded at maturity date when the issuer will repay them with the face value of the bonds. Consider the following example.

British Transco International Finance BV   USD 1500 million zero coupon bond due 2021

On 4 November 1991, British Transco (then an independent company but now a subsidiary of National Grid plc) issued these bonds with a total repayment value at maturity date of USD 1500 million. The bonds do not pay a coupon, instead they were issued at an issue price

---

3000 banks in the 25 member states of the European Union and in Iceland, Norway and Switzerland. Some of the other commonly used benchmark interest rates include LIBOR (London Interbank Offered Rate), TIBOR (Tokyo) and Federal Funds (USA).

of 8.77% of face value, and all the income comes at the maturity date (4 November 2021) when the bonds will be redeemed at 100% of face value.

From the bond issuer's perspective

The total amount paid to the issuer by the investors on 4 November 1991 was USD 131 550 million; and the amount that the issuer has to repay to them on 4 November 2021 (30 years later) is the face value of EUR 1500 million.

The investors of course do not receive any regular income payments in the form of coupons, but the issuer has to put aside the funds to repay them at face value. This amounts to USD 45 615 000 per year calculated as follows:

$$\text{Face value} - \text{Amount received on issue date}/30\,\text{years} = \text{Annual interest cost}$$

i.e.

$$1\,500\,000\,000 - 131\,550\,000/30 = 45\,615\,000$$

As we have already explained, this interest is not paid to the investors until maturity date.

From the investor's perspective

There are no regular coupon payments. All the income comes to the investor at maturity date. An investor that purchased face value 1,000,000 of the bond on issue date would have paid USD 87 700 for it, and will receive USD 1 000 000 on maturity date.

3.1.4   Asset-backed securities

Asset-backed securities are types of bond or notes that are based on pools of assets, or collateralised by the cash flows from a specified pool of underlying assets such as receivables from credit card payments, auto loans, and mortgages, or more esoteric cash flows such as aircraft leases, royalty payments and movie revenues.

Assets are pooled to make otherwise minor and uneconomical investments worthwhile, while also reducing risk by diversifying the underlying assets. Asset backed securities may be issued in the form of straight bonds, floating rate notes or zero coupon bonds.

Securitisation makes these assets available for investment to a broader set of investors. Typically, the securitised assets might be highly **illiquid** and private in nature, and sometimes difficult to value. Difficulty in valuing instruments of this kind led to the difficulties' in the market place in 2007 that have become known as the **credit crunch**.

Case study: The 2007 credit crunch and Northern Rock plc

In 2007, after 15 interest rate rises in 18 months, house prices in the USA began to fall and many homeowners on lower incomes were unable or unwilling to keep up their mortgage repayments. Lenders began to foreclose these mortgages that were in default. Many of these mortgages had been repackaged as asset-backed securities and sold on. Market participants became concerned that a significant number of asset-backed bonds might include **subprime** mortgages, and that there was insufficient information as to which securities issuers and individual instruments might be affected. As a result, trading in such instruments virtually ceased in August 2007, creating what is popularly known as the "credit crunch" but is more technically known as **liquidity risk**. In the UK, the highest profile corporate casualty of the credit crunch was Northern Rock Bank, a mortgage lender that had grown rapidly in the previous 10 years despite having a relatively small retail deposit base. The company had repackaged many of its mortgages in the form of asset-backed securities, and as these matured it could not refinance them. As a result, it was forced to borrow (ultimately) over £20 billion from the Bank of England, acting in its capacity as the lender of last resort. When news of the fact that the central bank had been forced to rescue Northern Rock reached the general public on 13 September, television viewers saw queues of several hundred people outside Northern Rock branches attempting to withdraw their savings. Several attempts were then made to find a commercial buyer to purchase Northern Rock's assets, but these proved unsuccessful. As a result, Northern Rock was nationalised by the UK government in February 2008.

3.1.5   Index linked bonds

An index linked bond is a bond whose interest rate and/or redemption proceeds are linked to an index, such as the Retail Price Index in the United Kingdom. Consider the following example.

National Grid Electricity Transmission plc   GBP 50 million 1.6574% RPI-linked instruments due 2056

On 28 July 2006 the UK utility National Grid plc issued bonds with a total value of GBP 50 million (the principal amount of the bond), which pay semi-annual coupons on 28 January and 28 July each year (the coupon dates), until 28 July 2056 (the maturity date). The issue price of these bonds was 100%, i.e. the issue price was the same as the face value.

The amount of each coupon is 1.6574% of face value plus the amount by which the UK Retail Price Index has changed since the last coupon payment. On maturity date (28 July 2056) National Grid will repay the proceeds of the bond, adjusted for changes in RPI since issue date to the investors. The key feature of these types of bonds is that both the semi-annual coupon payments and the redemption proceeds are adjusted for inflation in the period before the new coupon is fixed.

This means that neither the coupon payments nor the redemption proceeds are easily predictable. Organisations that are contemplating either issuing or investing in such securities need software applications that are capable of modelling a number of inflation predictions. Simplistically, if we assume that UK inflation is consistently 3% per annum for the life of this bond, then the coupon rates will be affected as follows:

• The first coupon payment on 28 January 2007 will be 101.5% of the quoted coupon rate of 1.6574% – i.e. 1.682261%.
• The second coupon payment on 28 July 2007 will be 101.5% of the coupon rate for the previous period (1.682261%) – i.e. 1.707495%.

- Each further semi-annual coupon payment (expressed as a percentage of face value) will increment by 1.5% of the quoted rate (compounded) on each payment date. This means that the final coupon payment will be equivalent to 4.180419% of face value.

Using the same assumption, we can predict the maturity proceeds as GBP 224 926 316.71 – the original amount borrowed plus 3% compounded for 50 years.

From the issuer's perspective

The issuer raised GBP 50 000.00 and needs to repay this amount adjusted for inflation 50 years later. It also needs to pay interest of 1.6754% adjusted for inflation, paid semi-annually.

From the investor's perspective

An investor who purchased GBP 1 000 000 face value will receive this amount, adjusted for inflation on maturity date 50 years later. It will also receive interest of 1.6754% adjusted for inflation, paid semi-annually.

3.1.6   Convertible bonds

A convertible bond is (usually) a straight bond that offers the investor the opportunity to surrender the bond in exchange for equity securities at a fixed price per share. The equity securities are usually issued by the same company that issued the bond. Consider the following example.

Cable and Wireless plc GBP 258 million 4% senior unsecured convertible bonds due 2010 which allow the holder to convert the bonds into Cable and Wireless ordinary shares, 145 pence per share, which represents a 48% premium over the reference price of 98 pence

On 16 July 2003 the UK telecoms company Cable and Wireless plc issued bonds with a total value of GBP 258 million (the principal amount of the bond), which pay semi-annual coupons of 4% on 16 January and 16 July each year (the **coupon date**), until 16 July 2010 (the **maturity date**) when Cable and Wireless will repay the proceeds of the bond to the investors. The bonds were issued at a price of 100%, i.e. at face value.

Alternatively, at any time during the life of the bond the investors can convert the bonds into equities issued by Cable and Wireless at a price of £1.45 per share. Therefore if the investor has bonds with a face value of GBP 10 000 it will be able to exchange these bonds for 6 896.55 shares in Cable and Wireless plc. At the time that these bonds were issued, Cable and Wireless shares were trading at 98 pence per share, so obviously conversion is only worthwhile when and if the price of Cable and Wireless shares has risen to more than £1.45.

This type of bond offers the benefit to the borrower that it can pay a lower coupon rate, and is attractive to an investor who thinks that the price of Cable and Wireless shares is likely to rise during the lifetime of the bond, but in the meantime wants to have the benefit of the coupon income.

From the issuer's perspective

1. If none of the bonds were converted: Cable and Wireless raised GBP 258 000 000 on issue date, and, assuming that no bonds are converted, will need to repay this amount to investors at maturity date. It also needs to pay investors semi-annual coupons of 4%, so its annual interest cost will be GBP 10 320 000.
2. The effect of conversion: Each GBP 1 000 000 face value that is converted reduces the amount to be repaid on maturity date by the same amount, and reduces the annual interest cost to the issuer by GBP 40 000.00.

From the investor's perspective:

1. *If none of the bonds were converted*: This bond is behaving like any other straight bond. Because the bonds were not issued at a discount to face value there is no opportunity for capital growth, but the investor will receive GBP 40 000 in interest each year for every GBP 1 000 000.00 purchased.
2. *The effect of conversion*: If bonds with a face value of GBP 1 000 000 are converted, the investor ceases to receive coupon payments and is not entitled to any repayment at maturity. Instead, it will receive 689,655 shares in Cable and Wireless plc and become entitled to any dividends paid by that company. If the shares are trading at GBP 1.50 each then it might choose to sell them, realising trade proceeds of GBP 1 034 482.50; and thereby making a profit of GBP 34 482.50 on its original investment in the bond.

3.1.7   Bonds with warrants attached

A **warrant** is a security that entitles the holder to buy stock of the company that issued it at a specified price, which is much higher than the stock price at time of issue.

Warrants are much like call **options** (see section 5.1) but the money goes to the issuer, not an option writer, and it initially has a lifespan of many years. When the warrant is exercised the company issues new shares of stock, so the number of outstanding shares increases.

Warrants are frequently attached to bonds as a sweetener, allowing the issuer to pay lower interest rates or dividends. A bond with warrants attached is also known as a **cum-warrant bond**. These warrants are detachable, and can be sold independently of the cum-warrant bond. If they are detached, then in effect the security is split into two new securities:

- The warrants – which can now be traded as an independent security, or exercised in the same way that a call option is exercised
- The underlying bond, known as the **ex-warrant bond**, which can continue to be traded as if it were a straight bond. Naturally the price of the ex-warrant bond will be lower than that of the cum-warrant bond.

3.1.8   Bills

Straight bonds that have an original maturity of less than one year are known as *bills*.

3.2 ACCRUED INTEREST ON BONDS IN THE SECONDARY MARKET

Bond issuers usually pay coupons annually or semi-annually, but sometimes at more frequent intervals. The coupon is paid to the investor that holds the bond on **record date**, which is usually one business day before the coupon date. Even if that investor only bought the bond a few days before record date, it will receive the coupon for the entire coupon period, and the investor that held the bond for the earlier part of the coupon period will receive nothing. For this reason, when bonds are bought and sold on the secondary market, the accrued interest on the bond for the coupon period is also bought and sold at the same time.

Example

The Cable and Wireless 4% convertible bond maturing 16 July 2010 last paid a coupon on 16 January 2008. On **trade date** 5 February 2008, for **value date** 8 February 2008, Investor A sells £100 000 **face value** of this bond to Investor B at a *trade price* of 96% of face value. Assuming that there are no **commissions** or **fees**, then the **consideration** that B has to pay A will be calculated as follows:

Principal amount: £100 000 face value @ trade price 96%	£96 000.00
Accrued interest £100 000 face value $*$ 4% for 23 days	£252.75
Consideration	£96 252.75

In this way Investor A receives the coupon (£252.75) that it is entitled to from Investor B on 8 February 2008. Investor B, in turn, will receive a semi-annual coupon payment of £2000.00 from Cable and Wireless on 16 July 2008.

Investor B had agreed to pay Investor A a trade price of 96% of face value, but because of the affect of accrued interest, it is actually paying a price of 96.25275% of face value. These two prices are known as the **clean price** (96%) and the **dirty price** (96.25275%), respectively. Clean and dirty prices are used in the bond market analytics which are examined in the section 3.4 and in Appendix 1.

There are a number of commonly used methods of calculating the accrued interest on bond trades. The most commonly used methods are:

- *30/360*: There are deemed to be 360 days in a year, and all months are deemed to be 30 days long. This method was used for many straight bonds that were issued before 1 January 1999. For example:

  We sell 100 000 of a bond bearing a 5% coupon for value date 7 April 2008. The bond last paid a coupon on 5 January 2008.
  The calculation of accrued interest is:

$$\text{Accrued interest} = \text{Face value} * t/360 * c$$

where

t = number of calendar days from, and including, the last interest payment date to and including the value date, assuming that each month is 30 days long
c = the annual rate of interest

This is extended as:

$$\text{Accrued interest} = 100\,000 * 92/360 * 5\% = 1277.77777$$

Rounded to two decimal places of the currency this comes to 1277.77.

The 92 days of T are comprised of 25 days in January, 30 days in February and March, and 7 days in April.

- *Actual/360*: There are deemed to be 360 days in a year, and we follow the conventional calendar for determining the days in a month. This method is used for most FRNs – except those denominated in pounds sterling and Japanese yen, which use the next method.
- *Actual/365*: We follow the actual calendar. Although this rule is usually expressed as "over 365", if there are 366 days in a year then 366 is used as the divisor.
- Actual/actual: The number of days in the coupon period – as distinct from the number of days in the year – is used for all calculations.

Nearly all straight and convertible bonds that have been issued since the advent of **Economic and Monetary Union** on 1 January 1999 use the actual/actual method.

The formula for calculating interest using actual/actual is:

$$\text{Accrued interest} = \text{Face value} * t/s * c/n$$

where

t = the actual number of calendar days from, and including, the last interest payment date to and including the value date
s = the actual number of calendar days in the current interest period
c = the annual rate of interest
n = the number of interest payments per annum

In the example of the Cable and Wireless bond above, the formula is therefore extended as

$$\text{Accrued interest} = 100\,000\,23/182 * 4\%/2 = 252.75$$

This formula is modified in the situation where there is an abnormally long or short first coupon period. Such a situation occurs when an issuer issues a bond for an irregular period of, say, 10 years and two months. In such a case the first coupon period (if coupons are to be paid semi-annually) would be for eight months. The modifications are:

- The first coupon period is deemed to start on the date which would have been the normal coupon date on or before the date on which interest starts accruing (i.e. four months before issue date in the example).
- If the date on which interest starts accruing is before the date that would have been the coupon date, then the period shall be split into two quasi interest periods for the purpose of the calculation.

Table 3.1   Additional debt instrument trade terminology

Term	Explanation
Accrued interest	In this context, the amount of interest that a bond purchaser pays a bond seller for the coupon income that the seller is entitled to for the period from the previous coupon date to trade value date
Benchmark rate	A rate such as LIBOR or EURIBOR that is used to determine the coupon rate on a floating rate note
Clean price	The price of a bond trade excluding accrued interest
Dirty price	The price of a bond trade including accrued interest
Coupon date	The dates on which the issuer pays interest on the bond
Next coupon date	The next date on which the issuer will pay interest on the bond
Previous coupon date	The previous date on which the issuer paid interest on the bond
Fixing date	The date on which the coupon rate on a floating rate note is fixed for the next coupon period. This is normally two working days before the next coupon date; i.e. the coupon date at the start of the coupon period
Coupon rate	The rate of interest on the bond
Coupon frequency	The number of times in the year that the issue pays interest
Coupon period	The difference (in days) between the last coupon date and the next coupon date
Accrued interest days	The difference (in days) between the previous coupon date and the value date of a bond trade

3.3   MORE TRADE TERMINOLOGY

Looking at the issue of accrued interest on bond trades has introduced us to more trade terminology (Table 3.1) to add to that listed Table 2.1.

3.4   HOW PRICES ARE FORMED IN THE SECONDARY MARKET

Bond prices fluctuate according to supply and demand. This is affected by investor sentiment as to the ability of an individual investor to continue to pay coupons and redemption proceeds, but to a larger extent bond prices vary according to the current level of short-term interest rates in the money markets as a whole. Simplistically, if a bond carries a 5% coupon at a time when short-term interest rates are less than 5%, then its price (quoted as a percentage of face value) will be greater than 100%, but if short-term interest rates rise to more than 5%, then its market price will be less than 5%. Bond market analytics is a complex subject.

3.4.1   The yield curve

The *yield curve* is the relation between the interest rate (or cost of borrowing) and the time to original maturity of the debt for a given borrower in a given currency. Normally, the longer the time to maturity of the debt instrument, the higher the yield to the investor, and the higher the interest rate cost to the borrower. Yield curves are commonly plotted on a graph such as the one in Figure 3.1, and typically show a gentle upward sloping pattern.

However, a positively sloped yield curve is not always the norm. A steep yield curve indicates the beginning of an economic expansion or the end of a recession. Economic stagnation will have depressed short-term interest rates; however, rates begin to rise once the demand for capital is re-established by growing economic activity. A flat yield curve is observed when all maturities have similar yields, whereas a humped curve results when short-term and long-term

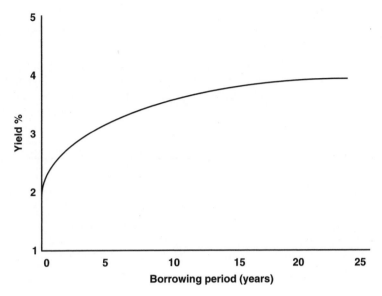

Figure 3.1 Example of a yield curve

yields are equal and medium-term yields are higher than those of the short term and long term. A flat curve signals uncertainty in the economy.

An inverted yield curve occurs when long-term yields fall below short-term yields. This implies that long-term investors will settle for lower yields now if they think the economy will slow or even decline in the future. An inverted curve may indicate a worsening economic situation in the future.

In order to value and compare the prices of bonds issued by a wide range of issuers in a wide range of currencies, a number of valuation methodologies have been developed, and these are described in Appendix 1.

3.4.2 The importance of a credit rating and the role of the rating agencies

In order for a bond issuer to be able to issue a bond, the issuer must obtain a **credit rating** from a **credit rating agency**. A credit rating measures the ability to pay back a loan, and affects the interest rate applied to loans. Interest rates are not the same for everyone, but instead are based on risk-based pricing, a form of price discrimination based on the different expected costs of different borrowers, as set out in their credit rating. There are more than 100 rating agencies worldwide, including:

- A.M. Best (US)
- Baycorp Advantage (Australia)
- Dominion Bond Rating Service (Canada)
- Fitch Ratings (Worldwide)
- Moody's (Worldwide)
- Standard & Poor's (Worldwide).

Issuers rely on credit ratings as an independent verification of their own creditworthiness. In most cases, a significant bond issuance must have at least one rating from a respected CRA for the issuance to be successful (without such a rating, the issuance may be undersubscribed or the price offered by investors too low for the issuer's purposes). Many institutional investors now prefer that a debt issuance has at least three ratings. Investment banks and broker/dealers also use credit ratings in calculating their own risk portfolios (i.e. the collective risk of all of their investments). Larger banks and broker/dealers conduct their own risk calculations, but rely on CRA ratings as a "check" (and double-check or triple-check) against their own analyses. Regulators use credit ratings as well, or permit these ratings to be used for regulatory purposes. For example, under the Basel II agreement of the Basel Committee on Banking Supervision, banking regulators can allow banks to use credit ratings from certain approved CRAs (called "ECAIs" or "External Credit Assessment Institutions") when calculating their net capital reserve requirements.

Credit ratings are expressed as a series of alphanumeric characters, and the exact codes that are used vary from agency to agency. Table 3.2 explains the codes that are used by Moody's.

These ratings are in fact further refined, so that there are three classes of each rating, i.e. Aaa1, Aaa2, Aaa3, etc.

Table 3.2 Moody's debt ratings

Rating	Explanation
Aaa	These bonds carry the smallest degree of investment risk. Interest payments are protected by a large or an exceptionally stable margin and principal is secure. While the various protective elements are likely to change, such changes as can be visualised are most unlikely to impair the fundamentally strong position of such issues
Aa	These bonds are judged to be of high quality by all standards. Together with the Aaa group they comprise what are generally known as high grade bonds. They are rated lower than the best bonds because margins of protection may not be as large as in Aaa securities or there may be other elements present which make the long-term risk appear somewhat larger than the Aaa securities
A	These bonds possess many favourable investment attributes and are considered as upper-medium-grade obligations. Factors giving security to principal and interest are considered adequate, but elements may be present which suggest a susceptibility to impairment some time in the future
Baa	These bonds are considered as medium-grade obligations (i.e. they are neither highly protected nor poorly secured). Interest payments and principal security appear adequate for the present but certain protective elements may be lacking or may be characteristically unreliable over any great length of time. Such bonds lack outstanding investment characteristics and in fact have speculative characteristics as well
Ba	These bonds are judged to have speculative elements; their future cannot be considered as well assured. Often the protection of interest and principal payments may be very moderate and thereby not well safeguarded during both good and bad times over the future. Uncertainty of position characterises bonds in this class
B	These bonds generally lack characteristics of the desirable investment. Assurance of interest and principal payments or of other terms of the contract over any long period of time may be small
Ca	These bonds are speculative in a high degree. Such issues are often in default or have other marked shortcomings
C	These bonds are the lowest rated class of bonds, and issues so rated can be regarded as having extremely poor prospects of ever attaining any real investment standing

The affect of ratings on bond prices is that the lower the credit rating, the higher the coupon rate that the borrower will need to pay. If two bonds with an identical original maturity and coupon rate are issued by two borrowers with different credit ratings, then the market price of the bond issued by the borrower with the lower rating will have lower market prices than the bond issued with the higher credit rating.

4

Cash

Cash is both an investment class in its own right, and of course the means of exchange that is used to pay for investments in the other asset classes such as securities and derivatives.

4.1 CASH AS A MEANS OF EXCHANGE

Cash is used to pay and receive funds as a result of trading in other instruments. In this context cash is a currency such as pounds sterling, United States dollars, Japanese yen, etc. Currencies are usually identified by a three character ISO currency code such as GBP, USD and JPY. Cash is held at bank accounts, and the location of these accounts is generally, but not exclusively, in the country that uses that particular currency as its own official currency. There are exceptions to this rule, for example all European Union countries offer bank accounts in euros, even if, like the United Kingdom, the euro is not the official currency of the country concerned.

The relationship between countries and currencies is a many (country) to one (currency) relationship. Even before the advent of the euro in 1999 there were examples (such as Panama which uses the United States dollar) of one country using the official currency of another country as its official currency.

For each currency there are associated working days and holiday calendars. Nearly all currencies use Monday to Friday as normal working days, and banks are closed at weekends. There are exceptions to this rule – some Islamic countries close their banks on Fridays and open them on Sundays.

Each currency is also linked to a calendar of public holidays when banks are closed and no transactions in that currency are able to settle across a bank account. For retail transactions there may be many such public holidays in the year; for wholesale transactions such as trading in securities and derivatives there may be very few. For example, the only days that are considered to be public holidays for settlement of trades using euros are 1 January and 25 December each year.

On a public holiday for the country concerned the following are generally true:

- Investment exchanges are closed, so that no new trades in instruments listed on those exchanges can take place.
- Banks are closed, so that:
  - No trades of an earlier trade date may settle
  - No coupons or dividends can be paid
  - No "fixings" of benchmark interest rates such as LIBOR or EURIBOR can take place.

Chapters 10 and 23 will examine the requirement to hold calendars and holiday calendars as part of static data in business applications.

4.1.1 Interest calculation methods for currencies

When calculating interest for fractions of years for currency transactions, the following calculation methods are used:

- *Actual number of days/360*: This method is used for all currencies except pounds sterling and Japanese yen. Calculate the difference between two dates, and divide the answer by 360.
- *Actual number of days/365*: This method is used for pounds sterling and Japanese yen. Calculate the difference between two dates, and divide the answer by 365, or 366 if the year concerned is a leap year.

4.2 CASH AS AN INVESTMENT CLASS

Investment industry participants use cash as an investment class in two ways, foreign exchange transactions and money market loans and deposits.

4.2.1 Foreign exchange transactions

The FX (**foreign exchange**) market exists wherever one currency is traded for another. It is by far the largest financial market in the world, and includes trading between large banks, central banks, currency speculators, multinational corporations, governments, and other financial markets and institutions. The FX market is by far the largest investment market in the world. In 2004, the Bank of International Settlements (BIS) estimated that the average daily turnover of this market was worth USD 1.9 trillion, which is equivalent to

- More than 10 times the average daily turnover of global equity markets
- 40 times the average daily turnover of the New York Stock Exchange
- USD 300 a day for every man, woman, and child on earth
- An annual turnover more than 10 times the value of all the world's goods and services combined.

More than 50% of this turnover is carried out in the United Kingdom and the United States. The daily turnover by transaction type is shown in Figure 4.1.

The different transaction types may be summarised as follows:

- **Spot transactions** occur when a **trading party** buys one currency with a different currency for immediate delivery, rather than for future delivery. The standard value date for foreign exchange spot trades is T + 2 days, i.e. two days from the date of trade execution. The price of a spot FX deal is known as the exchange rate of the transaction.
- **Forward transactions** are those where value date is greater than the standard two days for a spot transaction. The price of a forward FX transaction will be different to that of a spot transaction. The difference in price will reflect the fact that the two currencies concerned have different interest rates. The relationship between spot and forward prices is calculated by the following equation:

$$F = S\left(\frac{1 + r_T T}{1 + r_B T}\right)$$

where:

F = forward price
S = spot price
r_T = interest rate of the term (i.e. bought) currency
r_B = interest rate of the base (i.e., sold) currency
T = tenor (calculated according to the appropriate day count convention – see section 3.2 for more details of the day count conventions).

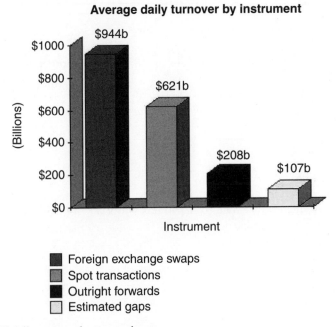

Figure 4.1 FX daily turnover by transaction type

Worked example

On 3 February 2008 a firm wishes to do a forward deal buying USD and selling GBP for value date 5 March 2008.

The normal spot value date for such a deal is 5 February 2008, so settlement is delayed for 29 days.

The spot exchange rate is USD 2.01 = GBP 1.

The current interest rate for the US dollar is 5.5%, calculated on an actual/360 day basis.

The current interest rate for the pounds sterling is 5.0%, calculated on an actual/360 day basis.

The calculation is as follows:

$F = 2.01 * (1 + 5.5 * 29/360)/ (1 + 5.0 * 29/365)$
   $= 2.75878$

FX swaps consist of two legs which are executed simultaneously for the same quantity, and therefore offset each other:

1. A spot foreign exchange transaction
2. A forward foreign exchange transaction.

Investors use forex swaps to speculate on changes in the interest rate differentials between two currencies. If the forward exchange rate for a particular currency was lower than the spot rate, an investor might sell a currency at the spot rate and buy it back at the forward rate.

4.2.2   Money market loans and deposits

Banks offer their clients the ability to place deposits or to take out loans for periods of up to 13 months. **Call and notice** loans and deposits have no agreed maturity date when the transaction is first agreed, while time deposits and **time loans and deposits** have an agreed maturity date. What one of the parties considers a loan, the other party of course considers a deposit. The rule is that if funds are received by Party A from Party B on the commencement date of the transaction then Party A has *attracted a deposit*, and Party B has *placed a loan*.

Worked example

On 5 February 2008 Bank A agrees to lend Bank B USD 1 000 000 for 31 days between 8 February 2008 and 10 March 2008 at 5% interest.

The amount of interest that Bank B has to repay to Bank A on 10 March is therefore USD 4305.56; which is calculated as:

Interest = Principal amount * Interest rate * Days difference between start date and end date/360

= 1 000 000.00 * 5% * 31/360

The divisor of 360 is used because the currency of the transaction is USD. If it had been GBP or JPY then a divisor of 365 would have been used

---

Because this is a time deposit/loan, two working days before the termination date of the transaction the two parties need to get in touch with each other and agree either that:

- They will terminate the transaction as originally agreed by Party B returning the principal amount plus the interest to Party A; or
- They may agree to roll over the transaction for a further period. In this case Party B needs to make payment of only the interest to Party A. Rolling over implies a renegotiation of the interest rate for the next period.

Some forms of loan and deposit transactions – known as sale and repurchase agreements or repos – involve the use of securities as collateral. These types of transactions will be examined in detail in Chapter 21.

4.3   MORE TRADE TERMINOLOGY

We now have some further trade terms from the FX and loan and deposit transactions (Table 4.1) to add to those that we have gathered from examining equity and bond trades.

Table 4.1 FX trade terminology

Term	Explanation
Spot date	The value date of a spot FX transaction, or the value date of the start leg of an FX swap
Forward date	The value date of a forward FX transaction, or the value date of the end leg of an FX Swap
Spot price	The exchange rate used in a spot FX transaction or the start leg of an FX swap
Forward price	The exchange rate used in a forward FX transaction or the start leg of an FX swap
Exchange rate	The price of an FX transaction
Deposit	When a financial institution borrows money from another institution, it is said to "attract a deposit"
Loan	When a financial institution lends money to another institution, it is said to "place a loan"
Call or notice	A loan or deposit that has no agreed maturity date
Start date	The value date of the first leg of a loan or deposit transaction
Maturity date	The value date of the end leg of a loan or deposit transaction

5
Derivatives

Derivative instruments (also known as derivative contracts) are financial contracts whose value depends upon the value of an **underlying instrument** or asset (typically a commodity, bond, equity or currency, or a combination of these).

There are two main classes of derivative contracts – exchange traded derivatives and OTC (over the counter) derivatives.

5.1 EXCHANGE TRADED DERIVATIVE CONTRACTS

As the name implies, these contracts are devised by and traded on investment exchanges, such as the **Euronext**.LIFFE exchange in London, the Chicago Board of Trade and the Eurex exchange in Frankfurt. These exchanges devise, standardise and provide trading facilities or a wide range of **futures** and **options** based on underlying instruments such as exchange rates, interest rates, government bonds, equity indexes, individual equities, as well as commodities such as wheat, copper and oil.

Exchanges provide two forms of derivative contracts – **traded options** and **futures.**

5.1.1 Traded options

There are two forms of traded options – put options and call options. A call option gives the buyer (or holder) the right (but *not* the obligation) to purchase the underlying instrument at a specified price (known as the **strike price**) on or before a given date known as the **exercise date**. A put option on the other hand gives the buyer (or holder) the right (but *not* the obligation) to sell the underlying instrument at a specified price on or before a given date. In order to acquire the rights to buy or sell the instrument at the agreed strike price the investor pays an **option premium**.

An investor that expects the price of a particular underlying instrument to rise in the near future will buy a call option while an investor that expects the price to fall would buy a put option.

Example

The price of Vodafone plc shares on 5 February 2008 on the London Stock Exchange is 164.4 pence per share. The Euronext.LIFFE exchange offers a variety of put and call options on Vodafone shares at different strike prices and exercise dates.

Investor A expects that the price will rise to 220 pence by June 2008. He therefore buys 10 **lots**[1] of the Euronext.LIFFE call option for June 2008 with a strike price of 200 pence. The option premium he pays is 5.25 pence per share.

---

[1] Exchange traded derivatives are traded in "lots". One lot is the minimum size of a trade on the exchange. Euronext has defined one lot in the context of Vodafone options as being equivalent to 1000 Vodafone shares.

He therefore pays a premium of (£.0525 + 10 lots * 1000 shares) £525.00. If, by the end of June, the price of Vodafone shares fails to reach 200 pence then he will allow the option to expire, and will lose £525.00. Alternatively, if the price is greater than 200 pence he could either exercise his option and purchase the shares at 200 pence each, or sell the option to another investor on the exchange.

If the price of the share had risen to 220 pence by the exercise date, and the investor did exercise the option and then sell the shares he had acquired, then the net result (exclusive of any commissions and expenses) would be:

Sale proceeds of 10 000 Vodafone plc @ £2.20 per share	£22 000.00
Less: cost of shares	£20 000.00
Less: exercise price of option	£525.00
Gross profit	**£1475.00**

Conversely, if the investor expected the price of Vodafone shares to fall below the current level of 164.4 pence, he could have purchased a put option at a lower price.

Investors that hold a **long position** in a particular underlying instrument often buy put options as a form of insurance against a fall in the price of the underlying instrument; while investors that hold a **short position** in the underlying often buy call options as a form of insurance against a rise in the price. This form of insurance is known as **hedging**.

Listed options may be either European style or American style:

- A **European style option** may be exercised only at the expiry date of the option, i.e. at a single pre-defined point in time.
- An **American style option** may be exercised at any time before the expiry date.

5.1.2   Exchange traded futures

A futures contract is a legally binding agreement to buy or sell a commodity or financial instrument in a designated future month at a price agreed upon today by the buyer and seller. Futures contracts are standardised according to the quality, quantity and delivery time and location for each commodity. A futures contract differs from an option because an option is the right to buy or sell, while a futures contract is the promise to actually make a transaction. Futures contracts, like options contracts, are used in hedging.

Example – the Eurex Bund Futures contract

Eurex's fixed income derivatives are the benchmark for the European yield curve and often serve as a standard reference when comparing, evaluating and hedging interest rates in Europe.

The Euro-Bund Futures allow investors to enter positions based on interest rate movements. Investors are able to use these products to take relative value positions between different maturity ranges or market segments as well as to **arbitrage** between the cash and futures markets. In other words, an investor who expects interest rates to rise in the future, and therefore the price of his existing bond portfolio to fall, will sell Bund Futures at today's price. Conversely, an investor who has a short position in his bond portfolio and expects interest rates to fall will buy Bund Futures at today's price.

Contract specifications – the Eurex Bund Futures contract

Euro-Bund Futures are based on a notional long-term debt instrument with a term of 8.5 to 10.5 years, bearing a notional coupon rate of 6% and are based on debt instruments issued by the Federal Republic of Germany. One lot of Euro-Bund Futures has a contract value of EUR 100 000 and minimum price changes of 0.01% – equivalent to a value of EUR 10.

There are contracts available for the three successive quarterly months within the March, June, September and December cycle. The **delivery date** is the tenth calendar day of the respective quarterly month, if this day is a working day; otherwise the following working day.

Trading volume

Eurex's Euro-Bund (FGBL), Euro-Bobl (FGBM) and Euro-Schatz (FGBS) Futures are the world's most heavily traded fixed income futures. The most actively traded product among them, the Euro-Bund Future, had a daily average volume of approximately one million lots during 2004.

Trade computations for the Bund contract

As one lot of Bund Futures is based on EUR 100 000 of the underlying government bond, then if an investor purchases 10 lots of the Mach contract at 108.64 the computation is:

$$10 \, \text{lots} * \text{EUR} \, 100\,000 * 108.64\% = \text{EUR} \, 1\,086\,400.00$$

No money actually changes hands when a futures contract is purchased or sold. Instead, the investor deposits collateral with a **clearing house** nominated by the exchange concerned. The mechanics of this will be dealt with in section 7.7 and section 19.3.

5.2 MORE TRADE TERMINOLOGY

We now have some further trade terms from the exchange traded derivative transactions (Table 5.1) to add to those that we have gathered from examining equity, bond and cash trades.

Table 5.1 Listed derivative trade terminology

Term	Explanation
Lot	The size of a futures or options trade is measured in lots. One lot represents a given amount of the underlying instrument, and the value of one lot is specified by the exchange that lists the contract
Exercise price	The price (of the underlying instrument) at which an option may be exercised
Exercise date	The latest date on which an option may be exercised. After this date the option expires and has no value
Strike price	See exercise price
Option Premium	The amount that the investor pays for the right to acquire an option
Underlying	The instrument on which a future or option is based

5.3   OTC DERIVATIVES

As well as listed futures and options there is a very wide variety of derivative contracts that are traded between investors and financial institutions without using an exchange. These include, *inter alia*:

- Interest rate **swaps**
- Currency swaps
- Credit default swaps
- Equity and equity index swaps
- Forward rate agreements
- Caps, collars and floors
- Credit default swaps
- OTC options.

It is beyond the scope of this book to provide a detailed explanation of all these contract types; see Appendix 3 for a list of publications that will provide further information. The book does examine interest rate swaps and currency swaps in detail, first, because an understanding of these instruments is the starting point for understanding most of the others, and second, because the size of the market for these instruments is huge – in 2006, the International Swaps and Derivatives Association estimated that the value of the outstanding contracts in these instruments was USD 285 728.14 billion. We shall also describe the other forms of OTC derivatives in brief.

5.3.1   Interest rate swaps

The essence of the transaction is that two parties agree to exchange (or swap) the cash flows from two payment streams. For example, a high street bank that takes retail deposits from customers at a variable rate of interest and wishes to provide fixed rate mortgages to other customers might "swap" the variable rate cash flows from its borrowings with another institution that has the opposite problem – it has fixed rate deposits but needs to make variable rate loans. In this way, the two institutions protect themselves from adverse movements in short-term interest rates.

Example

Bank A wishes to swap a **notional principal** of USD 100 000 000.00 with Bank B for two years from 1 February 2008 till 1 February 2010. Bank A will pay Bank B fixed interest of 5% annually on the notional principal while Bank B will pay Bank A interest at LIBOR semi-annually. LIBOR rates will not be fixed until two days before each interest period, so we are unable to predict the actual payments that B will need to make to A at the start date of the transaction.

Making some assumptions as to the actual LIBOR rates for the two years, the cash flows that the two institutions exchange will be as shown in Figure 5.1.

Example interest rate swap:
Notional principal   100 000 000.00 start date   **01 February 2008**

Bank A (pays 5% fixed, annually)			Bank B pays LIBOR, semi-annually		
Fixed interest rate	**Date**	**Amount paid by A to B**	**Assumed LIBOR rate**	**Amount paid by B to A**	**Net Cash Flow (+ve cash flow is A to B; –ve cash flow is B to A)**
	01 August 2008	0.00	5.10%	2 550 000.00	–2 550 000.00
5%	01 February 2009	5 000 000.00	4.80%	2 400 000.00	2 600 000.00
	01 August 2009	0.00	5.20%	2 600 000.00	–2 600 000.00
5%	01 February 2010	5 000 000.00	5.30%	2 650 000.00	2 350 000.00
Total cash flows		**10 000 000.00**		**10 200 000.00**	**–200 000.00**

Figure 5.1   Example of an interest rate swap

Note the following practical issues about the exchanges of cash flows:

- At no time do A and B exchange the principal – there would be no point in doing so, as they would both pay each other the same amount.
- At each interest payment date, the two cash flows are netted, and only one bank has a payment to make on each date. This is to avoid **delivery risk** – the risk that one payment is made correctly but the other cannot be made for any reason.

Alternative forms of interest rate swap

The interest rate swap in the above example can be considered a "classic" swap, in that the two parties are swapping a stream of fixed interest payments for a stream of floating rate interest payments. These types of swap are also known as "coupon swaps" where the term coupon is derived from the name of the interest payment on debt instruments. One of the common variations is **basis swaps,** where the two parties exchange two streams of payments that are based on benchmark interest rates. For example, they may swap a series of cash flows based on different tenors of the same benchmark (e.g. three-month LIBOR for six-month LIBOR), or they may swap different benchmarks (e.g. six-month LIBOR for six-month EURIBOR).

Currency swaps

A currency swap occurs when two parties exchange two payment streams in different currencies, calculated at a different interest rate, and also agree to return the original principal amount to each other at an exchange rate agreed at the start of the contract.

Example

On trade date 29 January 2008 the USD/GBP exchange rate is 2.00.

Banks A and B agree to swap the 5% fixed rate income streams on USD 100 000 00 with the floating rate LIBOR income streams on GBP 50 000 000 for two years from 1 February 2008. Bank A pays Bank B USD at 5%, while Bank B pays Bank A GBP LIBOR.

Example currency Swap:
Notional principal: Bank A   100 000 000.00 USD   start date   01 February 2008
Notional principal: Bank B   50 000 000.00 GBP   exchange rate 1 USD = 2 GBP
Bank A (pays 5% fixed, annually)   Bank B pays GBP LIBOR, semi-annually

Fixed interest rate	Date	Amount Paid by A to B (USD)	Assumed LIBOR rate	Amount Paid by B to A (GBP)	Net cash flow in USD (+ve cash flow is A to B; –ve cash flow is B to A)
Example Currency swap:	01/02/2008	100 000 000.00		50 000 000.00	0.00
	01 August 2008	0.00	5.10%	1 275 000.00	–2 550 000.00
5%	01 February 2009	5 000 000.00	4.80%	1 200 000.00	2 600 000.00
	01 August 2009	0.00	5.20%	1 300 000.00	–2 600 000.00
5%	01 February 2010	5 000 000.00	5.30%	1 325 000.00	2 350 000.00
Return of principal	01 February 2010	–100 000 000.00		0.00	
Total cash flows		**10 000 000.00**		**55 100 000.00**	**–200 000.00**

Figure 5.2   Example of a currency swap

Making some assumptions as to the actual LIBOR rates for the two years, the cash flows that the two institutions exchange will be as shown in Figure 5.2.

Unlike interest rate swaps, the principal amount of the transaction is exchanged at the start of the transaction, and returned at the end. The interest payments cannot be netted off against each other as they are denominated in different currencies.

5.3.2   Other OTC derivatives in brief

Credit default swaps

A **credit default swap** (**CDS**) is a contract under which two trade parties agree to isolate and separately trade the **credit risk** of one or more securities or other obligations issued by a third party.

Under a credit default swap agreement, a protection buyer pays a periodic fee to a protection seller in exchange for a contingent payment by the seller upon a credit event (such as a default or failure to pay) happening to the underlying securities. When a credit event is triggered, the protection seller either takes delivery of the defaulted security for the par value (physical settlement) or pays the protection buyer the difference between the par value and recovery value of the bond (cash settlement).

Credit default swaps resemble an insurance policy, as they can be used by debt owners to hedge against credit events. However, because there is no requirement to actually hold any asset or suffer a loss, credit default swaps can be used to speculate on changes in credit spread.

Credit default swaps are the most widely traded credit derivative product. The typical term of a credit default swap contract is five years, although being an over-the-counter derivative, credit default swaps of almost any maturity can be traded.

Equity and equity index swaps

An **equity swap** is where one of the payment streams is based on the return from holding an equity or equity index instead of being based on an interest rate.

For example, Party A swaps £5 000 000 at LIBOR + 0.03% against £5 000 000 exposure to the FTSE100 index with Party B for six months.

Party A receives from Party B any percentage increase in the FTSE applied to the £5 000 000 notional; while Party B receives interest paid at LIBOR + 0.03% from Party A.

If the FTSE at the six-month mark had risen by 10% from its level at trade commencement, the equity payer/floating leg receiver (Party B) would owe 10% * £5 000 000 = £500 000 to the floating leg payer/equity receiver (Party A). If, on the other hand, the FTSE at the six-month mark had fallen by 10% from its level at trade commencement, the equity receiver/floating leg payer (Party A) would owe an additional 10% * £5 000 000 = £500 000 to the floating leg receiver/equity payer (Party B).

Equity contracts for difference

A **contract for difference** (**CFD**) is a contract between two parties, buyer and seller, stipulating that the seller will pay to the buyer the difference between the current value of an equity and its value at a future date. If the difference is negative, then the buyer pays to the seller. CFDs allow investors to speculate on share price movements without the need for ownership of the underlying shares.

Contracts for differences allow investors to take long or short positions, and unlike futures contracts have no fixed expiry date or contract size. CFDs are often used by UK investors to gain exposure to the growth potential of an individual equity without the requirement to pay stamp duty.

Forward rate agreements

A **forward rate agreement** (**FRA**) can be thought of as a mini-swap, with only one interest payment date instead of many. It is a forward contract in which one party pays a fixed interest rate, and receives a floating interest rate equal to a reference rate (the underlying rate). The payments are calculated over a notional amount over a certain period, and netted, i.e. only the differential is paid. It is paid on the *effective date*. The reference rate is fixed at zero, one or two days before the termination date, dependent on the market convention for the particular currency. A swap is a combination of FRAs.

The payer of the fixed interest rate is also known as the borrower or the buyer, while the receiver of the fixed interest rate is the lender or the seller.

Caps, collars and floors

An **interest rate cap** is a contract where the buyer receives money at the end of each period in which an interest rate exceeds the agreed strike price. An example of a cap would be an agreement to receive money for each month the LIBOR rate exceeds 5%.

An **interest rate floor** is a contract where the buyer of the floor receives money at the end of each period in which an interest rate is lower than the agreed strike price. An example of a cap would be an agreement to receive money for each month the LIBOR rate is lower than 2.5%.

When a firm buys both an interest rate cap and an interest rate floor on the same index, it is known as a collar.

OTC options

As well as the traded (or listed) options that are traded on exchanges, there is also a large OTC market in put and call options based on a wide variety of underlying instruments.

The OTC option market enables firms to **write** and purchase put and call options on instruments that it would be uneconomic for exchanges to list, and at wider variety of strike prices and exercise dates than the exchanges could list. Trade parties benefit from avoiding the restrictions that exchanges place on options. The flexibility allows participants to achieve their desired position more precisely and cost effectively. However, the market for some of these options is far less liquid than its exchange traded equivalent.

Note that when an investor writes an option, its income is fixed but its downside risk is unlimited. For example, if an investor writes a call option on a share that is currently trading at £10 and receives a premium of £1 per share for doing so, then, if the buyer decides to exercise the option, the writer has to purchase the shares for the investor. At the time the option is exercised the share price could be £11, £15 or even higher – it is not predictable; but the maximum income that the writer will receive is the option premium of £1 per share.

More trade terminology

We now have some further trade terms from the OTC derivative transactions (Table 5.2) to add to those that we have gathered from examining equity, bond, cash and exchange trade derivative trades.

Table 5.2 OTC derivative trade terminology

Term	Explanation
Notional principal	The principal amount of a swap trade

6

Common Attributes of Financial Instruments

6.1 SUMMARY OF ALL TRADE TERMINOLOGY USED IN CHAPTERS 1 TO 5

Table 6.1 reiterates all the terms that we have learned about trades in the various instrument classes in the previous chapters and also categorises each term and shows to which instruments the term applies.

Table 6.1 Trade terminology summary

Term	Explanation	Instruments to which term applies	Category
Exercise date	The latest date on which an option may be exercised. After this date the option expires, and has no value	Options	Date
Fixing date	The date on which the coupon rate on a floating rate note is fixed for the next coupon period. This is normally two working days before the next coupon date, i.e. the coupon date at the start of the coupon period	Debt instrument, swap	Date
Forward date	The value date of a forward FX transaction, or the value date of the end leg of an FX swap	FX, money market	Date
Maturity date	The value date of the end leg of a loan or deposit transaction	FX, money market, swap, debt instrument	Date
Coupon date	The dates on which the issuer pays interest on the bond	Debt instrument, swap	Date
Next coupon date	The next date on which the issuer will pay interest on the bond	Debt instrument, swap	Date
Previous coupon date	The previous date on which the issuer paid interest on the bond	Debt instrument, swap	Date
Spot date	The value date of a spot FX transaction, or the value date of the start leg of an FX swap	FX, money market	Date
Spot price	The exchange rate used in a spot FX transaction or the start leg of an FX swap	FX	Date
Start date	The value date of the first leg of a loan or deposit transaction	FX, money market, swap	Date
Trade date	The date that the two parties agreed to carry out the trade	All instruments	Date

(Continued)

Table 6.1   (*Countinued*)

Term	Explanation	Instruments to which term applies	Category
Value date	The date that the seller will deliver the securities to the buyer and the buyer will pay the consideration to the seller. Also the date that the legal ownership of the securities changes from the buyer to the seller	All instruments	Date
Benchmark rate	A rate such as LIBOR or EURIBOR that is used to determine the coupon rate on a floating rate note	Debt instrument, swap	Instrument or transaction
Call or notice	A loan or deposit that has no agreed maturity date	Money market	Instrument or transaction
Coupon frequency	The number of times in the year that the issue pays interest	Debt instrument, swap	Instrument or transaction
Coupon period	The difference (in days) between the last coupon date and the next coupon date	Debt instrument, swap	Instrument or transaction
Deposit	When a financial institution borrows money from another institution, it is said to "attract a deposit"	Money market	Instrument or transaction
Loan	When a financial institution lends money to another institution, it is said to "place a loan"	Money market	Instrument or transaction
Underlying	The instrument on which a future or option is based	Futures, options	Instrument or transaction
Accrued interest days	The difference (in days) between the previous coupon date and the value date of a bond trade	Debt instrument	Instrument or transaction
Bid price	This is the price that a professional dealer is prepared to buy a given quantity of the security concerned from an investor	Equity, debt instrument	Price
Clean price	The price of a bond trade excluding accrued interest	Debt instrument	Price
Dirty price	The price of a bond trade including accrued interest	Debt instrument	Price
Exercise price	The price (of the underlying instrument) at which an option may be exercised	Options	Price
Forward price	The exchange rate used in a forward FX transaction or the start leg of an FX swap	FX	Price
Mid price	The average of bid price and offer price	Equity, debt instrument	Price
Offer price	This is the price that a professional dealer is prepared to sell a given quantity of the security concerned from an investor	Equity, debt instrument	Price
Option Premium	The amount that the investor pays for the right to acquire an option	Options	Price
Strike price	See exercise price	Options	Price

Table 6.1   (*Countinued*)

Term	Explanation	Instruments to which term applies	Category
Trade price	The price of this particular trade	Equity, debt instrument	Price
Accrued interest	In this context, the amount of interest that a bond purchaser pays a bond seller for the coupon income that the seller is entitled to for the period from the previous coupon date to trade value date	Debt instrument, money market, swap	Trade amounts
Commission	The amount that an agent will charge the investor for executing the trade	All instruments	Trade amounts
Consideration	Principal value + Accrued interest + Commission + Fees	All instruments	Trade amounts
Coupon rate	The rate of interest on the bond or one side of a swap	Debt instrument, swap	Trade amounts
Exchange rate	The price of an FX transaction	FX	Trade amounts
Fees	Any other charges levied on this trade other than commission	All instruments	Trade amounts
Lot	The size of a futures or options trade is measured in lots. One lot represents a given amount of the underlying instrument, and the value of one lot is specified by the exchange that lists the contract	Futures, options	Trade amounts
Nominal amount	The quantity of securities being purchased or sold	All instruments	Trade amounts
Notional principal	The principal amount of a swap trade	OTC derivatives	Trade amounts
Principal value	Nominal amount. The price of the trade	All instruments	Trade amounts

6.2   SUMMARY OF BASIC TRADE ARITHMETIC FOR TRANSACTIONS IN SECURITIES, FUTURES AND OPTIONS

6.2.1   Calculating the principal value of a trade

In Chapter 2 we learned that equity prices may be quoted in whole currency units or in "penny units" of the currency, while in Chapter 3 we learned that bond prices are usually expressed as percentages of the principal amount being traded. In Chapter 5 we learned that when dealing with futures and options we have to take into account the quantity of the underlying instrument when calculating the value of a trade in these instruments.

With this knowledge, we can build a generic formula to calculate the principal value of any security, future or option. The formula is:

$$\text{Principal value} = \text{Nominal amount} * \text{Price} * \text{Multiplier/Divisor}$$

Here are some examples:

- IBM shares are quoted in whole units of USD.
- HSBC shares are quoted in penny units of GBP.
- National Grid bonds are quoted in percentages of face value.
- Euro Bund Futures have to take into account the fact that one lot of this contract is equivalent to a bond quantity of 100 000.

Therefore, if the price of all four of these instruments is quoted as "97", and the quantity of a trade is 10 000, the calculation is as shown in Table 6.2.

Table 6.2   The interpretation of a price

Instrument	Instrument type	Price	Price multiplier	Price divisor	Principal value
IBM shares	USD share	97	1	1	970 000
HSBC share	Penny share	97	1	100	9 700
National Grid bond	Debt instrument	97	1	100	9 700
Eurex Bund future	Future based on 100k of underlying	97	100 000	100	9 700 000

6.2.2   Calculating the consideration

The consideration of a trade (i.e. the total amount payable by the buyer) is

$$\text{Consideration} = \text{Principal value} + \text{Accrued interest} + \text{Commission} + \text{Fees}$$

Chapter 3 told us how accrued interest is calculated on debt instruments.

Also, refer to Chapter 10 for more information on the static data that needs to be held to perform trade proceeds calculations accurately. Commissions and fees calculations and static data are covered in section 10.7.

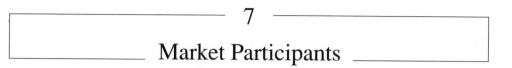

7

Market Participants

7.1 INTRODUCTION

This chapter explains the roles that various types of companies and individuals play in the investment industry, and describes how each of these organisations and individuals interact with one another in the processes of placing orders, executing them, confirming executions and settling the resulting trades. The different organisations may be divided into the following broad categories:

1. Investors, including:
   - Institutional investors such as pension funds and insurance companies
   - Private investors
   - Hedge funds
2. Institutional fund managers
3. Private client stockbrokers and investment managers
4. Investment banks that accept and execute orders from investors
5. Investment exchanges
6. Settlement agents, including
   - Central counterparties, also known as clearing houses
   - Central securities depositaries and international central securities depositaries
   - Commercial banks that provide payment and custodian services
7. Others, including:
   - Information vendors
   - Money brokers
   - Stock lending intermediaries
   - Registrars and transfer agents.

Note that some large organisations act in multiple roles – for example, a large bank may be an institutional fund manager, a private client stockbroker, an investment bank and a commercial custodian all at the same time.

7.2 INVESTORS

Institutional investors include pension funds, insurance companies and fund management companies that manage investment schemes such as mutual funds, unit trusts and investment trusts. In most countries, they are the largest investors in equities. Institutional investors usually delegate the actual investment decisions to **institutional fund managers** whose role is discussed in section 7.3. Traditional institutional investors usually only take **long positions** in securities, and avoid investment in complex derivatives. For this reason, they are sometimes known as "long only" investors.

Private investors include individuals and charities. Private investors place their orders through private client stockbrokers and investment managers, whose role is examined in section 7.4.

Hedge funds are pooled investment vehicles that are privately organised and administered by investment management professionals and not widely available to the public. Many hedge funds share a number of characteristics: they hold both **long and short positions**, use derivatives and **leverage** to enhance returns, pay a performance or incentive fee to their hedge fund managers, have high minimum investment requirements and target absolute (rather than relative) returns. Hedge funds usually deal direct with investment banks whose role is examined in section 7.5.

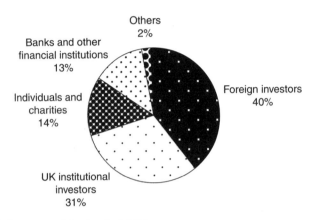

Figure 7.1 UK share ownership at end of 2006

Figure 7.1 (taken from data produced by the UK Office of National Statistics) shows the breakdown of ownership of equities listed on the London Stock Exchange at the end of 2006. Note that foreign investors (mainly long only institutional investors and hedge funds) accounted for the 40% of the value of LSE listed shares.

7.3   INSTITUTIONAL FUND MANAGERS

Institutional fund managers compete to win **investment mandates** from institutional investors. An investment mandate lists the types of investment (e.g. the geographical and industry sectors as well as the types of financial instruments) that the investor wishes the fund manager to invest in, sets performance targets for income and/or capital growth that the investor expects the fund manager to achieve, and describes how the fund manager will be remunerated. Within the guidelines of the mandate, the actual investment decisions are left to the fund manager.

A simplified example of an investment mandate might be as follows:

1. The Ethical Investment Pension Fund appoints XYZ Fund Managers to act on its behalf in investing in equities listed on exchanges in the United States of America and Canada.
2. Within the confines of (1), XYZ is not permitted to invest in the stocks of companies whose main business activities include the manufacture and/or distribution of alcohol, tobacco or armaments.
3. Within the confines of (1), XYZ is also authorised to lend securities provided that collateral is obtained from the borrower.

4. XYX may purchase or sell futures, and purchase put and call options on the equities that it has invested in, in order to hedge against falls in the market value of its portfolio, provided that such futures and options are listed on exchanges in the United States and Canada.
5. Ethical Investment Pension Fund expects XYZ to achieve capital growth of the portfolio equal to 100% of the growth of the Dow Jones US Large-Cap Index over the next three years.
6. Ethical Investment Pension Fund expects XYZ to achieve an annual income of 4% of the value of the fund over the next three years.
7. Ethical Investment Pension Fund will pay XYZ an annual fee of 1% of the fund value each year.

The fund manager will perform its own research into the United States and Canadian securities markets, and base its investment decisions on that research. When it makes a decision to purchase or sell a particular investment, it will place orders to buy or sell individual securities, futures and options with an investment bank – see section 7.5.

Institutional fund managers are often known as **buy-side firms**; and this term will be frequently used in the remainder of this book.

7.4   PRIVATE CLIENT STOCKBROKERS AND INVESTMENT MANAGERS

As their name implies, these organisations exist to serve the private individual. The services that such firms offer their clients may be divided into three categories. Some firms will only offer one or two of these services, while others will offer all three:

- *Execution only*: The investor takes sole responsibility for all investment decisions. When he is ready to buy or sell, he enters the order by telephone, letter or the firm's website; and the firm executes the order on the investor's behalf. The firm cannot be held responsible for the quality of the investment decision.
- *Advisory dealing*: When the investor is ready to buy or sell, he is able to talk it over with the firm, and he may or may not take the advice of the firm. The ultimate responsibility for the quality of the decision lies with the investor.
- *Discretionary dealing:* The investor signs an investment mandate with the firm, and the firm then manages the investor's portfolio according to the terms of that mandate. The ultimate responsibility for the quality of the decision lies with the firm itself.

In addition, these firms also provide other services to investors that normally include **safe custody services** and also **tax sheltered investments**, estate and pension planning:

7.5   INVESTMENT BANKS THAT ACCEPT AND EXECUTE ORDERS FROM INVESTORS

This book uses the term "investment banks" to describe institutions that accept orders from investors and/or their agents and execute them. The book also uses, in the context of order flows, the term "**sell-side firms**" to describe them. Not all investment banks offer all the services described in this section, and not all the firms that offer these services would describe themselves as investment banks.

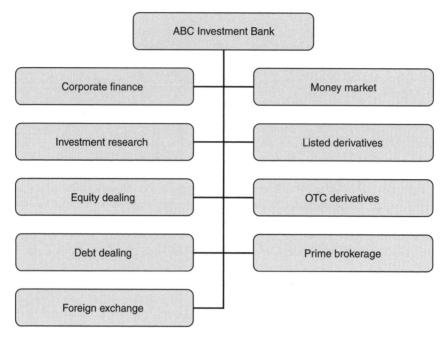

Figure 7.2   ABC investment bank organisation chart

7.5.1   Investment banks' business activities

An investment bank that offers all the services described in this section might be organised along the business lines shown in Figure 7.2.

- *Corporate finance*: The customers of this service are companies, central and local governments and supranational institutions. These customers use the bank's corporate finance department to advise and possibly also to provide finance to them when they are, *inter alia*:
  - Considering issuing new shares on the primary market, or making a primary market offering of debt securities
  - Considering acquiring other companies
  - Reacting to approaches from other companies to purchase some or all of their assets
  - Considering other corporate actions such as share splits, rights issues, bonus issues, etc.
- *Investment research*: This department researches the likely economic outlook for individual countries, business sectors and individual companies. The results of its research are made available to all the other business departments of the bank as well as to the bank's customers.
- *Equity dealing*: This department accepts orders to buy and sell equities from clients, as well as dealing on the bank's own behalf using its own capital. These orders may be executed either as **agency trades** or **principal trades**.
- *Debt dealing*: This department accepts orders to buy and sell debt securities from clients, as well as dealing on the bank's own behalf using its own capital. Debt trades are usually, but not exclusively, executed as principal.
- *Foreign exchange*: This department accepts orders to buy and sell currencies from clients, as well as dealing on the bank's own behalf using its own capital. Debt trades are almost always executed as principal.

- *Money market*: This department attracts deposits and makes loans.
- *Listed derivatives*: This department accepts orders to buy and sell listed futures and options from clients, as well as dealing on the bank's own behalf using its own capital. Listed derivative trades are always executed in an agency capacity.
- *OTC derivatives*: This department trades in instruments such as swaps, OTC options, forward rate agreements, etc. Investment banks risk their own capital in these transactions which are executed in the capacity of principal.
- *Prime brokerage*: This is a package of services offered to hedge funds. The business advantage to a hedge fund of using a prime broker is that the prime broker provides a centralised securities clearing facility for the hedge fund, and the hedge fund's collateral requirements are netted across all deals handled by the prime broker. The prime broker benefits by earning fees ("spreads") on financing the client's long and short cash and security positions, and by charging, in some cases, fees for clearing and/or other services.

The following "core services" are typically bundled into the prime brokerage package:

- Global custody (including clearing, custody and asset servicing)
- Securities lending
- Financing (to facilitate leverage of client assets)
- Customised technology (provide hedge fund managers with portfolio reporting needed to effectively manage money)
- Operational support (prime brokers act as a hedge fund's primary operations contact with all other broker/dealers).

7.5.2 A typical application systems configuration for an investment bank

An investment bank that is active in all of the business areas described in section 7.5.1 will need a number of specialised business application systems to process the transactions and manage the positions in financial instruments that result from the transactions. Figure 7.3 shows a *typical* systems configuration diagram for such a bank. No two banks will have the same configuration, and the configuration of many large banks will be much more complex than the one in this example.

The bank uses the following systems to process its transactions and manage the positions that arise as a result of these transactions.

Front-office systems

There are four of these, one for each instrument type. Each one of them is linked to sources of market data that enable the dealer to "see the market" – in other words, to be able to see the current levels of market prices, interest rates and exchange rates, economic and political news stories that may affect these rates and prices, and corporate announcements such as company results and merger and acquisition activity that may affect the share price of a single company.

Some of this data will also be fed into the individual front-office systems where it will be used in either automated or manual trading decision support. Suppliers of market data include Reuters, Bloomberg and the major stock exchanges.

The front-office systems also hold details of client orders that are awaiting execution. When these orders are executed, details of the trade are forwarded to the *main settlement system*, which is classed as a "back-office system".

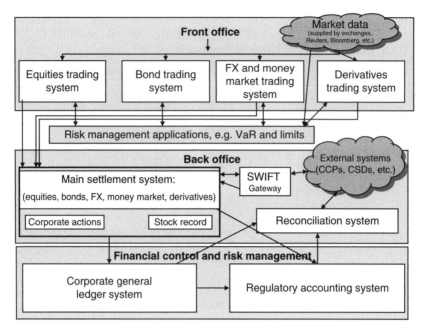

Figure 7.3   Simplified investment bank configuration

Risk management applications

These applications are used to measure and control market risk and credit risk, and are described in Chapter 24.

Back-office systems

Main settlement system
The functions of the main settlement system usually include:

1. Receiving real-time trade details from the front-office systems and enriching those trade details with client/instrument-specific settlement instructions
2. Sending trade confirmations to clients and counterparties, and "matching" confirmations received from counterparties with its own records of those trades
3. Reporting trade details to regulators, in real time and within the maximum allowed period demanded by the regulators
4. Sending settlement instructions to **settlement agents**
5. Receiving reports from settlement agents about which trades have settled and which have not, and updating its records as a result of such reports
6. Forwarding details of trades, settlements and positions to the reconciliation system
7. Forwarding details of all the activities listed in items (1)–(8) that affect the general ledger to the corporate general ledger system and the regulatory accounting system.
8. Position management activity for bonds, equities and currencies, including the maintenance of the stock record which is described in Chapter 15
9. Processing of changes to positions as a result of corporate actions, dividends, etc. – these activities are described in Chapter 23.

Because no two investment firms have the same configuration, it is often the case that the activities of dividend and corporate action processing, and the maintenance of the stock record, are carried out by separate applications to the main settlement system. In other firms, however, these activities will be an integral part of the main settlement system.

Reconciliation application

The purpose of this system is to take feeds from the main settlement system concerning transactions, balances and positions and compare them to data received from settlement agents so that the bank is able to prove that its records about transactions have settled today, and that the resulting position from such settlements agrees with the records of the external agents concerned.

SWIFT gateway

Most of the communications with the external systems will be in the form of **SWIFT** messages. The **SWIFT Gateway** system is the portal that validates, encrypts and transmits outgoing messages, and receives, de-encrypts and routes incoming messages to the appropriate applications or users. SWIFT is examined in Chapter 11.

Financial control systems

The *corporate general ledger* is the system that consists of the company's legal records. The general ledger records all the **assets**, **liabilities**, income and expenditure of the company. See Chapter 14 for more detailed information about investment accounting.

The *regulatory accounting* system is the system that is used to calculate the financial and statistical information that the firm needs to send to its regulator. The requirements of the regulators are examined in Chapter 8.

7.6   INVESTMENT EXCHANGES

An **investment exchange** (also known as **stock exchange**, **share market** or **bourse**) is a corporation or mutual organisation that provides facilities for stockbrokers and traders, to trade company stocks and other securities including bonds, derivatives and physical commodities such as precious metals and agricultural products. There are three economic functions of an investment exchange:

1. To provide a means for companies to raise new capital in the form of equities and debt instruments
2. To provide facilities for investors to trade company stocks and other securities
3. To create standardised derivative instruments such as futures and options which are based on the underlying securities, and to provide facilities for investors to trade in these derivative instruments.

7.6.1   The world's major investment exchanges

According to the World Federation of Exchanges, the 10 largest stock exchanges by market capitalisation as of 12 July 2007 (in trillions of US dollars, rounded to two significant figures) are as follows:

1. NYSE Euronext – $21[1]
2. Tokyo Stock Exchange – $4.7
3. NASDAQ – $4.2[2]
4. London Stock Exchange – $4.0[3]
5. Hong Kong Stock Exchange – $2.1
6. Toronto Stock Exchange – $2.0
7. Frankfurt Stock Exchange (Deutsche börse) – $2.0
8. Shanghai Stock Exchange – $1.7
9. Madrid Stock Exchange (BME Spanish exchanges) – $1.5
10. Australian Securities Exchange – $1.3.

7.6.2   Connecting to stock exchange trading systems

Buy-side firms that wish to trade instruments listed on an investment exchange have to route their orders to a sell-side firm – a stock exchange member. That member firm's IT department therefore needs to organise connectivity to a large number of stock exchange computer systems to facilitate trading.

Stock exchange trading systems may be classified in three ways.

Order-driven markets are designed to support markets in highly liquid, heavily traded securities, futures and options. They have no designated or official **market makers**. A member firm who wishes to buy a given stock at a given price submits a buy order to the relevant LSE market system, while at the same time other member firms who wish to sell the same stock submit sell orders to the relevant LSE system. When a buyer's bid meets a seller's offer (or vice versa) the stock exchange's matching system will decide that a deal has been executed. The identity of the buyer is not known to the seller, and vice versa.

Example

In Table 7.1, three firms have entered orders to a stock exchange system to buy shares in Company A with **price limits** – i.e. the maximum price that they are prepared to buy at and one firm has entered an order to sell securities in the same company with a price limit – i.e. the minimum price at which it is prepared to sell. Before the stock exchange trading system executes the trade, the order book looks like that shown in the table.

The stock exchange system will therefore be able to fill part of Firm 4's order to sell by matching it as follows:

- 4800 shares against the buy order issued by Firm 1
- 1500 shares against the buy order issued by Firm 2.

---

[1] NYSE Euronext comprises the following exchanges:
- The New York Stock Exchange
- Euronext Belgium
- Euronext France
- Euronext Netherlands
- Euronext Portugal
- Euronext.LIFFE – based in London, this division of NYSE Euronext handles all the group's European futures and options contracts.

[2] New York-based NASDAQ is currently in merger talks with the OMX exchange that services six Nordic countries.

[3] The London Stock Exchange has since acquired Milan-based Borsa Italiana.

Table 7.1 Orders placed on the stock exchange queue

	Orders to buy			Orders to sell	
Firm	No. of shares	Max. price	Firm	No. of shares	Min. price
Firm 1	4800	4.7	Firm 4	10 000	4.7
Firm 2	1500	4.7			
Firm 3	8700	4.69			
Total outstanding orders	1500		Total outstanding orders	10 000	

The remaining part of Firm 4's sell order and the whole of Firm 3's buy order cannot be filled immediately, so they will remain on the order book until such time as other firms place further orders. The state of the order book will now be as shown in Table 7.2.

Quote-driven markets are designed for less liquid, less heavily traded instruments. In these systems some of the exchange's member firms take on the obligation of always making a two-way price in each of the stocks in which they make markets. These firms are therefore known as market makers. If another member firm wishes to buy or sell a stock then they approach the market maker direct, either by telephone, or more likely electronically by using the stock exchange market system concerned. This system will display the **bid** and **offer prices** quoted by each market maker for trades in **normal market size**, and the firm that wants to execute the order will be able to use the stock exchange system to select the market maker that will provide **best execution**. In a quote-driven market, unlike an order-driven market, the identity of the buyer and seller are known to each other.

Hybrid markets offer both facilities – most orders are fulfilled through the order queue, but market makers exist side by side to guarantee trade execution if there is not enough liquidity in the order queue. Firms that have to execute orders may choose to place the order on the queue, or to approach a market maker. Depending on how the order was placed, the identity of the buyer and seller may or may not be known to each other.

All the systems that investment exchanges use to facilitate trading in listed futures and options are order-driven systems. Equities, which are less liquid than listed derivatives, may be traded on any one of the three types of platform.

Table 7.2 Orders remaining on the queue

	Orders to buy			Orders to sell	
Firm	No. of shares	Max. price	Firm	No. of shares	Min. price
Firm 3	8700	4.69	Firm 4	3700	4.7
Total Outstanding Orders	8700		Total outstanding orders	3700	

7.7 SETTLEMENT AGENTS

Once orders have been executed, then mechanisms need to be put in place to settle the resulting trade. **Settlement** is the process where the buyer pays the proceeds of the trade and receives legal title to the item it has purchased, while the seller receives the proceeds of the trade and has to deliver the item it has sold to the buyer.

Settlement date is the date on which settlement occurs. Settlement date should be the same date as value date. FX, money market and OTC derivatives deals usually do settle on value date unless there has been some kind of processing error by one of the parties. Securities trades are less likely to settle on value date, because of the affect of **short selling**.

Several different kinds of institution provide services whose end result is trade settlement. This book refers to them collectively as settlement agents, and there are four different types.

7.7.1   Clearing houses or central counterparties

In section 7.6 we learned that investment exchanges offer both order-driven markets and quote-driven markets, and that in an order-driven market the identity of the borrower is unknown to that of the seller, and vice versa. Clearly, then, the buyer and seller cannot settle the trade directly with each other in these circumstances. Therefore there is a role for a clearing house or **central counterparty** (CCP) in these markets.

In the example in section 7.6, the orders shown in Table 7.3 have been matched against each other.

Because Firms 1, 2 and 3 are not aware of each other's identity, as soon as the exchange has matched the orders, its systems inform a CCP that the trades have been executed. The CCP then takes over the obligations to make payments and/or deliver the instrument concerned – every other counterparty settles its obligations with the CCP, and not with each other.

This process – the substitution of one party to a contract by another party – is known as **novation**. The advantages to an exchange and its member firms in having a CCP include the following:

1. *Post-trade anonymity*: It is not necessary for the exchange to divulge the identity of Firm 1 to Firm 4 or vice versa; so there is no danger of one party learning the other party's commercial secrets as a result of discovering their trading pattern.
2. *Netting of positions*: Firm 1 may have carried out many trades in an identical instrument. The CCP nets these into a single position.

Table 7.3   Matched trades

Orders to buy			Orders to sell		
	No. of shares	Max. price	Firm	No. of shares	Min. price
Firm 1	4800	4.7	Firm 4	6300	4.7
Firm 2	1500	4.7			

Netting example

On 12 February Investor 1 placed an order to buy 5000 HSBC shares with Exchange Member 1 for £5 per share for value date 15 February. Exchange Member 1 placed this order on the London Stock Exchange **SETS** Queue and it was matched with a sell order from another member.

Exchange Member 1 also placed the four additional orders shown in Table 7.4 for HSBC shares on the SETS queue on 12 February, all for value date 15 February, and all the orders were matched by other member firms. The summary for all five additional orders is therefore as shown in the Table.

Without netting, Exchange Member 1 would have had to make two deliveries of HSBC shares and three receipts of the same stock, make three payments and receive two. Because of netting there is a single payment and a single delivery.

3. *A reduction in credit risk*: Because the buyers and sellers are unaware of each other, they are by definition unaware of each other's credit status. Once the CCP has novated the contract, sellers no longer have to worry about Firm 3's ability to pay for the securities on settlement date, and buyers no longer have to worry about the other Firms' ability to deliver. The CCP's ability to meet its obligations is monitored by the regulator in the country where the CCP is located. However, the CCP has to monitor the ability of its member firms to meet their obligations. It does this by requiring them to place **collateral** with the CCP to meet **margin** requirements.

Margin and collateral – an introduction

The following is an example of how the CCP uses collateral and margin to manage its credit risk:

1. On 1 February 2007 Party A bought a futures contract that obliges them to take delivery of 1000 shares in ABC plc on 30 March 2007 in return for payment by Party A of £10 per share. So the total amount they have to pay to the CCP if they still hold the contract on 30 March would be £10 000.

Table 7.4   Trade settlement netting by central counterparty

Trade no.	Operation	Share quantity	Share price £	Trade value £
1 (described above)	Buy	5000	5	−25 000
2	Buy	7500	5.1	−38 250
3	Buy	4000	5.05	−20 200
4	Sell	−6000	5.05	30 300
5	Sell	−2000	5	10 000
Net securities due to Member A		8500	Net cash payable by Member A	−43 150

2. However, by 7 February the price of ABC plc shares is only £8 per share. Party A stands to lose £2000 if it still holds the position on 30 March. The CCP therefore required Party A to make a margin payment of £2000 to cover the CCP's risk.
3. If, at some time between 8 February and 30 March, the price of ABC shares rises to £9 per share, then the CCP will refund £1000 to Party A. If, however, it falls to £7 per share then the CCP will demand another £1000 from Party A.

To avoid frequent margin calls immediately after the trade is agreed, CCPs require their member firms to pay an amount of **initial margin** that allows them to take positions of a given number of lots of each instrument. They follow this up with further margin calls to pay **maintenance margin** (also known as **variation margin**) which is the payment to cover the mark-to-market losses shown in the example.

When a member firm has many positions, some of which are showing losses and some showing profits, the maintenance margin is calculated on the net figure. Most exchanges use a methodology known as **SPAN** (Standard Portfolio ANalysis of risk). This is a leading margin system, which has been adopted by most options and futures exchanges around the world. SPAN is based on a sophisticated set of algorithms that determine margin according to a global (total portfolio) assessment of the one-day risk for a trader's account.

Instead of paying a margin call in cash, the CCP accepts the deposit of a wide variety of government bonds as collateral.

All investment exchanges that list contracts in futures and options use a central counterparty to handle the post-trade activities for these instruments. Some exchanges that list securities use a CCP to novate all securities trades, while some of them just use a CCP to settle those trades that are eligible to be executed on an order-driven market. Table 7.1 shows which CCPs are used in each of the world's 10 largest securities markets.

It is not necessary for every sell-side firm to be a member of every clearing house associated with every exchange of which it is a member. Derivatives exchanges provide three types of membership:

- A **clearing member** is an exchange member that clears *only* its own trades with the CCP appointed by the exchange.
- A **general clearing member** is an exchange member that clears both its own trades and also trades executed by other firms, who are known as:
- A **non-clearing member** – a firm whose trades are cleared by a general clearing member.

General clearing members will receive margin calls from the CCP for both their own positions and also the positions held by their clearing clients, and they have to pass those margin calls on to their clearing clients.

Diagrammatically, this is shown in Figures 7.4 and 7.5, which show the flow of a trade executed on the Euronext.LIFFE exchange in London; this is then cleared by LCH.Clearnet, the clearing house associated with the exchange.

Figure 7.4 shows the trade flow when the firm is clearing its own trades; Figure 7.5 shows the trade flows when the firm's trades are cleared by a general clearing member:

Once the LIFFEConnect system (the order-driven market system used by Euronext.LIFFE) has matched the orders, the exchange reports the matched trades to LCH.Clearnet and the transactions are novated. The clearing house then manages its credit risk with the member

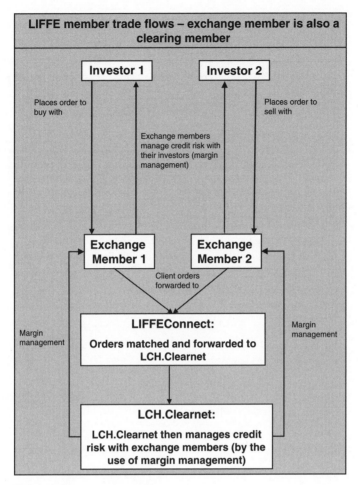

Figure 7.4   LIFFE trade flows – self clearing

firms by the use of margin management. If the member firm was not itself a clearing member, then two exchange members who are also clearing members would be involved, and the diagram now appears as shown in Figure 7.5.

The CLS Bank – netting for FX transactions

FX transactions are not executed through an investment exchange. Until 2001, each FX trade was settled separately, creating enormous volumes of individual payments and creating **operational risk**. CLS Bank was created to carry out transaction netting in this market. Firms who are CLS Bank participants advise the CLS Bank of the trades that they have to settle, and it nets all the movements in each of the currencies down to a single net payment or receipt for that currency. CLS Bank offers this service for 15 currencies. CLS Bank is headquartered in New York and regulated by the Federal Reserve Bank. An example of settlement netting using the CLS Bank is provided in section 18.1.5.

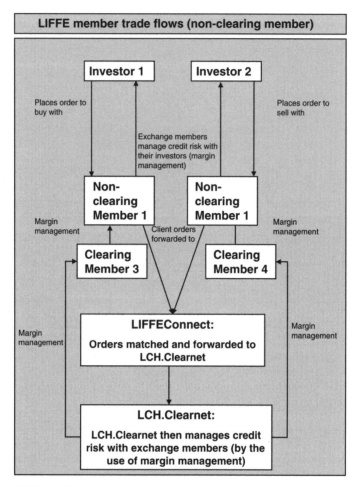

Figure 7.5   LIFFE trade flows – non-clearing member

7.7.2   Central securities depositaries and international central securities depositaries

Sell-side firms use **CSD**s and **ICSD**s to settle their trades in securities. Each country has a single CSD. A CSD is an organisation that serves the investment exchanges of a particular country by holding securities either in certificated or uncertificated (dematerialised) form, to enable transfer of securities between buyer and seller. The functions of a CSD include, *inter alia:*

- *Settlement*: The buyer instructs the CSD to deliver the securities to the seller, and the seller instructs the CSD to make payment to the buyer on value date. Provided that:
  - The seller's instructions and the buyer's instructions match
  - The seller has the securities to deliver
  - The buyer has either cash or credit to pay for the securities.
    Then the CSD will settle the trade on value date.
- *Safe custody*: The CSD holds the securities on behalf of its members.

Table 7.5 Major stock exchanges and their clearing arrangements

Exchange	World ranking (by market capitalisation)	Country	Instrument type	CCP	CSD
NYSE Euronext group, comprising:	1				
New York Stock Exchange		United States	Equities	National Securities Clearing Corporation (NSCC)	Depositary Trust Company (DTC)
		United States	Debt securities	Fixed Income Clearing Corporation (FICC)	Depositary Trust Company (DTC)
Euronext France		France	Debt and equity	LCH.Clearnet	Euroclear France
Euronext Belgium		Belgium	Debt and equity	LCH.Clearnet	Euroclear Belgium
Euronext Netherlands		Netherlands	Debt and equity	LCH.Clearnet	Euroclear Netherlands
Euronext Portugal		Portugal	Debt and equity	Interbolsa	Interbolsa
Tokyo Stock Exchange	2	Japan		Japan Securities Clearing Corporation	Japan Securities Settlement and Custody, Inc.
NASDAQ	3	United States		National Securities Clearing Corporation (NSCC)	Depositary Trust Company (DTC)
London Stock Exchange	4	United Kingdom		LCH.Clearnet	Euroclear UK and Ireland
Hong Kong Stock Exchange	5	Hong Kong		Hong Kong Exchanges and Clearing Ltd	Hong Kong Exchanges and Clearing Ltd
Toronto Stock Exchange	6	Canada		CDS Clearing and Depository Services	CDS Clearing and Depository Services
Frankfurt Stock Exchange	7	Germany		Eurex Clearing	Clearstream
Shanghai Stock Exchange	8	China	Equities	China Securities Depository and Clearing Corporation Limited	China Securities Depository and Clearing Corporation Limited
		China	Government debt	China Government Securities Depository and Clearing Corporation Limited	China Government Securities Depository and Clearing Corporation Limited
Madrid Stock Exchange	9	Spain		IBERCLEAR	IBERCLEAR
Australian Securities Exchange	10	Australia		Australian Clearing House (ACH)	ASX Settlement and Transfer Corporation Pty Limited (ASTC)

- **Dividend** and coupon processing as well as **corporate action** processing. Registrars as well as issuers are involved in these processes, depending on the level of services provided by the CSD and its relationship with these entities.
- *Other services*: CSDs offer additional services aside from those considered core services. These services include securities lending and borrowing, and repo settlement, which are examined in Chapter 21.

An **international central securities depository (ICSD)** is a central securities depository that settles trades in international securities and in various domestic securities, usually through direct or indirect (through local agents) links to local CSDs. ClearStream International (formerly Cedel), Euroclear and SegaInterSettle are considered ICSDs. While some view the New York-based Depository Trust Company (DTC) as the national CSD for the United States rather than an ICSD, in fact DTC – the largest depository in the world – holds over USD 2 trillion in non-US securities from over 100 nations.

Table 7.5 shows the relationship between exchanges, central counterparties and CSDs for the world's 10 largest securities exchanges.

The flow of trades in securities between sell-side firms, exchanges, CCPs and CSDs can be represented by Figure 7.6.

Note that trades in futures and options do not require the involvement of the CSD. The reasons why are explained in Chapter 8.

7.7.3 Commercial custodians

Institutional investors use custodian banks to settle their security trades. The role of a custodian is very similar to that of a CSD, i.e. to hold in safekeeping assets such as equities and bonds, arrange settlement of any purchases and sales of such securities, collect information on and income from such assets (dividends in the case of equities and interest in the case of bonds), process corporate actions, securities lending and borrowing and repo settlement, provide information on the underlying companies and their annual general meetings, manage cash transactions, perform foreign exchange transactions where required and provide regular reporting on all their activities to their clients. This reporting often includes "value added" services that are not provided by a CSD, such as performance measurement and peer group comparison.

Custodian banks are often referred to as **global custodians** if they hold assets for their clients in multiple jurisdictions around the world, using their own local branches or other local custodian banks in each market to hold accounts for their underlying clients.

Note that although the order to trade is given to the sell-side firm by the fund manager that is acting for the institutional investor, it is the investor itself that appoints the custodian. This can lead to the situation where a sell-side firm receives an order from a fund manager to buy or sell the same security for a number of investors, and the sell side firm has to settle separately with many custodians – one for each of the investors.

7.8 OTHER MARKET PARTICIPANTS

7.8.1 Information vendors

Investment firms depend on high quality, fast and robust feeds of real-time information covering market prices, company announcements and corporate actions, and economic and political

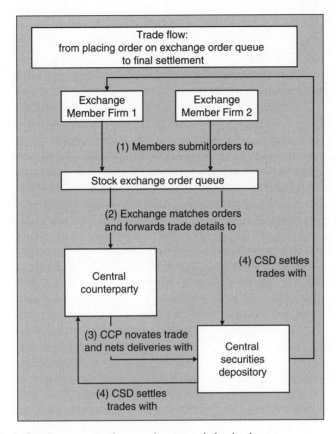

Figure 7.6 Trade flow between members, exchanges and clearing houses

events in order to make investment decisions. The two market leading suppliers of real-time market data are Reuters and Bloomberg.

The original missions of both Reuters –starting in the 1970s – and Bloomberg in the early 1980s were to deliver market data to securities professionals. Since then both companies have expanded enormously and diversified widely, and they both offer a very wide range of information services, media content and packaged software that is far beyond their original scope.

Reuters offers both conversational and automated trading in FX markets. Conversational dealing is where two dealers make use of the Reuters messaging facility to type requests for prices, and if the price is acceptable they type in their agreement to that price. A record of the conversation is printed out at each company's dealing room and is also written to the database, to act as an audit trail of the deal. A significant proportion of FX deals are originated in this way.

Reuters publishes APIs for software developers to enable them to integrate Reuters data with the firms' own applications. Most of this information may be downloaded from www.reuters.com. Registration is required.

7.8.2 Money brokers

Wholesale money brokers arrange deals in FX, money market loans and deposits, OTC derivatives and debt instruments. Sell-side firms pay them a commission for putting them into contact with investors and buy-side firms. Money brokers arrange deals by telephone, and through a variety of electronic networks and internet/intranet portals.

7.8.3 Stock lending intermediaries

Stock lending and **repos** are discussed in detail in Chapter 21. There are a number of specialised firms that find firms that are prepared to lend stock to those firms that wish to borrow, and they normally act as principal in these transactions.

7.8.4 Registrars and transfer agents

Where shares or bonds are issued in registered form, the function of the registrar is to keep the register updated, process corporate actions, ensure that holders receive the correct correspondence from the securities issuers, and pay dividends and coupons.

8

How Investment Firms are Regulated

8.1 INTRODUCTION

In all major economies, firms that play a part in the investment process have their activities monitored by one or more regulators. Regulators should not be confused with central banks, although in some countries the regulator and the central bank may be the same organisation. The precise way in which firms are regulated differs from country to country, although within the European Union, most regulations are harmonised. At a global level, regulators and central banks meet in supranational bodies such as the **Basel Committee**, which harmonises some aspects of regulation from a global perspective.

From an IT perspective, within the business applications used by investment firms, there are a number of functions that behave in the way they do because regulatory requirements have been built into their design. This matter is discussed further in section 8.3.6.

This chapter provides a brief overview of regulation from a global perspective, and then focuses on the main aspects of European, and then United Kingdom, regulation. Note that some authorities (such as the BIS – see section 8.3.1) refer to regulation as "supervision", and in this chapter the two terms have the same meaning unless otherwise stated.

8.2 OBJECTIVES OF REGULATION

The objectives of financial regulation can be summarised by looking at those of the UK regulator, the **Financial Services Authority (FSA)**. The FSA's four specific and equal objectives are:

- Maintaining market confidence
- Promoting public understanding of the financial system
- Securing the appropriate level of protection for consumers
- Reducing financial crime.

While other countries' regulators might express their objective using a different form of words, the FSA's objectives are typical of the objectives of regulators worldwide.

The Bank of England is the UK's central bank. It has two core objectives:

- Monetary stability, defined as stable prices and confidence in the currency. Stable prices are defined by the government's inflation target, which the Bank seeks to meet through the decisions on interest rates taken by the monetary policy.
- Financial stability, which entails detecting and reducing threats to the financial system as a whole. Such threats are detected through the Bank's surveillance and market intelligence functions. They are reduced by strengthening infrastructure, and by financial and other operations, at home and abroad, including, in exceptional circumstances, by acting as the lender of last resort.

There is obviously considerable overlap between the Bank's objective of financial stability and the FSA's four objectives, but it is the work of regulators – not central banks – that we are concerned with in this chapter.

8.3 THE GLOBAL PERSPECTIVE

Virtually every country that has functioning financial markets has appointed regulators. There may be a single regulator (the UK model) or several regulators. For example, in the United States some banks are regulated by the Comptroller of the Currency (a department of the federal government), while other banks are regulated by individual states; securities firms are regulated by the Securities and Exchange Commission (SEC), while trading in listed futures and options is regulated by the Commodity Futures Trading Commission (CFTC).

8.3.1 The Bank for International Settlements (BIS) and the Basel Accord

The **Bank for International Settlements (BIS)** is an international organisation of central banks, based in the Swiss city of Basel. One of its objectives is to act as "a forum for discussion and decision-making among central banks and within the international financial and supervisory community".

To this end, the BIS formed the Basel Committee on Banking Supervision in 1974. In 1988 this committee developed a unified set of minimum adequacy requirements (known as the **Basel Accord**) that central banks and regulators in participating countries agreed to implement. A second version of the Basel Accord (known as **Basel II**) was agreed by the committee in 2004, and is being implemented in over 100 countries at the time of writing.

Basel II has three "pillars":

1. Minimum capital requirements for all BIS members
2. Common approaches to the supervision of banks
3. Common approaches to market discipline.

This chapter is concerned with Pillar 1 – Minimum capital requirements. Regulators require that banks and other investment firms set aside an amount of their own capital to guard against three types of risk – credit risk, market risk and operational risk. Firms can only lend or invest a given multiple of this capital requirement. The Basel Accord sets out the rules for calculating this capital requirement.

The following paragraphs define these three risk categories in more detail.

Credit risk

Credit risk is the risk associated with one party not fulfilling its contractual obligations at a specific future date. Examples of credit risk include the possibility that a trading party might not have the funds to settle a trade in any kind of instrument, or that a securities issuer may be unable to pay dividends, coupons or redemption proceeds. Credit risk is covered by both Basel I and Basel II.

There are a number of commonly used ways in which an investment firm attempts to protect itself against credit risk, including:

1. *Trading party research*: Making credit checks about actual and potential trading parties.
2. *Use of central counterparties*: When trading on order-driven markets, the identity of the actual counterparty is unknown, and all trades are novated by a CCP. The CCP in turn has

the highest credit rating, and its creditworthiness is particularly closely monitored by the national regulator because the CCP's activities are critical to the stability of the financial markets.

3. Requesting parties to provide collateral for certain transactions: This topic is dealt with at length in Chapters 19 to 21.

4. Settling trades on a **delivery versus payment (DvP)** basis: DvP is the simultaneous delivery of securities by a seller and payment of sale proceeds by a purchaser of securities on settlement date. Both parties instruct their settlement agent to deliver or receive on a DvP basis. If the seller does not have the securities, and/or the buyer does not have the cash, then the agent will not settle the trade.

The various forms of credit risk are examined in more detail in Chapter 24.

Market risk

Market risk is the risk that the value of the investments owned by the investor might decline. There are a number of reasons why this may occur, including:

1. There is a general fall in prices of most classes of instrument caused by global economic or political uncertainty.

2. There is a fall in prices of shares issued by companies in a particular industry, which can be caused by either a poor economic outlook for that particular industry or a fall in prices of shares listed in a particular country because of economic or political uncertainty in that country.

3. There is a rise in interest rates for a particular currency (or indeed all currencies). This would cause a fall in bond prices, because for fixed income securities, market risk is closely tied to interest rate risk – as interest rates rise, prices decline and vice versa.

4. A fall in the exchange rate of a particular currency would cause a fall in the value of investments held in that currency when they were held by overseas investors who value in a different currency.

The various forms of market risk are examined in more detail in Chapter 24. Market risk is covered by both Basel I and Basel II. There are two commonly used ways in which an investment firm attempts to protect itself against market risk, including:

1. **Diversification**, which is simply defined as "not putting all your eggs in one basket" and means spreading the investment portfolio across a wide range of industries and/or countries. This protects against the possibilities of losses due to poor performance in a particular sector or country.

2. **Hedging**, which is the purchase or sale of one financial instrument (usually but not necessarily a derivative such as a future or option) for the purpose of offsetting the profit or loss of another security or investment. Thus, any loss on the original investment will be hedged, or offset, by a corresponding profit from the hedging instrument.

Operational risk

Operational risk was introduced in Basel II. It is defined as the risk of loss resulting from inadequate or failed internal processes, people and systems, or from external events. Basel II defines the following "operational risk events":

- *Internal fraud*: Misappropriation of assets, tax evasion, intentional mismarking of positions, bribery

- *External fraud*: Theft of information, hacking damage, third-party theft and forgery
- *Employment practices and workplace safety*: Discrimination, workers' compensation, employee health and safety
- *Clients, products and business practice*: Market manipulation, antitrust, improper trade, product defects, fiduciary breaches, account churning
- *Damage to physical assets*: Natural disasters, terrorism, vandalism
- *Business disruption and systems failures*: Utility disruptions, software failures, hardware failures
- *Execution, delivery and process management*: Data entry errors, accounting errors, failed mandatory reporting, negligent loss of client assets.

This is of course a very broad, sweeping list of potential problems that could cause an investment firm to lose considerable sums of money. Chapters 25 to 27 will discuss some of the risk mitigation techniques that should be used.

Basel II capital calculations for operational risk

Basel II has approved three methods of capital calculation for operational risk:

- *The basic indicator approach*: Simply, a percentage of the annual revenue of the financial institution needs to be set aside to cover operational risk. It is expected that smaller firms with a simple business model will adopt this approach.
- *The standardised approach*: Based on annual revenue of each of the broad business lines of the financial institution. This approach is more refined than the basic indicator approach because it divides a firm's activities into a number of standardised business lines, allowing different risk profiles to be allocated to each. This is intended to provide a more representative reflection of an organisation's overall operational risk. Like the basic indicator approach, it uses gross income as a broad indicator, but applies different percentages of annual income to reflect the assumed riskiness of each business. In order to qualify to use this approach, a firm must convince its regulator that it has the necessary management structure, expertise and systems to meet the measure and control its operational risk.
- *The advanced measurement approach*: Which is based on the firm's internally developed risk measurement framework adhering to the standards prescribed by the regulations. In order to qualify to use the advanced measurement approach the regulators require banks to comply with more stringent criteria than the standardised approach. They list generic, qualitative and quantitative criteria aimed at ensuring that the bank has satisfactory risk management processes, risk measurement systems and risk infrastructure in place to be able to use the AMA. In particular, firms that want to use this approach are required to calculate **Value-at-Risk (VaR)**, which is examined in section 24.1.6.

8.4 THE EUROPEAN PERSPECTIVE

All investment firms in the European Union (EU) are covered by rules issued by national governments and national regulators under the provisions of two EU directives – the Capital Adequacy Directive (**CAD**) and the Markets in Financial Instruments Directive (**MiFID**).

8.4.1 The European Capital Adequacy Directive (CAD)

The first EU-wide Capital Adequacy Directive (known as the Solvency Directive) was issued in 1989. Since then there have been a number of refinements, the latest of which came into force in 2006, although implementation by firms in the member states was not mandatory until 2007. Basically, the CAD is based on Basel II with some modifications.

It applies to all firms in the **European Economic Area** (the 27 EU states plus Iceland, Norway and Liechtenstein). The three states that are outside the EU itself play no part in formulating the directive, but they have agreed to implement it.

The EU's interpretation of Basel's standardised approach is that it does not require institutions to provide their own estimates of risks. It nonetheless incorporates enhanced risk sensitivity by permitting the use of, for example, external ratings of rating agencies and export credit agencies. It also permits the recognition of a considerably expanded range of collateral, guarantees and other "risk mitigants". It includes reduced capital charges for retail lending (6% as compared with 8% in the previous version of CAD) and residential mortgage lending (2.8% as compared with 4% previously).

The EU has renamed Basel's "Advanced Measurement Approach" as the "Internal Ratings-Based (IRB) Approach". This allows institutions to provide their own "risk inputs" – probability of default, loss estimates, etc. – in the calculation of capital requirements. The calculation of these inputs is subject to a strict set of operational requirements to ensure that they are robust and reliable. They are incorporated into a "capital requirement formula" which produces a capital charge for each loan or other exposure that the institution makes. The formula is designed to achieve a high level of soundness of the institution in the event of economic difficulties.

The IRB approach comes in two modes. The "Advanced" mode allows institutions to use their own estimates of all relevant risk inputs. This approach is likely to be chosen by the biggest and most sophisticated institutions.

The "Foundation Approach" requires institutions to provide only the "probability of default" risk input. This will enable a large number of less complex banks to reap the benefits of the risk sensitivity provided by the IRB approach.

Every month, investment firms have to produce a capital adequacy statement for their national regulator. Many firms will have built or purchased a dedicated regulatory accounting system (as shown in Figure 7.3) to fulfil this function.

8.4.2 The Markets in Financial Instruments Directive (MiFID)

The MiFID was enacted in 2004 and came into force on 1 November 2007, replacing the previous **Investment Services Directive** that was introduced in 1995. The legislation is detailed, prescriptive and wide ranging – MiFID's physical presence is twice the size of any of its predecessors. MiFID applies to all firms in the European Economic Area (the 27 EU states plus Iceland, Norway and Liechtenstein) and is concerned primarily with:

- Authorisation of investment firms
- Classification of clients
- Conflicts of interest
- Handling of client money
- Handling of client orders, including pre-trade and post-trade transparency.

Authorisation of investment firms

A firm that has its head office in one EEA state and branches in others will be regulated by the national regulator of the state in which its head office is located. As a result, a UK firm with a branch in France would have its French activities monitored by the FSA, and not by the French regulator.

Classification of clients

MiFID requires that each trading party be classified as one of the following:

1. Eligible counterparty – e.g. another regulated bank or stock exchange member firm
2. Professional client – e.g. a pension fund
3. Retail client – e.g. a private individual.

These points have increasing levels of protection. Clear procedures must be in place to classify clients and assess their suitability for each type of investment product, the appropriateness of any investment advice given or suitability of any transaction suggested to them.

Conflicts of interest

MiFID recognises that conflicts of interest may occur when an investment firm may, for example:

- Be acting for both investors in and issuers of the same security at the same time
- Be acting for more than one investor that has an interest in a particular security
- Be acting for investors that have an interest in a particular security at the same time that the firm itself has an interest in the same security.

MiFID requires firms to have a conflicts management policy which requires them to:

1. Take steps to prevent conflicts of interest giving rise to the material risk of damaging clients' interest
2. Proactively identify business areas where conflicts are likely to arise
3. Document each potential conflict and describe how its affect should be mitigated
4. Disclose its policy to clients on request.

Handling of client money and client assets

MiFID rules include a general requirement to make adequate arrangements to safeguard clients' money and client assets such as securities that the firm may hold on their behalf. There are specific rules about record keeping, segregation and reconciliation.

Handling of client orders and trade execution

Terminology
This is by far the most complex area of MiFID. It imposes different rules on different types of industry participant. It introduces two new terms that were not in common use before MiFID:

- **Multilateral trading facility(MTF)**, which is a system that brings together multiple parties (e.g. retail investors or other investment firms) that are interested in buying and selling financial instruments and enables them to do so. These systems can be crossing networks or

matching engines which are operated by an investment firm or a market operator. Instruments may include shares, bonds and derivatives. An investment exchange is a form of MTF.

- **Systematic internaliser (SI)**, which is a firm, which on a frequent and systematic basis, deals on its own account by executing client orders that are outside the scope of any "multilateral trading facility" (MTF) or exchange.

MiFID requirements

Pre-trade transparency   Investment exchanges, other multilateral trading facilities and systematic internalisers that operate continuous order-matching systems must make aggregated order information available at the five best price levels on the buy and sell side.

For quote-driven markets, the best bids and offers of all market makers must be made available. MiFID establishes minimum standards of pre-trade transparency for shares traded on regulated markets and MTFs.

MiFID also obliges an investment firm that is a "systematic internaliser" to undertake what is effectively a public market-making obligation. That is, the firm must provide a definite bid and offer quotes in liquid shares for orders below "standard market size".

Post-trade transparency   Investment exchanges and MTFs must publish the details of all trades executed in their systems. The exact detail of what information is to be published is left to the regulator of the country concerned.

Additionally, investment firms must publish details of trades in relevant instruments executed in the OTC markets.

Publication must be close to real time, and in any event within three minutes of trade execution. Exceptions are made for transactions taking place outside of a venue's normal trading hours, when publication must be made prior to the start of the next trading day. The full text of the rule about the timeliness of publication states

> Information which is required to be made available as close to real time as possible should be made available as close to instantaneously as technically possible, assuming a reasonable level of efficiency and of expenditure on systems on the part of the person concerned. The information should only be published close to the three minute maximum limit in exceptional cases where the systems available do not allow for a publication in a shorter period of time.

National regulators receive all the published post-trade details from all the publishers within their jurisdiction and enter them into a database that they use to monitor **market abuse** and **insider dealing**.

Best execution   Because of the complexity of the MiFID rules about best execution, this section is broken down into two subsections. The first explains the principles of best execution; the second describes the MiFID requirements.

The principles of best execution, timely execution and customer order priority   Broadly speaking, best execution places an obligation on the sell-side firm to get the lowest available price for its customer when the customer is buying, and the highest available price when the customer is selling. If a financial instrument is only quoted on one investment exchange, and that exchange trades it on a quote-driven system, then this obligation is usually fulfilled simply by placing an order on the order queue. The exchange's own systems will then match it with an opposite order appropriately.

Timely execution gives the firm an obligation to select the most opportune time to execute the order.

If a financial instrument is only quoted on one investment exchange, and that exchange trades it on a quote-driven system, then the best execution obligation is usually fulfilled simply by placing an order on the order queue. The exchange's own systems will then match it with an opposite order appropriately.

There are situations, however, where the sell-side firm needs to take more care and skill in handling the order. For example:

1. *When the order is above normal market size*: If the order is to buy or sell a very large amount of stock, then simply placing the entire order on the order queue in one operation will have the affect of moving the price adversely. In such a situation the sell-side firm has two alternatives:
   - It could split the order up into smaller parcels and feed it on to the order book over a few days. This may, however, conflict with its obligation to provide timely execution.
   - It could (if the order was to sell) purchase the stock from the investor as a principal transaction, and dispose of the stock that it now owns over a few days. If it does this it needs to be able to prove that the price it charged the investor was not lower than the prevailing order book price at the time. If the order was to buy, then it could sell the stock to the investor as a principal transaction, and purchase the stock that it is now obliged to deliver over a few days. If it does this it needs to be able to prove that the price it charged the investor was not higher than the prevailing order book price – in other words that it has in fact achieved best execution.
2. *When the instrument is quoted on more than one exchange*: The shares of large multi-national companies are often quoted on many stock exchanges. The main market for Sony Corporation shares, for example, is the Tokyo Stock Exchange (where Sony shares are priced in JPY), but Sony shares are also quoted on the LSE (both in JPY and GBP), the New York Stock Exchange (in USD) and the Deutsche Borse (in EUR). In such a case, a sell-side firm that has access to all of these exchanges should research the prevailing price levels on all of them to establish the most favourable price for the client. However, the two parties have also to take into account some other factors when deciding which exchange to route the order to:
   - Tokyo is the main market where most of the trades take place. There might be less liquidity in the other markets, meaning that the order might take longer to fill.
   - On the other hand, say that the investor is located in the USA, and has requested execution today. By the start of the working day in the USA, the Tokyo market has already closed, and therefore execution today is not possible. The NYSE will be open, and the European exchanges may also still be open.
   - The customer might want to pay for Sony shares in JPY. Because the Deutsche Borse prices Sony shares in EUR and the NYSE prices them in USD, there would be additional foreign exchange transaction costs in trading in New York or Frankfurt.
   - It is possible that the sell-side firm that receives the order is not, itself, a member of the exchange that is offering the best price and the most liquid market. For example, not all London-based firms are members of the Tokyo Stock Exchange. If this is the case, then the London firm might have to use another broker in Tokyo to place the order on its behalf. This would involve two lots of brokers' commission, and this could invalidate the price advantage if it was very slight to begin with.

The above examples show that there can be a practical conflict between "timely execution" and "execution at the best price".

The final rule that the sell-side firm needs to take into account is **customer order priority**. The firm is obliged to execute customer orders and own account orders fairly and in due turn. This rule exists because of the possibilities of conflict of interest between the sell-side firm and the investor. For example, a firm may wish to invest its own capital in purchasing Sony shares. If, at the same time, that firm has a client that wishes to sell a large quantity of Sony shares, which hits the market before the buy orders, it could have the affect of moving the price in the firm's favour.

MiFID best execution requirements   Article 21 of the MiFID regulations states that financial services firms carrying out transactions on their clients' behalf:

> must take all reasonable steps to obtain the best possible result, taking into account price, costs, speed, likelihood of execution and settlement, size, nature or any other consideration relevant to the execution of the order.

Article 21 goes on to say that firms need to:

1. Establish an execution policy, which must contain information on the venues firms used to execute client orders. Those venues must allow it to consistently obtain the best possible result for execution for their clients;
2. Disclose the policy to clients and obtaining their consent to that policy;
3. Monitor the effectiveness of arrangements in order to identify and correct any deficiencies and review the appropriateness of the venues in its execution policy at least yearly; and
4. Upon client request, be ready to demonstrate that the client's order has been executed in line with its execution policy.

8.5   THE UK PERSPECTIVE – THE ROLE OF THE FINANCIAL SERVICES AUTHORITY

Figure 8.1 shows the linkage between the work of Basel II, the European Union and the national regulator: legislation enacted by the EU is known as Level 1 legislation. Level 1 legislation is often at a high level; the detailed instructions that have to be complied with are usually found in the individual legislation of the member states. This is known as Level 2 legislation.

The UK regulator is the Financial Services Authority which was created by the **Financial Services and Markets Act (FSMA)** of 2000. The FSA undertakes both prudential regulation, which is concerned with ensuring that investment companies are financially sound, and business conduct regulation, which is concerned with the way business is transacted, in particular with the way that products are marketed and sold and investors are treated fairly. Broadly speaking prudential regulation comes under the auspices of the CAD, and business conduct regulation comes under the auspices of MiFID.

The FSA describes its approach to its work as "principles-based regulation", which it defines as:

> Placing greater reliance on principles and outcome-focused, high-level rules as a means to drive at the regulatory aims we want to achieve, and less reliance on prescriptive rules.

The 11 principles that it has established are:

1. A firm must conduct its business with integrity.
2. A firm must conduct its business with due skill, care and diligence.
3. A firm must take reasonable care to organise and control its affairs responsibly and effectively, with adequate risk management systems.

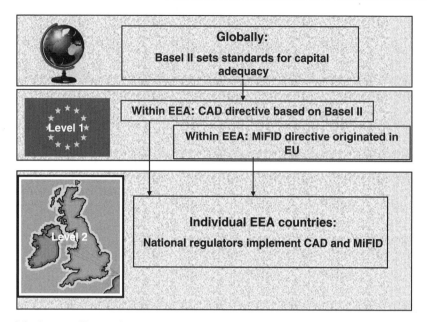

Figure 8.1   Layers of international regulation

4. A firm must maintain adequate financial resources.
5. A firm must observe proper standards of market conduct.
6. A firm must pay due regard to the interests of its customers and treat them fairly.
7. A firm must pay due regard to the information needs of its clients, and communicate information to them in a way which is clear, fair and not misleading.
8. A firm must manage conflicts of interest fairly, both between itself and its customers and between a customer and another client.
9. A firm must take reasonable care to ensure the suitability of its advice and discretionary decisions for any customer who is entitled to rely upon its judgement.
10. A firm must arrange adequate protection for clients' assets when it is responsible for them.
11. A firm must deal with its regulators in an open co-operative way, and must disclose to the FSA appropriately anything relating to the firm of which the FSA would reasonably expect notice.

Nevertheless, despite the fact that the FSA has adopted principles-based regulation, there are a large number of individual rules. These rules are published in the FSA Handbook, which is available online at http://www.fsa.gov.uk/Pages/handbook/.

8.6   SPECIFIC OFFENCES IN THE UNITED KINGDOM

IT practitioners working in the United Kingdom need to be aware of three specific offences of which investment firms and also employees of investment firms may be accused. The three offences are:

- Insider dealing
- Market abuse
- Money laundering.

Similar legislation exists in most countries; the UK legislation is quoted as an example of the type of legislation that exists globally.

8.6.1 Insider dealing

Insider dealing is a criminal offence in the United Kingdom under the Criminal Justice Act (CJA) of 1993. It is punishable by a fine or a jail term.

The offence of insider dealing is committed when an insider acquires or disposes of price-affected securities while in possession of unpublished price-sensitive information. The insider is also guilty of insider dealing if he encourages another person to deal in price-affected securities, or if he discloses the information to another person (other than in the proper performance of his employment). The acquisition or disposal must occur on a regulated market or through a professional intermediary.

To be found guilty of insider dealing, an insider in possession of inside information must commit the offence. The CJA provides the detail as to who is deemed to be an insider, what is deemed to be inside information and the situations that give rise to the offence. Inside information relates to particular securities or a particular issuer of securities (and not to securities or securities issuers generally) and:

- is specific or precise
- has not been made public
- if it were made public, it would be likely to have a significant effect on the price of the securities.

How price-sensitive information is made public

Listed companies have to announce price-sensitive information using a **regulatory news service** that disseminates it simultaneously to subscribers including the press and investment firms of all types. Regulatory news services are provided by a number of commercial organisations including stock exchanges and information providers such as Reuters and Thomsons. Listed companies have to announce price-sensitive information to these services as a condition of their listing. The type of information that they need to announce includes, *inter alia*:

- Final year end results and interim results
- Proposed dividends and other corporate actions
- Substantial changes of ownership
- Appointment and resignations of directors.

Any information of this type that has not yet been published on an RNS is, by definition, "unpublished, price-sensitive information".

IT implications of insider dealing

The standard way of preventing leakages of this type of information is by the implementation of Chinese walls, which is examined in section 25.3.1. However, it is worth noting that technical support staff often have access to many sources of information including production feeds when diagnosing production issues. The impact of this information entering the public domain should be considered, and risk assessed especially when work is being carried out offsite or offshore, where secure access is not assured.

8.6.2   Market abuse

Market abuse is an offence introduced by FSMA 2000; judged on what a "regular user" would view as a failure to observe the required standards. The offence includes:

- Abuse of information
- Misleading the market
- Distortion of the market
- Manipulating the market
- Disclosing inside information
- Failure to observe the required standards.

The FSA is empowered to impose financial penalties on the firms and also the individuals that it regulates if they are found guilty of market abuse.

8.6.3   Money laundering

Money laundering is an offence under a number of instruments, including the Proceeds of Crime Act 2002 (POCA), the Serious Organised Crime and Police Act 2005 (SOCPA) and the Money Laundering Regulations 2003.

Money laundering is the process of turning dirty money (money derived from criminal activities) into clean money (money that appears to be legitimate). Dirty money is difficult to invest or spend and carries the risk of being used as evidence of the initial crime. Clean money can be invested and spent without risk of incrimination. Money laundering is disguising the proceeds of illegal activities as legitimate money that can be freely spent. Increasingly anti-money laundering provisions are being seen as the frontline against drug dealing, organised crime and the "war against terrorism". Much police activity is directed towards making the disposal of criminal assets more difficult and monitoring the movement of money.

There are three stages to a successful money laundering operation:

- *Placement*: This stage typically involves placing the criminally derived cash into a bank or building society account.
- *Layering*: Layering involves moving the money around in order to make it difficult for the authorities to link the placed funds with the ultimate beneficiary of the money. This might involve buying and selling foreign currencies, shares or bonds.
- *Integration*: At this final stage, the layering has been successful and the ultimate beneficiary appears to be holding legitimate funds (clean money rather than dirty money). Broadly, the anti-money laundering provisions are aimed at identifying customers and reporting suspicions at the placement and layering stages, and keeping adequate records which should prevent the integration stage being reached.

The Money Laundering Regulations 2003 and the FSA rules require firms to adopt identification procedures for new clients (to "know your client") and keep records in relation to this proof of identity. The obligation to prove identity is triggered as soon as reasonably practicable after contact is made and the parties resolve to form a business relationship. Failure to prove the identity of the client could lead to an unlimited fine and a jail term of up to two years under the Money Laundering Regulations 2003.

The types of acceptable documentary evidence to prove the identity of a new client include the following:

For an individual

- An official document with a photograph (passport, international driving licence) will prove the name.
- A utilities bill (gas, water or electricity) with name and address will prove the address supplied is valid.

For a corporate client (a company)

- Proof of identity and existence would be drawn from the constitutional documents (Articles and Memorandum of Association) and sets of accounts.
- For smaller companies proving the identity of the key individual stakeholders (directors and shareholders) would also be required.

For a trust

The identity of the settlor (the person putting assets into trust), the trustees and the controller of the trust (the person who is able to instruct the trustees) would all be verified, along with a copy of the trust deed.

8.7 REGULATION AND ITS IMPACT ON THE IT FUNCTION

The impact of the regulatory environment upon an investment firm's IT functions may be summarised as follows.

8.7.1 Impact on the application configuration

Look again at Figure 7.3, which is repeated here as Figure 8.2 for clarity.

First, the reason that the regulatory accounting system is present in the configuration is that regulators require firms to produce a statutory capital adequacy report each month – if this were not required, then there would be no need for the application at all.

Second, in this chapter we have mentioned that there are rules concerning, *inter alia:*

- *Best execution, timely execution and customer order priority*: Therefore the design of the front-office systems (the applications that are primarily concerned with the management of order flow) has to take these rules into account in its business logic if these regulations are to be complied with.
- *Pre-trade publication of bid and offer prices*: If the firm concerned was a systematic internaliser, then it would need to build in the ability to broadcast these prices to its customers in the relevant front-office systems.
- *Post-trade publication of trade details within three minutes of execution*: Again, business logic needs to be built into the front-office systems concerned in order to comply with this requirement.
- *Client assets need to be reconciled*: This is one of the reasons for the existence of the reconciliation application. Another reason for the existence of this application is that it used to detect problems that can lead to operational risk – specifically those risks caused by internal fraud and errors in execution, delivery, and process management.

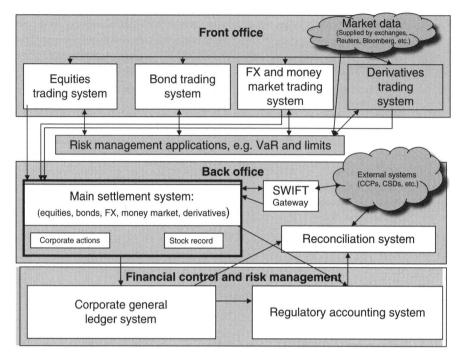

Figure 8.2   Simplified investment bank configuration

8.7.2   Impact on the way that the department is managed

Poor management of the IT function would be a major contributor to an unacceptable level of operational risk. Let us remind ourselves of the seven operational risk events as defined by Basel II, and examine how poor IT practice can increase operational risk, while good practice can mitigate it:

1. *Internal fraud*: Misappropriation of assets, tax evasion, intentional mismarking of positions, bribery

   These activities can be facilitated by practices that allow, *inter alia*, unauthorised access to applications and underlying data. They may be mitigated by the use of application password control and the deployment of systems that support the concept of segregation of duties.
2. *External fraud*: Theft of information, hacking damage, third-party theft and forgery

   As for (1) above, but in addition these problems can be mitigated by the deployment of antivirus software, anti-spyware software, firewalls, etc.
3. *Employment practices and workplace safety*: Discrimination, workers, compensation, employee health and safety

   There are no specific IT-related issues to this event, it is a company-wide issue.
4. *Clients, products and business practice*: Market manipulation, antitrust, improper trade, product defects, fiduciary breaches, account churning

   "Product defects" in this context includes defects in the software and hardware that is used to process the firm's data. Good IT practice involves the use of standardised, reliable methodologies to discover and document business requirements, select software vendors and packages, build, test and deploy software and manage projects. It also involves the use of configuration management and change control procedures to ensure that the right software versions are deployed. These topics are examined more deeply in Chapters 25 to 27.

5. *Damage to physical assets*: Natural disasters, terrorism, vandalism and:
6. *Business disruption and systems failures*: Utility disruptions, software failures, hardware failures

These risks may be mitigated by proper business recovery plans which are examined in Chapter 25. Software failures may also arise as a result of product defects (Basel II Event no. 4).

7. *Execution, delivery and process management*: Data entry errors, accounting errors, failed mandatory reporting, negligent loss of client assets

These events, in turn, may be caused by product defects.

8.7.3   Other regulations that affect the IT department

In addition to the regulations that are imposed on the firm by its financial regulator, there will be many other regulations imposed on them by other legislation that is common to companies of all kinds, such as legal restrictions concerning data retention and data protection, as well as general accounting and tax requirements. Some of these will be examined in more detail in Chapter 25.

9

Straight-Through-Processing

9.1 INTRODUCTION

Straight-through-processing (STP) is a set of working practices and systems that enable transactions to move seamlessly through the processing cycle, without manual intervention or redundant handling. Transactions in this context include not only orders and trades, but also the position-related activities such as corporate actions, accruals and mark-to-market processes, which are described in Chapter 23.

The key principles of STP are the following:

1. The transaction is entered into the firm's systems only once – it should never have to be rekeyed into another of the firm's systems.
2. As most investment firms need to record the transaction into more than one system, there need to be automated interfaces between all systems that need to store records of the order or trade.
3. Transaction processing should consist of a set of logical stages, each one being dependent on the satisfactory conclusion of the previous stage. No stage should commence until the previous stage has completed successfully.
4. Clerical intervention should be avoided as far as possible, but clerical staff should be enabled to manage by exception – that is to say that if one of the processing stages fails to complete satisfactorily, the fact that this has happened should be presented to skilled staff in a form in which they can deal with the exception in the most efficient manner.
5. Principles 1 to 4 above apply not just within the firm but also between the various firms involved in the transaction.

9.1.1 Client orders and their contents

As far as trades in financial instruments and their settlement are concerned, STP flow always starts with the placing of an order. An order is an instruction to:

- Buy or sell:
- A specific quantity or money value of a specific financial instrument such as an equity, bond, currency or derivative . . .

. . . as well as a number of instructions relating to the price of that instrument, such as:

- "At best" or "at market" – meaning buy or sell at the best available price the member firm can obtain
- Limit – where a price is specified, meaning:
  - If selling, do not sell for a price lower than the limit price
  - If buying, do not pay more than the limit price
- Stop loss – sell if and when the market price falls to this level . . .

... as well as a number of time related features such as:

- "Good till cancelled" or "open order" – there is no time limit on this order
- Expiry date – if the order cannot be filled by this date then it should be treated as cancelled
- "Fill or kill" – if the order is, say, to buy 10 000 shares of ABC plc, then either complete the order in full or reject it if the member firm can only obtain, say, 5000 shares.

9.1.2 Buy-side and sell-side connectivity

Orders may be placed by the buy-side (and therefore received at the sell-side) by a number of methods, including:

- By telephone or fax
- By entering the order details into a secure web page provided by the sell-side firm
- By sending the sell-side firm a SWIFT message. SWIFT is covered more fully in section 11.1.
- By entering the order details directly into the sell-side firm's order management system. This, in turn, may be facilitated by using a third-party "hub and spoke" order routing service. Providers of such services include:
  - Omgeo LLC, through its Oasys product
  - Thomson Financial, through its Autex product
  - Bloomberg, through its POMS and TOMS systems
  - Reuters
  - As well as many other package products and systems developed in-house by fund managers.

Consider the following example where an investor places an order with a broker who then places the order on a stock exchange order queue. The broker first needs to confirm the trade with the investor and then to send settlement instructions to its settlement agent, who will then settle the trade. These stages can be represented by Figure 9.1, and we shall look at the various stages of trade processing from the point of view of the broker.

> *Stage 1*: The investor places an order with a broker. In a truly STP compliant environment this order would be placed electronically. If it is placed electronically, then it is automatically recorded in the broker's front-office system without manual intervention. If, however, it were placed by telephone, then the broker would need to enter it into the system manually, and this is the only time that the trade is keyed into any of the broker's systems
>
> *Stage 2*: This order is then forwarded to a stock exchange order queue. The decision to do this *might* be taken automatically by the broker's front-office system because that system includes business rules that tell it which exchange order queue to forward it to. However, if the order was for more than normal market size for that security, and/or the security was quoted by more than one exchange, then decisions about whether to split it into a smaller number of orders, and/or which exchange to forward it to, might need to be taken by a dealer. In a truly STP-compliant environment, an order that required human intervention would be flagged as such by the system, and displayed to the dealer concerned in such a way that he could select the most appropriate actions.

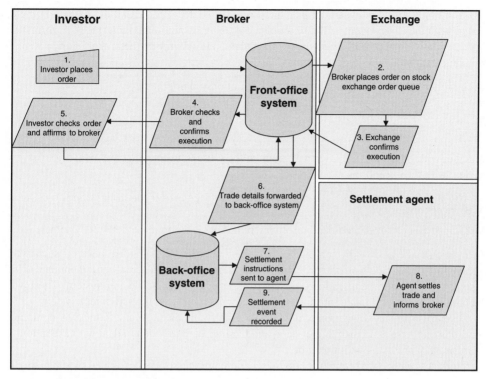

Figure 9.1   Simplified order flow

Irrespective of whether or not there has been human intervention of this kind, the order is placed on the exchange queue automatically by means of an interface between the broker and exchange systems concerned.

Stage 3: The exchange confirms that the deal has been executed by sending a message that is processed by the broker's front-office system. This system contains business rules to check executions against orders, and provided that the message from the exchange passes the required test, the process moves to Stage 4. If there is a discrepancy, then details of the trade are displayed to the relevant users who then decide what action to take.

Stage 4: The broker then confirms the execution to the investor, by means of an automated interface.

Stage 5: The investor repeats the checking process within its systems. If it is satisfied that the executed trade represents the order it placed, then it affirms it back to the broker, by means of an automated interface. If it disagrees with the execution, then it takes it up with the broker – this process is not usually automated.

Stage 6: Subject to satisfactory completion of Stage 5, the trade details are then forwarded to the broker's back-office (settlement) system.

Stage 7: The settlement system prepares the settlement instructions which are then sent to the broker's settlement agent by means of an automated interface. The settlement agent acknowledges receipt of these instructions, again by means of an automated interface.

From time to time between the date and time of trade execution, and the date and time of actual settlement, the agent will communicate – using an automated interface – information about the likelihood of settling on the contracted date. It will inform the broker of any potential problems that would delay settlement, such as:

- The seller's instructions and the buyer's instructions do not match
- The seller does not have the securities to deliver
- The buyer does not have sufficient cash or credit to pay for the securities.

In an STP-compliant settlement system there will be facilities to display these messages, together with other relevant information about the trade to users who can manually intervene to deal with the exceptions.

> *Stage 8*: The agent settles the trade and reports to the broker that it has done so using an automated interface.
>
> *Stage 9*: The broker records that settlement has occurred in its settlement system.

In addition to the steps shown on Figure 9.1, remember that each significant event – such as the generation of the trade from the order and the settlement event on actual settlement date – will also cause accounting entries to be posted to the broker's general ledger system. These will be handled by an automated interface to the general ledger from the settlement system – refer to Chapter 14 for an explanation of how this is usually achieved. Again, in the STP compliant environment there is no rekeying of data, and facilities are provided to deal with exceptions if there are any problems with this process.

Interfaces may be real-time or periodic scheduled processes, as demanded by the nature of the information being transmitted. In older applications, exceptions may be printed on paper or displayed on user interfaces which users have to check regularly, but in newer systems these exceptions are often displayed in "workbaskets" and automated email messages warn affected users that there are items that require their attention.

9.2   TO WHAT EXTENT IS STP ACTUALLY ACHIEVED IN PRACTICE?

The STP compliant environment described in section 9.1 is an ideal, and not all firms achieve 100% STP for all financial instruments. There is evidence that the more complex the instrument, the lower the STP rate.

In 2006 the Celent Group conducted a survey, based on interviews of over 80 senior executives from a cross-section of European institutions. The majority of respondents indicated that less than 50% of OTC derivatives processing is automated, according to the survey. The lack of STP in OTC derivatives was mainly attributed to the complexity of transactions and lack of standards. As a result, 35% of respondents cited derivatives as the number one priority for STP projects as opposed to other instrument classes. The study also illustrates that equities, fixed income and foreign exchange are benefiting from relatively high levels of STP but still need improvement. The current level of automation of OTC derivative processes involved in trade agreement, and the obstacles to improving it, is examined in section 12.1.1.

10

The Role of Accurate Static Data in the STP Process

The accuracy of static data is a significant factor in achieving STP. Incorrect or incomplete static information is a common cause of trade processing errors. The static data challenge for securities firms can be said to be to[1]:

- Gather the required data from disparate sources
- Store it securely
- Update it when necessary
- Utilise it appropriately.

This chapter explores the most important items of static data that need to be held regarding:

- The financial instruments that are traded
- The trading parties that the firm deals with
- The settlement agents used by the firm and its trading parties
- Divisions, departments and business units of the firm, including **trading books**
- Countries in which these various entities are located.

10.1 STATIC DATA OVERVIEW

In Figure 10.1, *ABC Investment Bank* has a number of dealing teams or *trading books*. The trading books buy and sell *financial instruments* that include *bonds, currencies, futures and options and equities*. The instruments, in turn have *parameters*, including *price calculation methods* – for all instruments – *and interest rates and interest calculation methods* – for bonds and currencies. There are also standard *identifiers* used throughout the industry to uniquely identify instruments, as well as rules that apply to the markets in which the instruments are traded.

In turn, all instruments are *denominated in a currency* – that is to say, bonds, equities, futures and options are normally traded and settled in a particular currency.

There is a *public holiday* calendar associated with each currency, and on the public holidays for that currency no trades can settle, and usually investment exchanges are closed.

The instruments are bought from or sold to *trading parties*. This term includes *exchanges, counterparties and clients*. Every one of these is resident in a particular country, as is ABC Investment Bank itself.

All of the trading parties, as well as ABC Investment Bank, have appointed *settlement agents* (this term includes central counterparties, CSDs and custodians) to settle trades in particular markets within a country. Settlement agents are unable to settle trades on a day which is a public holiday for the currency of the trade concerned.

---

[1] Michael Simmons provided this definition in *Securities Operations – A Guide to Trade and Position Management*; John Wiley & Sons, 2002. Reproduced by permission of John Wiley and Sons Ltd.

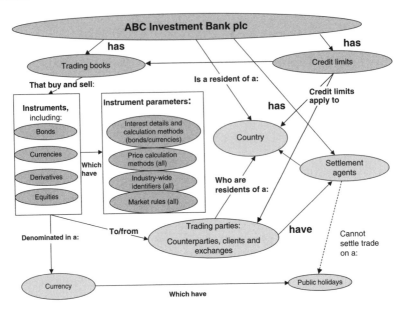

Figure 10.1   Static data overview

ABC Investment Bank also has credit policies and *credit limits* that restrict the total amount of exposure that the firm is prepared to tolerate for particular trading books, trading parties, clients and countries.

The following static data elements also need to be maintained, and are not shown on the figure for the sake of simplicity:

1. *Standard settlement instructions* (SSIs): Both ABC Investment Bank and its trading parties have standard settlement instructions. These control the selection of which settlement agent settles trades, in particular instruments for the two parties concerned. SSIs are examined in section 10.6.
2. *Commission rates*: When ABC is acting as agent it will charge customers commission. Commission rates will vary according to client and instrument class. Commission structures are described in section 10.7.

10.2   DUPLICATION OF STATIC DATA ACROSS SYSTEMS

One of the problems involved in managing the IT infrastructure of a large institution is that there may be a large number of individual business application systems in the configuration, all of which hold some of this large amount of static data, and some of the information may be duplicated across the different systems. Where there is duplication of static data, there is a danger that errors creep in – for example, the data about a particular instrument in one system is slightly different to that in another system. Figure 10.2 – a simplified version of Figure 7.3 – illustrates the problem. It is clear that, for example, every one of the systems in this configuration would need to hold details about all the currencies that the firm trades, so there is a danger that such data may become insistent between them.

To overcome these issues, some firms have built separate **static data repositories** which take in data from reliable sources such as Bloomberg or Reuters, and then feed this data to all the other systems in the configuration; those firms now appear as shown in Figure 10.3.

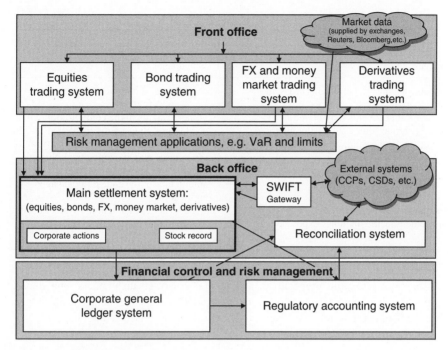

Figure 10.2 Simplified configuration

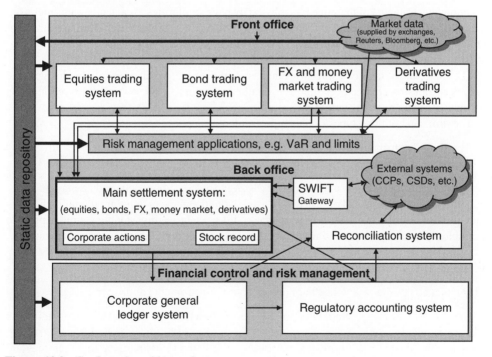

Figure 10.3 Configuration with repository

Table 10.1   Advantages and disadvantages of a repository

Static data repositories	
Advantages	Disadvantages
Ensures consistency of static data across all business applications	May be costly to build the system
Some static data elements may be fed from reliable external sources, e.g. Bloomberg, Reuters, exchanges and clearing houses	All other systems in the configuration will also need to be enhanced to utilise the SDR through the use of APIs – this may be costly, and in some cases may be impractical; this may be because the firm does not have the ability to amend the source code of a packaged application
Data is maintained by a dedicated data management team which has expertise in this area	May be costly to maintain the system itself and also to maintain the data in the system

If a firm chooses to build a repository, then it usually also sets up an operational department whose function it is to manage the collection and update of all static data. The advantages and disadvantages of using a static data repository may be summarised as in Table 10.1.

10.3   INSTRUMENT GROUP STATIC DATA

Individual instruments of the same type obviously have similarities to each other. It is therefore a useful concept in an investment industry application to hold a table of user-defined instrument groups, so that all individual instruments that are members of a group can inherit characteristics of that group.

The major advantage of using instrument groups are that when an attribute changes, the data need only be changed for the group, rather than for all the (potentially thousands of) instruments that are members of that group.

The firm can hold two types of data at instrument group level:

- "Hard data": Attributes of the group that all industry participants would agree with
- "Soft data": Attributes of the group that are specific to this firm.

Consider the following examples (Tables 10.2 and 10.3) of how default data may be maintained at group level instead of instrument level. Note that the examples are not all inclusive – they do not describe every item of data that could be held in this way, they simply provide examples of how an instrument group table could be utilised within a business application.

Example 1: UK equities quoted on the London Stock Exchange

This table tells us the following "hard data" about all instruments of this type:

- The *default* currency of trading is pounds sterling – although this could be over-ridden on any individual trade.
- By default, the currency in which the trades settle is the same currency in which they are traded.
- Normally, trades are expected to settle three days after trade date.

Table 10.2   Instrument group data for equities

Group name	Hard attributes		Soft attributes	
	Name	Value	Name	Value
UK equities quoted on London Stock Exchange	Default trade currency	GBP	Commission scheme	LSE_Comm
	Default settlement currency	GBP	Charge schemes	LSE_Charges
	Normal value date	T + 3	Market rules	LSE
	Normal quote	Pennies		
	Interest bearing	No		

- Normally, prices are quoted in penny units of the currency in which they are traded.
- Instruments of this type do not bear interest.

And it also tells us the following "soft data" about these instruments:

- This firm charges commission on trades in these instruments based on data held in a commission scheme called "LSE_Comm" – see section 10.7 for more information about commission schemes.
- As well as commission, there are other charges that may apply to trades in these instruments. Details of these charges are held in a charge scheme called "LSE_Charges" – see section 10.7 for more information.
- When this firm trades these instruments, it deals according to the rules of the London Stock Exchange – note that it is a regulatory requirement to print this information on trade confirmations.

Example 2: Straight Eurobonds

This table tells us the following "hard data" about all instruments of this type:

- As Eurobonds may be denominated in any currency, there is no default trade currency for the group. The data must be entered at individual instrument level.

Table 10.3   Instrument group data for debt instruments

Group name	Hard attributes		Soft attributes	
	Name	Value	Name	Value
Straight Eurobonds	Default trade currency	N/A	Commission scheme	No
	Default settlement currency	Trade currency	Charge schemes	No
	Normal value date	T + 3	Market rules	ICMA
	Normal quote	Percentage		
	Interest bearing	Yes		
	Interest calculation formula	Actual/actual		

- By default, the currency in which the trades settle is the same currency in which they are traded.
- Normally, trades are expected to settle three days after trade date.
- Normally, prices are quoted as a percentage of face value.
- Instruments of this type do bear interest.
- The normal interest calculation formula is actual/actual.

And it also tells us the following "soft data" about these instruments:

- This firm does not charge commission on trades in these instruments.
- There are no other charges on trades in these instruments.
- When this firm trades these instruments, it deals according to the rules of the **International Capital Markets Association (ICMA)** – note that it is a regulatory requirement to print this information on trade confirmations.

10.4   INSTRUMENT STATIC DATA

10.4.1   Instrument identification codes

In order that different industry participants are able to exchange messages between each other, standardised identification codes are needed for each instrument. For currencies, the ISO currency code is used almost universally.

For securities, a number of different coding schemes are widely used. This means that applications should be designed to have a one-to-many relationship between an individual security and the various identification coding schemes that may be needed to support STP in different markets in which the firm operates. These coding schemes are likely to include:

1. *ISIN code (International Securities Identification Number)*: This is a 12 character, alpha-numeric code where:
   - The first two characters are the country code of the country where the security was issued.
   - The next nine characters are the national securities identification number for that country.
   - The last character is a check digit that is used to verify the code.
   ISIN is the most commonly used code in financial messaging. **ISIN codes** are allocated to bonds and equities, but not to derivative instruments. There is only one ISIN code for each security, no matter on how many stock exchanges that security is listed. This can cause confusion when one firm sends a message to another firm about a particular security – the receiver is able to identify the security but not the country where it was traded or is to be settled. Because of this problem, two further coding schemes have been established that attempt to solve this problem:
2. *SEDOL code (Stock Exchange Daily Official List Code)*: This is a code which is issued by the London Stock Exchange. The LSE has allocated **SEDOL codes** to over 2 million individual debt and equity securities that are traded in a number of markets around the world; SEDOL codes are not restricted just to those securities that are listed on the LSE.
   The LSE allocates an individual SEDOL code to the combination of each individual security and country in which trading is carried out. For countries such as the United States

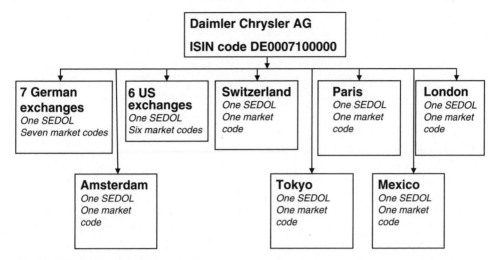

Figure 10.4 ISIN and SEDOL code allocation

and Germany where there is more than one stock exchange, further granularity is provided by the use of an additional market code. Figure 10.4 shows the example of Daimler Chrysler AG common shares which were quoted on 19 stock exchanges in eight countries.

As a result, Daimler Chrysler common shares had a single ISIN code, eight SEDOL codes and 19 **market identifier codes**. The market codes can, if necessary, be used to differentiate between shares traded on the various exchanges in the USA and Germany.

3. *ISIN code + market identifier code*: The same objective – of having a unique identifier for each individual security in the market where it is traded – may also be achieved by concatenating the security's ISIN code with the relevant market identifier code.

In addition to the ISIN code and SEDOL codes, several countries operate their own coding schemes, including those shown in Table 10.4.

10.4.2 Stock exchange ticker symbols

In addition to the security identification codes that are used in financial messaging, most stock exchange trading systems also identify securities by means of a ticker symbol, which is usually an abbreviation of the name. Investment firms may also need to store a number of

Table 10.4 Major country security coding schemes

Country	Coding scheme name
Australia	ASX
Canada	Cusip
Germany	WKN
Japan	Quick
USA	Cusip

ticker symbols for each security that they trade, each one will need to be associated with a particular market where the security is listed.

10.4.3   Static data needed to perform security calculations

The following items need to be stored for each security in order that the basic price calculations and interest calculations described in Chapter 6 can be performed accurately:

- For all instruments:
  - Price multiplier
  - Price divisor
- For interest bearing instruments:
  - For straight bonds – the coupon rate that will apply for the life of the bond
  - For floating rate notes – the benchmark interest rate and the margin above or below the rate that will apply to this bond issue
  - Interest calculation method
  - Rules for predicting coupon dates – for example, the legal documentation that accompanies a new bond issue will inform the reader of the following:
    - The first date on which the bond pays a coupon
    - The final date on which it pays a coupon, usually this is also the maturity date
    - The coupon frequency (e.g. annually, semi-annually, etc.)
    - For FRNs – the fixing dates when the benchmark rate will be determined for each coupon period
    - The business rules that are to be used (in conjunction with first coupon date and coupon frequency) to calculate future coupon dates. These rules are written in legal terms that provide specific instructions as to what the application should do when a predicted future coupon date falls on a non-working day for the currency concerned.

Example of the use of business rules to predict future coupon dates

A bond is issued on Wednesday 28 February 2007, paying semi-annual coupons until maturity date 28 February 2017. Business rules are needed to:

1. Establish whether the next coupon date is 28 August 2007 (exactly six months from 28 February 2007) or 31 August – i.e. the last day of the month which is six months after February
2. Tell the application what to do if any future coupon date falls on a non-working day for the currency of the bond issue. Possible actions are:
   - Ignore the fact
   - Move the coupon date forward to the next working day
   - Move the coupon date backward to the previous working day
   - Take some other action proscribed by the legal documentation

---

These business rules must be used in conjunction with holiday calendar and normal working day tables that are explained in section 10.8. They are also examined in more detail in sections 23.3.1 and 23.3.2.

10.4.4   Other instrument static data

In addition to the identification data, and any data that is held at group level, the firm needs to hold, *inter alia*, the following data about each instrument.

All instrument classes

- The correct name of the instrument
- The minimum denomination of the instrument that can be traded and settled
- The maximum number of decimal places that a price may be quoted to
- The maximum number of decimal places of a quantity that may be traded and settled
- Rules for defaulting the standard value date.

Currencies

- The holiday calendar that applies to this currency
- The normal working days in the week for this currency.

All instrument classes except currencies

- Trading currency
- Settlement currency
- Rules for defaulting the standard value date
- Issue date
- Issuers' business activities – this information is held for the following reasons:
    - The firm may wish to apply credit limits to different industrial sectors
    - Some business activities (e.g. defence and tobacco) are unsuitable investments for ethical investment funds and Islamic investors.

Equities

- Trading currency
- Settlement currency
- Issue date
- The identity of the issuer of the equity
- The exchange(s) where listed
- Number of shares in issue.

Debt instruments

- Trading currency
- Settlement currency
- Issue date
- The identity of the issuer of the debt instrument
- The identity of any rating agencies that have issued this instrument with a rating
- The rating(s) that each rating agency has awarded it
- Total size of issue.

Listed futures

- The identity of the underlying instrument
- The delivery date/expiry date
- Exchange where listed
- Underlying instrument
- Quantity of the underlying instrument represented by one lot.

Listed options

- The identity of the underlying instrument
- The expiry date
- Whether exercise can only take place on expiry date, or before expiry date
- The exercise price
- Exchange where listed
- Underlying instrument
- Quantity of the underlying instrument represented by one lot.

10.4.5   Instrument associations

Many instruments are "associated" with other instruments. These associations can have an impact on the **mark-to-market** process, which is examined in Chapter 23, and the Value-at-Risk calculation, which is examined in Chapter 24. In order to value these instruments correctly, the static data records need to hold relevant, up-to-date and accurate information about the other instruments with which they are associated.

Table 10.5 table gives examples of some **instrument associations** and their impact on these processes.

10.5   TRADING PARTY AND SETTLEMENT AGENT STATIC DATA

10.5.1   Trading party identifiers

Firms that offer **tax sheltered investments** to private individuals will need (subject to legislative variations between countries) to record their clients' National Insurance or Social Security numbers.

In order to identify corporate bodies it is necessary to record their company registration number and jurisdiction of registration.

On messages between investment industry participants parties are usually recognised by a **BIC code** or bank identifier code. This is the unique identification code of a particular bank. SWIFT handles the registration of these codes. For this reason, BIC codes are often called SWIFT addresses or codes. There are over 7500 "live" codes (for partners actively connected to the SWIFT network) and an estimated 10 000 additional BIC codes which are frequently used to refer to trade parties who are not themselves connected to SWIFT.

The code is 8 or 11 characters, made up of:

- 4 characters – bank code
- 2 characters – ISO 3166-1 alpha-2 country code
- 2 characters – location code
- 3 characters – branch code, optional ("XXX" for primary office).

Table 10.5 Instrument association static data

Main instrument type	Associated instrument type	Comment
Convertible bond	Other instrument (usually an equity) into which the convertible bond may be converted	The valuation of a convertible bond is dependent on the conversion terms (see section 3.1.6 for an example) and the current price of the associated instrument. Therefore the system needs to hold: 1. The unique ID of the instrument into which the bond may be converted 2. The conversion terms, including: • Conversion price • Conversion period dates.
Bond with warrants attached	1. The warrant	The price of a bond with warrant attached is the sum of the price of the warrant and the price of the ex-warrant bond. Therefore the system needs to hold:
	2. The ex-warrant bond	1. The unique ID of the ex-warrant bond 2. The unique ID of the warrant.
Warrant or OTC option	Other instrument (usually an equity) that will be obtained when the warrant or option is exercised	The value of a warrant or OTC option is dependent on the value of the underlying instrument. Therefore the system needs to hold: 1. The unique ID of the underlying instrument 2. The exercise price of the warrant 3. The exercise period of the warrant.

Where an 8-digit code is given, you may assume that it refers to the primary office.

For example, Deutsche Bank is an international bank; its head office is based in Frankfurt, Germany. Its BIC code for its head office is DEUTDEFF:

- DEUT identifies Deutsche Bank
- DE is the country code for Germany
- FF is the code for Frankfurt.

Using an extended code of 11 digits (if the receiving bank has assigned branches or processing areas individual extended codes) allows the payment to be directed to a specific office. For example, DEUTDEFF500 would direct the payment to an office of Deutsche Bank in Bad Homburg.

10.5.2   Other trading party static data

The following are the principal items of static data that the firm needs to hold about its trading parties:

- Party full name
- Party address

- Party type – e.g. private individual, bank, corporate, fund manager, etc.
- Regulatory information, including:
  - MiFID party classification. One of:
    - Eligible counterparty – e.g. another regulated bank or stock exchange member firm
    - Professional client – e.g. a pension fund
    - Retail client – e.g. a private individual
  - Date that the party commenced dealings with this firm
  - Information about party's risk tolerance, investment knowledge and financial position
  - Details of what steps were taken to verify client's identity.
- Any other addresses where copies of correspondence need to be sent. For example, fund manager customers may require confirmations to be sent to the investor as well as to the fund manager.
- Country of incorporation or residence.
- Details of any credit limits that are applied to this entity – this topic is covered in section 24.1.6.
- Details of relationships with other parties on the database. For example:
  - We may have accounts with Mr John Brown and Mrs Jane Brown, who are husband and wife.
  - XYZ Fund Managers may be wholly or partially owned by XYX Bank. We need to be able to track corporate ownership structures so that credit limits can be applied to groups of companies.

10.6   STANDARD SETTLEMENT INSTRUCTIONS (SSIs)

10.6.1   Overview

Standard settlement instructions (SSIs) are the main driver of the STP process from the point of **trade agreement** to final settlement. SSIs provide details of which settlement agents both the sell-side firm and the investors who use its services are going to use to settle the trade.

Both the cash side and the stock side of a securities trade will be settled – normally on a delivery-versus-payment basis – by the settlement agents chosen by the sell-side firm and the investor. Where a fund manager is acting for a number of investors, it is the investors – not the fund manager – that choose their settlement agent. Sell-side firms normally appoint CSDs such as CREST or ICSDs such as Euroclear as their settlement agents, while institutional investors normally appoint custodian banks.

In order to generate instructions both parties need to know who to send them to (our settlement agent) as well as details of the other party's settlement agent, as we need to advise our agent this information so that it can settle the trade. For this reason, firms hold details of the SSIs of those trading parties with whom it deals regularly as static data objects.

10.6.2   Examples of SSI data

Tables 10.6 and 10.7 show the SSI-related data held by ABC Investment Bank for itself, and also two of its investor clients for three major asset classes:

- UK listed equities settled in GBP
- Corporate bonds traded in London and settled in EUR
- Corporate bonds traded in London and settled in USD.

Table 10.6   Key to SSI table column headings

Column name	Purpose
Trading party	Identity of the party with which the firm is trading. The firm itself is also a trading party in this context
Instrument class	Identifies the type of asset concerned
Settlement currency	Identifies the currency of settlement
Stock depot	Identifies the settlement agent that will accept or make delivery of this type of asset on behalf of the trading party
Depot account code	Identifies the relevant account number at the stock depot
Cash nostro	Identifies the settlement agent that will accept or make payments for this type of asset on behalf of the trading party
Nostro account code	Identifies the relevant account number at the cash nostro
Instruction method	The method that the trading party will use to send instructions to the settlement agent

The tables introduce us to two new terms:

- **Depot**, which is the account with the settlement agent that is used to record transactions and balances in security quantities is often referred to as "the depot account".
- **Nostro** which is the account with the settlement agent that is used to record transactions and balances in money amounts is often referred to as "the nostro account".

10.6.3   Omgeo Alerts™ – centralised storage of SSI data

Traditionally, every trade party has had to maintain a file of the SSIs of every other trade party with whom it does business. This is clearly inefficient, as when one trade party changes its settlement instructions, it has to notify every other trade party that might be concerned. As a result, Omgeo LLC, a joint venture of the Depository Trust & Clearing Corporation (DTCC) and Thomson Financial, established Omgeo Alerts, a centralised database of the SSIs of over 9000 participants.

This database is updated by fund managers, global custodians and sell-side firms whenever new information is added or existing information is changed. Fund managers may also identify a list of sell-side firms with whom they wish to share this information for each of their investor clients. When any one of these organisations changes its SSIs for a particular instrument class then the other relevant parties are notified.

The product validates data as it is entered, for example invalid BIC codes are detected. It also allows fund managers to specify the method by which confirmation messages should be delivered, and allows them to specify the delivery addresses for each message.

The data that has been entered may be viewed in a web browser or printed out and entered into individual firms' settlement systems in order to update the SSI tables held in their internal systems. The functions of Omgeo Alerts are illustrated in Figure 10.5, which is reproduced by permission of Omgeo LLC.

Each party inputs details of any new or amended SSI data. For example, a fund manager inputs amended SSI data for one of its investor clients. The data is validated appropriately and then accepted by the application. When the sell-side firms that execute trades on behalf of that investor log on to Alerts, they are informed that the SSI details for that investor have been changed, and are able to inspect details of the change, and amend their own SSI records appropriately.

Table 10.7 Example SSI data

Trading party	Instrument class	Settlement currency	Stock depot	Depot account code	Cash nostro	Nostro account code	Instruction method
Ourselves	LSE listed equities	GBP	CREST	123456	CREST	654321	CREST
Ourselves	OTC bonds London desk	EUR	Euroclear	911222	Euroclear	466-911222-EUR	Euclid
Ourselves	OTC bonds London desk	USD	Euroclear	911222	Euroclear	457-911222-GBP	Euclid
Megacorp Pension Fund	LSE listed equities	GBP	State street London	256879	State street London	108-256879-GBP	SWIFT
Megacorp Pension Fund	OTC bonds London desk	EUR	State street London	256879	State street London	107-256879-EUR	SWIFT
Megacorp Pension Fund	OTC bonds London desk	USD	State street London	256879	State street New York	168-256789-USD	SWIFT
Minicorp Pension Fund	LSE listed equities	GBP	Société Généralé Paris	104867	Société Généralé London	0-0876554332	SWIFT
Minicorp Pension Fund	OTC bonds London desk	EUR	Société Généralé Paris	104867	Société Généralé Paris	0-0876554332	SWIFT
Minicorp Pension Fund	OTC bonds London desk	USD	Société Généralé Paris	104867	Société Généralé New York	0-0876554332	SWIFT

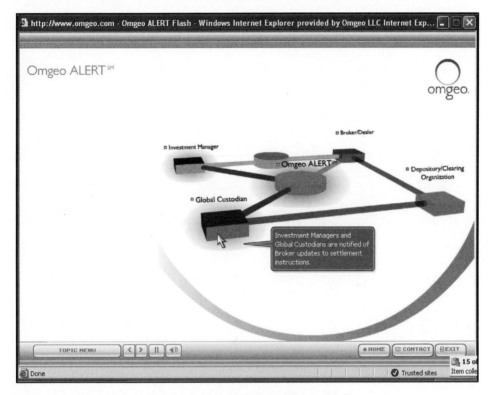

Figure 10.5 Omgeo Alerts. Reproduced by permission of Omgeo LLC.

10.6.4 Identification of depot and nostro account numbers

Bank account numbers have traditionally been expressed in different forms in different countries, which has made the storage of depot and nostro account numbers in applications somewhat imprecise.

As a result, in 2003 the European Union decided to adopt the *IBAN code* to overcome this problem. The IBAN was developed to facilitate payments within the European Union. The IBAN is not yet used as a standard in messaging, because the IBAN has not yet been widely adopted outside Europe. Adoption may take up to 10 years, so it remains necessary to use the current ISO 9362 Bank Identifier Code system (BIC code) in conjunction with the BBAN or IBAN.

At present, the United States does not participate in IBAN. Any adoption of the IBAN standard by US banks would likely be initiated by ANSI ASC X9, the US financial services standards development organisation.

Currently all European non-CIS countries, as well as some African countries and Turkey, participate in the IBAN system, while the rest of the world remains outside of it. British dependencies (except Gibraltar and the Crown Dependencies) don't participate in the IBAN system.

The IBAN consists of an ISO 3166-1 alpha-2 country code, followed by two check digits (represented by *kk* in the examples below), and up to 30 alphanumeric characters for the domestic bank account number, called the BBAN (Basic Bank Account Number). It is up to each country's national banking community to decide on the length of the BBAN for accounts in that country, but its length must be fixed for any given country.

Example of a UK IBAN code

Format: GBkk BBBB SSSS SSCC CCCC CC
  Example: GB65 LOYD 3000 0000 1195 87
  Where:
  GB is the country code for the United Kingdom
  65 is a check digit
  LOYD is the abbreviation for Lloyds TSB Bank
  3000 00 is the branch at Lloyds TSB where the account is held
  00 1195 87 is the account number concerned at that branch

The IBAN must not contain spaces when stored electronically. When printed on paper, however, the norm is to express it in groups of four characters, the last group being of variable length.

10.7   STATIC DATA THAT IS INTERNAL TO THE FIRM CONCERNED

The firm also needs to set up a number of static data elements that tell its business applications information about the firm itself. These "internal" static data objects will include, but are not limited to:

1. *Base currency*: A firm that invests in securities denominated in many currencies will wish to value them in the currency in which it produces its profit and loss account. Usually, but not exclusively, this means that a firm that is incorporated in the UK will have a base currency of GBP, a firm incorporated in the USA will choose USD, etc.
   The base currency will be used, *inter alia*, to:
   • Revalue foreign currency positions – refer to section 14.3.2
   • Convert foreign currency income and expenses into this currency
   • If required, Value at Risk (refer to section 24.6) will be measured in this currency.
2. *FX base currency*: A firm that trades foreign exchange needs to set up an FX base currency. This is the currency in which any profits on foreign exchange trades will be measured. The topic is examined in detail in section 18.1.
3. *Commission rates and calculation methods*: Relevant applications will need to store commission rates and commission calculation methods. The common methods of calculating commissions are as follows:
   • *Flat fee*: This method is used by many "execution only" stockbrokers that serve the private investor. For each trade there will be a fee of £x, no matter how large or small the value of the trade.
   • *Percentage*: This method is used for many equity transactions involving professional investors, the fee is x% of the principal value of the trade.
   • *Basis points*: This method is used in some bond and OTC derivative transactions. A basis point (often denoted as %∞) is a unit that is equal to 1/100th of 1%; and in this context commission is expressed as x basis points per 1 million nominal of face value (of the underlying instrument in the case of a derivative). For example, if the client is buying or selling $1 000 000 nominal of a corporate bond, and the commission is expressed as

"5 basis points per million" then the commission that applied to the trade would be $0.05% of the face value bought or sold – i.e. $500.00.

- *Per unit*: This method is widely used for futures and options contacts. The exchange concerned specifies, for each contract, how many units of the underlying instrument are referenced to "one lot" of the derivative. The commission is therefore expressed as "£x per lot".

- *Sliding scale:* A sliding scale may be applied to commissions that are based on percentages or basis points. The percentage reduces according to the size of the individual order. For example:
  - *Commission = 1% on individual orders with value below £50 000*
  - *Commission = 0.85% on individual orders with value between £50 001 and £100 000*
  - *Commission = 0.75% on individual orders with value between £100 001 and £150 000*
  - Etc., etc.

  Note that the size of the order – not the execution – determines the scale.

- *Reducing scale*: Again, the commission rate reduces for clients that place large amounts of business with the firm. However, using this method, the cumulative value of the orders that the client has placed over a period of time is added together, and the commission calculated according the commission rate is then multiplied by the cumulative value.

4. *Other fees and charges that may apply to trades*: These will depend on the jurisdictions that are relevant to the trade, and it would be impractical to list all the possibilities that could apply throughout the world. Using the United Kingdom as an example, the following fees apply to certain trades:

- *Stamp duty reserve tax* (commonly known as stamp duty or SDRT): Stamp duty is a tax payable by buyers (but not sellers) of most equity shares. The current rate is 0.5%. It is payable by any individual or corporation that is purchasing:
  - Shares in a company that is incorporated in the UK
  - Shares in a foreign company that maintains a share register in the UK
  - Options to buy shares as defined above
  - Rights arising from shares as defined above, like the rights under a rights issue

  Stamp duty is a tax that is paid by the final investor, so trades between stock exchange member firms are exempt from stamp duty. The dealing system database therefore needs to contain information about:
  - Which individual instruments stamp duty applies to
  - Which individual trade types and counterparties it applies to.

- *PTM Levy*: This is a charge automatically imposed on investors, and collected by their brokers, when they sell or buy shares with an aggregate value in excess of £10 000. The charge is £1, and the money raised goes to the Panel of Takeovers and Mergers. The Panel writes and enforces the rules by which takeovers of companies listed on the London Stock Exchange and Virt-x are conducted.

5. *Credit limits*: Any credit limits that the firm wishes to apply to its trading parties, trading books, countries in which trading parties are incorporated or resident need to be set up as static data objects. Some firms also set up limits that apply to individual issuers of securities, and stock market sectors such as pharmaceuticals, etc.

6. *Trading book/dealing desk structure*: Sell-side firms usually organise their dealing teams and trading books into a hierarchical "book structure" that corresponds to profit and loss attribution by business area. Each node in the hierarchy may have a credit limit applied to it.

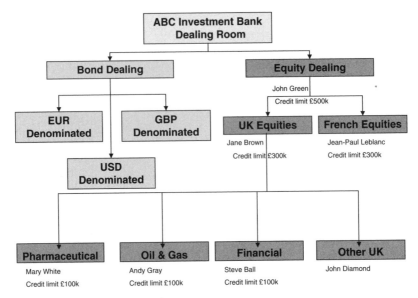

Figure 10.6   Example of a trading book structure

A sample hierarchy might look like Figure 10.6.

10.8   NORMAL WORKING DAYS AND PUBLIC HOLIDAYS

A firm needs to establish tables that informs it of:

- The various public holidays that apply across the globe. On these days stock exchanges and the banking systems in the countries concerned will be closed, so that no trades can settle. Note that in most jurisdictions there are very few public holidays that close exchanges or banking systems to large transactions. Although Italy, for example, had 11 public holidays in total in 2007, only two of those – 1 January and 25 December – were days on which the banking system was closed to transactions of this type.

In older investment industry applications, public holidays were traditionally associated with either currencies or countries, but this relationship is now considered over-rigid in the design of investment industry applications, as the following example will show.

Example: Impact of public holidays on a currency swap transaction

ABC Investment Bank has entered into a currency swap where it is exchanging semi-annual cash flows based on US dollar LIBOR and Japanese yen LIBOR.

Because LIBOR rates are determined in the United Kingdom, public holiday calendars of three countries – the United States, Japan and the United Kingdom – are relevant to this transaction.

The following activities cannot take place on a public holiday that affects the United States of America:

- Exchange of USD principal on start date of the swap
- Semi-annual interest payments in USD

- Exchange of USD principal on termination date of the swap.

  The following activities cannot take place on a public holiday that affects Japan:

- Exchange of JPY principal on start date of the swap
- Semi-annual interest payments in JPY
- Exchange of JPY principal on termination date of the swap.

  The following activities cannot take place on a public holiday that affects the United Kingdom:

- LIBOR fixings for USD and JPY – this normally occurs two days before the start of each interest period.

- For this reason, in modern business applications it is now considered "best practice" not to associate holiday calendars with countries or currencies, but to consider them as free-standing objects that may be associated as and when necessary with individual instruments and transactions as and when appropriate.
- *Normal working days:* Most countries use Monday to Friday as normal working days, and banks are closed at weekends. There are exceptions to this rule – some Islamic countries close their banks on Fridays and open them on Sundays.

10.9   COUNTRY INFORMATION

Countries are normally recognised by a two character ISO country code such as GB or US. Firms need to record the country of incorporation or residence of their trading parties and settlement agents so that:

- They can produce a number of statistical returns that may be demanded by their governments. Some of these returns are concerned with investment regulation; others may be concerned with data required by tax authorities and also requirements imposed on the industry to supply the government with data used to compile the home country's balance of payments data.
- Some firms will wish to apply credit limits that restrict their exposure to individual countries.

11

Communications Between Industry Participants

In Chapter 9 we learned that the principles of STP apply not just within the firm but also between the various firms involved in the transaction. In order to achieve STP individual firms have to be able to automate communications between other firms and other types of industry participants. This requires mutually agreed standards for the contents of messages as well as network facilities to transmit and receive these messages. All the world's investment exchanges and settlement agents provide proprietary facilities of this kind and publish **application programming interfaces** (APIs) that detail how to interact with these applications.

As well as these proprietary systems there are a number of open systems that are used widely in the investment industry. Some of them are specific to some areas of the industry, such as individual instruments or individual stages in the trade cycle. There is, however, one standard, the SWIFT standard, that is used by all types of industry participants for most instrument types and at all stages of the trade cycle. Section 11.1 examines the role of SWIFT in detail.

In 1992 several industry participants set up the FIX standard, which is also widely used in the pre-settlement phases of the trade cycle. The FIX Protocol is examined in section 11.2. Other message standards are covered in section 11.3.

11.1 SWIFT

11.1.1 Introduction

The Society for Worldwide Interbank Financial Telecommunication (SWIFT) was founded in 1973, with the mission of creating a shared worldwide data processing and communications link together with a common language for international financial transactions. This was an ambitious project that had the backing of 239 banks in 15 countries.

The next few years were spent defining the message standards and building a secure store and forward telecommunications network. The first SWIFT message was sent in 1977.

Originally, SWIFT services were only available to firms that were regulated as banks, and the message standards only related to foreign exchange, money markets and interbank transfers. The first securities-related message standards were introduced in 1987, and membership was not offered to non-bank investment firms and fund managers until 1992.

By 2007 there were 2792 SWIFT participants in 208 countries, exchanging over 2.2 billion messages annually, growing at an annual rate of 21.3%. On 31 July 2007 a record number of 15 912 693 messages were sent.

SWIFT now offers standard messages that support all stages of the transaction lifecycle for most instrument classes. The only instrument class where SWIFT does not have significant

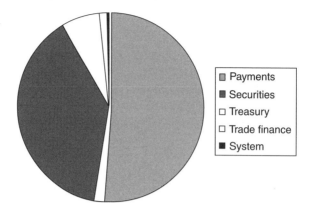

Figure 11.1   SWIFT message volume analysis

market share is exchange-traded futures and options, where the proprietary message formats of the various exchanges and clearing houses are dominant.

By business type, the breakdown of these messages is shown in Figure 11.1.

11.1.2   SWIFT connectivity

SWIFT connectivity is based on the presence of:

1. A secure IP-based network
2. SWIFTnet Link software that provides security and ensures interoperability between users
3. The store and forward principle

The secure IP-based network

This is a highly secure telecommunications network that, since 2005, has been based on the IP protocol; which in turn is the set of communications protocols that implement the protocol stack on which the Internet runs. It is sometimes called the TCP/IP protocol suite, after the two most important protocols in it: the **Transmission Control Protocol** (TCP) and the **Internet protocol suite** (IP), which were also the first two defined.

SWIFTnet Link

SWIFTnet Link is a suite of software products that ensures technical interoperability between users by providing the functionality required to communicate over these services. It is licensed both to SWIFT member firms directly, and also to software vendors who are able to embed it in their own products. When SWIFT supplies it directly, it is embedded in a packaged software application called **SWIFTAlliance**™. Both Windows and UNIX platforms are supported by SWIFTnet Link. SWIFTAlliance and the third party products that compete with it are often referred to as **SWIFT Gateway** Systems.

SWIFTnet Link incorporates a set of **XML**-based application programming interfaces (APIs) which enable communication with SWIFT services. One of the most important components is SWIFTnet PKI.

SWIFTnet PKI

SWIFTnet PKI is the part of SWIFTnet Link that provides the security layer. When a firm agrees with another firm that they will send and/or receive SWIFT messages with one another, the first thing that they do is to exchange *authenticator keys* with one another, using the SWIFT network for this purpose. Authenticator keys encrypt the outgoing message, and ensure that only the recipient that it was intended for is able to de-encrypt it. SWIFTnet PKI uses **digital certificates** to provide the highest levels of authentication of institutions, end-users and servers. Digital certificates convey the trust between institutions and SWIFT as the trusted third party. SWIFTnet PKI is additional to the network security provided on the protocol and the connection level.

Key exchange ensures:

- *Authenticity*: Correspondents are guaranteed the identity of the originator of any instruction, statement, query or response. By verifying the signature, the receiver of a message can confirm that the sender specified in the header of the message the private key used for signing the message.
- *Integrity*: Correspondents are guaranteed that the data they receive exactly matches the original as produced by the sender. By verifying the signature the receiver of a message can confirm that the message content has not been changed during transmission.
- *Non-repudiation*: Correspondents are able to prove that the claimed originator has effectively signed the message, as it can be proved that the originator is the sole owner of the unique signing key needed to produce the digital signature.
- *Confidentiality*: The message-level encryption guarantees that only the intended recipient can read and interpret the data as it can be proved that the originator is the sole owner of the unique decryption key.
- *Access control*: The access for an individual to his or her private key stored in a smart card is controlled through a private password.

The store and forward principle

SWIFT connectivity is based on the store and forward principle. This is a communications technique in which messages are sent to an intermediate station where they are kept and sent at a later time to the final destination or to another intermediate station. Reasons for using this method include:

- Origin and destination stations may not be available for communications at the same time. This, in turn, could be because of:
  - Time zone differences between the sender and the recipient
  - The sender's country and the recipient's country have different working days and/or public holidays

– The recipient's systems are not working due to hardware failure, software failure or "disasters" such as earthquake, civil unrest, etc.

• One or more circuits may not have enough capacity for peak traffic and there is a need to give priority to certain messages, without losing the others.

Interaction of the firm's systems with the SWIFT network

Figure 11.2 shows the interaction between the sending firm's systems, the SWIFT network and the receiving firm's systems. The assumptions are that the sending firm is based in London, and is generating settlement instructions to be sent to a settlement agent in Tokyo. Tokyo is, of course, in a different time zone and uses a different public holiday calendar to London.

At the sending firm

1. Trades are captured in the relevant front-office system, and forwarded to the firm's settlement system.
2. The settlement system enriches the trade with SSI details and any other relevant static data, and formats a settlement instruction message. This, in turn, is forwarded to the firm's SWIFT Gateway application, where:
   • The Gateway product validates the trade according to SWIFT's network validation rules, which deal with field specifications (e.g. whether alpha or numeric content is required, whether fields are mandatory or optional, etc.) If a message fails validation then it is sent to a repair queue.

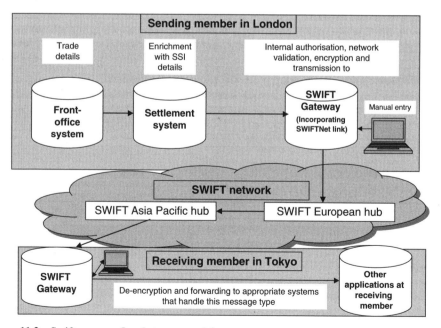

Figure 11.2   Swift message flow between participants

- The Gateway product provides facilities for manual authorisation of this instruction before it is sent out. The firm is able to set up business rules in the Gateway product to control policies that determine whether or not manual authorisation is required for different types and values of instruction.
- The Gateway product allows direct input through a user interface, shown in the figure. This allows users to set up business rules in the Gateway product, manually authorise transactions and repair transactions when necessary.
- Once the message has been validated and authorised it is then encrypted, and then sent to SWIFT. The message will, in fact, be received at one of SWIFT's European hubs (there is more than one of these for business resilience reasons) but this fact is transparent to the sender.

At SWIFT

1. The message is received at the European hub, and time stamped with the date and time of receipt.
2. It is then network validated. If network validation is successful, the SWIFT sends an ACK (meaning acknowledged) message back to the sender confirming that it is able to process the message. If the message fails network validation, then SWIFT sends a NACK (not acknowledged) message back to the sender. This process is known as the **ACK/NACK protocol**.
3. SWIFT identifies that this message is destined for a firm in Tokyo, so it forwards it to one of its Asia Pacific hubs in real time.
4. The Asia Pacific hub then verifies whether the Tokyo firm is online to SWIFT. If it is, it forwards it to the member; if the member is not online it stores the message until it detects that the member has come online.

At the receiving firm

1. The message is received at this member firm's Gateway system and de-encrypted.
2. The Gateway system then uses business rules that have been set up in this system to tell it what to do with the message. For example, if it is a settlement instruction message sent by one of the firm's custody clients it may need to be forwarded to one business application; if it is an FX trade confirmation sent by a counterparty it might need to be forwarded to another business application.
3. There will be some messages where the identity of the destination system will not be clear to the Gateway system. This may be due to the quality of the data in the incoming message, lack of clarity and coverage in the business rules entered into the gateway system, or for some other reason. For this reason Gateway systems provide a human interface that incorporates the ability to display messages held in a repair queue and manually deal with them, as well as the ability to input the business rules in the first place.

11.1.3   SWIFT message standards

SWIFT devises agreed standards for the content, sequence and validation rules for the messages used by its members. It does this by a process of consultation with its member firms and the various trade associations that they belong to. Once SWIFT has confirmed a standard, then this standard is then adopted by the **International Standards Organisation** (ISO). The ISO is a United Nations-sponsored organisation that sets international standards that can be used in any type of business and are accepted around the world as proof that a business can provide assured quality. The ISO has appointed SWIFT as the "registration authority" of standards for financial services messages.

FIN messages, also known as MT messages

The range of SWIFT messages that was developed before 2000 are known as FIN messages. They are represented as tagged data. Each FIN message is assigned a message identifier code, such as MT300, which is a foreign exchange trade confirmation message. For this reason, FIN messages are often referred to as MT messages.

There are 176 different business-related MT messages (as well as some system management messages) and there are two ISO standards that govern the content of these messages. The scope of the MT message series is summarised in Table 11.1.

In the relevant chapters this book will list the actual messages that are used by participants at each processing stage for each instrument type.

Table 11.1   SWIFT message series

Category	Nbr of individual messages in series	Purpose of the series	Examples	Relevant ISO standard
1	11	Customer payments and cheques	MT111 – Request to stop payment of a cheque	ISO7775
2	10	Financial institution transfers	MT202 – General financial institution transfer	ISO7775
3	20	Foreign exchange, money markets and derivatives	MT300 – Foreign exchange confirmation MT360 – interest rate swap confirmation	ISO7775
4	11	Collections and cash letters	MT400 – Advice of payment	ISO7775
5	57	Securities markets	MT502 – Order to buy or sell MT514 – Trade allocation instruction MT543 – Instruction to deliver against payment MT547 – Confirmation that DvP instruction has settled	ISO15022
6	13	Precious metals	MT600 – Trade confirmation	ISO7775
7	22	Documentary credits and guarantees	M700 – Issue of a documentary credit	ISO7775
8	11	Travellers cheques	MT810 – Travellers cheque refund request	ISO7775
9	21	Cash management and customer status	MT950 – Statement message	ISO7775

Communications Between Industry Participants   105

Underlying ISO standards for FIN messages

The ISO standard that governs all the series except for the MT500 series is ISO7775. This standard was developed during the 1980s and applied to all the messages that were developed up to 1997, including the then current MT500 series securities messages.

In the late 1990s SWIFT and its members realised that the original ISO7775 messages were too restrictive, did not reflect the full complexity of modern trading instruments and were still too ambiguous to ensure that full straight-through-processing could be achieved.

Thus was born the ISO15022 standard based on a data dictionary approach. Initially (in 1997) ISO15022 was applied to the securities message category as this represented the fastest growing usage of the SWIFT network. Old message types were replaced and many new ones introduced. ISO15022 trade initiation and confirmation messages were introduced in 1997 and settlement and reconciliation in 1998. There was no standards release in 1999 due to Y2K distractions, and the old MT500 series, ISO7775 standard message types were removed from the network in 2002.

Example of an FIN message

Figure 11.3 is an example of an FIN message. It is an MT950, which is a statement of a bank account sent by the account operator to the account holder.

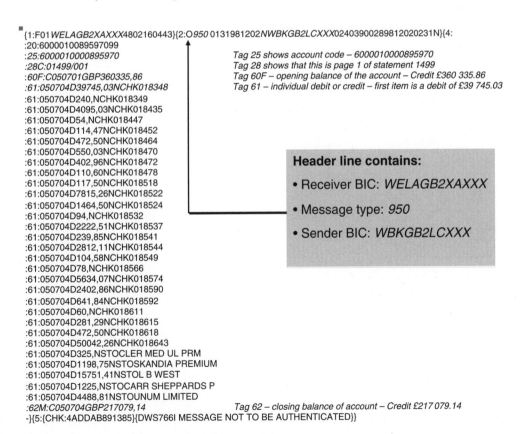

Figure 11.3   Analysis of a SWIFT MT950 message

61:050704D2402,86NCHK018590

61	The tag
050704	The date of the entry
D	Sign – D – debit; C = credit
2402,86	The amount debited or credited, "penny units" separated by commas
NCHK018590	Description of the entry

Figure 11.4   MT950 tag 61 explained

The message consists of:

1. A single header line that shows, *inter alia,* the BIC code of the sender and receiver, and the ID of the message type.
2. A single line of tagged data beginning with ":25:" – tag 25 shows the account number to which this message refers.
3. A single line of tagged data beginning with ":28:" – tag 28 shows the statement number and page number within this statement.
4. A single line of tagged data beginning with ":60F:" – tag 60 shows the opening balance of the account and the date of the opening balance.
5. Repeated lines of tagged data beginning with ":61:" – tag 61 shows each entry that was posted to the account. The format is as shown in Figure 11.4.
6. A single line of tagged data beginning with ":62M:" – tag 62 shows the closing balance of the account and the date of the closing balance.

If you add the money value of tag 60 – opening balance – to the money values of all the individual entries – the tag 61 rows – then the answer should be equal to the money value of the tag 62 line.

Although this is an example of an MT950 message, any other SWIFT message can be interpreted in this way. The explanations of the function of each message, together with the permitted contents of each tag within the message and the network validation rules, are available in the SWIFT Standards Documents that are made available to all SWIFT members.

New messaging developments – the MX messages

The tagged data structure of the MT message series has served the investment community well for many years, but many aspects of it are now somewhat dated. One of the main drivers for change is the growth of the use of Extensible Markup Language – better known as XML – throughout industry and commerce.

XML is a flexible way to create common information formats and share both the format and the data on the World Wide Web, intranets, and elsewhere. XML is a formal recommendation from the World Wide Web Consortium (W3C) similar to the language of today's web pages, the Hypertext Markup Language (HTML).

SWIFT's first implementation of XML and the new standard was in a series of messages designed for players in the mutual funds industry in 2003. SWIFT is currently in the process of developing XML-based message formats to replace all of the MT message series, in order to enable the transfer of richer data for more complex business transactions. The SWIFT website shows the current status of the migration program at any one time. There will be an indefinite coexistence period when members will be able to send and receive messages in either MT or MX formats. To support this coexistence period, SWIFT has developed translation rules in human readable form. The rules are provided for those MTs and MXs where equivalence is established and where the community of users has a need for translation support.

11.2   THE FINANCIAL INFORMATION EXCHANGE (FIX PROTOCOL)

The Financial Interface eXchange (**FIX Protocol**) was initiated in 1992 by a group of institutions and brokers interested in streamlining their trading processes. It is an open message standard controlled by no single entity, which can be structured to match the business requirements of each firm. At the time that the FIX Protocol was founded, institutions and brokers that were not banks had only recently become eligible to join SWIFT, and the founding firms were not satisfied with the ISO7775 securities messages that were then available on the SWIFT network.

FIX does not impose a single type of carrier (e.g. it will work with leased lines, private networks, Internet, etc.), or a single security protocol. It is, however, important to note that FIX is not a network in itself and that communication is made directly between each broker/institution pair by prior bilateral agreement. Thus a fund management institution may have 50 or 60 connections to brokers worldwide, some via the internet, others via direct dial or leased connections and still others connected via private networks such as Omgeo or Autex – see Chapter 12 for more information about Omgeo and Autex.

In summary each broker/institution connection can be thought of as a two-way conversational link taking place between applications at each end. These applications are often referred to as "FIX engines" and can operate either as standalone or fully integrated solutions.

The structure of the FIX Protocol organisation is based around a series of committees comprised of interested parties within the broking and institutional communities. These committees are focused on business, technical and regional issues with working groups examining the impact of new technology such as XML and potential expansion of the protocol to cover other users such as exchanges and ECNs (electronic crossing networks).

The protocol is defined at two levels: session and application. The session level is concerned with the delivery of data while the application level defines business-related data content. Broadly the business messages cover the communication between brokers and institutions of the following information:

- Indications of interest
- Orders and order acknowledgement
- Fills
- Account allocations

- News, Email, program trading lists
- Administrative messages

The protocol has been deliberately designed to support both domestic and cross-border trading in a varied spread of instrument and security types such as:

- Equities
- Bonds
- Depositary receipts
- Derivatives
- Futures
- Foreign exchange trading.

Because the FIX standards are "open source" they may be downloaded from the FIX Protocol website, www.fixprotocol.org.

The current version of the FIX Protocol is version 5.0, released in October 2006, but many market players will still be using version 4.4, released in April 2003. FIX Protocol Standard 4.4 and higher conforms to ISO15022. In 2001 the FIX Protocol organisation and SWIFT signed a memorandum of understanding which focused on convergence between pre-trade and post-trade processing in the use of ISO15022 XML.

11.3 OTHER MESSAGE STANDARDS

As well as the internationally recognised SWIFT and FIX standards, there are a number of proprietary message standards that are commonly used. Most commercial custodians, CSDs, ICSDs, exchanges and clearing houses publish APIs that enable member firms' systems to communicate with their systems. In particular, it is worth noting that SWIFT standards are not widely used for communicating with derivative exchanges and their associated clearing houses. The proprietary standards of the exchanges and clearing houses have traditionally been dominant. However, from 2008 the Eurex exchange will be supporting the FIX Protocol.

12

The Trade Agreement and Settlement
Processes

12.1 THE TRADE AGREEMENT PROCESS

Trade agreement is the process of the trade parties agreeing that orders have been executed in accordance with the ordering party's wishes. Generically, trade agreement is designed to detect and correct executed orders where either:

- The party concerned recognises the trade, but disagrees one or more details (e.g. incorrect price, value date, etc.); or:
- The party concerned does not recognise the trade at all.

There are four commonly used methods of trade agreement:

- Mutual exchange of confirmations
- The confirmation, affirmation and allocation model
- Use of a central matching engine
- Confirmation followed by no further action.

12.1.1 Mutual exchange of confirmations

This method of trade agreement is mostly used to agree foreign exchange, money market loan and deposit and OTC derivative transactions.

There are a number of variants of this model, but the basic workflow is captured in Figure 12.1. In this workflow, Party A sends Party B a confirmation note that begins "We confirm our purchase from you of . . . ." While Party B sends Party A a confirmation note that begins "We confirm our sale to you of . . . ." It is up to both parties to read the confirmation from the other party and check that their trade details agree to its trade details. If they do agree, there is no need for any further communication between the parties; if they don't agree, then one party takes the matter up with the other party.

Confirmation messages may be sent by mail, fax or telex – in which case message comparison is a manual process.

In high volume environments confirmation messages are sent in electronic format (usually in SWIFT format) and each party normally uses a dedicated confirmation matching application to compare the message that it has sent with the message that it has received. If the two records agree, then these applications move the workflow on to next stage in the STP process, where the two parties send their settlement instructions to their settlement agents. If the two records do not agree then the results of the matching process are delivered to a workbasket or input screen where a user will investigate and take the necessary action to resolve the dispute. This method of trade agreement only covers the post-execution stage of the trade flow; it does not provide any facilities for comparing orders.

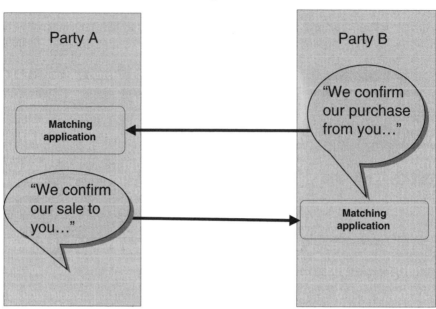

Figure 12.1   Mutual exchange of confirmations

The relevant SWIFT messages for mutual exchange of confirmations are shown in Table 12.1.

Trade agreement for OTC derivatives

Swaps and other OTC derivatives are agreed using this model. OTC confirmation messages (often referred to as contracts) are based on the **ISDA master agreement** which is a

Table 12.1   SWIFT messages used in mutual exchange of confirmations

Message number	Message name	Additional information
MT300	Foreign exchange trade confirmation	
MT305	Foreign currency option confirmation	Confirms information agreed to in the buying and selling of vanilla options on currencies
MT306	Foreign currency option confirmation	Confirms information agreed to in the buying and selling of exotic options on currencies
MT320	Fixed rate loan and deposit confirmation	
MT330	Call and notice loan and deposit confirmation	
MT360	Single currency interest rate derivative confirmation	Confirms the details of a single currency interest rate derivative swap, cap, collar or floor
MT361	Cross currency interest rate swap confirmation	Confirms the details of a cross currency interest rate swap transaction

standardised contract (drafted by the **International Swaps and Derivatives Association (ISDA)**. This master agreement contains general terms and conditions (such as provisions relating to payment netting, tax gross-up, tax representations, basic corporate representations, basic covenants, events of default and termination) but does not, by itself, include details of any specific derivatives transactions the parties may enter into. The ISDA master agreement is a pre-printed form which will not be amended itself (save for writing in the names of the parties on the front and signature pages). However, it also has a manually produced schedule in which the parties are required to select certain options and may modify sections of the master agreement if desired.

SWIFT format messages are available for OTC derivative confirmations, but due to the complexity and diversity of the transactions, printed confirmations that need to be read, interpreted and checked by qualified individuals are still extremely common. After confirmations are checked manually, they are then scanned into a database from where they may be retrieved if required. This variant of the mutual exchange model can be represented by Figure 12.2.

Each year the ISDA conducts an operations benchmarking survey among its member firms. Some of the salient points concerning trade agreement that were discovered in the 2007 survey are shown in Tables 12.2–12.4.

Table 12.2 shows that a high proportion of outgoing confirmations was not dispatched until T + 2 or later. As most OTC trades have a value date of T + 2, this means that the recipient cannot possibly check the confirmations until after the trade has settled. This breaches the third principle of STP, which states:

> Trade processing should consist of a set of logical stages, each one being dependent on the satisfactory conclusion of the previous stage. No stage should commence until the previous stage has completed successfully.

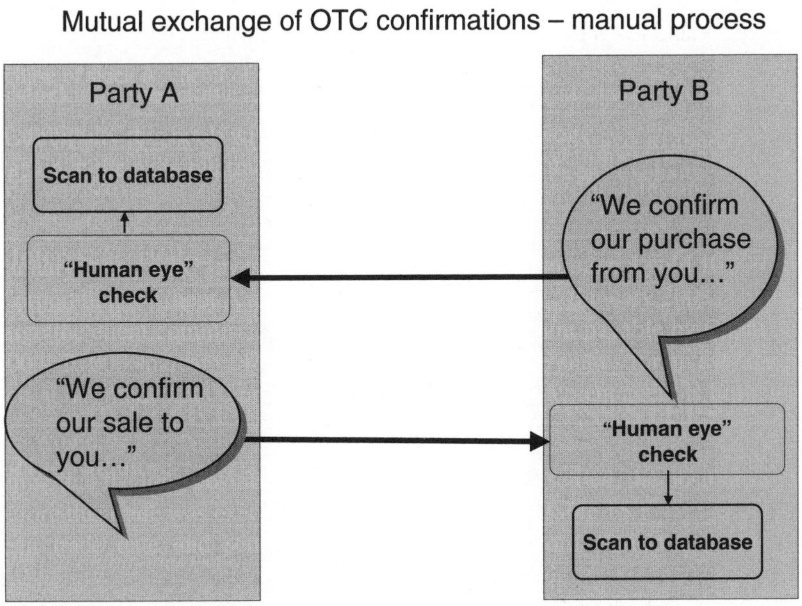

Figure 12.2   Manual agreement of OTC confirmations

Table 12.2   Promptness of dispatch of outgoing OTC confirmations

Product	Confirmation sent on trade date (%)	Confirmation sent on or before T + 1 (%)	Confirmation sent on or before T + 2 (%)	Confirmation sent after T + 2 (%)
Equity swaps	14	43	62	38
Interest rate swaps	22	68	86	14
Credit derivatives	31	69	88	12

Table 12.3   Percentage of trades that need to be rebooked as a result of confirmation checking

Product	% of trades needing to be rebooked
Equity swaps	15
Interest rate swaps	11
Credit derivatives	13
Currency options	6

Not surprisingly, the failure to send out and agree trade details on a timely basis results in a relatively high proportion of trades having to be amended, as shown in the Table 12.3.

The ISDA survey also asked respondents what levels of automation they had successfully applied to various processes. The responses to the questions concerning trade agreement processes were as found in Table 12.4.

Table 12.4   Level of automation of trade agreement – OTC derivatives

	Process automation
Activity	% of firms that had automated this activity
Production and dispatch of confirmations	56
Imaging outgoing confirmations	56
Imaging incoming confirmations	44
Matching confirmations	28

Trades that have been arranged by a money broker

If transactions have been arranged by a money broker (refer to section 7.8) then the money broker will also send both parties a confirmation; either in printed format or electronically. When it is sent electronically it is sent using a private telecommunications network operated by

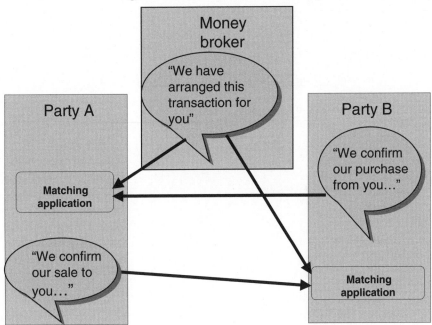

Figure 12.3 Mutual exchange of confirmations with money broker involvement

City Networks Limited on behalf of the Wholesale Money Brokers Association. This facility does not use SWIFT message formats; it has its own standards and APIs. When a money broker is involved, then Figure 12.1 is modified as shown in Figure 12.3.

The money broker also sends a confirmation note to both parties informing them that it has arranged the deal for them. Without the confirmation note from the money broker, both parties cannot start the transaction flow, as they are not yet aware that the deal has been completed. Most matching applications support three-way matching between the two trade parties and the money broker. Note that it is not necessary for Parties A and B to send a confirmation to the money broker, they only need to contact the money broker if the process results in a mismatch.

When building or buying a matching application, it is important to establish whether there is a business need to match money broker confirmations, as not all matching applications support this variant of the model.

12.1.2 The confirmation, affirmation and allocation model

This multi-stage process is the traditional process used to enable sell-side firms to agree trade details with buy-side firms when equities are traded (see Figure 12.4)

The steps on the process flow are as follows:

1. The buy-side firm sends the order to the sell-side firm.
2. The sell-side firm acknowledges it, and makes a decision as to how to execute it – i.e. whether to fill it by placing it with an investment exchange and which exchange to route

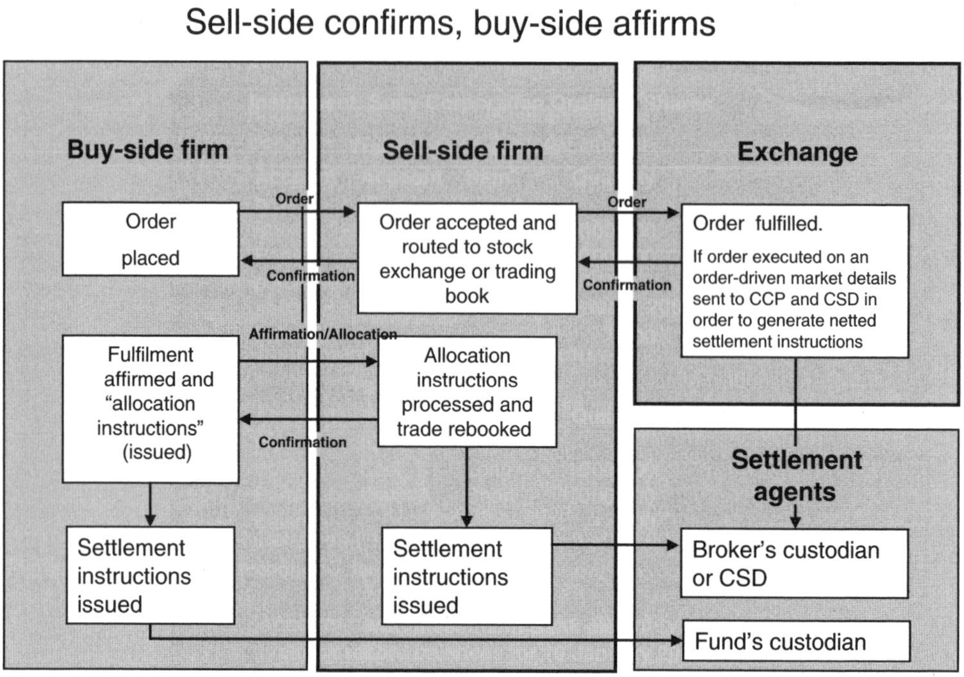

Sell-side confirms, buy-side affirms

Figure 12.4 Confirmation, affirmation and allocation

it to if there is a choice of exchanges; or whether to fill it by buying and selling from its own book. Article 21 of the MiFID regulations (see "The principles of best execution . . .", page 65, Chapter 8) requires the sell-side firm to have an execution policy that ensures that similar orders are always treated in the same fashion.

3. The sell-side firm then executes it, either as a single transaction (also known as a **block trade**), or if the order is for a large amount by breaking it down into smaller amounts.

4. When the sell-side firm has completed the order, it sends a confirmation to the buy-side firm. The confirmation will include, *inter alia*, details of:
   • The name of the client for whom the order was executed
   • The name of the stock and whether it was bought or sold
   • The trade date of the purchase or sale
   • The value date of the purchase or sale
   • The price of the trade – if the order was split into more than one order on an order queue this will be the average price of all the executed orders
   • The net amount to be paid or received by the investor, including any fees and charges, and for a bond sale any amount of accrued interest on the deal
   • Whether the firm acted as agent or principal
   • If it acted as agent, the name of the exchange that the deal was executed on.

5. The buy-side firm then checks the confirmation received from the sell-side firm. If it disagrees the details, it takes the matter up with the sell-side firm, otherwise it is said to **affirm** the confirmation.

6. At the same time that the buy-side firm affirms, it also advises the sell-side firm of the **allocation** details of this order. The fund manager itself has placed this order on behalf of its own clients – there may be just one of them or there may be many. At this stage the fund manager notifies the sell-side firm of the details of who its clients are, and how many shares are to be allocated to each client.

7. The sell-side firm then splits the **parent** trade into a number of **child** trades, one for each investor, and reconfirms the allocations to the fund manager. The confirmation repeats the information in the original confirmation of the "parent" trade (4 above).

8. The buy-side firm then reaffirms each of the individual fund transactions.

9. Both the buy-side firm and the sell-side firm then issue settlement instructions to their settlement agents.

10. All of these communications may be automated in the same way that the original order was automated, i.e. the confirmations, affirmations and allocations may be transmitted by any of the following methods:
   • By telephone or fax
   • By entering the information into a secure web page provided by the sell-side firm
   • By exchanging SWIFT messages
   • By entering the affirmation and allocation details directly into the sell-side firm's order management system. This, in turn, may be facilitated by using a third-party "hub and spoke" order routing service, which in turn usually involves exchanging FIX Protocol messages. Hub and spoke systems are provided by a number of vendors including Omgeo, Reuters and Bloomberg.

Figure 12.5, reproduced by permission of Omgeo LLC, shows how this is achieved using the Omgeo Oasys Global™ service provided by Omgeo LLC.

Step 1:
• The sell-side firm sends the confirmation of the block trade to the fund manager.
• If both firms are using Omgeo Alerts (see section 10.6.3) then the sell-side firm's settlement instructions will be appended to the message.

Step 2:
• The fund manager accepts or rejects details of the block trade.
• It affirms or rejects contract notes individually.
• If the details are accepted, then allocations are sent.

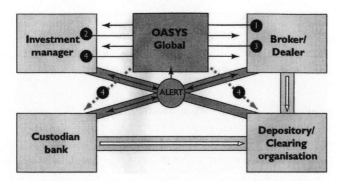

Figure 12.5   Trade agreement using Omgeo Oasys Global. Reproduced by permission of Omgeo LLC.

Table 12.5   SWIFT messages used in the confirmation/affirmation model

Message number	Message description	Sender	Receiver
MT202	Order to buy or sell	Buy side	Sell side
MT513	Advice of execution (of parent trade)	Sell side	Buy side
MT514	Allocation instruction	Buy side	Sell side
MT515	Client confirmation (of child trade) of purchase or sale	Sell side	Buy side
MT517	Affirmation (of either parent or child trade)	Buy side	Sell side

- If both firms are using Omgeo Alerts, then the investment manager's settlement instructions are appended to the allocation message.

Step 3:
- The sell-side firm accepts or rejects allocations individually.
- If accepted, then confirmation messages are created for each allocation.

Step 4:
- The fund manager affirms or rejects confirmation messages for each allocation.
- Copies of each confirmation message (if required) are generated.

Relevant SWIFT messages

The SWIFT messages shown in Table 12.5 are relevant to this model of order placing and trade agreement.

12.1.3   Use of a central matching engine

The traditional role of matching engines

Matching engines provide a further level of automation of the trade agreement process. They have been provided by investment exchanges and clearing houses for many years to automate the process of trade agreement between member firms. These traditional matching engines, however, have not been used by buy-side firms for a number of reasons.

The principles behind the traditional matching engines provided by exchanges and clearing houses are as follows:

1. Both parties input their trade details to the matching engine database in real time, as soon as possible after the trade has been struck. This is usually achieved by building a real-time interface from the firm's relevant business application to the matching engine.
2. The matching engine then compares the two trade reports, and provides the matching results to both parties in real time (see Figure 12.6).

Most matching engines also facilitate **post-trade publication** (also known as **regulatory trade reporting**). This is the process required in the EEA under the MiFID rules for post-trade transparency (see Chapter 8). Matching engines send a copy of each trade record to the regulator concerned so that it may monitor for insider dealing and market abuse. Because the regulators demand real-time trade reports, then trades need to be reported to the matching engine in near real time.

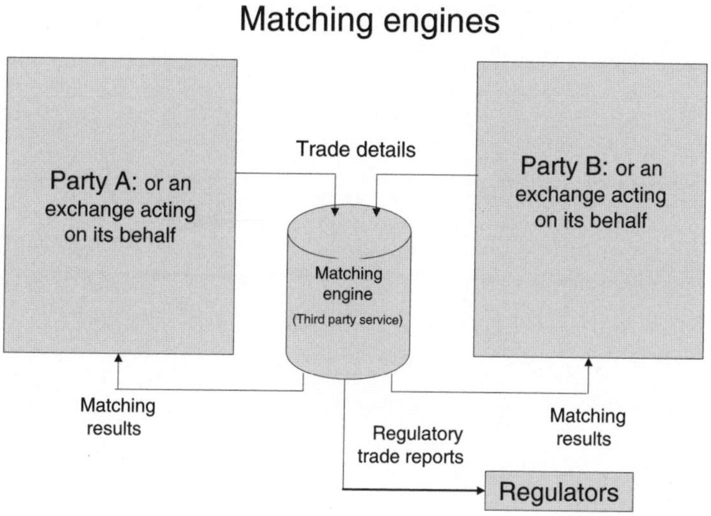

Matching engines

Figure 12.6 Central matching engine

However, traditional matching engines did not connect exchange member firms with non-member firms, nor did they support the confirmation/affirmation/allocation model, and nor did they store SSIs.

In 2002, Omgeo LLC launched the Central Trade Manager™(CTM), a central matching engine that involves the buy-side community and also supports block trades and allocations. The functions of CTM are shown in Figure 12.7, which is reproduced by permission of Omgeo LLC.

Steps 1a and 1b: After execution the sell-side firm sends a block/notice of execution (NOE) to their investment manager counterparty. The investment manager also sends their block and allocation messages to Omgeo CTM (this process is non-sequential). The sum of all the allocations have to agree to the total of the block trade confirmation. The investment manager can, optionally, send a block trade order first; if not, the system internally generates the block by grouping the allocation data.

Step 2: The fund manager and sell-side firm block trades are centrally matched.

Steps 3a and 3b: After the block trade is matched, allocations are sent to the sell-side firm for confirmation, after being enriched with standing settlement instructions via Omgeo Alert.

Step 4: To finalise the trade, the sell-side firm sends the allocation confirmations, Omgeo CTM matches them with the allocations and the trade moves to "match agreed" status.

Steps 5 and 6a: Throughout the process, status messages have been sent to the investment manager. This is done until a status of "match agreed" is achieved.

Step 6b: Once a matched status is achieved, an affirmation is also sent back to the broker/dealer.

Step 7: If required by either party, Omgeo CTM settlement notification functionality generates a SWIFT message based on the matched trades and then transmits the message to the settlement agent via SWIFT.

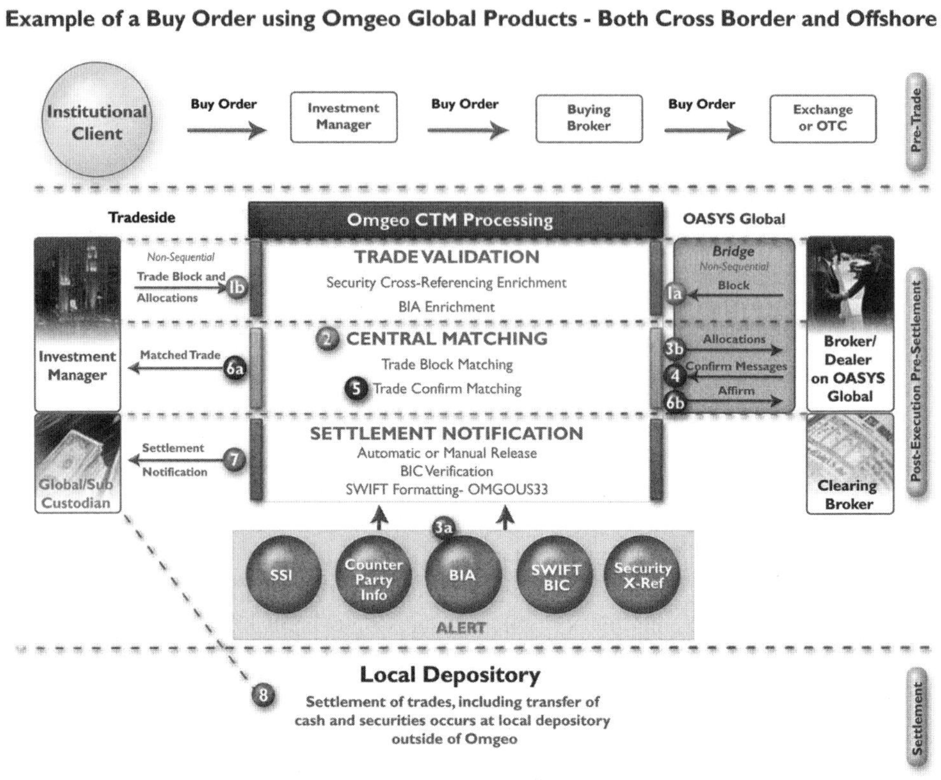

Example of a Buy Order using Omgeo Global Products - Both Cross Border and Offshore

Figure 12.7   Trade agreement using Omgeo CTM. Reproduced by permission of Omgeo LLC.

Step 8: Settlement of trades, including transfer of cash and securities, occurs at the local depository outside of Omgeo.

Message formats supported
The product supports a number of message standards, including SWIFT and FIX.

12.1.4   Confirmation followed by no further action

For private client (retail) trades, the executing firm simply sends a confirmation note by post or email to the client, who takes no action if it agrees with the contents.

12.2   COMMUNICATIONS BETWEEN THE TRADE PARTY AND ITS SETTLEMENT AGENT

12.2.1   Introduction

A settlement instruction is, as its name suggests, an instruction sent by a trading party to a settlement agent, instructing it to make or accept delivery of a financial instrument in exchange for receipt of payment of funds.

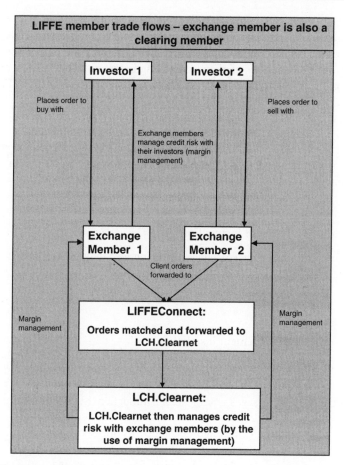

Figure 12.8 Trade flow with central counterparty

When the two trade parties have completed the trade agreement process, they both need to instruct their settlement agent to settle the trade. For an agency trade, the sell-side firm has to do this twice – first to settle the trade with the market counterparty, or stock exchange (the **market-side trade**), and second to settle the trade (the **customer-side trade**) with the investor.

If the market-side trade was for an instrument that is normally executed on a stock exchange order queue then there is no need to instruct it individually. The exchange concerned reports it to both the appropriate central counterparty, who novates it, and nets it with other trades in the same security; and also to the appropriate Central Securities Depository who will input settlement instructions for the net amount on behalf of both the firm concerned and the CCP. This concept was first examined in section 7.7.2, and is summarised in Figure 12.8.

For all other trades, each firm must send its settlement instructions for each individual trade to the relevant settlement agent. In this context "all other trades" includes:

- All trades for non-equity instruments
- Equity "market-side" trades in equities not normally traded on an order queue
- All "client-side" equity trades.

If the instruction relates to securities, and the delivery of the securities is to be inextricably linked to the receipt of funds, it is said to be a delivery-versus-payment or DvP instruction. If payment and delivery are not inextricably linked, then it is said to be **free of payment**, or FoP. DvP is the norm in the securities markets, as sending instructions FoP creates credit risk. For this reason, most firms have very strict rules as to under what circumstances an FoP instruction may be issued.

This means that many application systems that automatically generate settlement instructions are usually designed to require a second level of authorisation before an FoP instruction can be sent out. Each trade party will send its instructions to the settlement agent it has nominated for the particular asset class being traded. This information is stored in the SSI tables that were examined in section 10.6.

12.2.2 Contents of settlement instructions

Settlement instructions are *precise commands*, telling a settlement agent exactly what to do. No matter what message format is used, they follow a defined standard, which is illustrated in Table 12.6 for a principal trade.

12.2.3 Transmission of settlement instructions

Settlement instructions are usually transmitted in one of the following three ways:

• In the form of SWIFT messages – Table 12.11 in Section 12.2.9 for a full list of relevant messages.
• Using a proprietary standard message developed by the settlement agent, and transmitted using an "electronic banking system" designed by that settlement agent. Most commercial custodians, as well as the CSDs and ICS, supply systems to their customers that provide for secure communication. Traditionally, these were PC systems that required physical installation at the customer site, but increasingly these systems are web-based applications.
• Email, fax and telex: These traditional means of communication are being used less and less, as they do not lend themselves so readily to the STP concept as the other methods do.

In a high volume, STP-based environment the firm's settlement system usually generates settlement instructions automatically, and communicates directly with the firm's chosen method of transmission.

12.2.4 Information supplied by settlement agents between receipt of instruction and actual settlement event

Between the time that the settlement agent receives the instruction and the date that the trade actually settles, settlement agents usually send status messages relating to trades that are pending settlement to the firm concerned (see Figure 12.9).

Table 12.6   Contents of a settlement instruction

Field name	Explanation of contents	Example data
From:	Identity of the firm sending this instruction (note 1)	ABC Investment Bank
To:	Identity of the settlement agent receiving this instruction (note 1)	Euroclear Brussels
Value date	Earliest date on which this instruction should be carried out	5-Mar-07
Deliver/Receive	Whether securities are to be delivered or received	Deliver
Settlement basis	Whether to deliver-versus-payment or free of payment	Versus payment
Quantity of securities	The number of shares (equity) or face value of bonds to be delivered	1 000 000.00
Security reference	The ID of the security being delivered or received (note 2)	ICI plc 5% bond maturing 28 January 2010
Settlement currency	The currency of the cash to be paid or received	EUR
Net settlement value	The amount of cash to be paid or received	985 000.00
Our depot account	This firm's stock account number with the settlement agent	123456789
Our cash account	This firm's cash account number with the settlement agent	987654321
Counterparty depot details	Full details of the counterparty's stock settlement account, including account code (note 3)	Société Générale Paris, account no. 104867, in favour of Minicorp Pension Fund
Counterparty nostro details	Full details of the counterparty's cash settlement account, including account code (note 3)	Société Générale Paris, account no. 0-0876554332, in favour of Minicorp Pension Fund
Our reference	Our reference for this instruction. We would expect the settlement agent to quote this on all subsequent communications with us about this instruction	123456-01-02-03
Transmission date time	The date and time that the settlement instruction was sent	01/03/2007 10:33

Notes to Table 12.6:

1. The identities of the sender and receiver are usually represented by a BIC code – see section 10.5.1 .
2. The identities of the other party and its settlement agent are usually represented either by BIC codes or CSD/ICSD participant codes.
3. The identity of the security is usually represented by an ISIN code, SEDOL code, CUSIP code or some other standard identifier. The most widely used code in Europe is ISIN code – see section 10.4.1.

The format of such a status message will be based on Table 12.7.

Status codes

Each settlement agent will issue its customers with a list of status codes and their meanings. There may be several hundred individual codes, but the common ones (Euroclear codes are used in this example) are as shown in Table 12.8.

Communication with agents

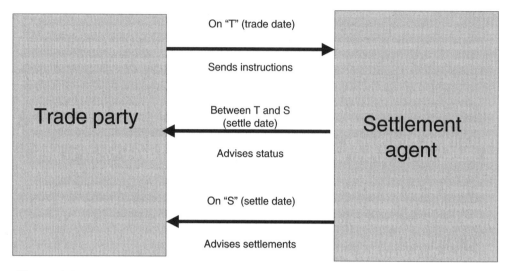

On "T" (trade date)

Sends instructions

Trade party

Between T and S
(settle date)

Advises status

Settlement agent

On "S" (settle date)

Advises settlements

Figure 12.9   Communication between trade party and settlement agent

Most CSDs and ICSDs make this information available to participants in real time; it is up
to business applications in the firm's configuration to access it. Some settlement agents make
it available in real time, but others only send it in the form of a SWIFT message once each
day, at the end of the day.

Table 12.7   Contents of a status message

Field name	Explanation of contents	Example data
From:	Identity of the settlement agent sending this status message	Euroclear Brussels
To:	Identity of the firm receiving this status message	ABC Investment Bank
Our trade reference	Euroclear's unique reference for this instruction	Kkee4455tt
Your trade reference	The reference that ABC quoted on the original settlement instruction	123456-01-02-03
Date and time of this message	The date and time that this message was sent	02/03/200/ 09:00:00
Brief details of the instruction	Action, security, security quantity, cash currency, cash amount	DvP 1 000 000 ICI plc 5% bond maturing 28 January 2010 to Société Génáralé in favour of Minicorp for EUR 985 000.00
Status code	A code to represent the status of the instruction	See below

Table 12.8   Explanation of status codes

Code	Meaning	Action to be taken by firm
UNM0	Unmatched – you have sent an instruction but your counterparty hasn't. Trade isn't due to settle until T + 2 or later	Take up with trade party
UNM1	Urgent unmatched – As above, but trade is due for settlement tomorrow or earlier	Take up with trade party – as a matter of urgency
CUNM	A trade party has alleged a trade against you, but you have not sent any instruction	Investigate internally/take up with trade party
USEC	Trade is matched, but you don't have any stock to deliver	Ascertain why you have no stock. Try to borrow if necessary
CSEC	Trade is matched, but counterparty has no stock to deliver	Take up with trade party
COLL	Trade is matched, but you don't have sufficient credit in your account with the settlement agent to pay for the stock	Investigate why. If the cash is held in a different bank account, transfer it, or else negotiate a line of credit
OTH	Other reason why this instruction might not take affect – usually this means that the other party has insufficient cash or collateral in his account to pay for the stock	Take up with trade party
OK	The instruction is OK for future settlement	No action is needed

Table 12.9   Status message history

Sequence	Date/Time	Event	Status now
1	01/03/2007 10:33	ABC sends the instruction. XYZ has not yet sent its instruction	UNM0
2	01/03/2007 12:14	XYZ sends its instruction, but ABC does not yet have the stock to deliver	USEC
3	02/03/2007 07:00	As a result of the successful settlement of another instruction, ABC now has stock to deliver	OK
4	02/03/2007 08:00	As a result of a processing error, ABC incorrectly cancels this instruction	CUNM
5	02/03/2007 11:00	ABC corrects the error that resulted in (4)	OK

The status of a trade may change many times between the time that the instruction was received by the agent and the date and time that it actually settles. For example, the status history of this trade might be as shown in Table 12.9.

12.2.5   The process of settling the trade – settling within tolerance

The settlement agent will settle the trade provided that:

1. Value date has been reached.
2. The seller has the stock to deliver.
3. The buyer has the cash or credit to pay for it.

4. Both the buyer's and the seller's instructions have been received by the agent's cut-off time for processing – this will usually be the close of business on the day before value date, or may be on value date itself depending on the market conventions for the instrument being traded.
5. The seller's instructions match the buyer's instructions. In determining whether instructions match, the settlement agent usually has the ability to settle within tolerance. That is to say, if the instructions match in every respect apart from a minor difference in the cash consideration, then the agent will settle the trade using the cash figure supplied by the seller. What is considered to be "a minor difference" varies from market to market; in the case of trades settling at Euroclear, for example, the threshold is set at the equivalent of USD 25.00.

A trade that has not settled by the agreed value date is known as a **failed trade.** The causes and consequences of failed trades are examined in Chapter 13.

12.2.6   Information provided by the agent when the trade settles

The settlement agent will provide the information shown in Table 12.10 when the trade settles.

12.2.7   The role of the unique reference number of the settlement instruction

When ABC sent the instruction, it provided its unique reference number (123456-01-02-03). Euroclear has quoted this number on all the messages it has sent back to ABC about this trade. The existence of this unique number facilitates STP; in particular it enables the update of the trade record in ABC's systems with the latest status of the instruction.

Table 12.10   Contents of a settlement message

Field name	Explanation of contents	Example data
From:	Identity of the settlement agent sending this status message	Euroclear Brussels
To:	Identity of the firm receiving this status message	ABC Investment Bank
Our trade reference	Euroclear's unique reference for this instruction	Kkee4455tt
Your trade reference	The reference that ABC quoted on the original settlement instruction	123456-01-02-03
Date and time of this message	The date and time that this message was sent	02/03/200/ 09:00:00
Deliver or receive	Whether stock has been delivered or received	Deliver
Security reference	The ID of the security being delivered or received	ICI plc 5% bond maturing 28 January 2010
Stock amount	Amount of stock actually delivered or received	1 000 000.00
Settlement currency	The currency of the cash that was received or paid	EUR
Settlement amount	The amount of cash that was received or paid	985 000.00

Some settlement systems simply quote the trade reference number in this field. There are a number of reasons why this is not "best practice", including the following:

1. Some trade types by definition will generate two or more instructions for different "events". For example, a stock loan – refer to Chapter 21 for more information – might generate the following event-based instructions:
   - An initial DvP instruction to settle the start leg
   - One or more (cash only) margin payments or refunds of margin payments as price movements create the need to increase or reduce collateral
   - One or more (cash only) interim payments of fees if the loan crosses several month ends
   - A final DvP instruction to close the transaction, returning the stock and the cash collateral.
        While an agency trade always has two components that settle independently of each other – the customer-side trade with the investor and the market-side trade with the exchange or market maker.
2. Sometimes it may not be possible to settle the whole transaction in one operation. The parties may agree to accept partial delivery in return for partial payment.
3. The affect of settlement netting – sometimes several trades will be consolidated into a single settlement.
4. If errors are made in trade processing, then sometimes settlement instructions need to be cancelled and reissued. Therefore a single trade has gone through multiple trade versions, each one creating changed settlement instructions.

For these reasons, it is generally considered "best practice" when designing a settlement system to have a many (trades) to many (instructions) relationship between trades and settlement instructions. As a result, many settlement applications build a unique reference number for a settlement instruction using this type of methodology:

Trade number	123456
Event number	01
Partial settlement number	02
Version number	03

Therefore the unique instruction for the third version of the second partial settlement instruction for the first event of trade number 123456 would be 123456-01-02-03.

12.2.8 Potential problems caused by the use of ISIN codes in status and final settlement messages

In section 10.4.1 we learned that an individual security may have a single ISIN code but many SEDOL codes or combinations of ISIN code and market identifier code. Therefore there may be a problem in interpreting messages from settlement agents when they only quote the ISIN code on these messages – the application processing the message does not know which unique security the message refers to. Therefore such applications need to provide an exception path that enables the correct security to be allocated by manual intervention.

12.2.9 Relevant SWIFT messages concerned with settlement

Note that the MT548 and the MT537 messages essentially provide the same information. The MT548 provides the information about a single instruction, while the MT537 provides the information for all the unsettled instructions for a particular account.

Table 12.11 SWIFT settlement messages

Business area	Message number	Message name	Additional information
All areas except securities	MT202	General financial institution transfer	This instructs a settlement agent to make a payment for any reason other than the settlement of a securities trade
All areas except securities	MT210	Advice to receive	This advises a settlement instruction that a third party will make a payment into the sender's nostro account – for any reason other than the settlement of a securities trade
Securities	MT540	Receive free	This advises the agent that a third party will deliver securities to the sender's depot account – free of payment
Securities	MT541	Receive against payment	This instructs the agent to receive securities in the sender's depot account and simultaneously make payment from the nostro
Securities	MT542	Deliver free	This instructs the agent to deliver securities from the sender's depot account free of payment
Securities	MT543	Deliver against payment	This instructs the agent to deliver securities from the sender's depot account and simultaneously receive payment in the nostro account
Securities	MT544	Receive free confirmation	The agent confirms that it has received an MT540
Securities	MT545	Receive against payment confirmation	The agent confirms that it has received an MT541
Securities	MT546	Deliver free confirmation	The agent confirms that it has received an MT542
Securities	MT547	Deliver against payment confirmation	The agent confirms that it has received an MT543
Securities	MT548	Status update and processing advice	The settlement agent uses this message to advise the current status of a particular instruction
Securities	MT536	Statement of transactions	The agent uses this message to advise which trades have settled today
Securities	MT537	Statement of pending transactions	The settlement agent uses this message to advise the current status of all the unsettled instructions for a particular depot account

13

Failed Trades – Causes, Consequences and Resolution

In section 12.2.4 we saw the settlement agent communicating details of settlement instructions that could not be fulfilled to its customer. When a settlement instruction cannot be implemented on value date it is known as a failed trade.

13.1 FAILED TRADES – CAUSES

The causes of failed trades fall into three categories:

- Problems with instructions
- The seller does not have the securities to deliver
- The buyer does not have sufficient cash or credit to make payment.

13.1.1 Unmatched settlement instructions

The settlement agent may be unable to match the buyer's and seller's instructions for any one or more of the following reasons:

- One of the parties has failed to send an instruction at all, or has sent it too late for processing on value date.
- The instructions sent by the two parties differ substantially from each other.

Instruction-related problems are almost always due to processing errors by one or other party. The possible causes of such a processing error include:

- *Human error at the data entry stage*: The order was entered for the wrong stock, wrong quantity of stock, wrong price, buy instead of sell, etc.
- *Computation error*: If the trade was entered correctly then the part of the process that calculates trade amounts such as principal amount, accrued interest, commission, fees (these elements sum to the trade consideration) may have failed for some reason. This type of problem may be caused by one or more of the following underlying problems:
  - Incorrect instrument-related static data in the system performing the computations
  - Application deficiencies – the business application is not able to perform the calculations for a complex transaction correctly.
- *Other data-related problems*: Such as incorrect SSI data that may lead the instruction either to be sent to the wrong agent, or quote incorrect nostro and depot accounts for one or other trade party.
- *Interfaces that fail:* For example, the trade is correctly entered into the front-office system but fails to reach the settlement system so no instruction is generated.

If the trade agreement process is working correctly, and if the different internal systems are reconciled with each other on a daily basis – as discussed in section 23.11 – then these types of problems *should* be detected and corrected before value date.

13.1.2   The seller has insufficient securities to deliver

This problem is caused by one or more of the following situations:

1. The seller has the securities in a depot account with the settlement agent, but they are not in the depot account that was quoted on the instruction.
2. The seller has "sold short" and does not have sufficient securities in its depot account to deliver.
3. The seller is depending on other parties to deliver securities to its depot account in order to make this delivery. One or more of those deliveries has failed, so the seller does not have sufficient securities in its depot account to deliver.

In the first case, it must be remembered that a settlement instruction is a precise command – the agent will only withdraw the securities from the depot account that was quoted in the instruction. If the firm has the same security in multiple depot accounts with the same agent, then it needs to issue a separate instruction to move them from one account to another.

In the second and third cases, the seller may be able to borrow the securities concerned. Stock borrowing is examined in detail in Chapter 21. In addition, in some markets the settlement agent will automatically arrange a partial delivery. In a partial delivery, the agent will deliver whatever proportion of the quantity instructed it can, against partial settlement of the cash – so if 40% of the stock is available the agent will deliver against 40% of the cash.

In other markets, it is necessary for the two trade parties to come to this type of agreement between themselves, and then cancel the original instruction and replace it with multiple instructions that bear a relationship to the quantities that the selling party estimates that it can deliver.

13.1.3   The buyer has insufficient cash or credit to make payment

Credit in this sense means the availability of an overdraft facility with the settlement agent. It is the buyer's responsibility to make sure that it is in a position to pay for its purchases.

Chapter 21 examines the need for the firm to be able to produce accurate cash flow projections, and also examines some of the common ways that portfolios are funded.

If a firm does not have sufficient cash or credit to pay for a purchase, then the trade will fail. Settlement agents do not arrange partial deliveries where the buyer has some – but not all – of the cash to pay for a purchase.

13.2   CONSEQUENCES OF FAILED TRADES

13.2.1   Purchases – cash perspective

The inability to pay for purchases creates **reputational risk**. It may lead to other trading parties reducing any credit limits that they apply to this party, which in turn can lead to liquidity risk. Both of these types of risk are examined in Chapter 24.

Additionally, depending on the rules that apply to the market the trade is executed in, either the seller may be entitled to make an interest claim against the purchaser for the loss of interest on the sale proceeds between contractual value date and actual settlement date, or the CSD may fine the purchaser for its inability to meet its contractual obligations.

13.2.2 Purchases – securities perspective

If a firm has the cash to pay for its purchases, and a purchase fails to settle, then it does not affect other aspects of the trade that are based on value date. It is still entitled to coupons, dividends and other corporate action benefits (examined in Chapter 23) that are based on the value date position.

If the buyer has bought the securities to add to an existing long position, and does not have any unsettled sale transactions that depend upon this receipt, then the failure of this purchase will not have any knock-on effects. However, if the buyer is depending on this receipt in order to make other deliveries, then a failed purchase does present problems. The buyer may be forced to borrow the stock (Chapter 21) in order to deliver its sales. The rules of most securities markets allow for the buyer to issue a **buy-in notice** to the seller if the seller is unable to deliver for an extended period of time.

Failure to act on the buy-in notice means the trading party that issued the notice may buy the securities from a third party and cancel the transaction with the original party. If the price has risen, then the selling party has to compensate the buying party for its losses.

13.2.3 Sales – cash perspective

The seller will naturally make every effort to ensure that its sales settle in full on value date, because until the trades settle it does not get paid and will not earn interest on the cash proceeds. If a buyer is unable to pay for securities due to lack of cash or credit then the seller may be entitled to make an interest claim against the buyer.

13.2.4 Sales – securities perspective

If the seller is selling out of a long depot position, then there should be no reason why sales fail provided that instructions are matched and purchasers have the cash or credit to pay for them. If the seller has sold short, then it may be able to borrow the securities concerned – this process is explained in Chapter 21.

13.3 THE PREVENTION AND RESOLUTION OF FAILED TRADES AND THE IMPACT ON IT APPLICATIONS

In order to minimise the number of failed trades, operations staff need to be able to monitor the status messages that the settlement agent sends prior to value date so that potential failed trades are handled as exceptions *before* value date. Settlement systems therefore need to be able to:

1. Automatically parse status messages and update the main trade record with the current status.

2. Provide real-time enquiries for operations personnel to inspect those instructions whose status is not "OK". These enquiries must be parameter driven, so that operations staff can view problem trades using a number of criteria such as:
   - Trading party
   - Instrument being traded value date
   - Settlement agent/depot account/nostro account
   - Current status
   - Combinations of the above.
3. Provide a history of status messages, so that the history of events may be used to make or defend interest claims and buy-in notices.
4. Provide operations personnel with the facilities to send and receive messages about actual and potential failed trades to trading parties and settlement agents.
5. Validate that the settlement instructions that the system has sent to settlement agents have in fact been received by those settlement agents. In other words, monitor the quality of the interfaces between systems and external suppliers.

14

An Overview of Investment Accounting

14.1 ROLE OF THE FINANCIAL CONTROL DEPARTMENT

As its name implies, the core function of the financial control department of a business is to manage its financial resources. The department is usually headed by a main board director who may have the title of chief financial officer. CFO job descriptions vary, but are likely to include:

- Overseeing all company accounting practices, preparing budgets, financial reports, tax and audit functions
- Directing financial strategy, planning and forecasts; conferring with chief executive officer, executive directors and department heads
- Managing investment and raising of funds for the business
- Studying, analysing and reporting on trends, opportunities for expansion and future company growth.

Within the department there are likely to be the following sections specialising in different activities:

- *Management accounting*, also known as product control: This section prepares budgets and produces the profit and loss accounts and balance sheets for individual business units, working closely with the managers of the business units to ensure that the income and expenditure of the business units is correctly recorded, and any financial risks are measured and appropriately contained.
- *Statutory reporting*: This section produces the firm's balance sheet and profit and loss account, which is then subject to both internal and external audit.
- *Regulatory reporting*: This section produces the financial and statistical returns demanded by the firm's regulator. In the UK this will be the Financial Services Authority (FSA).
- *Tax management*: This section will be concerned with organising the firm's activities so that its tax liabilities are (legally) minimised.
- *Treasury*: This section manages the company's cash resources, and, if the company's shares are listed on an exchange, it may be involved in decisions about raising additional capital in the form of equity or debt securities.
- *Financial operations*: This section makes payments to suppliers and payments of expenses to staff members, and in a non-financial company it would also control the sales ledger and credit control.

14.2 DEPARTMENTAL SYSTEMS

The department will have its own dedicated IT applications which include:

- A corporate general ledger system (section 14.3 examines the general ledger in more detail). This system will record all the assets, liabilities, income and expenditure of the firm, and is likely to include specialist modules which:

- Compare this year's P&L to the previous years P&L, and also to budgeted P&Ls
- Allocate expenses across departments. For example:
  - If the firm occupies a single building and 25% of the space in that building is occupied by the settlements department, then the settlements department needs to be charged with 25% of the rent, electricity, gas, water and property taxes.
  - The cost of the IT department itself needs to be recharged to those business units that benefit from it. There may be a number of bases for making this recharge. If, for example, there are five developers all working on an application used only by the settlements department, then the direct costs of these employees might be recharged directly to settlements. But other individuals in the IT department manage helpdesks, networks, desktop installations, etc. – from which all business units benefit – so the cost of these individuals may be recharged according to headcount – so if settlements employs 35% of all the firm's staff, then it would be recharged 35% of all these "general" IT costs.
- Manage the firm's purchase ledger and sales ledgers
- Translate profits and losses earned in foreign currencies into the firm's base currency.
- A regulatory accounting system – this system will be used to calculate the financial and statistical information that the firm needs to send to its regulator.

14.3   THE GENERAL LEDGER

The **general ledger**, sometimes known as the **nominal ledger**, is the main accounting record of a business which uses the double-entry bookkeeping convention. It will usually include accounts for such items as current assets, fixed assets, liabilities, revenue and expense items, gains and losses.

The general ledger is a summary of all of the transactions that occur in the company. It is built up by posting transactions to general ledger accounts as and when the business events occur.

The general ledger is based on the principle of **double-entry bookkeeping**, where each transaction is recorded in at least two ledger accounts. Each transaction results in at least one account being debited and at least one account being credited, with the total debits of the transaction being equal to the total credits.

For example, if a business purchases a desk for £100 cash, then its cash balances will decrease by £100 and the value of its office equipment will increase by £100. The cash account will be credited and the office equipment account will be debited with £100. Use of the double entry convention means that the accuracy of the accounts can be checked quickly – when all the accounts that have debit balance are summed, they should equal the sum of all the accounts which have a credit balance. Without this facility there would be no quick means to check accuracy.

However, the idea that a reduction in a bank balance is a credit does confuse the layman, who is used to talking to his bank about payments being debited, not credited. This is because the bank is talking from its point of view, not its customers. The customers account is a liability to the bank, and liabilities are credit balances. When a customer withdraws cash, he is reducing the bank's liabilities, and a reduction of a credit balance requires a debit.

Table 14.1   General ledger categories

General ledger account category	Accounting convention	Finance industry examples
Assets	Debit	Market value of securities purchased interest receivable Money due from counterparties and clients Cash in the bank account Premises, furniture, fittings and equipment
Liabilities	Credit	Market value of securities sold Interest payable Money due to counterparties and clients Overdrawn bank accounts
Revenue	Credit	Net interest income – i.e. interest received less interest paid Fees for client advice
Expense	Debit	Salaries and other employee benefits Rent, property taxes, heat, light, power, etc. All other expenses of running the business
Gains	Credit	Gains are profits (or increases in value) of an investment such as a stock or bond Gain is calculated by fair market value or the proceeds from the sale of the investment minus the sum of the purchase price and all costs associated with it. If the investment is not converted into cash or another asset, the gain is then called an unrealised gain
Losses	Debit	The opposite of gains – losses arise when the investment is sold for less than the purchase price, or when the fair market value is less than the purchase price
Shareholders' equity	Debit	The net value of the business to its shareholders. Based on the accounting equation: Shareholders, Equity = Assets – Liabilities

14.3.1   Assets and liabilities, income and expenses, gains and losses

There are seven basic categories in which all accounts are grouped. Table 14.1 shows the seven groups together with some examples of each group in the finance industry.

Shareholder's equity is the net value of the business to its owners, and is represented by the equation

$$\text{Shareholder's equity} = \text{Assets} - \text{Liabilities}$$

Assets and liabilities are collectively known as balance sheet accounts, while income, expenses, gains and losses are collectively known as P&L accounts. Some items (such as the notional principal of swap transactions) are known as **off-balance sheet items**.

14.3.2   General ledger account types for securities and investment firms

Firms in the financial sector will have (at least) the following account types within their general ledger. The concept of account types is used by applications that calculate the value of transaction- and position-related entries and post them to the ledger. There will be many individual unique accounts of each type, as discussed in section 14.3.3. The account types that are referenced in this book are shown in Table 14.2.

Table 14.2   General ledger account types

Account type	Category	Purpose of the account type
Security position	Balance sheet	To record the value of securities bought and sold in the firm's trading books or portfolios
Security trading party	Balance sheet	To record amounts payable or receivable for security purchases and sales
FX position	Balance sheet	To record the value of foreign currencies bought and sold in their original currency
Base currency cost of FX position	Balance sheet	To record the value of foreign currencies bought and sold in the firm's base currency
Money market deposits attracted	Balance sheet	To record the value of money market deposits attracted
Money market loans placed	Balance sheet	To record the value of money market loans placed
Swap notional principal	Off-balance sheet	To record the notional principal values of any swap transactions to which the firm is a party
Accrued interest on securities	Balance sheet	To record the value of interest due to the firm on its long security positions and payable by the firm on its short positions
Accrued interest on money market deposits attracted	Balance sheet	To record the value of interest payable by the firm on the money market deposits it has attracted
Accrued interest on money market loans placed	Balance sheet	To record the value of interest receivable by the firm on the money market loans it has placed
Accrued interest expense on swaps	Balance sheet	To record the value of interest payable by the firm on its outstanding swap transactions
Accrued interest income on swaps	Balance sheet	To record the value of interest receivable by the firm on its outstanding swap transactions
Collateral placed	Balance sheet	To record cash collateral placed by the firm
Collateral received	Balance sheet	To record cash collateral received by the firm
Accrued interest on collateral placed	Balance sheet	To record the interest receivable on collateral placed
Accrued interest on collateral received	Balance sheet	To record the interest payable on collateral received
Cash at bank	Balance sheet	To record the bank accounts used by the company
Coupon control	Balance sheet	To record any discrepancy in the value of coupons due to the company and the amount that it has actually received
Dividend control	Balance sheet	To record any discrepancy in the value of dividends due to the company and the amount that it has actually received
Corporate action control	Balance sheet	To record any discrepancy in the value of corporate action proceeds due to the company and the amount that it has actually received
Security fees and charges control	Balance sheet	To record the value of fees and charges (such as stamp duty and PM levy in the UK) that have been collected by the sell-side firm and need to be paid to the appropriate authorities
Swap gains and losses	Balance sheet	To record the mark-to-market gains and losses on swap trades
Security trading P&L	P&L	To record the income earned by the company from trading securities as principal

(Continued)

Table 14.2   *(Continued)*

Account type	Category	Purpose of the account type
Security commission income	P&L	To record the commission that the firm has charged its clients for executing agency trades
Security interest P&L	P&L	To record the interest that the firm has earned from its inventory of bonds
Money market loan interest income	P&L	To record the income earned from the deposits that the company has placed
Money Market Deposit interest expense	P&L	To record the cost of the deposits that the firm has attracted
Swap interest income	P&L	To record the interest income from the firm's swap transactions
Swap interest expense	P&L	To record the interest expense from the firm's swap transactions
Swap P&L	P&L	To record the mark to market gains and losses on swap trades
Stock lending income	P&L	To record the fees earned from stock lending
Stock borrowing expense	P&L	To record the fees payable from stock borrowing
Collateral interest income	P&L	To record the interest earned on collateral placed
Collateral interest expense	P&L	To record the interest paid on collateral received
Exchange fees	P&L	To record fees charged by exchanges
Settlement fees	P&L	To record fees charged by settlement agents
Option premium expense	P&L	To record the cost of options purchased or sold
Option premium income	P&L	To record income from writing options
FX trading P&L	P&L	To record gains and losses from FX trading

Examples of the use of account types in posting entries

Business applications use the concept of account types and trade amounts (refer to Chapter 6) to determine the money amounts that need to be posted to the general ledger.

Consider the following trade.

On 3 January 2008, ABC Investment Bank's trading book number 1 sold 10 000 shares in Sony Corporation to Client A at £11.30 per share, for value 7 January 2008. The Bank did not charge the client commission on this trade, so the amount payable by Client A is also £113 000 – 10 000 shares * £1130. As ABC purchased the shares for an average price of £11 each, it has made £3000 profit on this deal. ABC's settlement agent is Euroclear.

The entries that will be required on trade date will be as shown in Table 14.3.

Table 14.3   Example accounting entries for a securities principal sale

Debit or credit	Account type	Trade amount	Posted amount (£)
Cr	Security position	Principal amount	113 000.00
Dr	Security position	Trade P&L	3 000.00
Cr	Security trading P&L	Trade P&L	3 000.00
Dr	Security trading party	Consideration	113 000.00

Table 14.4   Example accounting entries for securities settlement

Debit or credit	Account type	Trade amount	Posted amount (£)
Cr	Security trading party	Settlement amount	113 000.00
Dr	Cash at bank	Settlement amount	113 000.00

The effects of these postings are that:

1. They have used the double-entry bookkeeping convention, the sum of the amounts debited less amounts credited is zero
2. They have recorded the profit as soon as it was made
3. They have recorded that a trading party – Client A – owes ABC £113 000.00

On the date that the trade settles the entries shown in Table 14.4 will be posted.

This entry reflects the fact that Client A no longer owes ABC the trade consideration, the trade has settled and the cash is now in the bank.

14.3.3   A unique general ledger account

The list of the accounts used by an individual general ledger system is called its **chart of accounts**. General ledger systems used by financial firms are usually multicurrency ledgers; that is to say that each individual account exists in all the currencies that it is possible for the user firm to trade in.

Each account code in the chart of accounts is given a unique account code. Sometimes this is a number, or it may be a meaningful alphanumeric code such as "SECPOS Book1".

In addition, user firms need to be able to see which entries apply to which individual securities, contracts or customer. Therefore, at account type level a decision needs to be made as to what further breakdown of the account postings and balances is required for each account code with this account type. The account types that were used in the example trade in section 14.3.2 of this chapter were:

- *Security position*: Accounts for this account type would normally be subdivided into an individual unique account for each individual security within each book, within each currency that the book trades.
- Security trading P&L: As for security position.
- Trading party: Each individual trading party would have at least one account in each currency that they have traded.
- Cash at bank: Each individual bank with whom the firm deals would require an individual account in each currency that the firm deposits with the bank concerned.

Table 14.5 Examples of unique accounts

Account code	Account type	Currency code	Further breakdown 1	Further breakdown 2
SECPOS book 1	Security position	GBP	Book 1	Sony shares
SECPOS book 1	Security trading P&L	GBP	Book 1	Sony shares
Client A	Security trading party	GBP	Client A	N/A
Euroclear	Cash at bank	GBP	Euroclear	N/A

Thus the individual identities of the four unique accounts that were used in the example might be as shown in Table 14.5.

14.3.4   Selecting the correct account to which an entry should be posted

Applications that decide to which general ledger account entries should be posted need to provide those users concerned with chart of accounts design with access to an account selection parameters table where they are able to build business rules that define:

1. Which trade amounts are posted to which account type, and to which individual account of that type
2. What further breakdowns are required.

It is not usually the general ledger system itself that decides what amounts are to be posted to which accounts. The decision logic is usually a part of the main settlement system. The exact methodology used will vary from system to system, but it is normally based on the principles described in this section.

Table 14.6 shows an example of the types of data found in the user interface to an account selection parameters table.

The explanation of the columns is:

1. *Trade amount*: The money amount connected with the trade, settlement or other event. A full list of these amounts needs to be defined in the system that is performing the account postings. The way that these objects are set up and defined in applications will vary. In older applications all of the definitions may be hard-coded; newer applications may make more use of metadata that provides users with more flexibility.

Table 14.6 Account selection parameters data input

Trade amount	Action	Sign	Account type	Breakdown I	Breakdown 2
Principal amount	Sell	Cr	Security position	Use book id	Use security id
Principal amount	Buy	Dr	Security position	Use book id	Use security id
Trade P&L	Profit	Cr	Security trading P&L	Use book id	Use security id
Trade P&L	Loss	Dr	Security trading P&L	Use book id	Use security id
Consideration	Sell	Cr	Security trading party	Use party ID	n/a
Consideration	Buy	Dr	Security trading party	Use party ID	n/a
Settlement amount	Receive	Cr	Security trading party	Use party ID	n/a
Settlement amount	Deliver	Dr	Security trading party	Use party ID	n/a

2. *Action*: The action that is being performed (e.g. buy, sell, profit, loss, receive, deliver). Once again, a full list of all possible actions needs to be defined in the system.

3. *Sign*: This tells the application whether a trade amount concerned with this action, which is a positive number, should be debited or credited to the account concerned. The converse will be true for negative numbers.

4. *Account type*: This tells the application to which account type data in this row should be posted.

5. *Breakdown 1 and Breakdown 2*: These columns tell the system how account types should be subdivided to create individual unique accounts. Subdivision is usually based on a defined list of suitable external objects such as trading books, currencies, securities and trading party IDs. Once again, a full list of available objects needs to be maintained, either in a hard-coded form or by the use of metadata.

   The example used in this chapter shows only two further levels of breakdown below account type, but many applications in use provide further levels of analysis. Very often a further level is used to allocate funding costs to particular business units. In the example trade that is used in this chapter, "book 1" sold the securities, and needs to fund the position until actual settlement date. Therefore breakdown 2 could be used to allocate the costs of funds to book 1.

14.3.5   A typical view of a general ledger account

A typical enquiry or report on a unique general ledger account will look similar to the example in Figure 14.1. It will contain the following data.

Static data items

1. The account type
2. The name of the account
3. The identity of the currency in which postings are made for this account.

Balance information items

1. The opening balance of the account
2. The date of the opening balance
3. The closing balance of the account on a value dated basis – this includes all postings where value date is equal to or earlier than the current date
4. The closing balance of the account on a forward basis – this includes all activity including those in (3) and also including those where value date is in the future
5. The date of the closing balances described in (3) and (4).

Transaction information items

1. The date that the transaction was carried out (business date)
2. The date that the transaction is expected to settle (value date)
3. The date that the transaction was entered into the general ledger system (entry date)
4. The money value of the transaction
5. A description of the transaction

ABC Investment Bank PLC general ledger postings and balances report

Account type: Security

					Date	31/01/2007
breakdown 1:	**Book 1**	**Currency GBP**			**Breakdown 2:**	**Sony Corp. shares**

Business date	Value date	Entry date	Trans. type	Origin code	Transaction description	Transaction reference number	Debit amount	credit amount
01/01/2007	**01/01/2007**	**01/01/2007**	**BAL**		**Opening balance of account**		0.00	
02/01/2007	05/01/2007	01/01/2007	PURCH	Equity	Purchased 20 000 shares at GBP 11 per share	222222	220 000.00	
03/01/2007	07/01/2007	03/01/2007	SALE	Equity	Sold 10000 shares at GBP 11.30 per share	333333		113 000.00
03/01/2007	07/01/2007	03/01/2007	Trade P&L	Equity	Profit on trade 333333	333333	3 000.00	
29/01/2007	01/02/2007	29/01/2007	SALE	Equity	Sold 1000 shares at 11.25	444444		11 250.00
29/01/2007	01/02/2007	29/01/2007	Trade P&L	Equity	Profit on trade 444444	444444	250.00	
31/01/2007	31/01/2007	31/01/2007	Reval	Setts	Revaluation of 9000 shares – current market price GBP 11.125	555555	1 012.50	
31/01/2007	**31/01/2007**	**31/01/2007**			**Closing balance of account – value dated**		**100 012.50**	
Forward dated entries on this account:								
31/01/2007	04/02/2007	31/01/2007	PURCH	Equity	Purchased 20 000 shares at GBP 12 per share	7777777	240 000.00	
31/01/2007	**04/02/2007**	**31/01/2007**			**Closing balance of account – forward dated**		**340 012.50**	

Figure 14.1 A unique general ledger account

6. A code to represent the type of the transaction (e.g. securities purchase, FX sale, etc.)
7. A "configuration origin code" – this tells the user of the general ledger which of the many systems in the configuration produced the transaction
8. A unique transaction reference number – ideally this reference number will be used by all the systems (front office, back office and FCD) that have recorded this transaction. This number should be meaningful in context. For example, if the user is looking at a general ledger account for a nostro account used for settlements, then the most useful transaction reference number for them to see is probably the unique instruction number that was described in section 12.2.7.

14.3.6 Posting errors and their possible causes

Because both the trade amounts and the account selection decisions will normally have been calculated by systems other than the general ledger system itself, dealing with a support call from a user of the general ledger application that is querying the amount of a posting (or indeed the lack of a posting or duplication of a posting) to a particular account can be complex. For example, consider the nature of this support call:

> I am looking at the security interest P&L account for book 1. For the past 10 months we have had the same bond portfolio, and the interest income has always been in the region of $100 000 per month. This month it is only $20 000.

Now look at the configuration diagram in Figure 14.2. A number of applications, services and interfaces between applications play a role in generating posting entries concerned with

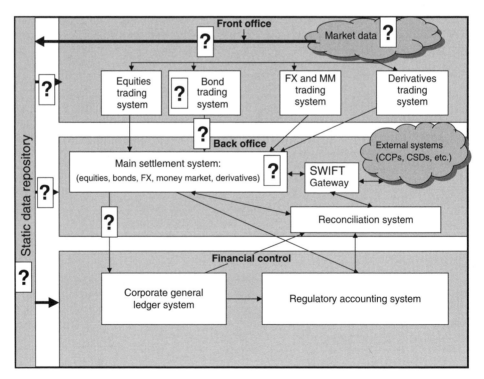

Figure 14.2   Where did the error occur?

bond interest, and the error – assume that it is a genuine error – could have occurred in any one of them. The applications, interfaces and services that are concerned with bond interest are highlighted by question marks.

And the cause of the error could include any one or more of the following:

- Human (data entry) errors, such as entering:
  - Buy instead of sell
  - Wrong stock
  - Wrong party
  - Wrong SSI or other static data
  - Etc.
- Technical errors including:
  - Interfaces that don't run/run twice/miss items out/duplicate data/run late
  - Incorrect static data obtained from an external information source
  - Systems that can not perform accurate trade computations/mark-to-market/interest accruals.

Because of the complexity of such a help desk call, it is recommended that general ledger reports and enquiries – such as the one illustrated in Figure 14.1 – always contain:

- The ID of the system that created the entry – the configuration origin code
- Meaningful – in context – transaction reference numbers
- Meaningful descriptions of entries
- The entry date of the entry – normally this will be the same as trade date, value date or settlement date – whichever date applies to entries of this type – but because of processing errors on earlier dates sometimes entries are passed late.

Effective, timely and comprehensive internal reconciliations between applications (as examined in section 23.11.2) can also be used proactively to detect problems of the sort that the user was reporting in this example.

14.3.7 Profits and losses in foreign currencies – translation into base currency

Any firm that invests in securities or other instruments that are denominated in foreign currencies will earn some of its profits, and incur some expenses in those currencies. As part of the accounting process, these P&L items need to be translated into its base currency at regular (usually monthly) intervals. If they are not translated, then their base currency value will fluctuate according to the exchange rate. This is known as **translation risk**, which is also covered in section 24.1.

The general ledger application usually contains specific functionality to automate the translation. At the end of the period defined by the user firm, accounting entries are passed that have the affect of reducing the balance of all the P&L accounts denominated in non-base currency to zero. The opposite entry debits or credits the sum of all the balances for that currency to a single balance sheet account.

Simultaneously, entries are passed that create the base currency equivalents of all the P&L accounts affected, using the exchange rate of the day. The opposite side of these entries is a single balance sheet account.

Consider the example in Table 14.7. ABC Investment Bank has a base currency of GBP and the following non-GBP balances in its P&L accounts.

$$\text{Total GBP equivalent} = 1190.48$$

Table 14.7   Non-base currency P&L balances

Account name	USD	CAD	EUR
Security interest	10 000.00	−5 000.00	−7 000.00
Security P&L	−5 000.00	−5 000.00	7 000.00
Swap interest	5 000.00	−5 000.00	5 000.00
Currency totals	10 000.00	−15 000.00	5 000.00
Exchange rate	USD 2 = GBP 1	CAD 2.1 = GBP 1	EUR 1.5 = GBP 1
GBP equivalents	5 000.00	−7 142.85	3 333.33

Table 14.8   P&L accounts after the translation process has run

Account name	USD	CAD	EUR	GBP
Security interest	0	0	0	−2 047.61
Security P&L	0	0	0	−214.29
Swap interest	0	0	0	3 452.38
Balance sheet FX translation account	10 000.00	−15 000.00	5 000.00	1 190.48

After the automated translation process has run, the balances for each currency will be as shown in Table 14.8.

The firm now needs to carry out FX deals for the FX translation account to sell USD 10 000.00 and EUR 5000.00 and buy CAD 15 000.00 for GBP. The base currency cost of these deals will be in the region of GBP 1190.48. If there has been a movement in the FX rates between the time that the translation entries were passed and the time that the deal is executed then there will be a further profit or loss on these deals.

15

The Stock Record – Using the Double-entry Convention to Control Positions and Security Quantities

Securities firms need to record stock (including listed futures and options in this context) quantities and balances as well as money amounts and balances. The business principles and software application structures (double-entry bookkeeping, unique accounts and the use of account selection parameter tables and the underlying data used by these tables) that have been used to record money amounts may also be used to record stock quantities.

The stock quantity equivalent of a general ledger is often known as the **stock record or stockrecord**. The stock record shows both the ownership of securities and the location of the stock. It is often a component of the main settlement system, but may also be a standalone application with interfaces to the main settlement system. Some packaged stock record applications employ the terminology of "long" and "short" as alternatives to "debit" and "credit", respectively, others use the debit/credit terminology. When they use debit and credit terminology different vendors do not use it consistently, as some applications are based in the premise that:

A purchase of stock is a debit of money and a credit of stock.

While the business logic of other applications is based on the premise that:

A purchase of stock is a debit of money and also a debit of stock.

To avoid ambiguity this book will use the long/short terminology.

Look again at the example trade that we used in Chapter 14.

On 3 January 2008, ABC Investment Bank's trading book number 1 sold 10 000 shares in Sony Corporation to Client A at £11.30 per share, for value 7 January 2008. The Bank did not charge the client commission on this trade, so the amount payable by Client A is also £113 000 – 10 000 shares * £11.30. As ABC purchased the shares for an average price of £11 each, it has made £3000 profit on this deal. ABC's settlement agent is Euroclear.

Assuming that the long position that was sold had already settled, the positions in the stock record before this trade was executed would be as shown in Table 15.1.

Between trade date and settlement date the stock record positions are as shown in Table 15.2.

On settlement date the stock record goes flat because we deliver the stock to Client A, and Euroclear no longer owes it to this firm.

Table 15.1 Stock record positions on trade date

Book 1	Long 10 000	The book is long because it owns the stock
Euroclear depot	Short 10 000	The depot is short because it owes this firm the stock

Table 15.2 Stock record positions on value date

Client A	Long 10 000	The client is long because we owe it the stock
Euroclear depot	Short 10 000	The depot is short because it owes this firm the stock

When the firm is processing coupons, dividends and corporate actions (see sections 23.3 to 23.6) it will use the stock record to ascertain which entities to pass the entitlements to, and which entities to claim the entitlement from.

The full list of account types within a typical stock record application is shown in Table 15.3.

It is necessary to produce two views of the stock record, one showing the positions for each account type on a trade dated basis, and the other on a value dated basis.

The trade dated version may be used to identify:

1. Book positions that require to be revalued – refer to section 23.8.
2. The actual position in the depot. This information is needed for dividend, coupon and corporate action proceeds (refer to sections 23.2 to 23.6) and also for depot reconciliation (refer to section 23.10).

While the value dated version may be used to identify:

1. Book positions on which coupon, dividend and corporate action proceeds are due – refer to sections 23.2 to 23.6
2. Safe custody positions on which coupon, dividend and corporate action proceeds are due – refer to sections 23.2 to 23.6
3. Trading parties (including borrowing and lending counterparties) to whom we owe or need to claim coupon, dividend and corporate action proceeds – refer to sections 23.2 to 23.6
4. Book positions on which interest needs to be accrued (refer to section 23.9).

Table 15.3 Stock record account types

Account type	Purpose of the account type
Book	To record the quantity of securities bought and sold in the firm's trading books or portfolios, and the identities of the books concerned
Depot	To record the position in the depot, and the identities of the depots concerned
Party purchase and sale	To record the value of securities bought and sold that have not yet settled, and the identities of the trading parties concerned
Custody	To record any security quantities that we are holding on behalf of clients, and the identity of the safe-custody clients concerned
Party borrow and lend	To record which trading parties this firm has borrowed stock from or lent stock to, and the quantities that have been borrowed or lent
Book borrow and lend	To record which trading books are borrowing or lending securities

The expected movements between the trade dated stock record and the value date stock record may be used to identify stock borrowing requirements and stock lending opportunities, which are discussed in Chapter 21.

Stock record example

On 3 January 2008, ABC Investment Bank's trading book number 1 purchased 10 000 shares in Sony Corporation to Client A at £11.30 per share, for value 7 January 2008. ABC's settlement agent is Euroclear. The trade does not settle until 10 January 2008.

Figure 15.1 to 15.3 show ABC Investment Bank's trade dated and value dated stock record balance reports for Sony shares on 3 January, 7 January and 10 January, respectively.

The trade dated and value dated stock record balances for 3 January are as shown in Figure 15.1.

There are no value dated balances as the trade has not yet reached value date. When the trade reaches value on 7 January, the stock record report looks like that shown in Figure 15.2.

No entries have been passed on 7 January, as no actual events took place (the trade did not settle); but the trade dated positions are now the same as the value dated positions. By the time that the trade settles, on 10 January, the stock record report looks like that shown in Figure 15.3.

The difference between the stock record of 7 February and that of 10 February is accounted for by the following entry:

Long: Client A 10 000 shares
Short: Depot Euroclear 10 000 shares

ABC Investment Bank plc
Stock record balances for 3 January 2008

Instrument: Sony Corporation Ordinary Shares

Trade dated balances

Account type	Account ID	Sign	Quantity
Book	Book1	Long	10 000.00
Party purchase and sale	Client A	Short	10 000.00
Balance			0.00

Value dated balances

Account type	Account ID	Sign	Quantity
Balance			0.00

Figure 15.1   The stock record on 3 January

ABC Investment Bank plc
Stock record balances for 7 January 2008

Instrument: Sony Corporation Ordinary Shares

Trade dated balances

Account type	Account ID	Sign	Quantity
Book	Book 1	Long	10 000.00
Party purchase and sale	Client A	Short	10 000.00
Balance			0.00

Value dated balances

Account type	Account ID	Sign	Quantity
Book	Book 1	Long	10 000.00
Party	Client A	Short	10 000.00
Balance			0.00

Figure 15.2   The stock record on 7 January

ABC Investment Bank plc
Stock record balances for 10 January 2008

Instrument: Sony Corporation Ordinary Shares

Trade dated balances

Account type	Account ID	Sign	Quantity
Book	Book 1	Long	10 000.00
Depot	Euroclear	Short	10 000.00
Balance			0.00

Value dated balances

Account type	Account ID	Sign	Quantity
Book	Book 1	Long	10 000.00
Depot	Euroclear	Short	10 000.00
Balance			0.00

Figure 15.3   The stock record on 10 January

Note that the stock record balance for an individual security is always zero, as the double-entry bookkeeping convention has been employed throughout the processing.

16

Example STP Flows of Equity Agency Trades – When Execution Venue is the London Stock Exchange

16.1 INTRODUCTION

There are a very large number of potential trade flows for equities, as the flow will vary according to whether the customer is an institutional investor or a private investor, and also according to what stock exchange the order is executed on. It is therefore not possible to provide examples of all the potential STP flows of equity trades in all the world's major markets.

Two examples are provided in this chapter, in each case the order is to be executed on the London Stock Exchange. The examples are:

1. An agency trade with an institutional customer
2. An agency trade with a retail customer in the United Kingdom.

The chapter finishes by examining the growth of orders being executed using **Direct Market Access (DMA)**.

16.1.1 Background to the London Stock Exchange and its trading platforms

In section 7.6.2 we learned that stock exchanges provide order-driven trading platforms, quote-driven trading platforms and hybrid trading platforms. Post-MiFID, the London Stock Exchange provides the following trading platforms.

LSE trading platforms for UK domestic securities

- *SETS (hybrid platform)*: SETS is the London Stock Exchange's hybrid trading service that combines electronic order-driven trading throughout the day with integrated market maker liquidity provision, delivering guaranteed two-way prices. It is used to trade all securities in the FTSE All Share Index as well as the more liquid AIM securities.
- *SETSqx (hybrid platform)*: SETSqx (Stock Exchange Electronic Trading Service – quotes and crosses) supports four electronic auctions a day (at 08.00am, 11.00am, 15.00pm and 16.35pm) along with continuous standalone quote-driven market making. It is used to trade all UK domestic equities not traded on SETS.
- *SEAQ (quote-driven platform)*: SEAQ is the quote-driven platform for fixed interest market and AIM securities not traded on either SETS or SETSqx.

LSE trading platforms for non-UK securities

- *International Order Book (order-driven platform)*: An electronic order book for trading depository receipts.
- *International Bulletin Board (order-driven platform)*: An electronic order book for trading international securities with a secondary listing on the London Stock Exchange.
- *EUROSETS (order-driven system)*: Dutch trading service offering secondary market trading in liquid, large and mid-cap Dutch equities in the AEX and AMX indices.
- *European Quoting Service (quote driven platform)*: Market making and trade reporting service for liquid MiFID securities not quoted on another exchange service.

Settlement agents involved in LSE trades and default value dates

All trades that are matched on the order book in an order-driven or hybrid platform need to be novated as the trade parties are anonymous. Therefore, all securities that *are eligible for trading* on the LSE's order-driven and hybrid platforms are cleared, novated and netted by the LSE's central counterparty, LCH.Clearnet Limited. Securities that are only eligible for trading on the LSE's quote-driven markets (where trade parties are not anonymous to each other) are not cleared by LCH.Clearnet Limited.

All trades on the LSE, whether or not they are cleared by LCH.Clearnet Limited, are settled by the CSD for the UK – Euroclear UK and Ireland.

The default value date for transactions matched on an order queue is T + 3.

16.2   EQUITY AGENCY TRADES WITH INSTITUTIONAL INVESTOR CUSTOMERS

16.2.1   Process overview

The process overview is summarised in Figure 16.1.

The figure shows two potential routes for the sell-side firm's settlement instructions, depending on whether or not LCH.Clearnet has cleared and novated the trade.

16.2.2   Order placement

Orders may be placed by any of the following means:

- By telephone or fax
- By entering the order details into a secure web page provided by the sell-side firm
- By sending the sell-side firms a SWIFT message. SWIFT is covered more fully in section 11.1
- By entering the order details directly into the sell-side firm's order management system. Typically, this would be facilitated by using a third-party "hub and spoke" order routing service. Providers of such services include Omgeo, Thomson Financial, Reuters and Bloomberg
- By using direct market access –see section 16.4.

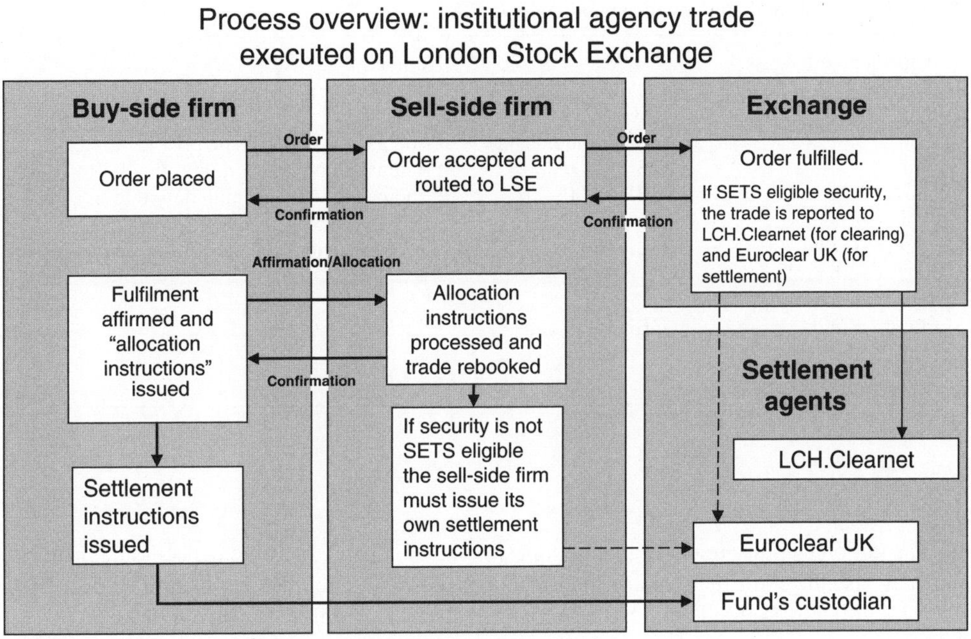

Figure 16.1 Process overview: LSE institutional agency trade

16.2.3 Order execution

The sell-side firm will have already decided to execute this trade in an agency capacity on the LSE. It will have decided this using its execution policy that is a requirement of the MiFID regulations. This requirement was examined in section 8.4.2.

The sell-side firm will charge the customer the same price that it obtained on the exchange, plus a commission for its services. The investor may also need to pay certain charges. If the trade is a purchase by the investor, then the end investor will also need to pay the stamp duty which was explained in section 10.7. If the trade (whether it is a purchase or a sale) has a principal value of GBP 10 000.00 or more, then the investor will need to pay PTM levy, which was also explained in section 10.7. These fees will be collected by the sell-side firm and held in a balance sheet account of the type "fees and charges". The sell-side firm will then be debited for these amounts by the CSD, who will pay them to the appropriate authorities.

16.2.4 Trade amounts

Example

On 4 February 2008 for value date 7 February 2008 ABC Investment Bank executed an agency trade on behalf of XYZ Fund Managers. XYZ purchased 10 000 shares in Megacorp at £1.50 per share, ABC charged XYZ a commission of 0.50% of the principal value.

The trade amounts are as shown in Table 16.1.

Table 16.1   Trade amounts for agency purchase on LSE

Principal amount	10 000 shares	Number of shares
Trade price	£1.50	Price per share
Commission rate	0.50%	
Principal value	GBP 15 000.00	Principal amount * Trade price
Commission	GBP 75.00	Principal amount * Commission rate
Stamp duty	GBP 75.00	Principal amount * Stamp duty rate
PTM levy	GBP 1.00	The PTM levy is always £1.00
Customer-side trade consideration (of XYZ's trade with ABC)	GBP 15 151.00	Sum of principal value + Commissions + Fees
Market-side trade consideration (of ABC's trade with the exchange)	GBP 15 000.00	Principal value

16.2.5 Trade agreement

For institutional equity trades, agreement between the buy-side firm and the sell-side firm will normally use the confirmation, affirmation and allocation model that was examined in section 12.1.2. For the market-side trade, the exchange acts as a central matching engine.

16.2.6 Regulatory trade reporting

Regulatory trade reporting is achieved by the exchange acting as a central matching engine.

16.2.7 Settlement

Market-side settlement

If the security is SETS eligible, then the exchange will report the trade both to LCH.Clearnet, who will clear it, novate it and settle it and to Euroclear UK and Ireland who will settle the net liability for that security by the member firms concerned. If it is not SETS eligible, then the sell-side firm that is executing it and the market maker that it dealt with will both need to issue settlement instructions.

Customer-side settlement

The buy-side firm (XYZ) will need to issue a settlement instruction to its custodian to receive 10 000 shares in Megacorp from ABC against payment of GBP 15 151.00 on value date 7 February 2008, and the sell-side firm (ABC) will need to issue instructions to Euroclear UK and Ireland to deliver 10 000 shares in Megacorp from XYZ against payment of GBP 15 151.00 on value date 7 February 2008. The format of the settlement instructions and the formats of the status and settlement messages that the settlement agents might send to the trade parties were provided in section 12.2.

Table 16.2   Trade date entries: institutional equity purchase

Sign	Ledger account type	Trading party ID	Trade amount	GBP amount
Dr	Security trading party	Customer (XYZ)	Customer-side consideration	15 151.00
Cr	Security fees and charges control	N/A	PTM levy	1
Cr	Security fees and charges control	N/A	Stamp duty	75
Cr	Commission income	N/A	Commission	75
Cr	Security position	N/A	Principal value of customer trade with XYZ	15 000.00
Dr	Security position	N/A	Principal value of market trade	15 000.00
Cr	Security trading party	Market counterparty or LCH.Clearnet	Market-side consideration	15 000.00

16.2.8   General ledger postings for the trade and the settlement

Trade dated postings

Using the example trade in section 16.2.4 the entries passed by ABC Investment Bank on trade date will be as shown in Table 16.2.

16.2.9   Settlement date postings

The sell-side firm expects that both sides of the trade will settle on the same day. However, this is not guaranteed as there could be an STP exception on either the market side or the customer side. On the date that the trades do settle (assuming that they settle in full) the entries – for the market side trade – where ABC has to pay for the securities – will be as shown in Table 16.3.

For the customer-side trade – where ABC will receive payment for the securities – the entries will be as shown in Table 16.4.

Table 16.3   Market-side settlement date entries

Sign	Ledger account type	Trading party ID	Trade amount	GBP amount
Dr	Security trading party	Market counterparty or LCH.Clearnet	Market-side consideration	15 000.00
Cr	Cash at bank	N/A	Market-side consideration	15 000.00

Table 16.4   Customer-side settlement date entries

Sign	Ledger account type	Trading party ID	Trade amount	GBP amount
Cr	Security trading party	Customer (XYZ)	Customer-side Consideration	15 151.00
Dr	Cash at bank	N/A	Customer-side Consideration	15 151.00

Table 16.5 Stock record postings on trade date

Sign	Stock record account type	Trading party ID	Trade amount
Long	Book	N/A	Principal amount of market-side trade
Short	Party purchase and sale	Market counterparty or LCH.Clearnet	Principal amount of market-side trade
Short	Book	N/A	Principal amount of customer-side trade
Long	Party purchase and sale	Customer (XYZ)	Principal amount of customer-side trade

16.2.10 Stock record postings for the trade and the settlement

Trade date postings

The postings on trade date will be as shown in Table 16.5.

As a result of these stock record postings, the stock record will look like Figure 16.2, reflecting the fact that on a trade dated basis ABC owes stock to XYZ and is owed stock by its market counterparty.

Settlement date postings

The postings that are made on the date that the trades settle will be as shown in Table 16.6.

If the market-side trader settled on time but the customer-side trade failed, then the stock record for 7 March would look like Figure 16.3.

The stock record is therefore now reflecting the fact that:

1. The market counterparty has delivered the 10 000 shares to our Euroclear account.
2. We owe the shares to XYZ, and if there were a dividend or a corporate action with a record date on any date prior to the actual settlement date then ABC will owe the proceeds to XYZ. Dividend and corporate actions processing are examined in sections 23.5 and 23.6.

ABC Investment Bank plc
Stock record balances for 4 March 2008

Instrument: Megacorp Ordinary Shares

		Trade dated balances	
Account type	**Account ID**	**Sign**	**Quantity**
Book	Book 1		0.00
Party purchase and sale	Market counterparty	Short	10 000.00
Party purchase and sale	XYZ	Long	10 000.00
Balance			0.00
		Value dated balances	
Account type	**Account ID**	**Sign**	**Quantity**
Balance			0.00

Figure 16.2 Stock record on trade date

Table 16.6 Stock record postings on settlement date

Sign	Stock record account type	Trading party ID	Trade amount
Short	Depot	N/A	Principal amount of market-side trade
Long	Party purchase and sale	Market counterparty or LCH.Clearnet	Principal amount of market-side trade
Short	Depot	N/A	Principal amount of customer-side trade
Long	Party purchase and sale	Customer (XYZ)	Principal amount of customer-side trade

ABC Investment Bank plc
Stock record balances for 7 March 2008

Instrument: Megacorp Ordinary Shares

Trade dated balances

Account type	Account ID	Sign	Quantity
Depot	Euroclear UK and Ireland	Short	10 000.00
Party purchase and sale	XYZ	Long	10 000.00
Balance			0.00

Value dated balances

Account type	Account ID	Sign	Quantity
Depot	Euroclear UK and Ireland	Short	10 000.00
Party purchase and sale	XYZ	Long	10 000.00
Balance			0.00

Figure 16.3 The stock record on settlement date

16.3 EQUITY AGENCY TRADES WITH PRIVATE INVESTOR CUSTOMERS

16.3.1 Order placement

Specialist securities firms that deal with the private investor may be known as private client stockbrokers, private banks or wealth managers. As stated in section 7.4, these firms often act in a discretionary capacity, which means that the firm itself generates the orders on behalf of the investor. In addition, firms of this type usually provide a safe-custody service for their clients, which means that securities are not normally delivered to them. When private investors place the orders themselves (rather than rely on their broker using its discretionary authority) they will normally use one of the following methods:

- By telephone
- By entering the order into a web portal provided by the firm concerned.

There are a number of significant differences between the way that orders are placed by private individuals and the way that orders are placed by buy-side firms acting for institutional investors:

1. Buy-side firms normally place orders in terms of an express share quantity, e.g. "buy (or sell) 1000 Tesco shares"; while retail customers may express the order in the same terms or may instead express a buy order as "Invest £1000 in Tesco" or a sell order as "sell £1000 worth of Tesco". £1000 in this context is the consideration (the net amount payable or receivable by the customer including commissions and fees).
2. Buy-side firms are usually content to express orders in terms of "at best" or "at limit" and wait for the confirmation message to tell it the exact price of the trade, but retail investors expect price certainty – they want to know the exact price of the shares concerned before they will agree to the order being executed.
3. Many retail investors have difficulty in meeting the T + 3 value date convention, as the UK banking system is not yet geared up for making relatively low value payments within three business days. If they want to pay the broker by cheque there is both a postal delay and a cheque clearing delay; if they want to pay using a debit card, then this form of payment usually clears on T + 4.

These issues make it impractical for the broker receiving the order to place it on the SETS queue, because:

1. There is no price certainty on SETS at the point of order – only when the order is matched.
2. There is no facility in SETS to enter an order in terms of its consideration – SETS orders can only be entered in terms of nominal amounts.
3. All SETS trades settle on T + 3.

As a result of these issues, private client brokers have developed web portals that are used both by clients entering trades directly and by the brokers' own call centre staff taking telephone orders that are able to:

1. Interface with software provided by **retail service providers (RSPs)**. RSPs are specialist principal dealers that:
   - Guarantee prices at the point of order entry
   - Provide extended settlement facilities – normal value date is usually T + 10.
2. Poll all the RSPs and determine which one is offering the best price.
3. Given the price supplied by the most competitive RSP, the target consideration supplied by the investor, the broker's commission schedule and the rules and rates of stamp duty and PTM levy, calculate the nominal amount that the client needs to buy or sell.
4. Provide a secure web portal for the investor to enter and authorise the order, and submit debit card or bank details to the broker.

The LSE defines RSPs on its website as:

> An RSP is an automated quoting system similar to a computerised market maker – it is electronically connected to brokers who normally request quotes from several RSPs and trade on the best price.

- RSPs trade in a principal capacity (i.e. trade on their own account) and these off book executions must be traded under the rules of, and reported to, a Recognised Organisation (investment exchanges recognised by the FSA and overseas equivalents) such as the London Stock Exchange.
- Though a broker is treated as a market counterparty and therefore can trade at any price, RSPs take on the best execution responsibility owed to a typical private investor and will always, at least, match the best bid and offer (BBO or touch) displayed by the Exchange.

This form of trading is aimed primarily at private investors, so maximum dealing sizes are restricted and there is no direct interaction with the order book.

16.3.2 Order execution

Figure 16.4 shows the interactions between the user of a web portal, the private client broker's systems and the RSP's systems.

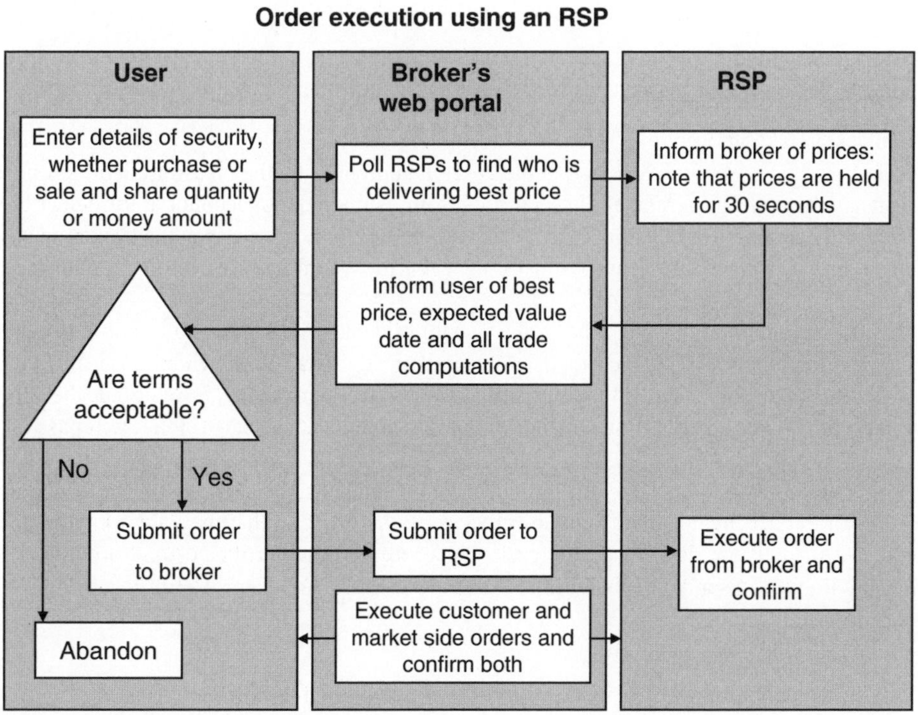

Figure 16.4 Execution of an order with an RSP

16.3.3 Trade agreement

The trade agreement for the customer-side trade is that the broker sends the customer a confirmation message (by post and/or email) and the customer takes no action if he agrees to its contents. The trade agreement process for the market-side trade is that the exchange acts as a central matching engine.

16.3.4 Regulatory trade reporting

Regulatory trade reporting is achieved by the exchange acting as a central matching engine.

16.3.5 Settlement

Market-side settlement

If the security is SETS eligible, then the exchange will report the trade both to LCH.Clearnet, who will clear it, novate it and settle it, and to Euroclear UK and Ireland, who will settle the net liability for that security by the member firms concerned. If it is not SETS eligible, then both the broker and the RSP need to submit settlement instructions to Euroclear. The settlement messages sent to and received from the firm's settlement agents were described in section 12.2.

Customer-side settlement

The investor takes no action. Because the normal practice is for the brokers to hold the securities in custody for the investor, in the case of a purchase by the investor the broker needs to issue an instruction to transfer the securities from its main depot account at Euroclear to its safe custody depot at Euroclear on value date. If the investor has sold, then the broker needs to issue an instruction to Euroclear to transfer the securities from its safe custody depot account at Euroclear to its main depot account.

Some investors may not wish the broker to hold the securities in custody on their behalf. They may require the securities to be registered in their name, in which case a physical certificate should be printed by the registrar and sent to them. If this is required, then for a purchase the broker needs to issue a **stock transfer form** to Euroclear which it will pass on to the registrar concerned.

If the investor is selling certificated securities, then most brokers will require physical delivery of the certificates in advance of processing the order so that they are not exposed to credit risk or delivery risk. When the broker has received the certificates and processed the order it will need to send the stock transfer form (signed by the client) to Euroclear.

16.3.6 General ledger postings for the trade and the settlement

The general ledger postings for a retail trade on trade date and settlement date are the same as those for an institutional agency trade. Refer to sections 16.2.8 and 16.2.9.

Table 16.7   Stock record postings on settlement date – safe custody purchase

Sign	Stock record account type	Trading party ID	Trade amount
Short	Depot	N/A	Principal amount of market-side trade
Long	Party purchase and sale	Market counterparty or LCH.Clearnet	Principal amount of market-side trade
Short	Depot	N/A	Principal amount of customer-side trade
Long	Custody	Customer name	Principal amount of customer-side trade

16.3.7   Stock record postings for the trade and the settlement

Trade date

The stock record postings on trade date for this type of trade are the same as those for an institutional agency trade. Refer to Section 16.2.10.

Settlement date postings

Assuming that the broker is holding the securities in custody for the client, the postings that are made on the date that the trades settle will be as shown in Table 16.7.

If this were a safe-custody sale then the signs would be reversed. The stock record after settlement of a customer purchase of 10 000 shares now looks like Figure 16.5.

The stock record now reflects the fact that this firm has to credit the customer with any dividends, coupons or corporate action proceeds while we are holding the securities in custody on its behalf.

ABC Investment Bank plc
Stock record balances for 7 March 2008

Instrument: Megacorp Ordinary Shares

Account type	**Account ID**	**Sign**	**Quantity**
	Trade dated balances		
Depot	Euroclear UK and Ireland: client's account	Short	10 000.00
Custody	Client ID	Long	10 000.00
Balance			0.00
	Value dated balances		
Depot	Euroclear UK and Ireland: client's account	Short	10 000.00
Custody	Client ID	Long	10 000.00
Balance			0.00

Figure 16.5   Stock record after safe-custody settlement activity

16.4   DIRECT MARKET ACCESS

16.4.1   Introduction

Direct Market Access (DMA) is defined as the automated process of routing a securities order directly to an execution venue, therefore avoiding intervention by a third party. Execution venues include exchanges, alternative trading systems and electronic communication networks. To simplify, DMA enables the buy-side firm or investor to place orders directly onto the order queues of investment exchanges, avoiding the need to submit the order to an exchange member firm in the traditional manner described in section 16.2.

DMA has the potential to "cut out the middleman"; or to put it another way, to disintermediate the exchange member firm. However, many of the providers of DMA services are themselves exchange member firms, others are technology suppliers that have acquired exchange membership for the purposes of opening it to investor clients.

One of the original drivers for the growth of DMA was the growth of **algorithmic trading**, which is defined as the "placing a buy or sell order of a defined quantity into a quantitative model that automatically generates the timing of orders and the size of orders based on goals specified by the parameters and constraints of the algorithm". If an investor is using algorithmic trading technology, then the timing of the order to the second is critical. Conventional order flow techniques are simply too slow to have the desired result. In addition, DMA is a more anonymous way of trading – it allows hedge funds in particular to offload large quantities of stock without tipping off the market.

DMA is available for listed futures and options as well as securities.

According to a survey conducted in 2004 by the Tower Group, DMA accounted for 33% of all orders originated by buy-side firms in the USA in that year. This was up from just 11% in 2000, and Tower Group expected DMA to account for 40% of all US-originated orders by the end of 2006. They found that commissions on DMA orders averaged only about one cent per share. For this reason, many sell-side firms were offering a range of services to their DMA customers including the supply of algorithmic trading analytics, often as part of a prime brokerage service. In the past few years, many investment firms have opened up their DMA trading platforms to private investors.

16.4.2   DMA technology

At the simplest level, DMA is just access to the sell-side firm's order execution technology. DMA changes the way that orders are placed and executed, but not the way they are agreed, reported to regulators, settled or accounted for.

There are a number of specialised DMA package applications available on the market, and a number of traditional front-office system packages have been adapted to provide DMA.

17
The STP Flow of Debt Instrument Trades

17.1 INTRODUCTION

Most trades in debt instruments are executed by sell-side firms as principal; there is no stock exchange involved. Instead, market makers publish bid and offer prices and compete with each other. Their bid and offer prices are published on Reuters and Bloomberg.

17.2 ORDER PLACEMENT

Orders may be placed by any of the following means:

- By researching best bid and offer prices and telephoning a market maker direct
- By researching best bid and offer prices and sending orders through hub and spoke services such as Omgeo Oasys or Autex
- By using the electronic bond trading platforms provided by information vendors such as Bloomberg, Reuters and Thomson Financial
- By using the services of a money broker. The money broker will aim to provide "best execution" subject to and taking into account the nature of the order, the prices available to the broker in the market and the nature of the market in question. The money broker will charge a fee for its services, which is usually invoiced at the end of the month in which the order was executed. Money brokers offer both telephone-based services and also electronic order entry and matching services.

17.3 ORDER EXECUTION

The sell-side firm will normally execute the trade as principal, and earn its income from the spread between the average price of its position in the securities and the price of the order. The sell-side firm may be running a short position in the security concerned.

17.4 TRADE AMOUNTS

Because trades in debt instruments are normally executed in a principal capacity, there are not usually any commissions or other fees charged on trades in these instruments. In section 3.2 we examined the reasons why accrued interest forms part of the trade computation. The different elements of a debt trade are therefore usually those shown in the following example and Table 17.1.

The Cable and Wireless 4% Convertible Bond Maturing 16 July 2010 last paid a coupon on 16 January 2008. On trade date 5 February 2008, for value date 8 February 2008, Investor A sells £100 000 face value of this bond to Investor B at a trade price of 96%.

Because Investor A had purchased these bonds earlier at an average price of 95.5%, it makes a profit of £500.00 on this transaction.

Table 17.1 Trade elements – debt principal trade

Trade date	05-Feb-08
Value date	08-Feb-08
Currency and face value of bonds bought or sold	£100 000
Principal amount: £100 000 face value @ trade price 96%	£96 000.00
Accrued interest days	23
Accrued interest £100 000 face value * 4% for 23 days	£252.75
Consideration	£96 252.75
Profit on trade	£500.00

Accrued interest needs to be calculated using the appropriate interest calculation formula for the particular bond. These formulae were described in Chapter 3.

17.5 TRADE AGREEMENT

All the components shown in the example in section 17.4 would need to be matched as part of the trade agreement process. In Europe, debt market makers are normally members of the International Capital Market Association (ICMA), a self-regulatory organisation and trade association representing the financial institutions active in the international capital markets worldwide.

ICMA provides a central matching engine known as **TRAX2** that may be used to compare trade records. Not all buy-side firms will be participants in TRAX2, so many sell-side firms will offer the following variants.

- Mutual exchange of confirmations in paper form
- Mutual exchange of conformations via SWIFT
- Variants of the confirmation, affirmation and allocation model including direct links between the two firms' systems and the use of hub and spoke service providers.

Note that not all sell-side firms will provide all the alternative methods of trade agreement.

If the transaction was arranged by a money broker, then the money broker will also send a confirmation that needs to be checked by the trade party.

17.6 REGULATORY TRADE REPORTING

TRAX2, the central matching engine, is typically used to fulfil the sell-side firm's trade reporting obligation.

17.7 SETTLEMENT

For many government bonds, standard settlement is T + 1, i.e. one business day after trade date. For corporate bonds it is usually T + 3.

Sell-side firms will normally use one of the following types of settlement agent:

- For securities issued by governments, they may use the CSD of the country concerned, e.g. for UK government securities they will use Euroclear UK and Ireland, for US government securities they will use the DTCC.
- For securities issued by corporate borrowers, they will normally use an ICSD such as Euroclear Bank in Brussels or Clearstream in Luxembourg.

Many corporate bond issues are relatively illiquid, therefore there can be a high proportion of failed trades in these instruments.

The settlement messages sent to and received from the firm's settlement agents were described in section 12.2.

17.8   GENERAL LEDGER POSTINGS FOR THE TRADE AND THE SETTLEMENT

As the example trade is a sale and it results in a realised profit, the entries posted on trade will be as shown in Table 17.2.

When the trade settles (the trade can of course settle in more than one event) the posting (for the settlement of a sale) will be as shown in Table 17.3.

The signs would of course be reversed for a purchase.

Table 17.2   Trade date accounting entries for bond purchase as principal

Item	Sign	Ledger account type	Trade amount name	Trade amount (£)
1	Cr	Security position account	Principal value	96 000.00
2	Cr	Accrued interest account	Accrued interest	252.75
3	Dr	Security position account	Realised P&L	500.00
4	Cr	Security trading P&L account	Realised P&L	500.00
5	Dr	Security trading Party account	Consideration	96 252.75

Notes:
1. If they were a purchase instead of a sale, then the signs of items 1, 2 and 5 would be reversed.
2. If the purchase or sale resulted in a loss instead of a profit, then the signs of items 3 and 4 would be reversed.

Table 17.3   Settlement date accounting entries – sale

Item	Sign	Ledger account type	Trade amount
1	Cr	Security trading party account	Settlement amount
2	Dr	Nostro account	Settlement amount

17.9   STOCK RECORD POSTINGS FOR THE TRADE AND THE SETTLEMENT

As the example trade is a sale, the stock record postings will be as shown in Table 17.4.

And when the trade settles, it will be as shown in Table 17.5

Table 17.4   Debt principal trade – stock record postings on trade date

Item	Sign	Stock record account type	Trade amount
1	Short	Book	Amount purchased
2	Long	Party purchase or sale	Amount purchased

Table 17.5   Debt principal trade – stock record postings on settlement date

Item	Sign	Stock record account type	Trade amount
1	Long	Party purchase or sale	Amount purchased
2	Short	Depot	Amount purchased

17.10   POSITION-RELATED EVENTS

A single principal transaction in a debt instrument gives rise to a position in that instrument. The position-related events for a debt instrument include coupon fixing, coupon payment, mark-to-market and interest accrual, and these are all examined in Chapter 23.

18

The STP Flow of Foreign Exchange and Money Market Trades

18.1 FOREIGN EXCHANGE

18.1.1 Order placement

Orders may be placed by any of the following means:

- By researching best bid and offer prices and telephoning a bank direct
- By researching best bid and offer prices and sending orders through hub and spoke services such as Omgeo Oasys or Autex
- By using any number of Reuters pre-trade services. Reuters is a major force in FX pre-trade services. Because the world's major FX market makers publish their prices on its services it is able to act as an electronic money broker, finding competitive quotes. It also provides analytical tools and conversational dealing.
- By using the services of a money broker. The money broker will aim to provide "best execution" subject to and taking into account the nature of the order, the prices available to the broker in the market and the nature of the market in question. The money broker will charge a fee for its services, which is usually invoiced at the end of the month in which the order was executed. Money brokers offer both telephone-based services and also electronic order entry and matching services. The major force in electronic money broking for foreign exchange is a company called Electronic Broking Services (EBS). EBS was created by a partnership of the world's largest foreign exchange (FX) market making banks. Approximately USD 145 billion in spot foreign exchange transaction, 700 000 oz in gold and 7 million oz in silver is traded every day over the EBS Spot Dealing System. It was created in 1990 to challenge Reuters' threatened monopoly in interbank spot foreign exchange and provide effective competition.

  EBS was the first organisation to facilitate orderly black box or algorithmic trading in spot FX, through an application programming interface (API). EBS was acquired by ICAP, the world's largest money broker, in June 2006.

  EBS claims to be the market leader for arranging deals in the EUR/USD, USD/JPY, EUR/JPY, USD/CHF and EUR/CHF currency pairs and Reuters is the leader for all other interbank currency pairs. In practice, banks that make markets in a wide variety of currency pairs need connectivity to both applications.

18.1.2 Order execution

Orders will be executed by the sell-side firm as principal; spot deals settle on $T + 2$ and forward deals settle on a date agreed by the trade parties. Section 4.2.1 explained how forward prices are calculated.

18.1.3   Trade amounts

Example

On 4 February 2008 for spot value date 6 February 2008, ABC Investment Bank plc purchases AUD 1 million (Australian dollars) from AN Other Investment Bank paying in GBP at an exchange rate of AUD 0.428458 to GBP 1.

This is an example of a cross-currency deal. In the London FX markets, banks normally buy and sell each currency against their FX base currency, which is usually the US dollar. Table 18.1 shows the rates (or prices) of the Australian dollar and the British pound versus the US dollar on 4 February, and the rate for this cross-currency trade is computed from the rates of the individual currencies against USD.

The trade amounts (from ABC Investment Bank's perspective) are as shown in Table 18.2.

The profit on the deal is the difference between the cost (measured in the base currency) of the bought currency and the sale proceeds of the bought currency.

18.1.4   Trade agreement

Trade agreement for FX trades is based on the "mutual exchange of confirmations" model that was examined in section 12.1.1. The relevant SWIFT message is the MT300. Where the deal has been arranged by a money broker, the money broker will also send a confirmation, and as a result it is necessary to agree both the confirmation received from the counterparty as well as the confirmation received from the money broker.

18.1.5   Settlement

The settlement agents of both trade parties will be held on each other's SSI tables, which were described in section 10.6. ABC Investment Bank needs to send the following messages:

- An instruction (SWIFT MT202) to its GBP settlement agent requesting it to deliver GBP 428 209.56 to AN Other's GBP settlement agent on 6 February.
- An instruction (SWIFT MT210) to its settlement agent for AUD requesting it to receive AUD 1 000 000.00 from AN Other's AUD settlement agent on 6 February.

Settlement netting

Both bilateral settlement netting and multilateral settlement netting are possible for FX transactions.

Bilateral settlement netting is where two parties agree to settle only the net proceeds for FX deals each day. For example, if ABC and AN Other had struck the FX deals shown in Table 18.3 all for the same value date then the settlements would only involve the net totals for each currency.

Multilateral settlement netting is made possible by the CLS Bank – refer to section 7.7.1. If these firms were CLS Bank participants then they each advise the CLS Bank of the trades that they have to settle, and it nets all the movements in each of the currencies down to a single net payment or receipt for that currency for each CLS participant.

Table 18.1 Determining the cross-currency rate

A	B	C	D	E	F	G	H	J
AUD quantity	USD (base currency) bid price of AUD 1	USD (base currency) offer price of AUD 1	USD quantity at bid price	USD quantity at offer price	USD profit on deal	GBP offer price of USD 1	GBP quantity	Derived exchange rate for GBP/AUD
1 000 000.00	0.863100	0.863600	863 100.00	863 600.00	500.00	2.015600	428 209.96	0.428210

Table 18.2   Foreign exchange trade amounts

Trade amount name	Currency name	Amount	Relevant column in Table 18.1
Bought currency principal amount	AUD	1 000 000.00	A
AUD to USD exchange rate (bid)		0.8631	B
AUD to USD exchange rate (offer)		0.8636	C
Cost of AUD	USD	863 100	D
Sale proceeds of AUD currency	USD	863 600	E
Profit on deal	USD	500	F (=D–E)
USD to GBP exchange rate		2.0156	G
Sold currency principal amount	GBP	428 209.56	H
Derived exchange rate AUD to GBP		0.42821	J (=H/A)

Table 18.3   Bilateral settlement netting example

Currency	ABC bought from AN Other	ABC sold to AN Other	Net amount to be received (+) or paid (−) by ABC
USD	721 200	1 442 400	−721 200
GBP		428 210	−428 209.9623
AUD	1 000 000		1 000 000
EUR	1 000 277	500 138.7	500 138.6963

The way that they advise CLS Bank about the trades to be netted is that they inform SWIFT of the fact they are CLS members. SWIFT then monitors all the FX trade confirmations that CLS members send to each other and passes the information on to the CLS Bank. Table 18.4 shows the net receipts and payments that ABC would make from and to the CLS Bank on 6 February if it and three other banks were CLS members.

18.1.6   General ledger postings

All FX trade-related general ledger postings are passed on value date, it is assumed that settlement will take place in full on contractual value date. The accounting entries generated by the example trade will be as shown in Table 18.5.

18.1.7   Stock record postings

The stock record is not used for trades where the instrument being traded is a currency.

18.1.8   Revaluing the position

As a result of this trade, ABC Investment Bank now has a long position in AUD and a short position in GBP. These positions need to be marked to market at the close of business each day using the closing exchange rates of this currency to the FX base currency, the US dollar. Marking to market is examined in section 23.8.

Table 18.4 Net settlement with CLS bank

Currency	ABC bought from AN Other	ABC sold to AN Other	ABC sold to CLS Member 1	ABC sold to CLS Member 2	ABC sold to CLS Member 3	ABC sold to CLS Member 4	Net amount to be received (+) or paid (−) by ABC
USD	721 200.00	1 442 400.00	1 947 240.00	2 452 080.00	3 310 308.00	6 620 616.00	−4 536 348.00
GBP		428 209.96	0.00	727 956.94	0.00	1 965 483.73	−3 121 650.63
AUD	1 000 000.00		1 700 000.00	0.00	2 890 000.00	0.00	5 590 000.00
EUR	1 000 277.39	500 138.70	1 700 471.57	850 235.78	2 890 801.66	2 295 636.62	1 945 539.53
ZAR	100 000.00			100 000.00			0.00

Table 18.5   FX trade account postings on trade date

Sign	Ledger account type	Trade amount	Currency	Cash amount
Cr	FX position	Bought currency principal amount	AUD	1 000 000.00
Dr	Cash at bank	Bought currency principal amount	AUD	1 000 000.00
Dr	Base currency cost of FX position	Bought currency principal amount at bid price	USD	863 100.00
Cr	Base currency cost of FX position	Bought currency principal amount at offer price	USD	863 600.00
Cr	FX P&L	Profit or loss on deal	USD	500
Dr	Base currency cost of FX position	Profit or loss on deal	USD	500
Cr	Base currency cost of FX position	Sold currency principal amount at bid price	USD	863 600.00
Dr	Base currency cost of FX position	Sold currency principal amount at offer price	USD	863 600.00
Dr	FX position	Sold currency principal amount	GBP	428 209.56
Cr	Cash at bank	Sold currency principal amount	GBP	428 209.56

18.2   MONEY MARKET

18.2.1   Order placement

Orders may be placed by any of the following means:

- By researching best bid and offer prices and telephoning a bank direct
- By researching best bid and offer prices and sending orders through hub and spoke services such as Omgeo Oasys or Autex
- By using the services of a money broker. The money broker will aim to provide "best execution" subject to and taking into account the nature of the order, the prices available to the broker in the market and the nature of the market in question. The money broker will charge a fee for its services, which is usually invoiced at the end of the month in which the order was executed. Money brokers offer both telephone-based services and also electronic order entry and matching services.
- By using any number of Reuters pre-trade services. Reuters is a major force in money market pre-trade services. Because the world's major banks publish their rates on its services it is able to act as an electronic money broker, finding competitive quotes. It also provides analytical tools and conversational dealing.

18.2.2   Order execution

Orders will be executed by the sell-side firm as principal. Executed trades are of two types:

- *Fixed rate deals* pay a fixed rate of interest and have a fixed maturity date. This is typically a period of one day, two days, one week or one month. However, two days before the agreed maturity date the two parties can agree to "roll it over". If a deal is rolled over, then:
  - The borrower will pay the interest due to the lender date on maturity date
  - A new maturity date is agreed
  - The interest rate is renegotiated for the next period.
- *Call or notice deposits* pay a variable rate of interest, and have no pre-agreed maturity date. The two parties may terminate the transaction by mutual agreement given two days' notice.

Table 18.6   Money market trade amounts

Trade amount name	Trade amount
Opening leg principal amount	GBP 1 000 000.00
Closing leg consideration	GBP 1 000 000.00
Interest rate	5%
Interest to maturity	GBP 4 109.59
Closing leg consideration	GBP 1 004 109.59

Opening leg transactions for both deal types usually settle on T + 2 but can settle on any forward date agreed by the trade parties.

18.2.3   Trade amounts

> **Example**
>
> On trade date 5 March 2007, value date 7 March 2007, ABC Investment Bank borrowed GBP 1 000 000 from AN Other for 30 days at 5% interest, calculated on the actual/actual basis. The maturity date is therefore 6 April 2007.
>
> On 6 April, ABC will repay the principal amount of GBP 1 000 000 + 30 days' interest:
> Repayment amount = 1 000 000 + (1 000 000 ∗ 30/365 ∗ 5%) = GBP 1 004 109.59

The trade amounts in this example are as shown in Table 18.6.

18.2.4   Trade agreement

Trade agreement for money market trades is based on the "mutual exchange of confirmations" model that was examined in section 12.1.1. The relevant SWIFT messages are the MT320 (used for fixed deals) and the MT330 (used for call and notice deals). Where the deal has been arranged by a money broker, the money broker will also send a confirmation, and as a result it is necessary to agree both the confirmation received from the counterparty as well as the confirmation received from the money broker.

18.2.5   Regulatory trade reporting

Regulatory trade reporting is not required for money market transactions.

18.2.6   Settlement

For the start leg, the borrower sends a SWIFT MT210 message to its settlement agent telling it to receive GBP 1 000 000.00 from the lender's settlement agent on 7 March and the lender sends an MT202 message to its settlement agent to make payment of GBP 1 000 000.00 to the borrower's settlement agent. The identities of the settlement agents will be held on the SSI tables described in section 10.6.

For the end leg, the borrower sends a SWIFT MT202 message to its settlement agent telling it to pay GBP 1 004 109.59 to the lender's settlement agent on 6 April and the lender sends an MT202 message to its settlement agent to receive GBP 1 004 109.59 from the borrower's settlement agent.

If the two parties agree to roll the deal over, then the borrower sends a SWIFT MT202 message to its settlement agent telling it to pay GBP 4109.59 to the lender's settlement agent on 6 April and the lender sends an MT202 message to its settlement agent to receive GBP 4109.59 from the borrower's settlement agent.

Business applications that build these messages need the ability to generate the start leg messages immediately, but hold the end leg messages until two business days before the maturity date. The concepts of bilateral or multilateral settlement netting do not apply to these transactions.

18.2.7 General ledger postings

These are the postings from the borrower's point of view. The start leg transactions are normally posted on trade date, and the end leg transactions are normally posted two business days before maturity date (see Tables 18.7 and 18.8).

If the transaction is looked at from the lender's point of view, then the entries become as shown in Tables 18.9 and 18.10.

Table 18.7 Money market deposit account postings – start leg

Sign	Ledger account type	Trade amount name	Trade amount (GBP)
Cr	Money market deposits attracted	Opening leg principal amount	1 000 000.00
Dr	Cash at bank	Opening leg principal amount	1 000 000.00

Table 18.8 Money market deposit account postings – end leg

Sign	Ledger account type	Trade amount name	Trade amount (GBP)
Dr	Money market deposits attracted	Opening leg principal amount	1 000 000.00
Dr	Accrued interest money market deposits attracted	Interest to maturity	4 109.59
Cr	Cash at bank	Closing leg consideration	1 004 109.59

Table 18.9 Money market loan account postings – start leg

Sign	Ledger account type	Trade amount name	Trade amount (GBP)
Dr	Money market loans placed	Opening leg principal amount	1 000 000.00
Cr	Cash at bank	Opening leg principal amount	1 000 000.00

Table 18.10 Money market loan account postings – end leg

Sign	Ledger account type	Trade amount name	Trade amount (GBP)
Cr	Money market loans placed	Opening leg principal amount	1 000 000.00
Cr	Accrued interest money market loans placed	Interest to maturity	4 109.59
Dr	Cash at bank	Closing leg consideration	1 004 109.59

18.2.8   Stock record postings

The stock record is not normally used in conjunction with trades in currencies.

18.2.9   Accrual of interest

During the life of the deposit or loan, interest needs to be accrued on a daily basis. Accrual of interest is explained in section 23.9.

The STP Flow of Futures and Options Transactions

19.1 INTRODUCTION

The examples in this section are based on futures and options listed on the Euronext.LIFFE exchange in London, which will be cleared by LCH.Clearnet Limited. However, the general principles that are described in the examples apply to all listed derivatives traded on any exchange, but when listed derivatives are traded on other exchanges the names of the exchanges, clearing houses and systems involved will vary from those used in the examples.

The following process steps are identical for futures and options:

- Order placement
- Order execution
- Trade agreement
- Regulatory trade reporting
- Settlement
- Mark to market
- Accrual of interest on collateral placed or received.

However, the trade amounts, as well as the general ledger and stock record posting process steps are different. Therefore the common processes are examined in section 19.2, and the instrument-specific process steps are examined in sections 19.3 for futures and section 19.4 for options.

19.2 FUTURES AND OPTIONS – COMMON PROCESS STEPS

19.2.1 Order placement

As each futures or options contract is unique to the exchange that developed it, the investor needs to submit the order to a sell-side firm that is a member of the exchange concerned. This may be achieved by any one of the following means:

- By telephone or fax
- By entering the order details into a secure web page provided by the sell-side firm
- By sending the sell-side firms a SWIFT message. SWIFT is covered more fully in section 11.1.
- By entering the order details directly into the sell-side firm's order management system. Typically, this would be facilitated by using a third-party "hub and spoke" order routing service. Providers of such services include Omgeo, Thomson Financial, Reuters and Bloomberg.
- By using direct market access – see section 16.4.

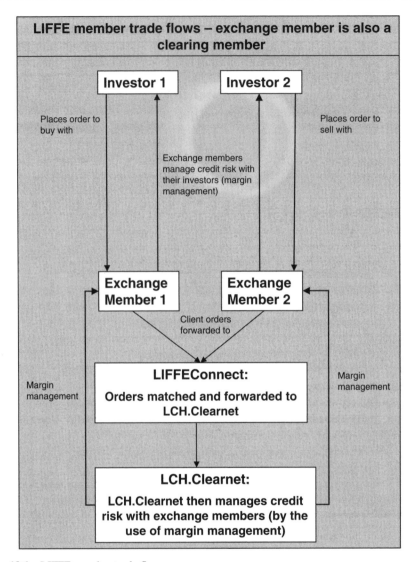

Figure 19.1   LIFFE member trade flow

19.2.2   Order execution

The order will always be executed by the sell-side firm as an agent. The process steps are explained by Figure 19.1, which was first seen in section 7.7.1:

1. The investor places its order with the exchange member firm.
2. The member firm then places it on the order queue maintained by LIFFEConnect™; the order-driven platform run by Euronext.LIFFE.
3. As soon as the order is matched on LIFFEConnect, then LIFFEConnect:
   - Informs the exchange member, who in turn needs to inform the investor
   - Informs LCH.Clearnet, who then novates the trade.

19.2.3 Trade agreement

Trade agreement between the member firm and the exchange is facilitated by the exchange acting as a central matching engine. Trade agreement between the member firm and its client may be achieved by any or all of the following methods:

- The confirmation, affirmation and allocation model using FIX protocol messages
- Sending an email, fax or mail confirmation to the investor or sell-side firm and relying on the investor to take action only if it disagrees with its content
- Mutual exchange of confirmations via SWIFT – this method of trade agreement is little used for exchange traded contracts.

19.2.4 Regulatory trade reporting

Regulatory trade reporting is achieved by the exchange acting as a central matching engine.

19.2.5 Settlement

Because the trade party in an order-driven market is anonymous, all settlement obligations have been novated by LCH.Clearnet Limited.

All the messages between the parties, the exchange and the clearing house will use message formats and APIs supplied by the exchange and clearing house. SWIFT and FIX standards do not apply.

Note that the exchange member firm is not necessarily a member of the clearing house. A firm that is a non-clearing member of an exchange will deal with a general clearing member of the exchange who is in turn a member of the clearing house. The relationships between the parties involved where trades are cleared by a third-party clearer were examined in section 7.7.1.

19.2.6 Marking to market

Positions in exchange traded futures and options should be marked to market each day as explained in section 23.8, using the closing prices published by the exchange concerned.

19.2.7 Interest accrual

Interest should be accrued on any collateral placed or received. Interest accrual is explained in section 23.9.

19.3 FUTURES-SPECIFIC PROCESS STEPS

19.3.1 Trade amounts

Example

ABC Investment Bank sells 10 lots of the LIFFE FTSE June 2008 Index future on a date when the value of the index is 6500. As, according to LIFFE's contract specification, 1 lot of the FTSE index future is worth £10 per index point we can extend the notional principal amount of the trade as:

Nominal amount ∗ Price ∗ Price multiplier/Price divisor = Notional principal

i.e.

10 lots ∗ 6500 ∗ 10/1 = 650 000.00

Margin and collateral calculations

Assuming that the clearing house requires an initial margin of 10% of notional principal,[1] then there will be an initial margin payable to the clearing house of GBP 65 000.00.

If, on T + 1, the price of the index has risen to 6600, then the clearing house will require ABC to deposit additional margin with a value of GBP 10 000.00, calculated as:

Notional principal at close today = Notional principal on previous working day

---

These calculations are summarised in Table 19.1.

Table 19.1 Futures trade amounts

Trade amount Date	Trade date	Trade date +1
Lots sold	10.00	10.00
Price	6500.00	6600.00
Position	−10.00	−10.00
Price multiplier	10.00	10.00
Price divisor	1.00	1.00
Notional principal amount	−650 000.00	−660 000.00
Initial margin rate	10.00%	n/a
Initial margin amount	−65 000.00	n/a
Maintenance margin	0.00	−10 000.00
Exchange fee (assume £1 per lot)	10.00	n/a
Clearing fee (assume £1 per lot)	10.00	n/a

19.3.2   General ledger postings

The only general ledger entries to be posted are concerned with the deposit of collateral and the payment of exchange and clearing house fees. The entry for the payment of the initial margin and fees to the clearing house on trade date is as shown in Table 19.2. and the entry for the payment of variation margin on T + 1 is as shown in Table 19.3.

If ABC Investment Bank was processing the trade on behalf of an investor, then it would need to ask the investor for collateral, and to process "mirror images" of these entries to reflect its position versus the investor (see Tables 19.4 and 19.5).

Collateral can of course be supplied in the form of securities instead of cash. Clearing houses accept high rated liquid government bonds as collateral. If securities were used instead, then

---

[1] Initial margin calculations are, in fact, more complex than this as they will be based on a SPAN margin calculation covering all the positions held by ABC Investment Bank for this exchange and clearing house. The assumption of 10% was made simply because a figure needs to be provided for section 19.3.3.

Table 19.2 Futures account postings on trade date – market side

Sign	Ledger account type	Trade amount name	Amount (GBP)
Dr	Exchange fees	Exchange fee	10.00
Dr	Settlement fees	Clearing fee	10.00
Dr	Collateral placed	Initial margin	65 000.00
Cr	Cash at bank	Sum of above	65 020.00

Table 19.3 Futures account postings for payment of maintenance margin – market side

Sign	Ledger account type	Trade amount name	Amount (GBP)
Dr	Collateral placed	Maintenance margin	10 000.00
Cr	Cash at Bank	Maintenance margin	10 000.00

Table 19.4 Futures account postings on trade date – customer side

Sign	Ledger account type	Trade amount name	Amount (GBP)
Cr	Exchange fees	Exchange fee	10.00
Cr	Settlement fees	Clearing fee	10.00
Cr	Commission income	ABC's commission for processing the trade, say £20	20.00
Cr	Collateral received	Initial margin	65 000.00
Dr	Cash at bank	Sum of above	65 040.00

Notes:
[1] There is an additional charge to the investor – ABC Investment Bank's own commission for carrying out the trade, shown in row 3.
[2] ABC is free to charge its customer a different amount of initial margin to that charged by the clearing house to ABC – the numbers have been left unchanged in the table for the sake of simplicity.

Table 19.5 Futures account postings for payment of maintenance margin – customer side

Sign	Ledger account type	Trade amount name	Amount (GBP)
Dr	Collateral received	Maintenance margin	10 000.00
Cr	Cash at bank	Maintenance margin	10 000.00

the entry would be passed in the stock record, see section 19.4.2 for an example of such an entry.

19.3.3 Stock record postings

Postings to reflect the establishment of the position

The entry to be passed on trade date is as shown in Table 19.6.
  After posting this entry, the stock record now looks like Figure 19.2.

Postings to reflect the use of securities as collateral

A government security could be used instead of cash to provide collateral. If this were the case, and ABC used 100 000 of the bond concerned as collateral, then the stock record before collateral was placed for the security concerned might look like Figure 19.3.

Table 19.6 Stock record posting to establish a futures or options position

Sign	Account type	Trade amount name	Amount
Short	Book	Nominal amount	10
Long	Depot	Nominal amount	10

ABC Investment Bank plc
Stock record balances for 3 January 2008

Instrument: FTSE 100 index future

Trade dated balances

Account type	Account ID	Sign	Quantity
Book	Book 1	Long	10.00
Depot	LCH.Clearnet	Short	10.00
Balance			0.00

Value dated balances

Account type	Account ID	Sign	Quantity
Book	Book 1	Long	10.00
Depot	LCH.Clearnet	Short	10.00
Balance			0.00

Figure 19.2 Stock record on completion of posting

Stock record balances for 3 January 2008

Instrument: UK Treasury 5% 2012

Trade dated balances

Account type	Account ID	Sign	Quantity
Book	Book 1	Long	100 000.00
Depot	Euroclear	Short	100 000.00
Balance			0.00

Value dated balances

Account type	Account ID	Sign	Quantity
Book	Book 1	Long	100 000.00
Depot	Euroclear	Short	100 000.00
Balance			0.00

Figure 19.3 Stock record before collateral deposit

Table 19.7   Stock collateral entry

Sign	Account type	Trade amount name	Amount
Short	Depot – LCH.Clearnet	Nominal amount	100 000.00
Long	Depot – Euroclear	Nominal amount	100 000.00

Stock record balances for 3 January 2008

Instrument: UK Treasury 5% 2012

Trade dated balances

Account type	Account ID	Sign	Quantity
Book	Book 1	Long	100 000.00
Depot	LCH.Clearnet	Short	100 000.00
Balance			0.00

Value dated balances

Account type	Account ID	Sign	Quantity
Book	Book 1	Long	100 000.00
Depot	LCH.Clearnet	Short	100 000.00
Balance			0.00

Figure 19.4   Stock record after collateral deposit

If collateral is to be used then Euroclear will need to be instructed to deliver it to LCH.Clearnet, and the entry shown in Table 19.7 (known as depot transfer) must be passed in ABC's stock record.

And the stock record for the government bond would now be as shown in Figure 19.4.

19.4   OPTIONS-SPECIFIC PROCESS STEPS

19.4.1   Trade amounts

Example

ABC Investment Bank sells 10 lots of a call option on the FTSE 100 index with a strike price of GBP 8176.00 and an option premium price of GBP 110.75 per lot. As, according to LIFFE's contract specification, 1 lot of the FTSE index future is worth £10 per index point we can extend the principal amount of the trade as:

Nominal amount $*$ Price $*$ Price multiplier/Price divisor $=$ Principal

i.e.

10 lots $* 110.75 * 10/1 = 11\,075.00$

Margin and collateral calculations

Assuming that the clearing house requires an initial margin of 10% of notional principal, then there will be an initial margin payable to the clearing house of GBP 1 107.50.

If, on T + 1, the price of the option has risen to GBP 115.00, then the clearing house will require ABC to deposit additional margin with a value of GBP 425.00, calculated as:

Notional principal at close today = Notional principal on previous working day

---

These trade amounts are summarised in Table 19.8.

19.4.2   General ledger postings

The trade date entries for the example trade in section 19.4.1 will be as shown in Table 19.9.

And the entries to reflect the payment of maintenance margin will be as shown in Table 19.10.

Table 19.8   Options trade amounts

Trade amount Date	Trade date	Trade date +1
Strike price	6 175.00	6 175.00
Option price	110.75	115.00
Lots sold	10.00	10.00
Position	−10.00	−10.00
Price multiplier	10.00	10.00
Price divisor	1.00	1.00
Principal amount	−11 075.00	−11 500.00
Initial margin rate	10.00%	n/a
Initial margin amount	−1 107.50	n/a
Maintenance margin	0.00	−425.00
Exchange fee (assume £1 per lot)	10.00	n/a
Clearing fee (assume £1 per lot)	10.00	n/a

Table 19.9   Options account postings on trade date – market side

Sign	Ledger account type	Trade amount name	Amount (GBP)
Dr	Exchange fees	Exchange fee	10.00
Dr	Settlement fees	Clearing fee	10.00
Dr	Option premium expense	Principal value of option sold	11 075.00
Dr	Collateral placed	Initial margin	1 107.50
Cr	Cash at bank	Sum of above	12 202.50

Table 19.10   Futures account postings for payment of maintenance margin – market side

Sign	Ledger account type	Trade amount name	Amount (GBP)
Dr	Collateral placed	Maintenance margin	425.00
Cr	Cash at bank	Maintenance margin	425.00

If ABC executed this trade on behalf of a client, then they may also need to process the further "customer-side" entries that were shown in Tables 10.3 and 10.4, with the trade amounts relevant to this example.

19.4.3 Stock record postings

The stock record postings for options are the same as those for futures.

20

The STP Flow of Swap and other OTC Derivative Trades

20.1 INTRODUCTION

The examples provided in this chapter are for interest rate swaps and currency swaps, but the text also refers to the other instrument types that were introduced in section 5.3.2 if and where there is variation in the trade flow.

20.2 ORDER PLACEMENT

Orders may be placed by any of the following means:

- By researching best bid and offer prices and telephoning a bank direct
- By researching best bid and offer prices and sending orders through hub and spoke services such as Omgeo Oasys or Autex
- By using any number of Reuters pre-trade services. Reuters is a major force in FX pre-trade services. Because the world's major FX market makers publish their prices on its services it is able to act as an electronic money broker, finding competitive quotes. It also provides analytical tools and conversational dealing
- By using the services of a money broker

20.3 ORDER EXECUTION

Orders are normally executed as principal by market makers.

20.4 TRADE COMPONENTS AND AMOUNTS

The following is an example of a currency swap that was originally quoted in section 5.3.2.

On trade date 29 January 2008 the USD/GBP exchange rate is 2.00.

Banks A and B agree to swap the 5% fixed rate income streams on USD 100 000.00 with the floating rate LIBOR income streams on GBP 50 000 000 for two years from 1 February 2008. Bank A pays Bank B USD at 5%, while Bank B pays Bank A GBP LIBOR.

The trade components and amounts, from Bank A's point of view,[1] are as shown in Table 20.1.

---

[1] If this table had been produced from Bank B's point of view, then of course the sterling cash flows would be the "Pay side" and the dollar cash flows the "Receive side".

Table 20.1   Currency swap trade components and trade amounts

Side of transaction	Trade amount or component	Value
Common to both sides	Trade date	29-Jan-08
	Start leg value date	01-Feb-08
	End leg value date	01-Feb-10
Pay side	Notional principal currency	USD
	Notional principal	100 000 000.00
	Interest frequency	Annual
	Interest basis	Fixed
	Interest rate	5%
	Interest margin over/under basis rate	0%
	Interest calculation	Actual/360
	Date of first interest payment	01-Feb-09
	Rule for determining date of next interest payment if predicted date is a non-working day (note 2)	Leave unchanged
	Rule for determining fixing dates (note 3)	
Receive side	Notional principal currency	GBP
	Notional principal	50 000 000.00
	Interest frequency	Semi-annual
	Interest basis	Floating
	Interest rate	Six-month LIBOR
	Interest margin over/under basis rate	0%
	Interest calculation	Actual/365
	Date of first interest payment	01-Aug-08
	Rule for determining date of next interest payment if predicted date is a non-working day (note 2)	Roll forward
	Rule for determining fixing dates (note 3)	Interest payment date – two working days

Notes:
1. *Interest basis*: The different interest calculation methods were examined in section 3.2.
2. *Rule for determining date of next interest payment if predicted date is a non-working day*: This issue is examined in section 23.3.
3. *Rule for determining fixing dates*: Interest rate fixings are described in section 23.3.1.

20.5   TRADE AGREEMENT

The usual model of trade agreement for all types of OTC derivative transaction is based on the mutual exchange of confirmations model. SWIFT format messages are available for OTC derivative confirmations, but due to the complexity of many of the transactions, the sending of printed confirmations that need to be read, interpreted and checked by qualified individuals and then scanned into a database is still extremely common. Refer to section 12.1.2 for more discussion about the process.

20.6   REGULATORY TRADE REPORTING

The regulatory trade reporting requirements for OTC derivatives are somewhat complex, and there may be slight variations between countries. In the EEA they depend on MiFID Level 2 legislation, which was explained in section 8.4.

Broadly speaking, OTC derivative transactions are *reportable* to the regulators if one or more of the underlying instruments of the transaction are any of the following:

- Purchases and sales of individual equities or individual bonds
- Purchases and sales of listed and OTC derivatives where one of the underlying instruments is an individual equity or individual bond
- Purchases and sales of listed and OTC derivatives where the underlying instrument is an equity index or basket of individual equities.

While, broadly speaking, the following transactions are not reportable:

- Foreign exchange and money market transactions
- OTC derivatives where all the underlying instruments are currencies
- Some securities funding transactions
- The exercise of options and warrants
- Certain primary market transactions in equities and bonds.

This list is provided for guidance only. It was accurate at the time of writing, but may not be accurate at the time of reading. Readers who are in any doubt should consult their firm's compliance office or national regulator at the time.

20.7   SETTLEMENT

20.7.1   Principles

The key principles involved in settlement of swaps are that:

1. Where the notional principals of both sides of the swap are denominated in the same currency (as in an interest rate swap) then the notional principal is not settled; as settlement would be pointless – all it would do is add additional layers of credit risk, delivery risk and operational risk. If the notional principal amounts are denominated in different currencies (as in a currency swap), then they need to be exchanged.
2. On dates when both parties have to make interest payments to each other, if these payments are denominated in the same currency, then they are netted. The party that has to pay the larger cash flow deducts the value of the smaller cash flow which it is owed and pays the difference to the other party.
3. Firms can agree bilateral netting with each other – so if two firms have to make and receive payments for a number of different swap transactions on the same day, then they can agree that the cash flows of all the swaps are netted.

Multilateral netting is also available through clearing houses. For example, LCH.Clearnet Limited provides the SwapClear™ service. SwapClear is a central counterparty service for interest rate swaps of up to 10 years' maturity in USD, EUR, JPY and GBP. The service has since been extended to provide clearing facilities for compounding interest rate swaps with the following tenors:

- USD, EUR, JPY and GBP up to 30 years
- CHF, AUD, DKK, CAD and SEK up to 10 years
- HKD, NOK and NZD up to five years.

SwapClear's objectives are to free up credit lines, risk and use of capital, thus increasing return on investment and trading opportunities. These benefits depend on the individual bank, but are likely to include:

- Lower counterparty risk
- Lower operational risk
- Reduced credit line utilisation
- Reduced regulatory capital requirements
- More secure and standardised collateral handling procedures
- Standardised processing of swaps, simplifying documentation and operations, enabling back offices to handle higher volumes at lower cost
- Fewer payments.

There are no transaction fees for SwapClear. Members pay a fixed annual clearing fee to participate in the SwapClear service.

20.7.2   Practice

For OTC payments and receipts that are not subject to multilateral netting, the party that needs to make a payment sends a SWIFT MT202 message to its settlement agent advising it to make the payment to the trade party's settlement agent, and the party that is receiving funds sends an MT210 message to its settlement agent advising it that the other trade party's settlement agent will make payment on the party's behalf.

The identities of the two parties' settlement agents are stored in the SSI tables that were examined in section 10.6.

20.8   GENERAL LEDGER POSTINGS

20.8.1   Interest rate swap

Start leg value date postings

The general ledger postings for an interest swap on trade date are as shown in Table 20.2.

If the transaction was a currency swap the postings would be as shown in Table 20.3, assuming that the transaction were a (pay) GBP/(receive) USD swap, and 2USD = 1GBP.

Table 20.2   Interest rate swap – start date postings

Sign	Ledger account type	Trade amount name	Trade amount (£)
Dr	Swap notional principal – book	Pay-side notional principal amount	100 000 000.00
Cr	Swap notional principal – trade party	Receive-side notional principal amount	100 000 000.00

Table 20.3   Currency swap – start date postings

Sign	Ledger account type	Trade amount name	Trade amount
Cr	Cash at bank	Pay-side notional principal amount	£100 000 000.00
Dr	Swap notional principal	Pay-side notional principal amount	£100 000 000.00
Dr	Cash at bank	Receive-side notional principal amount	$200 000 000.00
Cr	Swap notional principal	Receive-side notional principal amount	$200 000 000.00

Table 20.4   Swap interest payment date postings

Sign	Ledger account type	Trade amount name
Cr	Accrued interest on swaps	Value of interest payment on the receive side
Dr	Accrued interest on swaps	Value of interest payment on the pay side
Dr or Cr (as required)	Cash at bank	Interest payment on the pay side *less* interest payment on the receive side

During the life of the transaction – periodic interest payments

The entries shown in Table 20.4 need to be passed on the value date that interest payments become due.

End leg value date postings

On the value date of the end leg, the postings that were made for the start leg are reversed.

20.9   STOCK RECORD POSTINGS

The stock record is not used for these transactions.

20.10   MARKING TO MARKET

Swap and other OTC derivatives need to be marked to market daily – refer to section 23.8.

20.11   DAILY ACCRUAL OF INTEREST

Swap interest also needs to be accrued during the life of the transaction – see Section 23.9.

21

Stock Lending, Repos and Funding

21.1 INTRODUCTION

As well as being bought and sold, securities may be lent and borrowed, and also used as collateral for firms that need to borrow cash. There are two broad categories of transactions of this type – **stock loans** and **repos**. The word repo is short for **sale and repurchase agreement**.

The term "stock lending" is usually used to describe a transaction where:

1. The motivation of the borrower (of stock) is to acquire a specific quantity of a given stock to meet a commitment to deliver.
2. The motivation of the lender (of stock) is to provide the securities the borrower requires, and to attract collateral to protect itself against default.

A repo transaction, by contrast, is one where:

1. The motivation of the lender (of stock) is to borrow cash at a better rate of interest than it would if it borrowed on an unsecured basis.
2. The motivation of the borrower (of stock) is to lend cash on a secured basis.

In other words the business purpose of a stock loan is to enable one party to lend securities to another, and the business purpose of a repo is to allow one party to use securities as **collateral** for its cash borrowing. In processing terms the two transaction types share the following characteristics:

- They both use collateral to reduce the lender's credit risk
- They both employ the concepts of **nominal ownership** and **beneficial ownership** which preserve the lenders rights to any income or other benefits provided by ownership of the security being lent.

21.1.1 Stock loan conceptual example

The underlying concept behind a stock loan may be expressed by Figure 21.1

The transaction has a start leg and an end leg. On the value date of the start leg the lender delivers securities to the borrower in exchange for collateral. The purpose of the cash collateral is to provide the lender with security in case the borrower does not return the securities that were borrowed. On the value date of the end leg the securities are returned to the borrower and the collateral is returned to the lender. At the same time, the lender is paid a lending fee, and the borrower is paid interest on the collateral.

21.1.2 Repo conceptual example

Conceptually, a repo is slightly different, as shown by Figure 21.2.

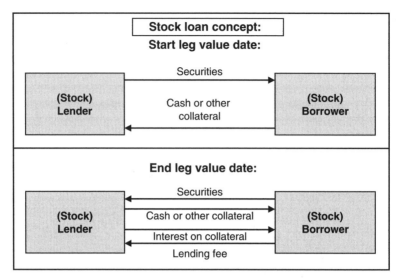

Figure 21.1   Stock loan conceptual example

The repo also involves an exchange of cash for securities in both legs of the transaction, but this time the lender of cash is using the securities as collateral in case the borrower is unable to return the cash at the end of the loan period.

This exchange of cash for securities in both transaction legs is the underlying principle of all forms of stock loan and repo, but there are a number of differences between different forms of transactions which are examined in the appropriate sections of this chapter. However, the principle is that the lender of securities is also the borrower of cash and the borrower of securities is also the lender of cash.

Stock lending is a large and growing business. The international trade organisation for the securities lending industry is the **International Securities Lending Association (ISLA)**.

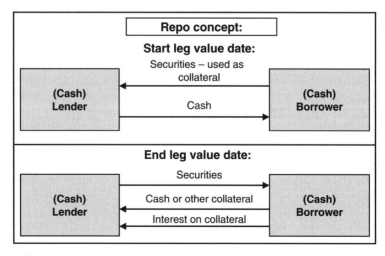

Figure 21.2   Repo conceptual example

According to a June 2004 survey, their members had EUR 5.99 billion worth of securities available for lending. In the US, the Risk Management Association publishes quarterly surveys among its (US-based) members. In June 2005, these had USD 5.77 billion worth of securities available.

21.1.3   Who are the borrowers and why do they borrow securities?

Investment firms borrow securities for a number of reasons, including:

1. They have sold short, and therefore need to borrow stock in order to settle their sales on the correct value date. Market makers sell short as part of their function of providing liquidity to the market, but stock may also be sold short because the seller expects the price of the stock to fall, and therefore it will be able to buy it back later at a lower price.
2. Hedge funds in particular use stock lending as part of strategies to influence the management of the company concerned; particularly in matters relating to mergers and acquisitions. If a hedge fund borrows stock, then it can vote the borrowed stock at company meetings.
3. Any buy-side or sell-side firm may have a situation where securities that it has bought cannot be delivered for some reason. If they have, in turn, sold the stock to another party, then they of course will be unable to deliver what they have not received. They therefore borrow stock to cover for delivery failures.

21.1.4   Who are the lenders and why do they lend securities?

1. Traditional fund managers do not sell short, and are sometimes referred to as "long only" fund managers in this context. They are prepared to lend stock because of the fee they receive for doing so.
2. The fee they receive has to be offset against the interest they pay on the collateral they hold, so it may seem that the returns are not great. However, the fund manager is then able to reinvest the collateral and so enhance the total return of the fund.
3. Market makers have to finance their inventory of long positions. One of the ways they can do this is to use those long positions as collateral for funds they borrow to finance their trading books. If they supply securities as collateral, then they will normally expect to pay a lower rate of interest than if they had no collateral to supply. For example, ABC Investment Bank may be rated Baa by Moody's, and with this rating it would expect to pay 6% interest on a bank loan. However, if it supplies securities issued by the US government as collateral, then because the US government is rated Aaa it might be able to attract funds at 5.5%.
4. Central banks use repos to provide liquidity to financial institutions. They will lend cash to the institutions in the country for which they are responsible, provided that the institutions supply securities as collateral.
5. Settlement agents lend securities to their customers in order to earn fees for providing the service.

21.1.5   Legal and beneficial ownership

Under UK law, the borrower of the securities becomes the **nominal owner** of them – if the securities are in registered form, then they are registered in the name of the borrower; if they are in certificated form, then the name of the borrower appears on the certificate.

The rights of the lender are protected, however, as it remains the **beneficial owner**, which means that although the borrower receives all dividends, coupons and any other corporate action proceeds that are paid during the period of the loan, it has an obligation to repay any proceeds received of this kind to the lender.

There is no doubt in law about the responsibility of the borrower to return any benefits paid to it during the course of the loan to the lender.

However, the borrower also acquires the right to vote at any company meetings that take place during the life of the loan. This is why hedge funds borrow stock to influence the companies whose shares have been borrowed. There is considerable debate about whether this practice is good for corporate governance. In January 2004 Paul Myners produced a report "Review of the impediments to voting UK shares", one of the conclusions of which was:

> [Beneficial owners] should also have a clear voting policy and be aware of the implications of other activities and arrangements on their ability to exercise voting rights. For example, stocklending affects the voting rights attached to the shares, as the lender does not retain the right to vote. When a resolution is contentious I recommend that the stock lent is automatically recalled, unless there are good economic reasons for not doing so.

21.1.6   Collateral and margin

Both stock lending and repo transactions require the borrower to pay collateral to the lender. Collateral may be supplied in one of three forms:

- Cash
- Other securities to the same value as the amount borrowed
- A letter of credit.

21.1.7   Cash as collateral

Where cash is supplied, then the two parties agree that the amount of cash should be equal to the market value of the securities (including accrued interest to the start leg value date) plus a "safety margin" known as **haircut**.

The lender of the securities pays interest on this collateral to the borrower. During the life of the transaction the securities lent and the collateral placed are revalued each day. If the value of the securities lent has increased, then the lender can demand that the borrower supplies it with additional collateral in the form of a margin payment. This is illustrated by the sample transaction in section 21.2.1.

21.1.8   Securities as collateral

In the case of a stock loan, instead of supplying cash as collateral, the borrower may supply other securities as collateral provided that they have the same or higher market value as the cash. Lenders may have other requirements in this respect, for example they may specify that the securities have to be government bonds issued by an **OECD** country or corporate bonds issued by companies resident in an OECD country with a specified minimum credit rating.

In the case of a repo it is cash that is borrowed, and securities are normally used as collateral. Lenders (of cash in this context) usually have quite stringent specifications as to which securities they are prepared to accept as collateral.

Use of multiple securities

Both transaction types support the possibility of using more than one security as collateral at the same time.

Collateral substitution

When securities are supplied as collateral, they may be substituted during the life of the transaction. If the borrower finds that it needs the securities it has supplied to be returned (usually because it has sold them) it may agree for the original securities to be returned and replaced with other securities of a similar quality and value.

21.1.9   Letters of credit as collateral

In this context a **letter of credit** is a document issued by the borrower's bank that essentially acts as an irrevocable guarantee of payment to the lender, should the borrower not be in a position to return the securities.

Understandably, most lenders prefer cash. Therefore there is a role for specialised stock lending intermediaries, one of whose functions is to convert non-cash collateral to cash collateral. The role of the intermediaries is examined in section 21.5.

21.2   STOCK LENDING AND BORROWING TRANSACTIONS

Stock lending and borrowing transactions may involve just one borrower and one lender, or they may involve a borrower, a lender and a lending intermediary. One of the main differences between stock loans and repos is that for stock loans, the lender is paid a fee for lending the stock. There is no such fee involved in a repo transaction.

Stock loans may be agreed for a fixed period (term loans) or for an indefinite period (notice loans). Many types of securities may be borrowed and lent including a wide range of government bonds, corporate bonds and equities of all kinds.

21.2.1   A simple stock lending transaction

Stock loans can be complex transactions, especially if they use securities or letters of credit as collateral but this example transaction covers all the common elements of such a trade:

1. On 3 March 2008, XYZ Fund Managers agrees to lend 10 000 shares in Tesco plc to ABC Investment Bank "until further notice". Value date for the commencement of the loan is agreed as 6 March 2008. On 3 March, the bid price of Tesco shares is £5.00 per share.
2. The parties agree that:
   - ABC is to supply XYZ with collateral of 102% of the current market price of Tesco, in the form of cash. XYZ will pay ABC 5% interest on this cash; calculated on an actual/365 day basis. The 2% difference between the market value and the collateral required is known as the "haircut"
   - ABC will pay XYZ £0.001 per share per day lending fee.
   - The settlement of the interest and the lending fee will be netted against each other when the loan is concluded, or on 1 April, whichever is the earlier.
   - If the price of Tesco rises above £5.00 per share, XYZ has the right to ask ABC to make a margin payment of 10 000 shares $*$ (market price $-$ £5.00) $*$ 102%.

3. The loan starts, as agreed, on 6 March.
4. On 17 March, the price of Tesco rises to £6.00 per share, and XYZ asks ABC to make a margin payment on 18 March.
5. On 24 March, the two parties agree to terminate the loan, with value 25 March.

Such a transaction would cause the deliveries of securities and payments of cash by the two parties shown in Figure 21.3. The example shows only a single price change, on 17 March, but in the real world the securities lent would be revalued each day, and this might cause additional margin payments to be made every working day if the price of Tesco shares were rising, or collateral to be refunded if the price were falling. Additional margin payments may be made in cash, or, if the original collateral was placed in the form of securities, by depositing additional securities with the lender.

We can summarise these cash flows as follows:

Cash value of start leg = Market value of amount borrowed + Haircut
Cash value of end leg = Cash value of start leg * (1 + (Interest rate % * Interest days/Interest year) − Agreed lending fee per day * Duration of transaction)

21.2.2   Automated lending services provided by settlement agents

Settlement agents such as CSDs, ICSDs and custodian banks offer automatic borrowing and lending services to those participants that require them. If the agent sees that Member A is unable to deliver 500 shares of a particular stock to meet a sale commitment, it will find another participant (Member B) that can lend the stock to Member A. Member A will be charged a fee by the agent, the majority of which will be paid to the other party. When the agent sees that Member A no longer needs the borrowing, it will automatically be repaid to Member B. Members A and B are unaware of each other's identity, and in the event of the default of Member A, the agent has to purchase the stock to return to B. For this reason, members that wish to participate in automated borrowing services have to "pledge" their depot positions to the agent. In other words, the member firm's entire depot positions in all securities are treated as collateral. This allows the agent, in the event of default by Member A, to sell any securities in its account to provide the funds to purchase the stock that has to be returned to the lender.

21.3   REPO TRANSACTIONS

Repo is short for "sale and repurchase", and as its name implies it is a sale of stock with an agreement to repurchase it at a later date and:

• The seller is lending (or selling) stock and borrowing cash
• The purchaser is borrowing (or buying) stock and lending cash – from this party's perspective, the transaction is known as a "reverse repo".

Because the aim of the transaction is to reduce the interest costs of the lender, a much smaller range of securities is acceptable to purchasers. The repo market is mainly concerned with highly rated government debt.

There are two forms of repo transaction – classic repo and buy-sellback.

		XYZ Fund Managers		ABC Investment Bank	
Date	Event description	Tesco shares	GBP cash	Tesco shares	GBP cash
06-Mar	Settlement of start leg – XYZ delivers 10 000 shares to ABC against payment of GBP 51 000.00	–10 000	51 000.00	10 000	–51 000.00
18-Mar	ABC makes an additional margin payment of GBP 1.00 per share to XYZ		10 200.00		–10 000.00
24-Mar	Settlement of end leg – ABC delivers 10 000 shares to XYZ against payment of GBP 115 213.47	10 000	–61 153.97	–10 000	61 153.97

Calculation of amount to be paid by XYZ to ABC on 23 March:

Return of original collateral	51 000.00
Return of additional margin paid 18 March	10 200.00
Interest on original collateral	125.75
Interest on margin call collateral	8.22
Less: Lending fee of GBP 0.001 per share per day:	–180.00
Total cash to be repaid	**61 153.97**

Calculated as 51 000 * 5% * (Date difference 6 March to 24 March/360
Calculated as 102% of 10 000 * 5% * (Date difference 17 March to 24 March)/360
Calculated as 10000 shares * 0.001 * (Date difference 6 March to 24 March)

Figure 21.3 Simple stock lending transaction

21.3.1 Classic repo

Classic repo example

On trade date 3 March 2008 ABC Investment Bank enters into a repo agreement with XYZ Fund Managers. ABC is the borrower of cash and XYZ is the lender of cash.

ABC wishes to use EUR 60 000 000 face value of a German government bond paying a 5.5% annual coupon on 1 March each year as collateral. Coupons on this bond are calculated on the actual/actual basis:

Value date of the start leg is 6 March 2008
Value date of the end leg is 3 April 2008
The clean market price of the government bond on trade date is 98.9%

The two parties agree the *repo rate* (the interest on the cash borrowing at 5%), calculated on the actual/360 basis.

Such a transaction would cause the deliveries of securities and payments of cash by the two parties shown in Figure 21.4.

We can summarise these cash flows as follows:

Cash value of start leg = Nominal amount of bond ∗ (Clean price + Accrued coupon)/100
Cash value of end leg = Cash value of start leg ∗ (1+ Repo rate% ∗ Repo days/Repo year)

In this example, we have started with a nominal amount of a bond, and given the market price and coupon rate of that bond we have calculated that ABC is able to borrow EUR 59 385 205.48.

This would be useful if the seller (cash borrower) wanted to fund a position in this particular security, but many repo deals are predicated on the fact that a seller (cash borrower) wishes to use repos to raise an amount of cash to fund positions in general. In that case, the parties need to calculate the nominal amount of the bond that is to be used in the transaction.

The formula for calculating "cash-driven repos" is:

Nominal amount required = Cash amount to be borrowed/Dirty bond price on trade date

Hence if a firm wished to borrow EUR 100 000 000.00 using the same government bond that has a clean price of 98.9% then the calculation is:

Nominal of EUR 101 122 234.50 = 100 000 000/0.989

This nominal amount would of course need to be rounded up or down to the nearest denomination in which this particular bond can be traded and settled.

Other characteristics of classic repos

- *Fixed date or notice*: Like stock loans, classic repos may be for either a fixed term or "until further notice".
- *Haircuts*: Classic repo trades, like stock loans, also include a haircut. This is not shown in the example in Figure 21.4 for the sake of simplicity.
- *Margin calls*: Both trade parties to a classic repo manage credit risk by issuing margin calls to each other. The seller will require extra cash if the price of the security rises; the buyer can require extra securities if the price falls.
- *Collateral substitution*: This is possible for classic repos.

Date	Event description	XYZ Fund Managers		ABC Investment Bank	
		German government bond	GBP cash	German government bond	GBP cash
06-Mar	Settlement of start leg – ABC delivers EUR 60M bond to XYZ against payment of EUR 59 340 000	60 000 000	−59 385 205.48	−60 000 000	59 385 205.48
03-Apr	Settlement of end leg – ABC returns EUR 60M bond to XYZ against payment of EUR 59 340 000	−60 000 000	59 616 147.95	60 000 000	−59 616 147.95

Calculation of amount to be paid by XYZ to ABC on 6 March (start leg)

Security quantity * Clean price of 98.9%	59 340 000.00
Accrued interest on security paying 5.5% coupon from 1 March to 6 March	45 205.48
Total cash to be repaid	**59 385 205.48**

Calculation of amount to be paid by ABC to XYZ on 3 April (end Leg)

Return of amount borrowed	−59 385 205.48
Interest on amount borrowed at 5%	−230 942.47
Total cash to be repaid	**−59 616 147.95**

Figure 21.4 Simple classic repo transaction

- *No separate stock lending fee*: Unlike stock loans, classic repos do not involve the buyer (lender of cash) paying the seller a stock lending fee. The only charge payable is the interest on the amount borrowed calculated at the repo rate.

21.3.2   Buy-sellback

A **buy-sellback** is a form of repo where the two legs of the transaction (although they are dealt on the same trade date) are treated as separate transactions, and the purchaser does not directly pass any coupon payments back to the seller. Instead, the price of the second leg is adjusted by the value of the coupon that the seller did not receive.

The cash values of each leg of a buy-sellback transaction that did not involve a coupon period during its term are identical to those of a classic repo, but the calculation of the trade price is expressed using the following formulae:

End-leg clean price = End-leg dirty price – Accrued coupon to end leg value date
= Cash repaid at the end/Bond nominal amount $*$ 100 − Accrued coupon to end data

- *Fixed date or notice*: Buy-sellbacks are always for a fixed period, open transactions are not permitted.
- *Haircuts*: Buy-sellbacks, like classic repos and stock loans, may include a haircut.
- *Margin calls*: As the two legs of the transaction are not linked, it is not possible for either party to issue margin calls to the other party. As a result, both parties may be exposed to a higher degree of credit risk than in the other transaction types.
- *Collateral substitution* is not possible for buy-sellbacks.
- *No separate stock lending fee*: Unlike stock loans, buy-sellbacks do not involve the buyer (lender of cash) paying the seller a stock lending fee.
- *Single security per transaction*: Unlike classic repos and stock loans, buy-sellbacks can only be concerned with a single security per transaction.
- *Coupon compensation*: In the case of stock loans and classic repos, the nominal owner makes a separate payment to the beneficial owner of any coupon proceeds received by the (stock) borrower during the life of the transaction. For buy-sellbacks, however, the end leg cash amount repayable is adjusted as follows.

Without a coupon payment the formula would be:

End leg cash amount = Cash value of end leg = Cash value of start leg $*$ (1 + repo rate% $*$ Repo days/Repo year)

But this is now adjusted to become:

End leg cash amount = Cash value of start leg $*$ (1 + Repo rate% $*$ Repo days/Repo year) − Coupon received $*$ (1 + Repo rate $*$ Days from date of coupon payment to repo maturity/Days in year)

Deliveries by value

Securities firms of all kinds, but market makers in particular, often want to use their whole inventory as collateral to fund that inventory. Their problem is determining which stock they can lend. They are obviously not in a position to lend stock that they need to deliver today for their sales that reach value today. CSDs operate a special service for such firms, called

delivery by value (DbV). The way that DbV works is that the market maker and a specialised intermediary (see section 21.5) agree that the market maker needs to borrow, say, £10 000 000 to finance its trading book "overnight" (i.e. for one day). Both parties input a special DbV transaction that just quotes this amount, and the collateral amount (say, £10 500 000 including haircut) that the intermediary needs. That evening the CSD selects securities to the value of £10.5 million in the market maker's account that are:

1. Not needed for delivery to clients; and
2. Do not have a record date or payment date for coupons, dividends or corporate action proceeds today

and transfers them, against payment, to the intermediary's account. The following day the CSD returns the securities to the market maker and the cash to the intermediary. The market maker then re-evaluates its funding requirements for the next day and the process is repeated.

In essence, then, a delivery by value (although it is technically considered as a stock loan rather than a repo) can be thought of as a fixed term repo for one day where multiple securities of many kinds (not just highly rated government bonds) are acceptable as collateral.

Tri-party repo

Settlement agents also provide **tri-party repo** facilities for their customers, where they act as the "third-party" custodian for the securities held as collateral. Instead of delivering the securities to the buyer, the seller delivers them to the third party, which acts as the buyer's custodian. The advantages of tri-party are:

- Administrative simplicity, especially for fund managers and corporates who may lack the administrative and systems capabilities that banks use to process repos
- Easier administration of collateral substitutions and margin calls.

However, there is a disadvantage to the buyer. Because the seller does not itself hold the collateral, and the buyer can substitute collateral so easily, the buyer is unable to use the securities in a reverse repo transaction.

The services offered by the third-party settlement agent include:

- Providing daily collateral valuation reports to both the buyer and the seller
- Ensuring that the securities used as collateral conform to the buyer's requirements for currency of issue, credit rating, haircut and liquidity.

All tri-party fees are paid by the seller.

21.4 SUMMARY OF THE DIFFERENCES BETWEEN THE VARIOUS TRANSACTION TYPES

The differences between the various transaction types examined in this chapter can be summarised in Table 21.1.

Table 21.1 Summary of transaction attributes

Transaction attributes	Stocklending transactions		Repo transactions	
	Stock loan	Delivery by value	Classic repo	Buy-sellback
Usual business purpose – stock borrower	To borrow securities in order to deliver them or vote them	To provide collateral for loans granted	To provide collateral for loans granted	To provide collateral for loans granted
Usual business purpose – stock lender	To enhance returns on portfolio	To reduce interest expense	To reduce interest expense	To reduce interest expense
What form of collateral is acceptable to cash provider?	Wide range of securities including both equities and bonds	Wide range of securities including both equities and bonds	Usually only high grade bonds	Usually only high grade bonds
What form of collateral is acceptable to securities provider?	Cash or securities	Cash	Cash	Cash
Fixed term or open ended?	Both	Fixed – one day	Both	Fixed only
Are margin calls made during the life of the transaction?	Yes	No – term is too short	Yes	No
Can collateral be substituted?	Yes	No – term is too short	Yes	No
Can a single transaction handle multiple securities?	No	Yes	Yes	No
How are benefits paid to beneficial owners?	The stock borrower must make immediate payment direct to the lender	Not applicable – stocks paying benefits would not get selected for the DbV transaction	The stock borrower must make immediate payment direct to the lender	The end leg price is adjusted for the coupon received

21.5 THE ROLE OF SPECIALIST LENDING INTERMEDIARIES (SLIs)

There are a number of firms that act as **specialist lending intermediaries** (**SLIs**). There are several reasons why their presence is required. Let us extend the examples in sections 21.2.1 and 21.3.1 to see how their presence makes a deeper and more liquid market.

The examples both covered two parties dealing direct with each other for a short period for relatively small transactions. This could only be possible if ABC and XYZ know of each other's existence, but it is often the case that a borrower is not aware of the identities of the potential lenders. But if ABC wanted to borrow 1 million Tesco shares for seven months and use German government bonds as collateral then it might run into some or all of these problems:

1. It can't find a lender willing to lend such a large amount
2. It can't find a lender willing to lend for such a long period
3. It can't find a lender prepared to accept non-cash collateral
4. It *may* become aware of a suitable lender, but it has no credit information about that lender, and neither does the lender have any credit information about ABC Investment Bank. As neither party has granted a credit limit (credit limits are examined in section 24.5.1) to the other, it may not be possible to carry out the transaction very swiftly.

In any of these circumstances, it can put the lending request to an SLI. SLIs include stock lending divisions of investment banks, as well as specialist niche firms. SLIs have a list of fund manager clients who are prepared to lend securities and will divide a large loan request into a number of smaller parcels, and/or for shorter periods. If one of its clients needs its stock back after, say, one month, then it will reassign that part of the loan to another client.

It also deals with the problem that the borrower doesn't want to provide cash collateral, but the lenders insist on it. It takes the government bond and does a repo transaction with it with the cash to provide to the lenders.

SLIs act as principal in transactions, making a small margin on collateral interest rates and stock lending fees. Because they act as principal, then their customers only need to grant a single trading party credit limit – to the SLI itself.

The following example shows how the SLI would meet the requirements of three of its customers by carrying out a series of linked stock lending transactions.

The scenario

1. ABC Investment Bank wishes to borrow 1000 shares in Company A. It is not willing to provide cash collateral but is willing to provide 1000 shares in Company B.
2. XYZ Fund Managers is willing to lend 1000 shares in Company A but insists on GBP 100 000 cash collateral.
3. AN Other & Co. wishes to borrow 1000 shares in Company B and is prepared to provide GBP 100 000 in collateral.

Assume that 1 share in Company A has the same (constant) price as 1 share in Company B.

The SLI will act as party to the stock lending transactions shown in Figure 21.5. As a result of these transactions, both ABC and AN Other are able to borrow the stock they require,

The solution involving the stock lending intermediary	Collateral flow (GBP)	Company A shares	Company B shares
The SLI			
Borrows 1000 shares in Company B from ABC paying cash collateral £100 000	-100 000		1000
Lends 1000 shares in Company A to ABC receiving cash collateral £100 000	100 000	-1000	
Borrows 1000 shares in Company A from XYZ paying cash collateral £100 000	-100 000	1000	
Lends 1000 shares in Company B to AN Other receiving cash collateral £100 000	100 000		-1000
Totals for the SLI	**0**	**0**	**0**
ABC Investment Bank			
Lends 1000 shares in Company B to the SLI receiving cash collateral £100 000	100 000		-1000
Borrows 1000 shares in Company A from the SLI paying cash collateral £100 000	-100 000	1000	
Totals for ABC Investment Bank	**0**	**1000**	**-1000**
XYZ Fund Managers			
Lends 1000 shares in Company A to the SLI receiving cash collateral of £100 000	100 000	-1000	
Totals for the SLI	**100 000**	**-1000**	**0**
AN Other Investment Bank			
Borrows 1000 shares in Company B from the SLI paying cash collateral of £100 000	-100 000		1000
Totals for AN Other	**-100 000**	**0**	**1000**

Figure 21.5 Linked transactions involving an SLI

ABC's transactions are neutral in terms of cash collateral and XYZ gets the cash collateral it requires. All the transactions are neutral from the SLI's perspective – it holds no cash or security positions. The type of operation that the SLI is running is often known as "matchbook lending".

On a larger scale, this is the type of activity that the SLI is doing when it borrows stock in the delivery-by-value transaction that was described earlier in this chapter.

21.6   BUSINESS APPLICATIONS TO SUPPORT STOCK LENDING AND REPOS

Firms that are active in the stock lending and repo markets often use dedicated front-office applications to support these activities. In other firms, the functionality may be provided by the main settlement system.

The key requirements of the application used to support these activities are the abilities to:

- Project future cash flow
- Project future depot positions
- Mark borrowed, lent and repo positions to market
- Support the relevant messages to trade parties and settlement agents
- Post the appropriate financial accounting entries in the general ledger
- Post the appropriate stock movement entries in the stock record.

21.6.1   Cash flow projections

Once the settlement instructions for all trade types have been sent out, both trade parties have to ensure that they will have the cash available to pay for their purchases, and the stock available to deliver for their sales.

However, the aims of cash management are broader than this. Cash flow management aims to optimise the use of the firm's cash, so that:

- Overdrawn nostro accounts are avoided wherever possible. Positions should instead be funded by repos or money market loans which generally charge a lower rate of interest than an overdraft.
- If it is not possible to avoid overdrafts, the overdrawn balances are held on accounts that charge the lowest rates of interest.
- Excessively large positive cash balances are also avoided – under normal market conditions the firm can expect to receive higher interest on money market deposits and reverse repos than it can on nostro accounts.

Therefore most main settlement systems incorporate a cash flow projection module. This may be presented to users as either a report or a real-time enquiry.

Figure 21.6 shows examples of a cash flow projection produced at the close of business on 5 March 2007 for ABC Investment Bank's USD bank account with Euroclear Brussels for the next three working days.

In the real world, the cash flow projection would show the expected cash movements for all the firm's bank accounts in all currencies (one page for each individual currency bank account) for the next five working days. The figure only shows three days, the last two days have been omitted in this example in order to simplify it.

ABC Investment Bank plc – cash flow projection

Nostro name:		Euroclear Brussels		Currency: USD	Date	05 March 2008
Cash balance on account as at:	nbr of items	**05/03/08** 2 000 000.00	nbr of items	**06/03/08** 3 614 944.00	nbr of items	**07/03/08** −8 385 056.00
Items due for settlement on:		06/03/07		07/03/07		08/03/07
Overdue security purchases	0	0.00	0	0.00	0	
Overdue security sales	1	500 000.00	0	0.00	0	
Security purchases	1	−1 000 000.00	6	−13 500 000.00	1	−1 250 000.00
Security sales	4	1 500 000.00	3	1 500 000.00	10	1 750 000.00
Stock lending open leg transactions	2	750 000.00	0	0.00	0	0.00
Stock borrowing open leg transactions	1	−250 000.00	0	0.00	0	0.00
Stock lending return leg transactions	2	−400 000.00	0	0.00	0	0.00
Stock borrowing return leg transactions	3	300 000.00	0	0.00	0	0.00
Repo open leg transactions transactions	0	0.00	0	0.00	0	0.00
Repo closing leg transactions transactions	0	0.00	0	0.00	0	0.00
Money market transactions	0	0.00	0	0.00	0	0.00
FX purchases	1	250 000.00	0	0.00	0	0.00
FX sales	0	0.00	0	0.00	0	0.00
Other cash movements	0	0.00	0	0.00	0	0.00
Coupons due	1	50 200.00	0	0.00	0	0.00
Dividends due	2	−10 000.00	0	0.00	0	0.00
Other cash movements	1	−75 256.00	0	0.00	0	0.00
Cash flow projection for		**06/03/07** 3 614 944.00		**07/03/07** −8 385 056.00		**08/03/07** −7 885 056.00

Figure 21.6 Cash flow projection before funding activities

We can see the following information in the cash flow projection:

1. The closing balance of our USD account at Euroclear for today (5 March) is USD 2 000 000.00.
2. The enquiry then lists the numbers of trades and total net values of all the various trade types (security purchases, sales, stock lending transactions, FX transactions, etc.) that are due to settle on 6 March. Included among these are one overdue security purchase with a value of USD 1 million, and one overdue unsettled security sale with a value of USD 1.5 million. These trades should have settled on or before 5 March but have failed to settle for some reason.
3. If you add the value of all the transactions that should settle on or before 6 March to the 5 March cash balance, then we have a projected balance on this account for 6 March of USD 3 614 944.00.
4. The process is then repeated for 7 March when the projected balance of the account is USD 8 385 056, and 8 March when it becomes USD 7 885 056.

21.6.2   What the cash flow projection shows us

The conclusions we can draw from looking at this cash flow projection are:

1. On 6 March, we have excess funds of USD 3.61 million on this account.
2. On 7 March, we have a shortage of USD 8.35 million on this account
3. On 8 March we have a shortage of USD 7.85 million on this account.

21.6.3   Possible actions the firm could take to fund the account correctly

Excess funds on 6 March

For 6 March, the firm's treasurer could put USD 3 million on overnight deposit for 6 March, to earn a higher rate of interest than Euroclear pays on a nostro account. If we assume that the firm could earn 4% overnight, then the following day (when the deposit matures) USD 3 000 333.33 will be paid back into the account (interest being calculated as 3 000 000 ∗ 4% ∗ 1 day/360 days in a year).

Inadequate funds on 7 and 8 March

The firm may be able to resolve this issue by any one of the following means:

1. Perhaps it has excess funds on another nostro that it could transfer into the account.
2. It could borrow USD 8.5 million for two days on the money markets at, say, 5%.
3. If it has government bonds that it could use as collateral, it could borrow USD 8.5 million indefinitely by using these bonds as collateral for a repo transaction, paying only 4% interest.

If it takes the third option – the repo – then the revised cash flow projection is shown in Figure 21.7. The new transactions are highlighted. You will see that the treasurer has been able to keep the projected balances on this account at between USD 0.11 million and USD 0.61 million for the period – ensuring that the account is funded adequately for the period, and that any excess funds are swept into higher interest bearing vehicles.

ABC Investment Bank plc – cash flow projection

	Euroclear Brussels		Currency: USD		Date	
Nostro name:						
Cash balance on account as at:	**05/03/08**	**2 000 000.00**	**06/03/08**	**614 944.00**	**07/03/08**	**05 March 2008**
						115 227.00
	nbr of items		nbr of items		nbr of items	**115 227.00**
Items due for settlement on:	06/03/07		07/03/07		08/03/07	
Overdue security purchases	0	0.00	0	0.00	0	
Overdue security sales	1	500 000.00	0	0.00	0	
Security purchases	1	-1 000 000.00	6	-13 500 000.00	1	-1 250 000.00
Security sales	4	1 500 000.00	3	1 500 000.00	10	1 750 000.00
Stock lending open leg transactions	2	750 000.00	0	0.00	0	0.00
Stock borrowing open leg transactions	1	-250 000.00	0	0.00	0	0.00
Stock lending return leg transactions	2	-400 000.00	0	0.00	0	0.00
Stock borrowing return leg transactions	3	300 000.00	0	0.00	0	0.00
Repo open leg transactions	0	0.00	1	8 500 000.00	0	0.00
Repo closing leg transactions	0	0.00	0	0.00	0	0.00
Money market transactions	1	-3 000 000.00	1	3 000 333.00	0	0.00
FX purchases	1	250 000.00	0	0.00	0	0.00
FX sales	0	0.00	0	0.00	0	0.00
Other cash movements	0	0.00	0	0.00	0	0.00
Coupons due	1	50 200.00	0	0.00	0	0.00
Dividends due	2	-10 000.00	0	0.00	0	0.00
Other cash movements	1	-75 256.00	0	0.00	0	0.00
Cash flow projection for	**06/03/07**	**614 944.00**	**07/03/07**	**115 277.00**	**08/03/07**	**615 277.00**

Figure 21.7 Cash flow projection after funding activity

21.6.4   Depot movement projections

A firm that is active in these markets needs to know at all times:

• Which securities it needs to borrow to cover short positions and delivery failures
• Which borrowed securities it is now in a position to return
• Which securities are available to lend to others
• Which securities it is in a position to use as collateral for repos
• Which securities it has used in repo transactions that it now needs to return.

Therefore a firm will require a depot movement projection that serves the same function for securities as the cash flow projection. However, while it is a viable option to present the cash flow projection in the form of a printed report, the depot movement projection needs to be presented in the form of a screen-based enquiry because the sheer number of individual securities concerned makes a printed report impractical.

Such an enquiry will be based on the stock record described in Chapter 15 and might be presented in the form shown in Figure 21.8.

21.6.5   Marking positions to market

In order to ensure that the value of collateral placed with the firm is at least equivalent to the value of securities and cash lent by the firm then the firm needs to mark the net value of stock loan and repo positions with each trading party to market. The mark-to-market process is explained in section 23.8. Part of the mark-to-market process is the accrual of interest on both the cash collateral and also any bonds involved in the transactions. Accrual of interest on positions is examined in section 23.9.

21.6.6   Relevant SWIFT messages for repo and stock ending activities

The messages shown in Table 21.2 are used between the trade parties for stock loans and repos.

There are no specific settlement messages for these transactions – the messages that the trade party sends to and receives from its settlement agent are the same messages that were described in section 12.2.

21.6.7   Accounting entries to be posted in the general ledger

Start leg entries – from the perspective of the securities borrower

On trade date the entries shown in Table 21.3 are passed. If the firm was lending securities, the entries would be reversed.

On settlement date the entries shown in Table 21.4 are passed.

Entries posted on payment of a margin call

If the firm is required to deposit additional collateral as a result of a rise in the price of the securities borrowed then the trade date entries are as shown in Table 21.5.

ABC Investment Bank plc – depot movement projection

Depot name:	Euroclear London		Instrument: Tesco plc ordinary shares		Date 05 March 2008	
Depot balance on account as at:	**05/03/08**	**10 000.00**	**06/03/08**	**2 500.00**	**07/03/08**	**2 500.00**
	nbr of items		nbr of items		nbr of items	
Items due for settlement on:	06/03/07		07/03/07		08/03/07	
Overdue security purchases	0	1 000.00	0	0.00	0	
Overdue security sales	1	−2 000.00	0	0.00	0	
Security purchases	1	3 500.00	6	5 500.00	1	0.00
Security sales	4	−4 500.00	3	−5 500.00	10	0.00
Stock lending open leg transactions	2	−10 000.00	0	0.00	0	10 000.00
Stock borrowing open leg transactions	1	0.00	0	0.00	0	0.00
Stock lending return leg transactions	2	4 500.00	0	0.00	0	0.00
Stock borrowing return leg transactions	3	0.00	0	0.00	0	0.00
Repo open leg transactions	0	0.00	0	0.00	0	0.00
Repo closing leg transactions	0	0.00	0	0.00	0	0.00
Depot balance projection for	**06/03/07**	**2 500.00**	**07/03/07**	**2 500.00**	**08/03/07**	**12 500.00**

Figure 21.8 Depot movement projection

Table 21.2 SWIFT messages relevant to stock lending and repo activity

Message no.	Message name	Additional information
MT503	Collateral claim	Requests new or additional collateral, or the return or recall of collateral
MT504	Collateral proposal	Proposes new or additional collateral
MT505	Collateral substitution	Proposes or requests the substitution of collateral held
MT506	Collateral and exposure statement	Provides the details of the valuation of both the collateral and the exposure
MT507	Collateral status and processing advice	Advises the status of a collateral claim, a collateral proposal, or a proposal/request for collateral substitution
MT516	Securities loan confirmation	Confirms the details of a securities loan, including collateral arrangements. It may also confirm the details of a partial recall or return of securities previously out on loan
MT526	General securities lending/borrowing message	Requests the borrowing of securities or notifies the return or recall of securities previously out on loan. It may also be used to list securities available for lending
MT581	Collateral adjustment message	Claims or notifies a change in the amount of collateral held against securities out on loan or for other reasons

Table 21.3 Trade date postings when securities borrowed

Item	Sign	Ledger account type	Trade amount
1	Dr	Collateral placed	Collateral amount
2	Cr	Security trading party account	Collateral amount

Table 21.4 Settlement date postings when securities borrowed

Item	Sign	Ledger account type	Trade amount
1	Dr	Security trading party account	Collateral amount
2	Cr	Nostro account	Collateral amount

Table 21.5 Accounting entries to be passed on trade date for a margin call

Item	Sign	Ledger account type	Trade amount
1	Dr	Collateral placed	Collateral amount
2	Cr	Security trading party account	Collateral amount

Table 21.6   Accounting entries to be passed on value date for a margin call

Item	Sign	Ledger account type	Trade amount
1	Dr	Security trading party account	Collateral amount
2	Cr	Nostro account	Collateral amount

Table 21.7   Trade date entries for end leg

Item	Sign	Ledger account type	Trade amount
1	Cr	Collateral placed	Total collateral amount
2	Cr	Accrued interest on collateral	Interest earned on collateral
3	Dr	Stock borrowing fees	Fees due to date on amount of stock borrowed
4	Dr	Security trading party amount	Total consideration (sum of items 1 to 3)

Note: If the trade was a repo instead of a stock loan, then there would be no separate fee to post in item 3.

If the price of the securities had fallen and the firm was in a position to claim a return of collateral then the signs would be reversed. The entries to be passed on actual settlement date are as shown in Table 21.6.

End leg entries – from the perspective of the securities borrower

On the trade date of the end leg of the transaction the entries shown in Table 21.7 are passed.
On the actual settlement date of the transaction the entries in Table 21.8 would be posted.

21.6.8   Stock movement entries to be posted in the stock record

Start leg entries – from the perspective of the securities borrower

The stock record entry shown in Table 21.9 will be passed on the trade date of the start leg of the loan.
And the entry shown in Table 21.10 will be passed on the settlement date of the start leg.

Table 21.8   Settlement date entries for end leg

Item	Sign	Ledger account type	Trade amount
1	Cr	Security trading party account	Collateral amount
2	Dr	Nostro account	Collateral amount

Table 21.9   Stock record postings on trade date – stock borrow start leg

Item	Sign	Stock record account type	Trade amount
1	Long	Party borrow and lend	Quantity borrowed
2	Short	Book borrow and lend	Quantity borrowed

Table 21.10   Stock record postings on settlement date – stock borrow start leg

Item	Sign	Stock record account type	Trade amount
1	Long	Book borrow and lend	Quantity borrowed
2	Short	Depot	Quantity borrowed

Entries posted when quantity borrowed is substituted, increased or decreased

When collateral is substituted, then the entries shown in Tables 21.9 and 21.10 are repeated for an increase in the amount borrowed and repeated with the signs reversed if there is a decrease in the amount borrowed. If the transaction is a repo and the instrument being used as collateral is substituted, then there will be a reversal of the entries passed for the original instrument shown in Tables 21.9 and 21.10, and replacement entries for a new instrument.

End leg entries – from the perspective of the securities borrower

On the trade date and settlement date of the end leg the entries that were passed on the start leg (adjusted by any collateral substitutions entries posted since then) need to be reversed.

22

The Impact of Islamic Finance

22.1 INTRODUCTION

Islamic finance is a system of banking activity that is consistent with Islamic law (Sharia) principles and guided by Islamic economics. In particular, Islamic law prohibits the collection and payment of interest (commonly called **riba**) in Islamic discourse. In addition, Islamic law prohibits investing in businesses that are considered unlawful, or **haraam** (such as businesses that sell alcohol or pork, or businesses that produce media such as gossip columns or pornography, which are contrary to Islamic values). In the late 20th century, a number of Islamic banks were created to cater for this particular banking market. Because of the very large number of individuals and corporations that wish to raise or invest capital according to Sharia principles, many of the world's leading financial institutions such as HSBC, UBS and Citicorp, as well as institutions whose origins lie in Islamic countries, offer Sharia compliant products to their customers. Conservative estimates suggest that over USD 500 billion of assets are managed according to Islamic investment principles. Such principles form part of Sharia, which is often understood to be Islamic law, but it is actually broader than this in that it also encompasses the general body of spiritual and moral obligations and duties in Islam.

An investor who wishes to invest according to Sharia principles may not:

- Be a party to any transaction that, however indirectly, involves the payment or receipt of riba (interest)
- Be a party to any transaction whose nature is **gharar** (contractually ambiguous). Gharar is defined as "a situation where one party to a contract has information regarding some element of the contract which is withheld from the other party, and/or the subject of the contract is something which neither party has control". Some Islamic scholars argue that most derivative contracts are, by their nature, gharar, and are therefore prohibited instruments.
- Invest in securities issued by any company whose business activities include activities that are haraam (forbidden). The following list of business activities has been deemed inconsistent with the principles of Sharia:
  - Alcohol
  - Pork-related products
  - Conventional financial services (banking, insurance, etc.)
  - Entertainment (hotels, gambling, cinema, pornography, music, etc.)
  - Tobacco
  - Weapons and defence.
- Invest in any company that finances itself mainly by the use of conventional debt instruments, or depends upon interest for a substantial proportion of its income
- Sell a stock short.

22.2   DELIVERING ISLAMIC FINANCIAL SERVICES

Islamic financial services are delivered not only by banks that have their origins in Islamic countries, but also by banks that have their origins in North America and Europe. These banks are delivering both wholesale and retail services both to international and domestic customers through **Islamic windows** – departments that only offer Sharia compliant products. Such an Islamic window must be supervised by a **Sharia Supervisory Board** – a group of Sharia scholars that also understand the financial services industry. It is this board that decides what products may be offered to customers, and also how those products are to be financed by the institution offering them, and what types of instruments (such as derivatives) may be used to hedge the firm's positions.

22.3   SHARIA COMPLIANT INSTRUMENTS

As both borrowers and lenders are prohibited from investing in conventional debt instruments that pay interest, the market has evolved a wide range of products that have similar characteristics to conventional bonds, but do not involve the payment of interest *per se*. Many of these instruments are designed for the retail financial services sector, in particular for the residential mortgage market.

To avoid the issue of paying interest, Islamic mortgages usually involve the bank buying the property and then the buyer purchasing it from them over a length of time at a slightly increased price. Islamic mortgages also involve making other aspects of the mortgage Sharia compliant, for instance making sure that the money the banks use to buy the property comes from permissible sources.

Until July 2002 only one financial institution in the UK offered Islamic mortgages (the United Bank of Kuwait). The shortage of Islamic mortgages was due to a combination of technical and cultural problems. Stamp duty was one of the biggest problems. Stamp duty is a one-off tax that is charged on every property sold. But stamp duty was being charged twice on Islamic mortgages because in a Muslim mortgage the property is in theory bought twice (once by the bank and once by the buyer).

The law on stamp duty has been altered – double stamp duty was abolished on Islamic mortgages in April 2003 – and the government has been urging banks to work with Muslims. One of the first results came in July 2003 when HSBC, one of the biggest banks in the UK, brought out a range of Sharia compliant mortgages. By the end of 2005 there were five banks offering Islamic mortgages including Lloyds TSB and the Islamic Bank of Britain.

The main Sharia compliant instrument that this book is concerned with is the Sukuk, which is an alternative to interest bearing debt securities.

22.3.1   Sukuk instruments

Sukuk is the Arabic name for a financial certificate but can be seen as an Islamic equivalent of a bond. However, interest bearing bonds are not permissible in Islam, hence Sukuks are securities that comply with the Islamic law and its investment principles, which prohibits the charging, or paying of interest. The first Sukuk instrument was issued by the Jordan Islamic Bank in 1978, and many governments, banks and corporate entities have issued Sukuks since then. The steps involved in creating a Sukuk are as follows:

1. An asset, such as land, quoted investments or other property that belongs to the entity wishing to raise capital (the borrower), is identified. These assets are then sold (together with an agreement to buy them back at a predetermined price after a given period) to a corporate entity (the special purpose vehicle or SPV) specially created for the purpose of the Sukuk.
2. The SPV then sells certificates (the Sukuk) to investors representing their share of the assets acquired.
3. The SPV then leases the assets back to the borrower from whom it acquired them, in exchange for periodic lease payments. It passes these payments back to the holders of the Sukuk, less a small deduction for its administrative expenses.
4. During the life of the Sukkuk, the borrower makes the periodic payments in the same way that it would make coupon payments on a traditional bond. However, the difference between Sukuk periodic payments and coupon payments is that coupon payments have to be made irrespective of the economic performance of the assets that service them, but Sukuk payments are only made if there is sufficient income generated by the underlying assets. Most Sukuks can, like conventional bonds, be traded in the secondary markets.
5. At the end of the period agreed in Step 1, the SPV sells the assets back to the borrower at the price that was agreed in Step 1, and uses the proceeds to repay the investors in the Sukuk.

22.4 THE VALUATION AND RISK MANAGEMENT OF ISLAMIC FINANCING INSTRUMENTS

Because Sukuk cash flows are based on periodic predetermined lease payments, these cash flows may be accrued in the same way that bond interest is accrued, and used in yield to maturity calculations as if they were coupon payments.

However, firms that hold positions in Sukuks and other Islamic instruments must be aware of the following issues:

1. Sukuk investors also have to monitor the quality of the performance of the underlying assets. If they are not providing the income to make the periodic payments, then these payments cannot, under Sharia law, be made.
2. Under Sharia, no penalties such as additional interest payments can be imposed on borrowers or other trade parties for late payment; as such a penalty would be considered as riba which is haraam. Therefore, firms that take positions in Sukuks and similar instruments need to monitor and manage credit risk and market risk differently to the way that they monitor and manage these risks for conventional financial instruments.
3. Many of the commonly used tools (for example, certain types of derivatives which are used for hedging against currency, interest rates and other risks) are not acceptable to almost all Sharia scholars. In the past, this has made risk management more difficult for wholly Islamic firms as Sharia compliant substitutes have been slow to develop. However, new products and techniques are gradually emerging – for example, Sharia compliant, derivative-like products for managing foreign exchange and interest rate risk.
4. An issue that was highlighted by the UK FSA in a paper entitled "Islamic finance in the UK: regulation and challenges", published in November 2007, is the fact that both wholly

Table 22.1   IFSB credit risk principles

Principle 2.1	Islamic financial institutions shall have in place a strategy for financing, using the various Islamic instruments in compliance with Sharia, whereby it recognises the potential credit exposures that may arise at different stages of the various financing agreements
Principle 2.2	Islamic financial institutions shall carry out a due diligence review in respect of counterparties prior to deciding on the choice of an appropriate Islamic financing instrument
Principle 2.3	Islamic financial institutions shall have in place appropriate methodologies for measuring and reporting the credit risk exposures arising under each Islamic financing instrument
Principle 2.4	Islamic financial institutions shall have in place Sharia compliant credit risk mitigating techniques appropriate for each Islamic financing instrument

Table 22.2   IFSB market risk principles

Principle 4.1	Islamic financial institutions shall have in place an appropriate framework for market risk management (including reporting) in respect of all assets held, including those that do not have a ready market and/or are exposed to high price volatility

Islamic banks and also conventional banks that provide Islamic services are suffering from a scarcity of experienced professionals in the Islamic finance sector. Resources that are in short supply include not only operations and risk management professionals, but also Sharia scholars with relevant banking experience who are therefore qualified to join the Sharia Supervisory Board.

The **Islamic Financial Services Board (IFSB)** is an international standard-setting organisation that promotes and enhances the soundness and stability of the Islamic financial services industry by issuing global prudential standards and guiding principles for the industry, broadly defined to include banking, capital markets and insurance sectors.

Full membership of the IFSB is open to regulators, but investment firms may join as observers. The IFSB has developed credit risk and market risk management principles, shown in Tables 22.1 and 22.2 respectively.

22.5   THE IT IMPLICATIONS OF PROVIDING ISLAMIC INSTRUMENTS

In principle Sukuks can be valued as if they were straight bonds, as the periodic payments by the borrower can be accrued as if it were interest. However, firms that are offering these products need to be aware of the specific risks that they are incurring, which were described in section 22.4. As the market in Sharia compliant instruments is a young and emerging one, it is likely to be a source of application enhancement requests in the trade processing and risk management areas.

The Management of Positions

23.1 INTRODUCTION

Once trades have been executed, they create positions. If the quantity purchased of a particular instrument exceeds the quantity sold, then the position is a long position; if the quantity sold exceeds the quantity purchased, then it is a short position.

During the life of a position, there are a number of events that take place. Some of these events are externally driven and result from actions taken by the issuer of a security, or by the nature of a derivatives contract or the legal agreement underpinning a debt instrument, while others are internally driven and arise from good financial practice. Table 23.1 summarises all the events that are examined in this chapter.

Before we examine each of these events in detail, we shall first of all cover the difference between trade dated, value dated and settlement dated positions.

23.2 TRADE DATED, VALUE DATED, SETTLED AND DEPOT POSITIONS

The **trade dated position** is the net quantity of an instrument or contract bought or sold up to and including the most recent trade, while the **value dated position** is the net quantity bought or sold where value date is equal to or earlier than today. The **settlement dated** position is the net quantity that has settled on or before today. If trades always settle on the correct value

Table 23.1 Position events

Event description	Event driver	Instrument types affected
Interest rate fixing	Legal documentation of contract or debt issue	Swaps, floating rate notes
Interest (coupon) payment	Legal documentation of contract or debt issue	Swaps, all types of debt instruments, money market loans and deposits
Collection of maturity proceeds	Legal documentation of contract or debt issue	Swaps, all types of debt instruments, money market loans and deposits
Dividend payment	Equity issuer	Equities
Corporate actions	Equity issuer	Equities
Contract expiry	Exchange that developed the contract	Futures and options
Funding of positions	Internal process/good accounting practice	All instruments
Mark to market	Internal process/good accounting practice	All instruments
Reconciliation	Internal process/good accounting practice	All instruments
Interest accrual	Internal process/good accounting practice	All instruments except equities

date, then the value dated position and the settlement dated position would be one and the same. The **depot position** is the actual amount of an instrument that a settlement agent holds on behalf of its customer, and the depot position is the sum of the settlement date position + stock borrowed − stock lent.

It is essential to understand the difference between these concepts because some of the events need to be applied to the trade dated position, some to the value dated position, some to the settlement dated position and some to the depot position.

Many firms employ the use of a stock record, usually part of the main settlement system, that enables them to view positions on a trade dated and value dated basis. The stock record was examined in Chapter 15.

23.3   INTEREST PAYMENTS AND INTEREST RATE FIXINGS

Most forms of debt instruments, as well as OTC derivatives such as swaps, pay periodic interest payments or coupons at regular intervals. The only exceptions to this rule are zero coupon bonds which were issued at a deep discount to face value, bonds that were issued by companies that are no longer able to fund the interest payments (in other words bonds where the issuer is in default) and swaps where the counterparty is in default. For floating rate notes and the floating side of swaps, the interest rate for the next coupon period also needs to be "fixed" a few days before the end of the current interest period.

23.3.1   Interest rate fixings

Example

National Grid plc EUR 750 million floating rate instruments due 2012.

This bond pays quarterly coupons of EURIBOR + 35 basis points (one basis point is 1/100 of 1%) on 18 January, 18 April, 18 July and 18 October) each year.

---

18 January 2008 is a Friday, a normal working day for the euro. Shortly after 11am on Wednesday 16 January (**fixing date**) – two *working* days before the start of the next coupon period – the value of three-month EURIBOR will be published on pages 248 and 249 of Reuters. This is the rate that will apply to the next coupon period. In the case of the National Grid bond, the interest rate that applies will be the published EURIBOR rate plus 35 basis points. Firms that trade instruments based on benchmark rates such as EURIBOR and LIBOR will need to access these Reuters pages, update the static data about the bond issue concerned in the relevant systems and use this rate for any transactions that settle during the next coupon period. The same applies to bonds that are fixed on other benchmark rates such as LIBOR or US Federal funds – these rates will also be published by Reuters, Bloomberg and other information providers.

For swap cash flows, the process is identical. Two working days before the start of the next coupon period the firm needs to access the relevant page, update the contract data in the relevant systems and use this rate to determine the coupon payment to be paid or received at the end of the next coupon period.

Note that fixing dates are usually two *working* days before the start of the next coupon period. Business applications that are concerned with interest rate fixings include diary functions that predict the fixing dates for the life of the bond or the derivative contract. These applications need to use working day calendars and holiday calendars to predict these dates. Refer to section 10.8 for more information.

23.3.2   Interest payments on bonds

Determining entitlements

On the coupon date – the first day of the next coupon period – holders of bonds will be paid the regular coupon payments that they are owed by the issuer. Holders are *owed* the amount based on their value dated positions on record date, which is usually one day before coupon date. However, these payments are made to them by their settlement agent acting in its role as custodian of their assets, and the settlement agent will pay the coupon amount based on their depot position. This means that the coupon amount paid may differ from the amount owed by the net value of any overdue unsettled deals, and also by the net borrowing/lending position.

Where a firm's depot position is not the same as its value dated position, it will need to claim any coupons due to it, and pay any coupons due to others, from the trading parties concerned. Sometimes this process is automated for the firms by their settlement agents who automatically adjust the settlement amount of trades that settle late by the value of any coupons that have been paid to the wrong party, but on other occasions there may be the need to make a claim from or proactively organise payment to the trading parties concerned.

Firms that use a stock record as part of their settlement system will use the stock record to identify the internal trading books, external trading, lending and borrowing parties and depots that need to be debited or credited with coupon proceeds. Consider Figure 23.1, which is an example of a value date stock record report.

ABC Investment Bank plc
Stock record balances for 3 January 2008

Instrument: National Grid plc EUR 750 million floating rate instruments due 2012

Account Type	Account ID	Value dated balances Sign	Quantity
Book	Book 1	Short	7 000.00
Book	Book 2	Long	5 000.00
Party purchase and sale	Party A	Short	3 000.00
Party borrow and lend	Party B	Long	7 000.00
Depot	Euroclear main	Short	2 000.00
Depot	Euroclear custody	Short	20 000.00
Custody	Client B	Long	5 000.00
Custody	Client C	Long	5 000.00
Custody	Client D	Long	5 000.00
Custody	Client E	Long	5 000.00
Total short			32 000.00
Total long			32 000.00
Balance			0.00

Figure 23.1   Stock record used to identify beneficiaries

In this example, Euroclear will pay this firm the coupon on face value of 2000 for the settled position in its main depot account and face value 20 000 for the depot position in its custody account. The 20 000 received for the custody depot needs to be distributed to the four custody clients – B, C, D and E.

Book 1 needs to be debited with the coupon on its short position of 7000 and Book 2 needs to be credited with the coupon on its long position of 5000. Party A has failed to settle a sale to ABC before record date, so ABC needs to claim the coupon on face value 3000 from that trading party. Finally, ABC needs to pay a coupon on face value 7000 to Party B, from whom it has borrowed the bonds.

Coupon calculations for FRNs

There are a small number of differences between the way that coupons are calculated and paid for straight bonds and for floating rate notes:

1. *The affect of non-working days on payment date*: For FRNs, if a predicted coupon date falls on a non-working day, the date is adjusted according to rules laid out in the legal documentation of the bond concerned. The most common rules are as follows, but any bond issuer is free to mandate an alternative rule:
   - *Roll forward until end of month*: Assume a coupon date of the 25th of the month. The first time that this falls on a non-working day (say a Saturday), the coupon rolls forward to Monday the 27th. The next coupon will also fall on the 27th, and the same test is made for the next coupon date, which may cause it to roll forward again. However, once the roll-forward process has reached the last calendar day of the month, it stays there – it never rolls forward into the following month.
   - *Roll backward until start of month*: The same principle as roll forward, but the first time that the coupon falls on a non-working day it is rolled backward to the previous working day, and the next coupon date will also be based on this day. However, once the roll-backward process has reached the first calendar day of the month, it stays there – it never rolls back into the previous month.
   - *Roll forward, express dates*: Assume a coupon date of the 25th of the month. The first time that this falls on a non-working day (say a Saturday), the coupon rolls forward to Monday the 27th. The next coupon date, however, will revert to the 25th of the month because this date has been expressly written into the legal documentation.
   For straight bonds the date remains unchanged, even though the holder will receive the coupon one day later. Adjusting the coupon date on an FRN affects the number of days in the interest period.

   Fixing dates are also amended using the same rules as coupon dates.
2. *The amount of coupon to be paid where the coupon period is less than one year*: For FRNs the amount of coupon to be paid in a particular interest period depends upon the number of days in the period. Refer to section 3.2 for the common methods of determining how many days there are in an interest period.

   For straight bonds that pay semi-annual or quarterly coupons, the amount paid on each coupon date is not affected by the length of the coupon period; a bond bearing a 4% coupon and paying semi-annual interest will simply pay 2% at each coupon date.

23.3.3   Interest payments on swaps

Interest payments on swaps work in the same way as interest payments on bonds, the fixed side of the swap behaves like a fixed rate bond and the floating side behaves like an FRN, with the following exceptions:

1. Swap interest payments for each side are netted, the party that has the most to pay makes a net payment to the other party – refer to the swap examples in section 5.5.3.
2. There is no party acting in the role of custodian, so it is up to each party to ensure that payments are made and received on a timely basis.
3. When swap floating side coupon dates and/or fixing dates fall on non-working days, they are adjusted in the same way as they are adjusted for FRNs.

23.3.4   Accounting for interest payments

In order to ensure that the amount received for a particular coupon payment is the same as the amount due, most settlement systems incorporate coupon control accounts. Consider the following example.

> Bond A pays a 4% coupon. On record date, two trading books of ABC Investment Bank each have a value dated position of 50 000. The depot position is only 80 000. The difference is caused by a single overdue (purchase) settlement of 20 000.

On coupon date, the settlement system automatically credits the interest income account and debits the coupon control account with two lots of 2000 (50 000 ∗ 4%). The settlement agent will actually pay the firm 3200 (80 000 ∗ 4%) which will be credited to the coupon control account. The balance of this account will therefore be 800.00 debit, which is the amount owed to it by the trading party that has failed to deliver 20 000 face value of the bond concerned. When the firm manages to collect the 800.00 that it is owed, it will credit it to the coupon control account, which will then have a zero balance.

In accounting terms, the entries that pass across the general ledger for this type of account may be represented as shown in Figure 23.2.

23.4   COLLECTION OF MATURITY PROCEEDS

Bonds and swaps mature at the end of the borrowing period. For an interest rate swap, there is no maturity event as such as no principal amounts are exchanged, but for a currency swap it is up to both parties to return the principal amount to each other. Refer to the example transactions in section 5.3.

	Coupon control account for Bond A. Coupon date 18 January 2008			
Date	Debit description	Debit Amount	Credit description	Credit amount
01/01/2008		opening balance		0.00
18/01/2008	Book 1 −vd position 50,000	2 000.00		
18/01/2008	Book 2 −vd position 50,000	2 000.00		
18/01/2008			Received from Euroclear	3200.00
18/01/2008	net balance of account	800.00		

Figure 23.2   Coupon control account entries

For bonds, the firm's settlement agent will arrange for the securities to be withdrawn from the firm's depot account on maturity date and the cash to be credited to its nostro account. The amount withdrawn should be the same as the form's value dated position according to the stock record.

Most settlement systems incorporate the use of a redemption control account to control the collection of maturity proceeds. The redemption control account works in the same way as the coupon control account illustrated in Figure 23.2. On maturity date, the settlement system automatically debits the position account with the maturity proceeds and debits the same amount to the redemption control account. When the settlement agent pays the maturity proceeds, the amount paid is credited to redemption control, which now has a zero balance. If, one day after maturity date, there is still a non-zero balance on the redemption control account, then the matter requires investigation.

23.5   DIVIDEND PAYMENTS

Dividend payments are the distribution of earnings to shareholders, and are the result of a decision made by the directors of the issuing company. Dividends are usually paid in cash denominated in the issue currency, but may sometimes be paid in other currencies or sometimes paid in the form of stock. Depending upon the country of issue, dividends may be paid once, twice or four times each year. The directors may, of course, choose not to pay a dividend.

Dividends are paid on **dividend date** to holders based on their value dated positions as of **record date**, which may be several weeks before dividend date. **Ex-dividend date** varies according to the rules of the market in which the securities are listed, but in many markets it is usually two working days before record date. After the stock exchange closes on the day before the ex-dividend date and before the market opens on the ex-dividend date, the price of all open good-until-cancelled, limit, stop and stop limit orders are automatically reduced by the amount of the dividend, except for orders that the customer indicated "Do Not Reduce". This is because these trades cannot settle until after record date, and the new owners will not receive the dividend concerned.

Dividends are paid by the firms' settlement agents based on the depot position, so the same problems that were described for bond coupons also apply to equity dividends when the value dated position and the depot position on record date are not identical. The stock record may be used to work out the entitlements to dividends in the same way that it was used to work out coupon entitlements in the example described under "Determining entitlements", page 219.

Unlike bond coupons, neither the dates nor the amounts of dividend payments are predictable until the dividend is announced by the issuer. Firms use a large number of information services such as those provided by Reuters, Thomson, Bloomberg, the various stock exchanges and also their settlement agents to advise them which issuer is paying a dividend (and how much they are paying) on which dates.

This information is usually uploaded into each firm's settlement system or static data repository, so that automatic postings may be made to a dividend control account that serves exactly the same purpose as the coupon control account described in section 23.1.5.

23.6   CORPORATE ACTIONS

Corporate actions are events initiated by a public company that affect the securities issued by the company. Coupons and dividends may be considered examples of corporate actions.

Equities may be subject to corporate actions. The primary reasons for companies to use corporate actions are:

1. *To return profits to shareholders*: Cash dividends are the classic example.
2. *To influence the share price*: If the price of a stock is too high or too low, the liquidity of the stock suffers. Stocks priced too high will not be affordable to all investors and stocks priced too low may be delisted. Corporate actions such as stock splits or reverse stock splits increase or decrease the number of outstanding shares to decrease or increase the stock price, respectively. Buybacks are another example of influencing the stock price where a corporation buys back shares from the market in an attempt to reduce the number of outstanding shares thereby increasing the price.
3. *Corporate restructuring*: Corporations restructure in order to increase their profitability. Mergers are an example of a corporate action where two companies that are competitive or complementary come together to increase profitability. Spinoffs are an example of a corporate action where a company breaks itself up in order to focus on its core competencies.

Corporate actions may be classified into two types – mandatory and voluntary.

A mandatory corporate action is an event initiated by the corporation by the board of directors that affects all shareholders. Participation of shareholders is mandatory for these corporate actions. The shareholder does not need to do anything to get the benefits of the corporate action – it is just a passive beneficiary.

A voluntary corporate action is one where the shareholders either elect to participate in the action, or have a choice as to how they will receive the benefits provided. A response is required by the issuer to process the action. The shareholder may or may not participate in the tender offer; if it wishes to it sends its instructions to the corporation's registrars, and the issuer will send the proceeds of the action to the shareholders who elect to participate. Sometimes a voluntary corporate action may give the option of how to get the proceeds of the action. For example, in case of a cash/stock dividend option, the shareholder can elect to take the proceeds of the dividend either as cash or additional shares of the corporation.

23.6.1   Corporate action examples

Table 23.2 shows examples of the most common forms of corporate actions.

23.6.2   Corporate action processing

Introduction

Corporate actions processing has traditionally been a function of core settlement systems, but in recent years a number of software vendors have produced dedicated packaged applications designed to manage and control this activity. The firms that have adopted them are often those that have a large number of client (usually safe-custody) positions to manage. This means that communicating the nature of voluntary actions to each client, establishing which option each client wishes to take, and then consolidating the results to the settlement agent represents a significant cost that may be reduced by automation. The dedicated corporate actions packages are usually based on **workflow applications**, which deliver exceptions to the desks of individuals who can manage them. The use of workflow technologies is very

Table 23.2   Common forms of corporate actions

Name	Description	Investor action required?
Bonus issue	Additional shares are given to existing shareholders in proportion to their existing shareholding free of cost. This has no effect on the valuation of the holding. If a holder owned 100 shares with a market price of £6 each and received a bonus issue of 50 shares, then the share price would fall to £4 per share	None – mandatory
Share split or stock split	The total number of shares in issue is increased, and the additional shares are given to existing shareholders in proportion to their existing shareholding free of cost. Like a bonus issue, a share split has no affect on the valuation of the holding	None – mandatory
Reverse share split	The total number of shares in issue is reduced, and shares are taken from existing shareholders in proportion to their existing shareholding free of cost. Like a bonus issue, a reverse share split has no affect on the valuation of the holding	None – mandatory
Merger or takeover	Company A offers to acquire Company B. It may pay shareholders in cash, or in securities issued by Company A, or by a combination of both	Voluntary – shareholders have to elect whether they want to sell or not, and if they do whether they want cash or stock.
Spinoff	Company A divests itself of one or more activities by forming Company B, and giving shares in Company B to Company A's shareholders in proportion to their existing shareholding free of cost	None – mandatory
Rights issues	The company offers existing shareholders the rights to acquire new shares in the company at a discounted price	Voluntary – if the shareholder does not take up its rights they may be sold on the stock exchange concerned
Share buy-backs	The company offers to buy back shares of existing holders and cancel them	Voluntary
Exercise of warrants or options	The investor decides to acquire new shares in a company by exercising warrants or options over those shares	Voluntary
Conversion of convertible bonds	The investor decides to acquire new shares in a company by exercising its right to convert some or all of its holding in a convertible bond	Voluntary

helpful in tracking correspondence between the firm, its customers and its settlement agents, and dealing with situations where customers are not giving their instructions for voluntary corporate actions in the correct timeframe.

Figure 23.3 is an illustration of the functionality of one such system, Smartstream TLM Corporate Actions[TM].

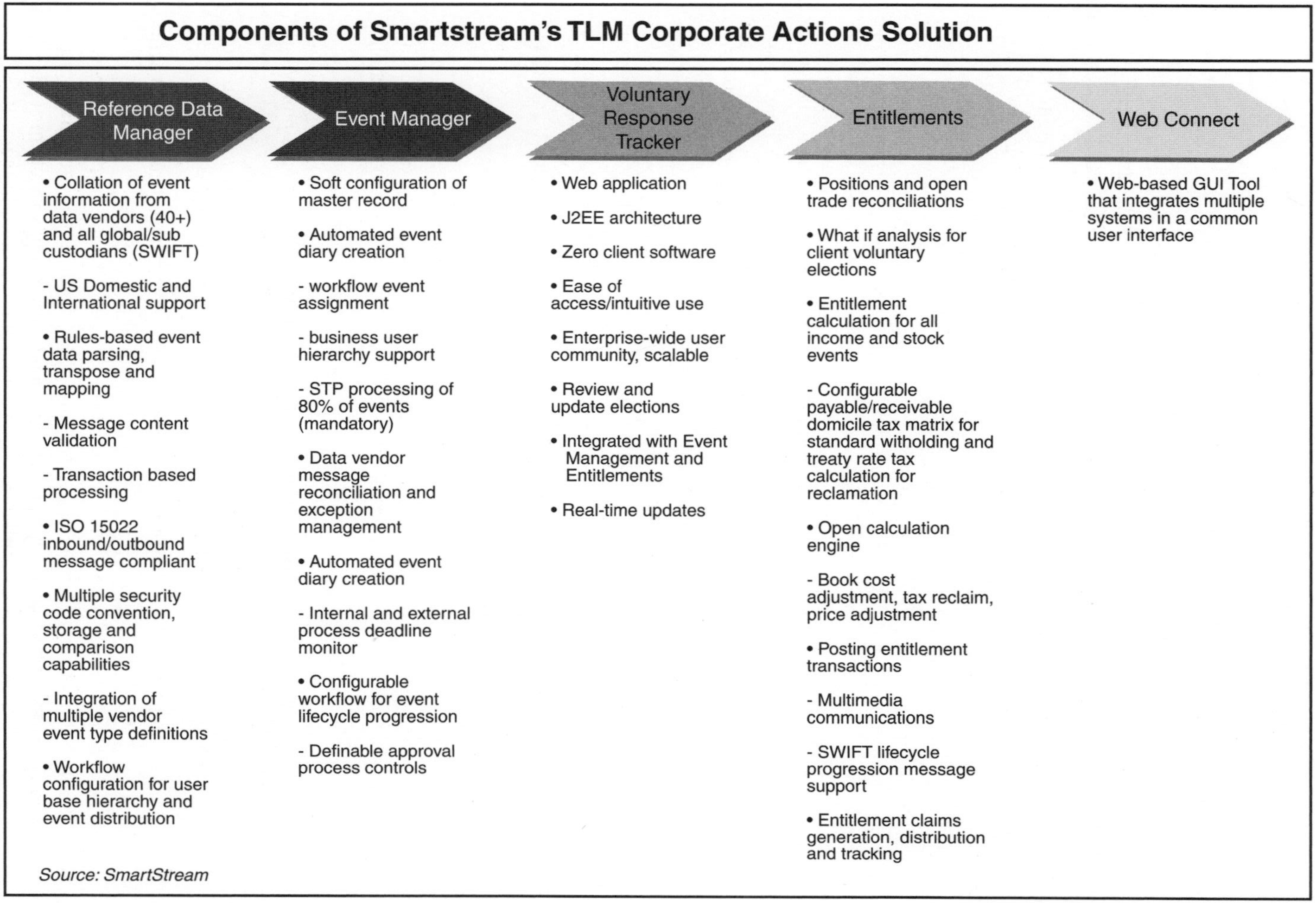

Components of Smartstream's TLM Corporate Actions Solution

Reference Data Manager	Event Manager	Voluntary Response Tracker	Entitlements	Web Connect
• Collation of event information from data vendors (40+) and all global/sub custodians (SWIFT)	• Soft configuration of master record	• Web application	• Positions and open trade reconciliations	• Web-based GUI Tool that integrates multiple systems in a common user interface
- US Domestic and International support	• Automated event diary creation	• J2EE architecture	• What if analysis for client voluntary elections	
• Rules-based event data parsing, transpose and mapping	- workflow event assignment	• Zero client software	• Entitlement calculation for all income and stock events	
- Message content validation	- business user hierarchy support	• Ease of access/intuitive use	- Configurable payable/receivable domicile tax matrix for standard witholding and treaty rate tax calculation for reclamation	
- Transaction based processing	- STP processing of 80% of events (mandatory)	• Enterprise-wide user community, scalable		
• ISO 15022 inbound/outbound message compliant	• Data vendor message reconciliation and exception management	• Review and update elections	• Open calculation engine	
• Multiple security code convention, storage and comparison capabilities	• Automated event diary creation	• Integrated with Event Management and Entitlements	- Book cost adjustment, tax reclaim, price adjustment	
- Integration of multiple vendor event type definitions	- Internal and external process deadline monitor	• Real-time updates	• Posting entitlement transactions	
• Workflow configuration for user base hierarchy and event distribution	• Configurable workflow for event lifecycle progression		- Multimedia communications	
	- Definable approval process controls		- SWIFT lifecycle progression message support	
			• Entitlement claims generation, distribution and tracking	

Source: SmartStream

Figure 23.3 Components of a corporate actions package system

These standalone corporate action systems also support the messaging standards used by the major providers of corporate action information. The relevant SWIFT standards are shown under Table 23.3.

Processing stages

The steps involved in corporate action processing are similar to those of dividend processing, except where voluntary actions are concerned. Corporate actions have an announcement date (the date on which the company announces its intentions) as well as a record date and payment date. When corporate actions are voluntary there is an additional step involved in finding out the wishes of the holders of the security concerned. Depending on the business profile of the firm processing the action, "the holders" might include any or all of the following:

- The firm's own trading books
- Clients for whom it is holding securities in safe custody
- Clients for whom it is providing investment advice
- Trading parties from whom it has borrowed stock, and therefore has a responsibility to provide the right outcome for them.

The stock record may be used to work out the entitlements to corporate actions in the same way that it was used to work out coupon entitlements in the example in Section 23.3.2. When the firm has ascertained the holders' intentions, it then has to communicate them to the firm's settlement agent, who will process the action in the firm's depot account. Once again, each holder's entitlement to corporate action proceeds will be based on its value dated position, so if there is any discrepancy between the value dated position and the depot position, there will be a discrepancy in the amount paid or received. A corporate actions suspense account (which behaves like the coupon and dividend suspense accounts) is used to control this discrepancy. The settlement agent will notify a "closing date" – the latest date that it can accept its customers' instructions – and often a default action – the choice that it will elect if it doesn't receive any instructions in time.

The steps involved in processing corporate actions are illustrated in Figure 23.4.

> *Step 1 (announcement date) Capture details of the action*: The firm will receive details of the corporate action from its settlement agent very shortly after it is announced by the issuer. In addition, a large number of information vendors supply corporate actions information in electronic form.
>
> *Step 2 (announcement date) Decide whether it is voluntary*: This step involves reading the message content. If it is voluntary, and the firm processing it has a large number of clients affected, then it needs to go to Step 3, else it goes to Step 5.
>
> *Step 3 (between record date and closing date) Ascertain the holders' wishes*: This step may be broken down into the following:
>
> > - *Step 3a Identify the holders*: Firms that use a *stock record* (see Chapter 15) will identify the holders from this part of the settlements application.
> > - *Step 3b Decide how to communicate with the holders*: If this firm's holders are retail investors, it might decide to send them a letter or an email, paraphrasing the information that it has received. If, in turn, these clients are advisory clients (refer to section 7.4), then it may go further and make a recommendation to them. If on the other hand the firm's clients are institutional investors, then it may simply forward the

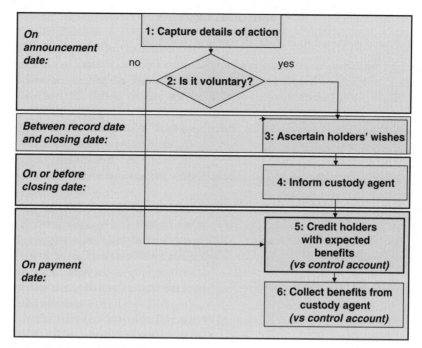

Figure 23.4 Corporate action workflow

messages that it has received in substantially the same form. However, the message carrier may change on a case-by-case basis; for example, this firm may have received notification by a SWIFT message, but not all of its investors are SWIFT members.

This message needs to include a closing date – the latest date that it is possible for the firm to execute the holders' instructions. This may need to be earlier than the closing date that was advised to this firm by its own settlement agent in order for the firm to be able to complete Step 4 in time.

- *Step 3c Send the message to the holders and await responses*
- *Step 3d Follow up any missing or ambiguous responses*: The modern corporate actions packages usually provide workflow-based facilities to support this stage.

Step 4 (on or before closing date) Inform the settlement agent of the actions that it needs to take: This step usually involves responding to the electronic message that the settlement agent sent in Step 1 with an appropriately formatted electronic message.

Step 5 (payment date) Process the corporate actions: This step involves crediting the holders' accounts with the benefits that are due to them and ensuring that the settlement agent credits our firm. The other side of these accounting entries is the corporate actions suspense account.

Relevant SWIFT messages for corporate actions

The relevant messages are as shown in Table 23.3.

Table 23.3   SWIFT messages relevant to corporate actions

Message ID	Message contents	Sender	Receiver
MT564	Notification	Account servicing institution	Customer
MT565	Instruction	Customer	Account servicing institution
MT566	Confirmation of instruction	Account servicing institution	Customer
MT567	Processing advice	Account servicing institution	Customer
MT568	Additional narrative	Either party	Either party

Because of the textual complexity involved in describing corporate actions, the MT568 is used to provide any supplementary information that cannot be contained within the structural constraints of the other messages.

Business applications used to process coupon, dividend and corporate action activity

Traditionally, coupons, maturities, dividends and corporate actions processing capabilities have been provided by the firm's main settlement system. In the past 10 years several software vendors have produced dedicated corporate action processing applications to provide these facilities. Most of these new dedicated applications are based on workflow technology.

23.7   LISTED DERIVATIVES – CONTRACT EXPIRY AND DELIVERY DATES

23.7.1   Listed options

Listed options have an expiry date. If the option is not exercised before this date, then it expires and has no value. The exchange that developed the contract will provide details of the expiry dates of each option, and the relevant clearing house that services the exchange will provide message formats that are used to exercise the option if required. If the holder wishes the option to lapse, then it need take no action.

23.7.2   Listed futures

Expiry date is the time when the final price of the future is determined. For many equity index and interest rate futures contracts (as well as for most equity options), this happens on the third Friday of certain trading months. After the expiry date of a futures contract the key date is known as delivery date or final settlement date. Because a futures contract gives the holder the *obligation* to deliver or receive the underlying instrument, when delivery date is reached the holder of a long position must deliver, and the holder of a short position must receive. In practice, delivery occurs only on a minority of contracts. Most are cancelled out by purchasing a covering position – that is, buying a contract to cancel out an earlier sale (covering a short), or selling a contract to liquidate an earlier purchase (covering a long).

Settlement is the act of consummating the contract, and can be done in one of two ways, as specified by the exchange concerned for each futures contract that it lists:

- *Physical delivery*: The amount specified on the underlying asset of the contract is delivered by the seller of the contract to the exchange, and by the exchange to the buyers of the contract. Physical delivery is common with commodities and bonds.
- *Cash settlement*: A cash payment is made based on the underlying reference rate, such as a short-term interest rate index such as EURIBOR, or the closing value of a stock market index.

The exchange that developed the contract will provide details of the expiry dates, settlement prices and delivery dates of each futures contract, and the relevant clearing house that services the exchange will provide message formats that are used to make cash or physical settlement as required.

23.8   MARKING POSITIONS TO MARKET

Mark to market is an accounting procedure by which assets are "marked", or recorded, at their current market value, which may be higher or lower than their purchase price or book value. As a result of a mark-to-market calculation, all investments are valued in the dealing system at their current market value, and all profits and losses that result from price rises or falls are recognised on the day that they happen. This is accounting "best practice". Consider the following example.

On 22 February, ABC Investment Bank carries out three trades in Megacorp plc:

1. It buys 10 000 shares at £10 each at 9am.
2. It buys an additional 10 000 shares at £9.50 each at 10am. At this point its position is 20 000 shares and its **average price** per share is £9.75.
3. It sells 12 000 shares at £9.95 per share at 11am. Its position is now 8000 shares, and it has made a **realised profit** of £1800.00. This is calculated as:

Realised P&L = Number of shares sold ∗ (Sale price − Average cost price)

At the close of business the **bid price** of Megacorp on the exchange is 9.95 per share and the **offer price** is £10.00 per share. Because ABC has a long position in Megacorp, it marks the **trade dated position** to market at the bid price. If the position were short, it would mark it to the offer price. As a result, it calculates an **unrealised profit** of £1600.00. This is calculated as:

Unrealised P&L = Position ∗ (Mark-to-market price − Average price)

In addition, as a result of the mark-to-market calculation, it is now holding the position in its book at a new price – £9.95 per share, the current bid price.

If it were to sell some or all of its holding in Megacorp on 23 February, then it would calculate the realised P&L for that day as:

Realised P&L = Number of shares sold ∗ (Sale price − 9.95)

In other words, the close of business mark-to-market price on day 1 becomes the opening average price on day 2. The profits and losses (both realised and unrealised) are posted to the firm's general ledger on the day that they occur.

In this example, the revaluation (or marking to market) of the portfolio was based on the **weighted average price (WAP)** method of revaluation, which is usually expressed by the following formulae:

For a long position:

$$\text{WAP} = \text{Cumulative principal amount of purchases/Cumulative position}$$

And the cost of an amount sold (which reduces the long position) is expressed as:

$$\text{Principal amount of sale} = \text{Amount sold} * \text{WAP}$$

For a short position:

$$\text{WAP} = \text{Cumulative principal amount of sales/Cumulative position}$$

And the cost of an amount purchased (which reduces the short position) is expressed as:

$$\text{Principal amount of sale} = \text{Amount sold} * \text{WAP}$$

When a transaction takes the position from long to short, or from short to long, then the weighted average price of the resulting position is the same as the price of the trade.

The transactions in this example are summarised in Figure 23.5.

23.8.1   Mark to market: practical issues

Which transactions and positions are normally marked to market?

Positions in bonds, equities and listed derivatives are normally marked to market in the manner described in this section, using closing bid and offer prices for the instrument concerned. FX positions also need to be marked to market in the same way, this time using the closing exchange rates of the currencies concerned to the firm's FX base currency. Swaps are marked to market using the procedure described in "Marking swap transactions to market", page 232

Determining accurate bid and offer prices

The closing bid and offer prices of liquid equities are published each day by the stock exchanges on which the shares are quoted. For illiquid equities that are traded over the counter, and for many corporate bonds, finding an accurate independently verifiable source of bid and offer prices is more difficult. MiFID (see "Post-trade transparency", Section 8.4.2) introduced requirements for market makers to publish pre-trade quotes and also mandated post-trade publication of all executed OTC trades, and a number of exchanges and central matching engines collect such data and publish the results in summary form. The information that they publish may be used to ascertain realistic bid and offer prices for many instruments.

As far as illiquid corporate bonds are concerned, many investment firms will base their decision as to what the accurate closing price of an individual security is by referencing the individual bond to a liquid government security denominated in the same currency. For example, if the yield on a 30-year US Treasury bond is currently 4.5%, then the yield on all

Event	Date	Amount purchased or sold	Trade price	Trade value	Cumulative position	Cumulative cost	Average price	Realised P&L	Unrealised P&L
(1) Purchase of 10000 shares in Megacorp at £10 per share	22-Feb	10000.00	10.00	100000.00	10000.00	100000.00	10.00		
(2) Purchase additional 10000 shares in Megacorp at £9.50 per share	22-Feb	10000.00	9.50	95000.00	20000.00	195000.00	9.75		
(3) Sale of 12000 shares in Megacorp at £9.90 per share	22-Feb	-12000.00	9.90	-118800.00	8000.00	78000.00	9.75	1800.00	
(4) Mark the remaining position of 8000 shares to market at the current bid price - £9.95 per share	22-Feb				8000.00		9.95		1600.00

Figure 23.5 Mark-to-market example

AAA rated straight corporate bonds with a similar maturity might be 60 basis points higher, while the yield on AA rated straight corporate bonds might be 90 basis points higher. FRNs are usually benchmarked to the swap curve for the index on which their interest rates are based.

Most debt instrument front-office systems include the facilities to track individual issues to a benchmark bond issue or benchmark interest rate in this way. If the firm has a dedicated risk management department (section 24.1.5), then this department will monitor the accuracy of the sources of bid and offer prices that the firm is using, and the assumptions about benchmark issues that are used as reference points.

Alternatives to using weighted average price

The weighted average price method of calculating P&L is probably the most widely used method of calculating P&L and valuing positions, but there are other methods that may be used, including:

- *FIFO (First-In-First-Out)*: In this method of P&L calculation, the 12 000 shares that were sold at 11am are deemed to comprise the 10 000 bought at 9am and 2000 of the 10 000 shares bought at 10am. This method is not widely used because of its complexity – it needs a history of the price of every trade that has taken place since the position last went flat, which could, in theory, be many years ago.
- *LIFO (Last-In-First-Out)*: In this method of P&L calculation, the 12 000 shares that were sold at 11am are deemed to comprise the 10 000 bought at 10am and 2000 of the 10 000 shares bought at 9am. Firms such as private client stockbrokers that handle investments on behalf of UK resident private individuals will need to take into account the investor's liability to pay capital gains tax if and when investments are sold. Note that UK tax law requires them to use the LIFO P&L method when calculating liability to pay this tax.

Marking swap transactions to market

Swaps are marked to market by calculating their **present value (PV)**. The present value of a plain vanilla (i.e. fixed rate for floating rate) swap is calculated using standard methods to determine the present value of the fixed side and the floating side. The steps in the computation are as follows:

1. Calculate the present value of the fixed side. The value of the fixed side is given by the present value of the fixed coupon payments known at the start of the swap, i.e.:

$$PV_{fixed} = C \times \sum_{i=1}^{M} \left(P \times \frac{t_i}{T_i} \times df_i \right)$$

where:

- C is the swap rate
- M is the number of fixed payments
- P is the notional amount
- t_i is the number of days in period i
- T_i is the basis according to the interest calculation method
- df_i is the discount factor.

2. The value of the floating side is given by the present value of the floating coupon payments determined at the agreed dates of each payment. However, at the start of the swap, only the actual payment rates of the fixed side are known in the future, whereas the forward rates (derived from the yield curve) are used to approximate the floating rates. Each variable rate payment is calculated based on the forward rate for each respective payment date. Using these interest rates leads to a series of cash flows. Each cash flow is discounted by the zero-coupon rate for the date of the payment; this is also sourced from the yield curve data available from the market. Zero-coupon rates are used because these rates are for bonds that pay only one cash flow. The interest rate swap is therefore treated like a series of zero-coupon bonds. Thus, the value of the floating side is given by:

$$PV_{float} = \sum_{j=1}^{N} \left(P \times f_j \times \frac{t_j}{T_j} \times df_j \right)$$

where:

- N is the number of floating payments
- f_j is the forward rate
- P is the notional amount
- t_j is the number of days in period j
- T_j is the basis according to the day count convention
- df_j is the discount factor.

The discount factor always starts with 1. It is calculated as follows:

[Discount factor in the previous period]/1 + [(Forward rate of floating side asset in previous period ∗ No. of days in previous period/360 or 365)][1]

3. The fixed rate offered in the swap is the rate which values the fixed rates payments at the same PV as the variable rate payments using today's forward rates, i.e.:

$$C = \frac{PV_{float}}{\sum_{i=1}^{M} \left(P \times \frac{t_i}{T_i} \times df_i \right)}$$

Therefore, at the time the contract is entered into, there is no advantage to either party, i.e:

$$PV_{fixed} = PV_{float}$$

Thus, on the value date of the start leg the swap requires no upfront payment from either party. During the life of the swap, the same valuation technique is used, but since, over time, the forward rates change, the PV of the variable rate part of the swap will deviate from the unchangeable fixed rate side of the swap.

The daily mark-to-market accounting entry is the sum of

Present value of transaction today − Present value of transactionon previous day

Accounting entries for mark-to-market activity

Tables 23.4 to 23.6 show the accounting entries to be posted in the general ledger for mark-to-market profits. If the process results in a loss, then the signs are reversed.

---

[1] The divisor of 360 for all currencies except GBP and JPY which use the 365-days convention. Refer to section 4.1.1.

Table 23.4   Posting entry for unrealised profit on securities and listed derivatives

Sign	Account type	Trade amount name	Currency of posting
Dr	Security position account	Unrealised profit or loss	Currency in which instrument is normally traded
Cr	Security trading P&L	Unrealised profit or loss	Currency in which instrument is normally traded

Table 23.5   Posting entry for unrealised profit on FX position

Sign	Account type	Trade amount name	Currency of posting
Dr	Base currency cost of FX position	Unrealised profit or loss	FX base currency
Cr	FX trading P&L	Unrealised profit or loss	FX base currency

Table 23.6   Posting entry for unrealised profit on swap transactions

Sign	Account type	Trade amount name	Currency of posting
Dr	Swap gains and losses	Unrealised profit or loss	FX base currency
Cr	Swap trading P&L	Unrealised profit or loss	FX base currency

Securities and listed derivatives
Each individual position within each book for which the firm holds a position, the entry shown in Table 23.4 should be passed.

Foreign exchange positions
Each currency within each book for which the firm holds a position, the entry shown in Table 23.5 should be passed.

Swaps
Each outstanding swap contract for which the firm holds a position, the entry shown in Table 23.6 should be passed.

23.9   ACCRUAL OF INTEREST

When a firm enters into any of the following types of transactions:

- Purchase or sale of bonds
- Stock borrowing, lending and repos
- Money market loans and deposits
- Swaps

it needs to account for the interest that will be paid on the next coupon date of the bond or the termination date of the other types of contract. This process is known as interest accrual.

Accrual is an accounting term. It is defined as a method of accounting in which each item is entered as it is earned or incurred regardless of when actual payments are received or made.

Accrued interest is defined as the interest that has accumulated on a transaction since the last interest payment date or start date, up to but not including the current date.

23.9.1 Example of accrued interest calculation

On trade date 5 March 2007, value date 7 March 2007, ABC Investment Bank borrowed GBP 1 000 000 for 30 days at 5% interest; calculated on the actual/actual basis. The maturity date is therefore 6 April 2007.

On 6 April, ABC will repay the principal amount of GBP 1 000 000 + 30 days' interest: Repayment amount = 1 000 000 + (1 000 000 * 30/365 * 5%) = GBP 1 004 109.59.

However, as part of the mark-to-market process ABC needs to account for this interest expense on each day that it occurs – not all in one amount at the end of the loan period.

The firm is therefore required to process the interest accrual amounts shown in Table 23.7 on each working day between 7 March and 6 April, so that the interest cost is recorded in the general ledger on the day that it is incurred.

Table 23.7   Daily interest accruals

Day of week	Date	Cumulative days	No. of days accrued today	Accrual to date	Accrual for the day	Cumulative accrual for month	Cumulative accrual for transaction
Wednesday	39148	0	0	0.00	0.00	0.00	1.00
Thursday	39149	1	1	136.99	136.99	136.99	136.99
Friday	39150	4	3	547.95	410.96	547.95	547.95
Monday	39153	5	1	684.93	136.99	684.93	684.93
Tuesday	39154	6	1	821.92	136.99	821.92	821.92
Wednesday	39155	7	1	958.90	136.99	958.90	958.90
Thursday	39156	8	1	1,095.89	136.99	1,095.89	1,095.89
Friday	39157	11	3	1,506.85	410.96	1,506.85	1,506.85
Monday	39160	12	1	1,643.84	136.99	1,643.84	1,643.84
Tuesday	39161	13	1	1,780.82	136.99	1,780.82	1,780.82
Wednesday	39162	14	1	1,917.81	136.99	1,917.81	1,917.81
Thursday	39163	15	1	2,054.79	136.99	2,054.79	2,054.79
Friday	39164	18	3	2,465.75	410.96	2,465.75	2,465.75
Monday	39167	19	1	2,602.74	136.99	2,602.74	2,602.74
Tuesday	39168	20	1	2,739.73	136.99	2,739.73	2,739.73
Wednesday	39169	21	1	2,876.71	136.99	2,876.71	2,876.71
Thursday	39170	22	1	3,013.70	136.99	3,013.70	3,013.70
Friday	39171	24	2	3,287.67	273.97	3,287.67	3,287.67
Monday	39174	26	2	3,561.64	273.97	273.97	3,561.64
Tuesday	39175	27	1	3,698.63	136.99	410.96	3,698.63
Wednesday	39176	28	1	3,835.62	136.99	547.95	3,835.62
Thursday	39177	29	1	3,972.60	136.99	684.93	3,972.60
Friday	39178	30	1	4,109.59	136.99	821.92	4,109.59

The following business rules apply to interest accruals:

1. It is the convention that no interest is payable or receivable on the start date of a transaction, but it is payable for the end date. For money market loans and deposits the practice is to accrue interest from (and not including) the value date of the start leg of the transaction to (and including) the effective date of the accrual. For bonds, the practice is to accrue from (and not including) the date of the start of the current interest period to (and including) the effective date of the accrual.
2. For bonds, the accrual is based on the value dated position (according to the stock record used).
3. When making an accrual it is necessary to use the correct interest calculation method for the currency or debt instrument concerned. The different methods were examined in section 3.2.
4. Most financial sector firms have their statistical month ends on the same day as the calendar month end, and most systems that are concerned with interest accrual do not run at weekends.
5. Because of item (3), the daily accrual convention is one day's interest on Tuesdays through Thursdays, and three days' interest is to be accrued on Fridays, unless any or all of the days of the weekend following fall into the next month. If that is the case, the system should accrue to the month end date – Saturday 31 March in this example. The date that is used is the **effective date** of the accrual.
6. On Mondays, the practice is to accrue interest from the previous day, or from the start of the month, whichever is earlier. Hence if three days' interest (to Sunday) had been accrued on the previous Friday, then one day's interest would be accrued on Monday; if two days' interest (to Saturday) had been accrued, then two days' interest would be accrued on Monday; and if only one day's interest had been accrued on Friday, then three days' interest would be accrued on Monday.

Therefore, if the firm had a financial month end of Saturday 31 March, then the firm would account for the total interest of GBP 4109.59 as:

- 24 days – GBP 3287.67 forming March expenses; and
- 6 days – GBP 821.92 forming April expenses.

The daily interest accruals for the example transaction are therefore as shown in Table 23.7.

23.9.2 Accrual and de-accrual

In practice, most applications that accrue interest will, each working day:

1. De-accrue (i.e. reverse) any interest that was accrued the previous day
2. Accrue interest from the relevant start date to the relevant effective date.

In other words, in the example transaction, on Friday 9 March the application would reverse the previous day's accrual of GBP 136.99 and re-accrue GBP 547.95, instead of accruing an additional GBP 410.96. The reason that most applications work in this way are:

1. This methodology allows for the automatic correction of any processing errors. For example, if this money market transaction had been entered into the system with the wrong interest rate, principal amount or interest calculation method, and the transaction had not

Table 23.8   Interest P&L account postings

	Interest expense account for money market deposit attracted			
Date	Debit description	Debit amount	Credit description	Credit amount
02/04/2007	opening balance	**2.00**		**0.00**
02/04/2007	accrual	273.97	de-accrual	−2.00
03/04/2007	accrual	410.96	de-accrual	−273.97
04/04/2007	accrual	547.95	de-accrual	−410.96
05/04/2007	accrual	684.93	de-accrual	−547.95
06/04/2007	cash payment	821.92	de-accrual	−684.93
06/07/2007	totals	2 741.73		−1 919.81
06/07/2007	net balance of account	821.92		

been corrected until 9 March, then the process of de-accruing automatically corrects any consequent interest mispostings.

2. On the maturity date, it is not in fact necessary to make an accrual, because on this date the firm will actually pay (in this example) or receive (if it were a loan placed instead of a deposit attracted) the interest for the entire transaction. If the accrual were not reversed, then the interest expense would be duplicated in the profit and loss account. This point is illustrated in Table 23.8 for the accounting entries for the month of April that would be passed in the firm's general ledger account for interest expense for the example transaction.

23.10   OTHER ACCRUALS

Dividends and corporate action proceeds can also be accrued, but such accruals cannot be made before the record date for the dividend or corporate action concerned.

23.11   RECONCILIATION

Reconciliation is the process of proving that the firm's books and records are accurate. It is an essential tool in controlling operational risk, in particular the risks caused by operational errors, as well as the risks of internal and external fraud. For this reason, the UK FSA recommends that reconciliation is usually carried out by persons who have not played any role in processing the transactions.

External reconciliation is the act of reconciling data such as cash movements on nostro accounts and stock movements on depot accounts with the settlement agents that operate those accounts on the firm's behalf.

Internal reconciliation is the act of reconciling data held in one of the firm's business applications (such as its settlement system) with data held on one or more of its other business application systems.

23.11.1   External reconciliation

Each firm needs to decide what information it needs to reconcile with third parties such as exchanges, central counterparties and settlement agents, but the following are the minimum requirements that apply to all firms:

- Bank reconciliations – with settlement agents and other banks that service the firm.
- Depot reconciliations – covering all depot positions for which the firm is responsible, i.e. both its own proprietary positions as well as any client positions that it may be responsible for. The regulators in most countries have specific rules that require firms to reconcile client assets.

Bank reconciliations

The purposes of a bank reconciliation are to ensure that:

- All the receipts and payments that the bank customer has posted to its general ledger account are reflected by the bank that is providing the account
- There are no entries on the bank statement that were not expected
- The balance of the account in the ledger – open transactions in the ledger and open transactions in the statement – is equal to the balance of the account on the bank statement.

In high volume financial institutions, bank reconciliations are usually performed daily. The bank that is providing the account normally sends the statement in electronic form and the statement is then passed to a dedicated reconciliation application that compares it with data provided by the appropriate internal system – usually the main settlement system. Section 23.11.3 provides more details about how these applications work.

The relevant SWIFT messages for bank reconciliation are the MT940 and the MT950. The MT950 message was examined in section 11.1.3. The difference between the two forms of statement is that the MT940 provides a longer narrative tag. The equivalent data needs to be extracted from the appropriate internal system (either the main settlement system or the corporate general ledger) so that the two sets of records may be compared.

When extracting balance data from the general ledger it is important that the value dated balance is used and not the forward balance, and that only account postings that have reached value today or earlier are extracted, or else the data that is extracted will include items that have not yet been posted by the external party. Refer to section 14.3.3 for an explanation of the difference between the trade dated balance and the value dated balance.

In a bank reconciliation, both the account balances and the individual transactions are compared. There may be many transactions of the same amount on the same day, and the aim of the reconciliation is to "tick off" the correct transaction in the internal record against its external equivalent. Consider the example shown in Table 23.9.

All the items that are shown on both sides of the reconciliation, which have the same amount, reference number and value date, are "good matches". The importance of the unique reference number was examined in section 12.2.7. If we use automated reconciliation software to eliminate the good matches, we are left with the items shown in Table 23.10, which require user inspection.

Depot reconciliation

The purposes of a depot reconciliation are to ensure that the firm's record of the **depot position** is the same as that of the institution providing the depot account. In addition, some firms will also wish to reconcile and compare the values of any unsettled instructions with the depot institution.

Table 23.9 Bank reconciliation – all items

Bank				Internal application			
Value date	Description	Reference	Amount	Value date	Description	Reference	Amount
03 December 2007	settlement	123456	80 000.00	03 December 2007	settlement	123456	80 000.00
03 December 2007	settlement		80 000.00	03 December 2007	settlement	123457	80 000.00
03 December 2007	settlement	123458	80 000.00	03 December 2007	settlement	123458	80 000.00
03 December 2007	settlement	123459	80 000.00	03 December 2007	settlement	123459	80 000.00
03 December 2007	settlement	123461	80 000.00	03 December 2007	settlement	123461	79 999.99
03 December 2007	bank charges		– 100.00	04 December 2007	settlement	123460	80 000.00
				04 December 2007	reversal of incorrect entry	123460	– 80 000.00

Table 23.10 Bank reconciliation – unmatched items

Bank				Internal application			
Value date	Description	Reference	Amount	Value date	Description	Reference	Amount
03 December 2007	settlement		80 000.00	03 December 2007	settlement	123457	80 000.00
03 December 2007	settlement	123461	80 000.00	03 December 2007	settlement	123461	79 000.00
03 December 2007	bank charges		– 100.00	04 December 2007	settlement	123460	80 000.00
				04 December 2007	reversal of incorrect entry	123460	– 80 000.00

Notes:

1. The "Bank" item in the first row has no reference number, but it probably relates to the internal item with reference number 1234567. This needs to be verified by a user.
2. The bank charges in the third row will not yet have been posted in the internal records, as this is probably the first time that the firm was aware of it. When it is posted, it will enter the reconciliation application on the next run, and provided there is a business rule to match on the description of "bank charges", it should be automatically matched.
3. The transaction with reference number 123461 has a different amount on each side and requires investigation and correction.
4. There are two items on the internal side with the same reference number – 123460 – that cancel each other out; in other words they can be matched against each other.

In high volume financial institutions, depot reconciliations are usually performed daily. The bank that is providing the account normally sends the data in electronic form and the statement is then passed to a dedicated reconciliation application that compares it with data that is provided by the appropriate internal system.

The relevant SWIFT messages for depot reconciliation are the MT535 (Statement of Holdings), MT536 (Statement of Transactions) and MT537 (Statement of Pending Transactions). The equivalent data needs to be extracted from the appropriate internal system (usually the main settlement system) so that the two sets of records may be compared. Firms that use a stock record would extract the data from the stock record and make the comparisons in the following manner.

- *Balance information*: This is found by extracting all the depot balance records from the value dated stock record and comparing it to the data on the MT535 messages from each settlement agent.
- *Transaction information*: This is found by extracting all the individual stock record entries of the day and comparing them to the entries shown on the MT536 messages for each settlement agent. In order to perform this reconciliation, the unique reference number described in section 12.2.7 is used to link the two record sets.

A potential problem within depot reconciliation is that most settlement agents identify securities in their messages by ISIN code. In section 10.4.1 it was pointed out that where securities are traded in more than one market, there is only one ISIN code allocated to that security, but that single ISIN code may be used by more than one unique instrument in the firm's internal records. This can lead to ambiguity, where, for example, an MT535 message is quoting the ISIN code of Sony Corporation shares, but the firm has perhaps four or five unique instruments with that ISIN code, depending on which markets Sony shares are traded and in which currency the shares are quoted.

23.11.2   Internal reconciliation

The purpose of internal reconciliation is to ensure that data that is represented in more than one business application is represented consistently across all those applications. Consider the affect of a single equity principal trade being executed and settled in the applications in the configuration diagram in Figure 23.6.

The elements of this trade shown in Table 23.11, and the position that results from it, will be represented in the applications coloured in grey in the figure.

If these amounts are not consistent across the applications, then the firm may be exposed to operational risk, as users of the systems that are showing the incorrect data will base decisions on that data. Therefore each firm has to decide which trade and position elements it needs to reconcile between applications. Making such decisions may be one of the responsibilities of the centralised risk management department, which is discussed in Chapter 24. The equivalent data needs to be extracted from the appropriate internal systems so that the two or more sets of records may be compared.

23.11.3   Reconciliation software applications

There are a number of specialised reconciliation packages on the market that perform automated internal and external reconciliations of both cash and stock. The components of such

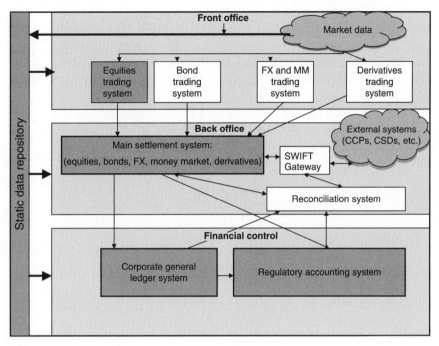

Figure 23.6 Flow of an equity trade through the configuration

systems usually include:

1. The ability to process the relevant SWIFT messages required for reconciliation
2. Defined APIs to extract equivalent data from internal systems
3. The ability to define data relationships between systems, e.g.:
   - The general ledger account code 123456 is the same entity as the nostro account number 654321 with JP Morgan

Table 23.11 Flow of an equity trade through the configuration

Application	Trade elements	Position elements
Equities trading system	Nominal amount	Trade dated position
	Principal value	Value dated position
	Trade price	
	Fees such as stamp duty	
	Consideration	
Settlement system	Nominal amount	Trade dated position
	Principal value	Value dated position
	Trade price	Settled position
	Fees such as stamp duty	Depot position
	Consideration	Bank account balance
	Settlement (cash) amount	
	Settlement (stock) amount	
Corporate general ledger	Principal value	
	Fees such as stamp duty	
	Consideration	
	Settlement (cash) amount	Bank account balance

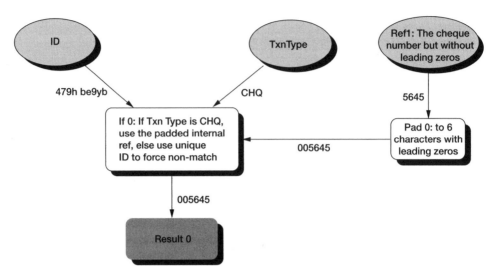

Figure 23.7   Reconciliation business rules development. Reproduced by permission of City Networks Limited.

- The depot account code "Euroclear Main" in the stock record is the same as the depot account number 77665544 with Euroclear
4. A security cross-reference table that provides a cross-reference between the ISIN code used by most external agents and the internal identifiers of each security
5. The ability for users to create business rules that the system will use to match transactions on combinations of data fields such as amount, value date, description, reference number, etc.
6. The ability to display items that cannot be matched automatically and for users to manually match them and investigate them
7. The ability to escalate items that are user defined thresholds such as transaction age and transaction size.

Figures 23.7 and 23.8 are provided by City Networks Limited and reproduced with their permission, in order to show some of these abilities.

Figure 23.7 shows a user developed business rule. The problem that it is designed to solve is that the one application provides cheque numbers as unique reference numbers with six digits (e.g. 005645) while the other one does not provide leading zeros. In order for the transactions to match on reference the data supplied by the second application must be manipulated to be presented in the same format as the first application.

Figure 23.8 shows a list of the items in a bank reconciliation that could not be automatically matched. Users are able to work through this list and either:

- Manually match some items for which their was not an appropriate business rule
- Propose matches for another senior user to approve or
- Commence investigation and follow-up of unmatched items that cannot be explained.

The different symbols in the first column show the status of each item. Items with the rectangular symbol are currently unmatched, while items with the triangular symbol have been proposed as matches, and await approval from another user.

	Source Code	Ccy	Their	Our	Diff	Debit/Credit	Reference	Linked	Matching Scheme Rule	Close Batch Ref	Close Batch Status
Currently Unmatched Txns - for selected Objectives of External Cash											
◁	LEDGER	GBP	0.00	28.54	-28.54	DR	101501			EBOEEAB	Proposed
◁	STATEMENT	GBP	28.54	0.00	28.54	CR	101501			EBOEEAB	Proposed
▣	STATEMENT	GBP	-117.50	0.00	-117.50	DR	018518	Yes	3:Match Manual Cheques		
▣	LEDGER	GBP	0.00	-240.00	240.00	CR	M665352				
▣	STATEMENT	GBP	-240.00	0.00	-240.00	DR	018349				
▣	LEDGER	GBP	0.00	-843.06	843.06	CR	5879567				
▣	LEDGER	GBP	0.00	-1,117.50	1,117.50	CR	M665352	Yes	3:Match Manual Cheques		
◁	LEDGER	GBP	0.00	1,424.65	-1,424.65	DR	IP2MC9811227000812			78252A8	Proposed
◁	STATEMENT	GBP	1,424.65	0.00	1,424.65	CR	IP2MC9811227000812			78252A8	Proposed
▣	LEDGER	GBP	0.00	-2,400.86	2,400.86	CR	M665352	Yes	3:Match Manual Cheques		
▣	STATEMENT	GBP	-2,402.86	0.00	-2,402.86	DR	018590	Yes	3:Match Manual Cheques		
▣	LEDGER	GBP	0.00	-5,000.00	5,000.00	CR	J655909				
▣	LEDGER	GBP	0.00	10,335.86	-10,335.86	DR	PBMC9812010100748				
▣	LEDGER	GBP	14,630.65	14,630.65	-14,630.65	DR	PBMC9812010100748				
▣	STATEMENT	GBP	14,630.65	0.00	14,630.65	CR	PBMC9812010100748				
▣	LEDGER	GBP	0.00	350,000.00	-350,000.00	DR	STARTUP				
▣	STATEMENT	GBP	360,335.86	0.00	360,335.86	CR	STARTUP				
			373,659.34	366,818.28	6,841.06						

Figure 23.8 Reconciliation user interface for manual matching and investigation. Reproduced by permission of City Networks Limited.

24

The Management of Risk

Chapter 8 introduced the concepts of market risk, credit risk and operational risk. This chapter examines market risk and credit risk in more detail, examines the role of a centralised risk management function and provides a brief introduction to credit control and Value-at-Risk (VaR). VaR is one of the analytical techniques that are used by investment professionals to measure and control such risks.

24.1 FORMS OF MARKET RISK

Currency risk is the risk caused by movements in exchange rates. It is often subdivided into **transaction risk**; the risk that exchange rate movements affect the values of individual transactions; and **translation risk**, the risk that foreign currency assets held on the balance sheet decline due to exchange rate movements. Accounting procedures designed to avoid translation risk were examined in section 14.3.7.

Interest rate risk is the risk to a portfolio caused by fluctuating interest rates. All investors and borrowers are affected by changes to the levels of interest rates, but some parties run positions that are affected by changes in the shape of the yield curve (refer to section 3.4.1). For example, a firm that has borrowed money for short-term periods and invested it in long dated bonds would be adversely affected if the yield curve rapidly inverted.

Equity risk is the general market risk of rises or falls of individual share prices or stock market levels in general.

Volatility risk is the risk in the value of options portfolios due to the unpredictable changes in the **volatility** of the underlying asset.

Basis risk results from hedging activity. It is the risk that one position has been hedged with another position which behaves in a similar, but not identical, fashion. For example, a firm that had invested in the UK stock market might hedge its positions using futures or options based on the FTSE100 Index, but unless the firm owned all the constituent stock of the index in the correct proportions, the use of these contracts would be an imperfect hedge.

24.2 FORMS OF CREDIT RISK

Credit risk may be divided into the following main categories.

Counterparty risk is the risk that a trading party cannot meet its obligations to settle trades or make other transaction-related payments (such as swap cash flows) in the future.

Issuer risk is the risk that a security issuer may not be able to pay coupon, dividend or maturity proceeds at some time in the future. The issuer risk of a bond issued by the government of a developed country is very low, but the risk of default by a developing country government is relatively high. The risk of default by a government risk is known as **sovereign risk**.

Delivery risk is the danger that in a transaction that is settled free of payment (FoP), the expected incoming payment or delivery is not received as a result of a transaction processing error by one or other party or a settlement agent.

24.3   OTHER FORMS OF RISK

Liquidity risk is the risk that a firm may be unable to refinance its borrowings as they mature and need to be renegotiated. For securities firms, this may be because the market for the instruments that it uses for its borrowings becomes too thin to enable efficient and fair trading to take place. The most public and dramatic example of liquidity risk in recent years is the 2007 "credit crunch" that was examined in section 3.1.4.

Reputational risk is damage to an organisation through loss of its reputation or standing. Loss of reputation usually occurs when the organisation concerned has failed to manage some other form of risk effectively. IT managers in particular need to be aware that failure of business recovery efforts (Chapter 25) and high profile business change programmes and projects (Chapter 26) is often reported by the banking and IT trade press and sometimes the national press and television, and that failure of these types of activities can lead to reputational risk events.

Project risk is the risk of over-run or failure to complete a change project. This is examined in more detail in Chapter 26.

24.4   THE ROLE OF THE BOARD OF DIRECTORS IN MANAGING RISK

Most large financial institutions have set up an independent risk committee, made up of independent non-executive directors of the company. The committee meets regularly without management present, and has the authority to engage independent advisors, paid for by the company, to help its decisions making. Its main responsibilities are usually to:

- Identify and monitor the key risks of the company and evaluate their management.
- Approve risk management policies that establish the appropriate approval levels for decisions and other checks and balances to manage risk
- Satisfy itself that policies are in place to manage the risks to which the company is exposed, including market, operational, liquidity, credit, insurance, regulatory and legal risk, and reputational risk
- Provide a forum for "big picture" analysis of future risks including considering trends
- Critically assess the company's business strategies and plans from a risk perspective.

24.5   THE ROLE OF THE RISK MANAGEMENT DEPARTMENT

Many large investment firms have a centralised risk management department. While there is no standard definition of its role, this department usually has an independent "middle office" function headed by a senior manager who reports to, or may be, a member of the executive board. The department's duties are likely to include:

1. Monitoring the separation of duties between front-, middle- and back-office functions
2. Monitoring of, and reporting to, management the firm's overall risk exposure and adherence to risk control policies
3. Communicating risks and risk strategy to shareholders and/or the board risk committee
4. Defining and monitoring the use of credit limits
5. Independent sourcing and validation of closing bid and offer prices used to mark positions to market and calculate profits and losses

6. Independent validation of Value-at-Risk (VaR) models
7. Defining and implementing escalation procedures to deal with realised and unrealised trading losses and internal "stop-loss" limits.

24.5.1 Credit control and the application of credit limits

The risk management department is usually responsible for allocating credit limits to various internal and external entities, monitoring that these credit limits are not exceeded without authorisation, and perhaps authorising temporary extensions to these limits. Credit limits are, in turn, affected by regulatory requirements derived from Basel II and (in the EEA) the Capital Adequacy Directive, which were first examined in Chapter 8.

Basel II states that the minimum capital ration is 8%. The practical affect of this regulation is that if, for example, a dealer is given a trading limit for his or her trading book of GBP 10 000 000, then this means that 8% of that 10 million (GBP 800 000) represents the firm's own capital. So if the firm has total capital of GBP 80 000 000, then the sum of all the limits granted cannot exceed GBP 1 billion.

Different firms will have different credit policies, but typically firms grant credit limits to the following entities:

• Internal departments and trading books
• Securities issuers
• Market counterparties and clients
• Countries where counterparties, clients and issuers are incorporated or resident
• Parent companies of counterparties, clients.

These different types of limits will be examined individually in the individual subsections of this section; but first of all it should be noted that a limit can be applied and measured in a number of ways, including:

• *Limits that are based on current mark-to-market value*: If a trade or position has a mark-to-market value (including accrued interest if applicable) of GBP 100 000, then a limit of GBP 100 000 has been used.
• *Limits that are based on mark-to-market exposure less collateral placed*: If a trade or position has a cost of GBP 100 000 but a current market value of GBP 90 000, then only GBP 10 000 (the expected loss) contributes to the limit. If, however, the party to the trade has supplied collateral worth GBP 5000; then the limit utilisation is reduced by the collateral value, so it becomes GBP 5000.
• *Limits that are based on the Value-at-Risk of the entity concerned*: Value-at-Risk is examined in section 24.6.
• *Stop-loss limits*: If the firm purchased a position for GBP 100 000 and has a stop-loss limit of 10%, then as soon as the position falls to GBP 90 000 it must be sold to stop the loss. This is a simplistic application of a stop-loss limit; a more realistic example would be as follows:
  – The firm purchases the position for 100 000 and the stop-loss limit is 10%.
  – If after trade date the value of the position rises to 120 000 and then starts to fall, the stop-loss limit is measured against the highest market value it has achieved.
  – Therefore, if the value falls by 12 000 (10% of 120 000), then it must be sold.

Department and book limits

Investment firms use books or portfolios to hold their positions. Figure 24.1 shows a typical "book hierarchy".

Note that the Equities Dealing Division has a total limit of GBP 500 000. There are two sections within the division, UK Equities and French Equities, both of which have individual limits of GBP 300 000. Obviously both sections cannot each use their entire limit, or else they would exceed the overall limit for the division. It is up to John Green, the head of the division, to arbitrate between his managers if they both wish to use their individual limits to the full. The same is true further down the tree; the four subsections of UK Equities have individual limits that exceed the limit for the section as a whole, and the section manager may need to arbitrate between her dealers.

Department and book limits are usually measured against the mark-to-market value of the portfolios. As well as an overall limit for each book, some firms may also issue additional limits based on criteria such as:

• A maximum limit for the value of total short positions
• A maximum limit for the value of total long positions
• Stop-loss limits for the individual instruments in the book
• Quality-based limits and restrictions – for example, for a bond portfolio there may be separate limits based on issuer credit ratings (refer to section 3.4.2).
• Concentration limits – for example, no individual security position can exceed x% of the total value of the book

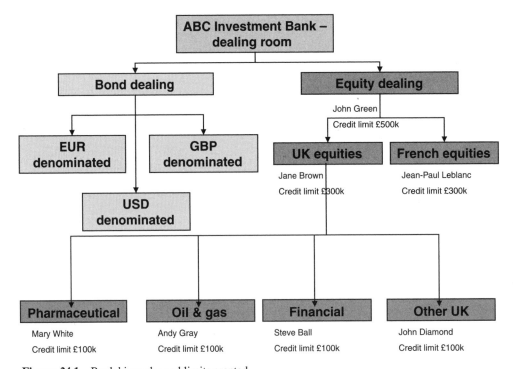

Figure 24.1   Book hierarchy and limits granted

- Sector limits – for example, the value of pharmaceutical stocks may not exceed x% of a particular limit, banking sector y%, etc.

Issuer limits

In Figure 24.1, it is possible that several trading books trade securities issued by the same issuer. For example, GlaxoSmithKline plc's shares may be traded in the pharmaceuticals book, and its bonds may be traded in a number of different books depending on the issue currency. Many firms would apply an issuer limit to ensure that its total exposure to securities of all kinds issued by GlaxoSmithKline plc across all books was not greater than a pre-defined limit.

Counterparty and client limits

The same trading party may be a trading party for a number of different trade types in a number of different instruments. For example, Institutional Investor A may be a bond trading party, equity trading party, FX trading party, swap trading party, stock lending and repo counterparty, etc. The firm may wish to grant an absolute limit to the exposure that we are prepared to allow for Institutional Investor A, and additional limits for each business type. Counterparty limits are usually based on mark-to-market exposure less collateral placed, but not all firms will set up limits in the same way.

Country limits

Security issuers, trading parties and settlement agents must all be residents of a particular country, and some firms will wish to apply country limits to control and monitor the total exposure that the firm is willing to have to a particular country.

Parent limits and large exposures

An individual corporation in the financial sector could have (either directly or through subsidiaries) all of the following roles at the same time in relation to the firm that is managing limits:

- It is a securities issuer
- It is a trading party
- It is a settlement agent or payment bank.

Parent limits attempt to monitor the total exposure that the firm has to this type of complex organisation. European regulators require each firm to monitor its large exposures and to submit a quarterly return describing such exposures.

Software used to manage limits

There are a number of packaged applications designed to manage credit limits. The typical functions of such applications include:

- Limit type definition
- Limit basis definition

- Conglomerate ownership structure definition
- Real-time collection of trade data and current market prices from front-office systems to update limit utilisation records
- Ability to monitor trades pre-execution for potential limit breaches
- Real-time advice of limit breaches delivered to credit risk staff for them to take action
- Facilities for credit management to authorise temporary limit breaches
- Calculation of Value-at-Risk – refer to section 24.6.

If such an application is deployed, then many of the firm's other systems will require real-time interfaces with that application.

24.6   AN INTRODUCTION TO VALUE-AT-RISK (VAR)

24.6.1   Overview of VaR

Value-at-Risk (VaR) is an *estimate* – not a precise measurement – of how the market value of an asset or of a portfolio of assets is likely to decrease over a certain time period (usually over one day or 10 days) under usual conditions. It was initially used by securities firms but was widely adopted by banks and corporates after 1994 when JP Morgan offered its RiskMetrics™ VaR measurement service over the internet in 1994. Firms that want to use the Basel Committee's Advanced Measurement Approach (see "Basel II capital calculations for operational risk", page 62, Chapter 8 to calculating their capital ratio are required to use the VaR technique.

A VaR statement is commonly expressed in the following way:

Our 20-day VaR is $4 000 000 with a 95% confidence level.

This means that the maximum that this firm would expect to lose over a 20-day period under "normal" market conditions is $4 000 000. However, they are only 95% confident of this estimate, which means that there is a 5% chance (one day out of the 20) that they could lose more than $4 000 000.

Normality in this context is a statistical concept and its importance varies according the VaR calculation methodology being used. Essentially VaR measures the **volatility** of a company's assets, so the greater the volatility the higher the probability of loss.

24.6.2   The VaR calculation

The steps to setting up an application to perform a VaR calculation are as follows:

1. *Determine the time horizons to use*: Traders are often interested in calculating the amount they may lose in a single day. Basel II requires a 10-day horizon.
2. *Select the degree of certainty required*: Basel II requires 99%.
3. *Create a probability distribution*: There are several methods; the simplest depends upon collecting a history of price changes for the portfolio for the time horizon.
4. *Gather the position data into a centralised database*: Static data, position and price information for all the different instruments (which may be held and processed in a number of different business applications) must be gathered together in a single normalised database so that the calculation may be performed. Accurate static data is vital in this context; in particular quality of the instrument associations data (described in section 10.4.4) can have a considerable affect on the accuracy of the VaR prediction.

5. *Make correlation assumptions*: VaR requires that the user decides which exposures are allowed to offset each other and by how much. For example, are prices of physical commodities correlated to inflation rates; are crude oil prices correlated to natural gas prices, and to what degree?

6. *Decide on the statistical model*: There are three to choose from:

   • *Historical simulation method*: This method assumes that asset returns in the future will have the same distribution as they had in the past (historical market data). It therefore uses actual historical data which means that rare events and crashes can be included in the results. It is the simplest and most transparent methodology.

   • *Correlation method*: This method (also known as the variance–covariance method) assumes that risk factor returns are always (jointly) normally distributed and that the change in portfolio value is linearly dependent on all risk factor returns.

   • *Monte Carlo simulation method*: Future asset returns are more or less randomly simulated using volatility and correlation estimates chosen by the risk manager. Monte Carlo simulation is often used to compute VaR for portfolios containing instruments such as options that have non-linear returns. Because the computational effort required is non-trivial, it is less often used for simpler portfolios.

24.6.3   Benefits, disadvantages and risks of using VaR

Benefits

• It provides a statistical probability of potential loss.
• It can make an assessment of the correlation between different assets.
• It translates all risks in a portfolio into a common standard – that of potential loss, allowing the quantification of firm-wide, cross-product exposures.

Disadvantages

• It does not account for liquidity risk.
• It is dependent on good historical price data. For this reason, it is most useful for financial instruments that have accurate and comprehensive records of market values for all instruments.

Risks

VaR has been developed as a means of predicting, or anticipating, future events. This is an imperfect process and the models can break down if the assumptions that they are based upon are violated. The risk of this happening is called **model risk** – the risk that models are applied to tasks for which they are inappropriate or are otherwise implemented incorrectly. For example, a firm is expanding operations into Asian emerging markets. It fails to modify its pricing models to reflect the lack of liquidity in these markets and underestimates the cost of hedging its positions.

An important aspect in the application of complex models is to understand the assumptions and test their accuracy as far as possible. This is achieved by performing back testing and stress testing.

Back testing is the practice of comparing the actual daily trading results to the predicted VaR figure. It is a test of reliability of the VaR methodology and ensures that the approach is of sufficient quality. It is usually performed on a daily basis by the risk management department and if the differences between reality and estimation are found to be unacceptable the VaR model must be revised. Back testing of course assumes that what happens in the past will happen in the future, and this assumption itself can create risks for the model.

Stress testing means testing the model against "extreme" market conditions. It can be thought of as capturing and considering particular risks that may, or may not, have been captured by the VaR calculation. Stress tests are not designed to generate worst case results. Stress testing is normally performed by the risk management department and is designed to improve the appreciation of market risk. The results can be fed back into the VaR model to improve it.

Stress testing scenarios can be constructed in either an ad hoc manner or a systematised manner. If the firm is concerned about the effect of an inverted yield curve or a breakdown in a specific correlation, an ad hoc scenario can be constructed specifically to assess that eventuality. Alternatively, firms may specify certain fixed scenarios (defined in terms of per cent changes in applicable risk factors) and then perform periodic stress testing with those scenarios. In this manner, a firm might present stress test results in its daily risk report.

Part Two

Good IT Practice in the
Investment Industry

25
The Role of the IT Department in Daily Operations

25.1 INTRODUCTION

The information technology department of an investment firm has two primary responsibilities:

- *Managing "business as usual" activities*: These activities include:
  - Ensuring that applications are stable
  - Ensuring that applications can cope with normal business volumes
  - Documenting deficiencies, fixing them and devising and documenting workrounds
  - Ensuring appropriate data security
  - Ensuring that system development keeps pace with user requirements
  - Ensuring that systems integrate effectively
  - Minimising manual intervention
  - Dealing with data integrity issues appropriately
- *Managing business change*: These activities include:
  - Aligning the IT strategy with business strategy
  - Aligning delivered solutions with strategic business drivers
  - Managing and monitoring the risks of introducing change
  - Providing visibility of risk to stakeholders.

The department needs to manage these activities in such a way that it minimises operational risk. In Chapter 8 we saw the seven operational risk events that had been defined by Basel II:

- *Internal fraud*: Misappropriation of assets, tax evasion, intentional mismarking of positions, bribery
- *External fraud*: Theft of information, hacking damage, third-party theft and forgery
- *Employment practices and workplace safety*: Discrimination, workers' compensation, employee health and safety
- *Clients, products and business practice*: Market manipulation, antitrust, improper trade, product defects, fiduciary breaches, account churning
- *Damage to physical assets*: Natural disasters, terrorism, vandalism
- *Business disruption and systems failures*: Utility disruptions, software failures, hardware failures
- *Execution, delivery and process management*: Data entry errors, accounting errors, failed mandatory reporting, negligent loss of client assets.

IT managers also need to be aware that major problems of the types described by the Basel Committee are often reported by the trade press, national press and television, which can lead to another type of risk – reputational risk.

25.2   USER SUPPORT AND HELPDESK MANAGEMENT

As part of its "business as usual" activity the department will normally need to set up a **helpdesk** to handle requests for assistance from its users. In a large organisation these requests will cover a very wide range of topics, which may be divided into the following categories:

- Planned administrative activities, such as:
  - Provide a new user with a PC and/or appropriate software to run on that PC and/or usernames and passwords to run software applications
  - Move one or more PCs or servers or other hardware items within the office
  - Upgrade an item of hardware or software at an agreed date in the future
- Unplanned emergency activities, such as:
  - An item of hardware or an application is not performing correctly and needs to be fixed to enable the user to continue normal daily operations
  - An item of hardware or software has failed in the recent past and action needs to be taken to recover the problems that were created.

Such requests are often referred to as **issues**. The role of the helpdesk is therefore

1. To receive issues from users
2. To prioritise them
3. To pass them to the appropriate individuals for action
4. To monitor whether the issue has been actioned to the satisfaction of the requestor, and:
   - If they have, to close the issues
   - If they have not, to escalate them to management
5. To provide a database of "Frequently Asked Questions" that can be used by helpdesk staff in the future to deal with common queries
6. To provide statistical reports to management about the numbers of issues, and the severity of issues that are recorded:
   - By different business units
   - For different applications.

25.2.1   Recording and actioning issues

In many firms, issues are now recorded directly into a helpdesk management system by the users affected. Such systems have business rules that allow for the automatic logging of issues by the user concerned, and also:

- Provide a predefined series of issue types, priority codes, applications and environments for the reporting user to select from
- Based on the input into these predefined lists, automatically assign the problem to the correct individual or section
- Provide facilities for the section dealing with the issue to respond to the requestor by automated email when the issue has been actioned
- Provide facilities for the responder to provide details of the time spent dealing with a particular problem
- Provide facilities for issues of a particular type to follow a particular workflow pattern. For example, an issue that requires a software enhancement needs to be directed to:
  - An analyst to decide what the software change needs to be, then
  - A developer to make the change, then

– A test analyst to test the change, then
– The user who reported the issue to sign it off.

Figure 25.1 shows an example of an issue that has been entered into a helpdesk management system by a user. In this case, the item was entered into the JIRA system developed by Atlassian Software Systems Pty Ltd and is reproduced with Atlassian's permission.

As soon as the user makes the entry in the helpdesk system the assignee will receive an email informing him of the new issue. Depending on the nature of the issue, the assignee will take one or more of the following actions:

1. Action it immediately
2. Diarise it for action at a later date
3. Respond to the user with requests for clarification
4. Delegate it to another individual
5. Provide an estimate for the effort required to handle the issue
6. Split the issue into two or more issues, or create subissues
7. Attach further documents to the issue.

The assignee records each action taken in the helpdesk system, and each time he makes an entry an email is automatically generated to the requestor informing him of the current state of the issue.

Note that in the example, the assignee is required to take two actions:

• To stop the problem occurring again
• To deal with the knock-on effects of the problem on 29 October – there are 3500 unwanted duplicate transactions in the settlement system that need to be removed before the close of business on 30 October.

The issue is therefore reporting two problems, both of which need to be addressed urgently. For this reason, it may be a good idea to split the issue into two issues, and delegate the handling of one of them to another individual.

If this problem was caused by a software or hardware fault, then the remedy may be a code change. If so, then the code needs to be changed, then tested, and finally released before the problem can be said to be resolved. Therefore, this issue may be assigned to several individuals during its lifecycle.

The final assignee (the person responsible for release) will then reassign it to the requestor, who will be notified by email. If the requestor is satisfied with the solution, he will close the issue; if he is not satisfied then he will note the reasons on the face of the issue report, and reassign it to the original assignee.

25.2.2   Helpdesk management

An effectively managed helpdesk is a prerequisite for minimising operational risk. If the helpdesk is being established for the first time, then the following information needs to be collated. This type of information is often known as an **infrastructure catalogue**, and includes full details of all the:

• Users that the desk supports. Key details include:
  – Name, department, telephone number, email address and physical location
  – Normal working hours and working days

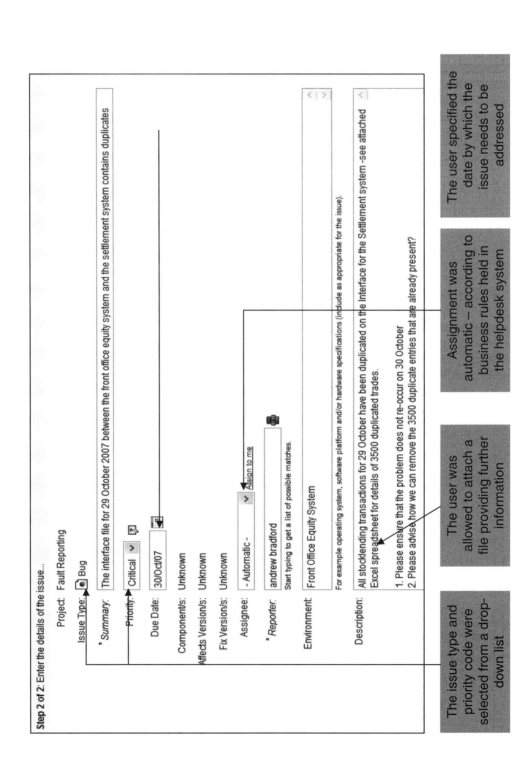

Figure 25.1 Entry of an issue in a helpdesk system. Reproduced by permission of Atlassian Software Systems Pty Ltd.

- Applications that the desk supports. Key details include:
  - Name of application
  - Details of its role in the business
  - Name and full contact details of the organisation that is responsible for supporting it. Note that this may be the firm's IT department, or an external vendor. If it is an external vendor, then full details of any **service level agreements** need to be available to the helpdesk.
  - Technical details – is it a PC application such as Word or Excel, or is it a web-based application that does not require installation in a user PC, or is it a client–server application employing a database?
  - If it is a client–server application, what database is used, and what specific servers does it run on?
  - Any requirements for specific version numbers for database and operating system software
  - Hours during the day and days of the week on which there is expected to be activity. If there is a great deal of night-time activity in this application, then the desk will need to hold out of hours contact details, and perhaps rotas for support staff who may need to be contacted at home.
  - An assessment as to how critical the loss of this application for an extended period would be to the business
- Hardware that the desk supports. Key details include:
  - Locations of all servers and routers
  - Whether they are used for production, testing or disaster recovery
  - Which applications are running on each server.

Once the infrastructure catalogue has been built up, IT management needs to decide:

- Which applications are "critical" to the business
- Which applications need to be supported "around the clock" on normal working days and which need to be supported for shorter periods
- Which applications need to be routinely supported at weekends and on public holidays
- If round the clock support is required, then what is the best way to achieve it? The following models are commonly used.
  - "*Follow the sun*": This model is widely used by firms that have operations in more than one time zone, and users accessing the same applications and servers from different countries. During normal European working hours support for all users worldwide is provided from a European location. When Europe closes, support moves to a North American support centre, and when North America closes, support is handled by an Asian support centre.
  - *Extended working hours*: This model is widely used when a firm is doing business in a single time zone, but is using applications that are working throughout the day and night. A singe helpdesk works in shifts. One shift coincides with normal working hours for the majority of the users, and is more heavily manned than the other shift, which only deal with emergency calls.
  - *Partial outsourcing*: If the number of out of hours calls is expected to be very few in number but may be critical, then overnight manning of the helpdesk could be outsourced to a third party specialist firm. Outsourcing is examined in more detail in Chapter 27.

25.2.3 Service level agreements

The role of the helpdesk in supporting its users may be formally expressed in a service level agreement (SLA). An SLA is that part of a service contract in which a certain level of service is agreed upon. Level of service in this context refers to both the quality of the service and the time deadlines for performing the service. It may also specify penalties to be paid by either party if the level of service provided fails to reach the minimum standards in the agreement for an extended period of time.

The SLA is a fundamental tool from the perspective of both the supplier and the recipient in provision of a service. The quality of the service level agreement is a critical matter as it defines the relationship between all concerned parties.

The SLA itself must be of sufficient detail and scope in relation to the service being offered and the scale thereof.

Typical SLA sections are as follows:

- Introduction (parties, signatures, service description)
- Scope of work (service hours, support)
- Performance
- Tracking and reporting (content, frequency)
- Problem management (change procedures, escalation)
- Penalties and compensation payable when the actual service level falls below the agreed level
- Customer duties and responsibilities
- Warranties and remedies
- Security
- Intellectual property rights and confidential information
- Legal compliance and resolution of disputes
- Termination and signatures.

An SLA is a contract between the customer and the service provider. Internal SLAs are agreements set out among two groups within the same organisation while external SLAs involve external parties. Some securities companies provide a service to an external customer where they are assessed on their compliance to the SLA while other securities companies might outsource some of their non-essential business to an external vendor who is able to provide an agreed service.

Even if there is no formal (internal) SLA between the helpdesk and its customer business units, then the work of the helpdesk may be impacted by other external SLAs between the business units and the software vendors and outsourced service providers that supply the firm.

25.3 DATA SECURITY, DATA RETENTION, DATA PROTECTION AND INTELLECTUAL PROPERTY

25.3.1 Data security

The IT department is responsible for the safe storage of the firm's data. Failure to do so may result in operational risk events such as internal fraud, external fraud and market manipulation. Market manipulation includes the offences of insider dealing and market abuse that were examined in Chapter 8.

ISO 17799 the international standard for information security

ISO 17799 is the de facto standard for the information security code of practice. It includes a number of sections, covering a wide range of security issues. In terms of legislation, the standard covers:

- Data protection and privacy of personal information
- Protection of organisational records
- Intellectual property rights.

In terms of defining common practice, the standard covers:

- Use of an information security policy document
- Allocation of information security responsibilities
- Information security awareness, training and education
- Correct processing in applications
- Technical vulnerability management
- Business continuity management
- Management of information security incidents and improvements.

The standard suggests that security requirements should be established through:

- Risk assessment
- Legal and regulatory contractual obligations
- Internal principles (objectives and requirements).

The standard also advises that a simple management model should be used consisting of "plan-do-check-act" (PDCA):

> PLAN: Establish the objectives and processes necessary to deliver results in accordance with the specifications
> DO: Implement the processes
> CHECK: Monitor and evaluate the processes and results against objectives and specifications and report the outcome
> ACT: Apply actions to the outcome for necessary improvement. This means reviewing all steps (Plan, Do, Check, Act) and modifying the process to improve it before its next implementation.

Chinese walls, insider dealing and market abuse

In Chapter 7 we learned that an investment bank will normally have a corporate finance department that is working with clients that may be issuing securities, attempting to acquire other companies or performing some corporate activity that may be price sensitive, and in Chapter 8 we examined the specific offences of insider dealing and market abuse. The corporate finance department that is advising the issuer cannot help but acquire inside information as part of its normal daily operations. If this information were to be made known to the dealing desks that buy and sell securities before it were made known to the general public, then it could very well result in insider dealing and/or market abuse. Both of these are offences in the United Kingdom, and similar legislation is enacted in many other jurisdictions.

Most securities firms will therefore need to implement **Chinese walls** between the relevant departments. Chinese walls are information barriers implemented within firms to separate and isolate people who make investment decisions from people who are privy to undisclosed material information which may influence those decisions.

In general, all firms are required to develop, implement and enforce reasonable policies and procedures to safeguard insider information, and to ensure no improper trading occurs. Although specific procedures are not mandated, adopted practices must be formalised in writing and must be appropriate and sufficient. Procedures should address the following areas: education of employees, containment of insider information, restriction of transactions and trading surveillance.

Depending on the policies that the firm has adopted, the role of the IT department in developing and implementing these policies is likely to include:

- Identifying the particular business applications where unauthorised or unrestricted access by individuals or other business applications would be likely to breach the wall
- Ensuring that all these applications utilise appropriate user access controls (usernames, passwords, etc.)
- Ensuring that user access to these systems is correctly monitored, and that the privileges that are granted to particular groups of users (for example, which accounts they can view from a particular enquiry) do not breach the principles of the Chinese wall.

25.3.2 Data retention

The firm will find itself subject to many different legal requirements concerning the preservation and retention of data. Most (but by no means all) legal requirements demand that records be retained for five years from the date of the event that created them. There are, however, exceptions to this. For example, some correspondence with private individuals about their pension arrangements has to be kept indefinitely and information about client categorisation under the MiFID regulations has to be kept for five years "after the firm ceases to carry on business with or for that client".

The firm's senior management is responsible for implementing data retention policies. Data in this context includes written materials, recordings of telephone conversations, microfiches, and electronic records of orders received and executed. Such electronic records include SWIFT messages, FIX protocol messages, files transferred by FTP and similar techniques and emails. It is the responsibility of the IT department to organise the safe storage of such records.

Records must be retained for the statutory period in a form that enables them to be accessed at any time before the end of that period. Because the statutory retention periods are very long, IT departments need to consider the problems that can be created by the introduction of new technologies. For example:

- Certain records may have, at some time in the past, been moved to offline storage in a form that is no longer widely used. For example, at the time when the record was first created, tape cartridges may have been a popular offline storage device, but most modern equipment does not read most of the tape cartridges that were in use in the early 1990s.
- Certain records are being held online, in a business application that is to be replaced. It is not practical to migrate every historic record from the old system to the new one because of the sheer number of records the old system holds. Once the new system is implemented there will no longer be any user access to the old system. If that is the case, then data may have to be extracted from the old system and stored, say, in a specially created **SQL** database in order that the firm's data retention policies and legal requirements may be complied with.

There are now many companies that offer outsourced services connected with paper and electronic records management and consultancy services to help firms develop "compliant records management" policies. Many of the practical issues around records management are linked to the issues involved in developing a business continuity plan. Business continuity planning is covered in section 25.5.

25.3.3   Data protection

All countries in the EEA have data protection legislation. In the United Kingdom, the relevant Act is the **Data Protection Act 1998.** This act details how personal data should be managed by any kind of organisation (government, corporate, charity, etc.) to protect its integrity and to protect the rights of the persons concerned.

Any firm holding and processing personal data must appoint a **data controller** who takes responsibility for compliance with the Data Protection Act; the data controller must be registered with the **Information Commissioner.**

Principles of the Act

The Data Protection Act lays down eight principles of good data protection practice. It states that personal data shall:

- be processed fairly and lawfully;
- be obtained for one or more specified and lawful purposes, and shall not be further processed in any manner that is incompatible with those purposes;
- be adequate, relevant and not excessive in relation to the purpose or purposes for which it is processed;
- be accurate and, where necessary, kept up-to-date;
- not be kept for longer than is necessary for its purpose or purposes;
- be processed in accordance with the rights of the subject under the Act;
- be safeguarded by the use of appropriate technical and organisational measures to prevent unauthorised or unlawful processing of personal data, and against accidental loss or destruction of, or damage to, the personal data;
- not be transferred to a country or territory outside the European Economic Area (EEA), unless that country or territory ensures an adequate level of protection in relation to the processing of personal data.

Penalties for non-compliance with the Data Protection Act

The Act states that:

(1) An individual who suffers damage by reason of any contravention by a data controller of any of the requirements of this Act is entitled to compensation from the data controller for that damage.
(2) An individual who suffers distress by reason of any contravention by a data controller of any of the requirements of this Act is entitled to compensation from the data controller for that distress if–
   (a) The individual also suffers damage by reason of the contravention, or
   (b) The contravention relates to the processing of personal data for the special purposes.

(3) In proceedings brought against a person by virtue of this section it is a defence to prove that he had taken such care as in all the circumstances was reasonably required to comply with the requirement concerned.

But in addition to the compensation that a data owner may claim under the provisions of the Act itself, companies that are regulated by the FSA may face additional sanctions, as demonstrated by the following case study.

On 14 February 2007 the Financial Services Authority (FSA) fined Nationwide Building Society (Nationwide) £980 000 for failing to have effective systems and controls to manage its information security risks. The failings came to light following the theft of a laptop from a Nationwide employee's home in 2006.

During its investigation, the FSA found that the building society did not have adequate information security procedures and controls in place, potentially exposing its customers to an increased risk of financial crime.

The FSA also discovered that Nationwide was not aware that the laptop contained confidential customer information and did not start an investigation until three weeks after the theft.

In a press release, the FSA said "Nationwide is the UK's largest building society and holds confidential information for over 11 million customers. Nationwide's customers were entitled to rely upon it to take reasonable steps to make sure their personal information was secure."

"Firms' internal controls are fundamental in ensuring customers' details remain as secure as they can be and, as technology evolves, firms must keep their systems and controls up-to-date to prevent lapses in security. The FSA took swift enforcement action in this case to send a clear, strong message to all firms about the importance of information security."

By agreeing to settle at an early stage of the FSA's investigation Nationwide qualified for a 30% discount under the FSA's executive settlement procedures – without the discount the fine would have been £1.4 million.

25.3.4 An IT perspective on the legal aspects of data management

It is useful within firms for information to be classified internally so that it is clear how the information needs to be protected, managed and destroyed. Typical classifications are generally accessible, internal use only, confidential and secret. Generally, the accessibility of information by users and systems should be safeguarded so that data is only disclosed on a need to know basis.

The retention of data is an issue that the securities industry is currently trying to tackle. While the Data Protection Act states that customer information should not be retained for longer than necessary, money laundering or anti-terrorism regulation might require that this information is stored for a significant length of time. In the maintenance of systems, the decision not to retain data or to delete it might lead to prosecutions, fines or reputation risk. The risk that data retention may be unmanageable because of technology changes is a real one.

Unfortunately, the potential data that can be requested for recall by authorities or regulators is also increasing in scope and can include emails, chat conversations, voice message and phone call records and recordings.

25.3.5   Intellectual property rights management

Intellectual property rights (IPR) are rights to intangible property that is the product of the human intellect. Intellectual property may be protected by copyright, trademark or patent.

Computer software is normally, but not exclusively, protected by copyright. The holder of intellectual property rights is usually the person or persons who developed the product or the organisation that funded it.

Any investment firm that is using any kind of packaged software will usually find that the vendor retains the IPR to the software. In the contract, there is usually an obligation on the firm (as the customer) to ensure that the vendor's rights are maintained, and that confidentiality clauses are not breached.

This can become an issue if the firm wishes to outsource or offshore an activity that is dependent on the vendor's package. The firm may need to ask the express permission of the vendor, or to sign a further agreement that protects the vendor's interest.

The IPR for software that the firm developed itself, or commissioned an external vendor to produce explicitly for them, will normally belong to the firm itself. The application that has been created is the firm's IPR, and this IPR may provide the firm with a competitive advantage.

In order to protect the IPR of both the firm itself and its package, vendors include a confidentiality clause in their employment contracts and contracts with external IT consultants. These contracts oblige the employee or consultant to keep IPR confidential. The clause that deals with these matters usually requests that such information be kept confidential *indefinitely* – not just for the period of the employment or consultancy assignment.

25.4   CHANGE MANAGEMENT

Change management or **change control procedures** are processes designed to prevent software or hardware objects from being amended without auditability and review of the impact by all interested parties. There are two aspects to change management; the use of **version control systems** to control access to items that need to be changed and the development of procedures that ensure that only authorised changes are made to software or hardware items.

25.4.1   Symptoms of inadequate change control management

Poor change control creates operational risk. In particular, they can create the following operational risk events as defined by Basel II:

> Product defects, software failures, hardware failures, accounting errors, failed mandatory reporting, negligent loss of client assets.

The symptoms of poor change control include:

- The latest version of source code cannot be found.
- A difficult defect that was fixed at great expense suddenly reappears.
- A developed and tested feature is mysteriously missing.
- A fully tested program suddenly does not work.
- The wrong version of the code was deployed.
- The wrong version of the code was tested.
- There is no traceability between the software requirements, documentation and code.
- Programmers are working on the wrong version of the code.

- The wrong versions of the configuration items are being baselined.
- No one knows which modules comprise the software system delivered to the customer.

25.4.2 Version control systems

Version control systems (**VCS**) are software applications that manage multiple revisions of the same unit of information. In particular, they:

1. Prevent more than one developer working on a change to a program or other software object at the same time
2. Ensure that when a program or other object is selected for modification, there is an audit trail of who is modifying it
3. Ensure that the modifications are being made to the right version of the program
4. In the event that the wrong version of an object is released, these applications provide the ability to "roll back" to a prior version.

There are at least 50 different packaged systems that perform version control. Some of them are open source software that may be downloaded for no cash payment, and some are proprietary packages. Some are suitable for a wide variety of operating systems, while others are deigned for specific operating systems such as MS Windows or UNIX.

It is not only source code that may be protected by a version control system. Version control may be applied to user and technical documentation, key static data files and virtually any object within an application that needs to be protected.

A simplified view of how version control software applications work is shown by Figures 25.2 and 25.3.

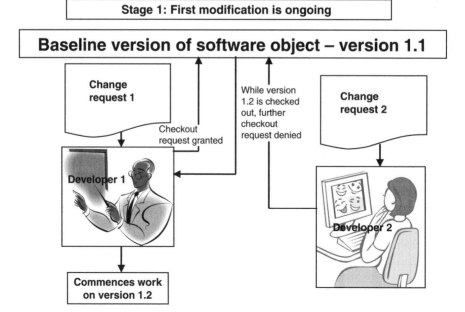

Figure 25.2 Version control software – stage 1

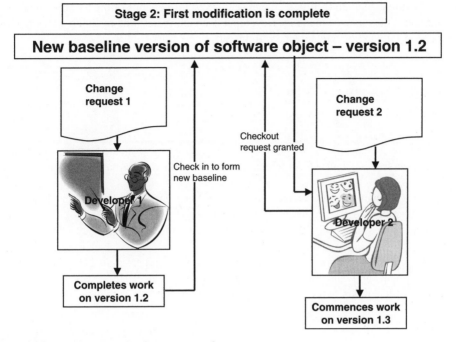

Figure 25.3 Version control software – stage 2

1. The VCS stores the current, latest version of the program (version 1.1 in this example) as the **baseline** version. All changes will be applied to this version so long as it remains the baseline version.
2. Developer 1 receives a change control request that requires amendment to this program. He requests the VCS to allow him to check it out, and starts work.
3. The VCS records the fact that Developer 1 is working on this object.
4. Developer 2 then receives a change request that applies to the same unit. She attempts to check the unit out, but permission is denied as Developer 1 has the record locked. She is left with two choices:
   • To wait until Developer 1 has completed his work before she can commence her work; or
   • To make a branching request to the VCS. A set of files under version control may be branched or forked at a point in time so that, from that time forward, two copies of those files may be developed at different speeds or in different ways independently of the other. Branching requests are usually only made when emergency fixes are needed, as versions that are branched will later on have to be merged. This may not be an easy process to control.
      Assuming that there was no branching request, the next steps are illustrated in Figure 25.3.
5. Developer 1 completes his work, and checks in the new version (version 1.2) which becomes the new baseline version.
6. Developer 2 is now free to checkout the baseline version and commence work on it. The version she is working on will become version 1.3. When she checks this version in it will become the new baseline.

VCS applications include facilities to regress to previous versions of the baseline in an emergency. Should the changes made by Developer 1 create issues when version 1.2 is released, then version 1.1 can be recreated and re-released if necessary.

25.4.3   Change control procedures

Change control procedures are business practices that are designed to:

- Allow changes to accepted work products to be proposed and evaluated, schedule and quality impact assessed, and approved or rejected for release into production systems in a controlled manner
- Provide a mechanism for management to accept and sign off changes that improve the product overall while rejecting those that degrade it
- Notify all parties materially affected by a proposed revision of the need to accept the new version
- Notify interested parties on the periphery of development regarding change proposals, their assessed impact and whether the changes were approved or rejected
- Facilitate efficient deployment of changes to environments where they are required.

Many firms hold periodic (often weekly in the case of large organisations with complex configurations) change control meetings to ensure that these aims are achieved. The participants will include representatives of all the business areas affected. Change control meetings may be guided by a change management policy. An example of such a policy might be as follows:

ABC Investment Bank plc – change control policy for client–server applications

1. Changes are normally deployed after the close of business on Tuesday evenings unless the nature of the change demands a different time.
2. As the bank's financial year end is 31 December, only emergency fixes will be released after the first Tuesday in December. This is to avoid destabilising the preparation of the bank's annual accounts.
3. No significant changes will be applied to critical systems in the last week of any accounting month. This is to avoid destabilising the preparation of the bank's monthly accounts.
4. No changes will be applied to critical systems in weeks when the key individuals concerned with the change are unavailable due to sickness, holiday or other absence.
5. No change will be released if there are any Grade A issues outstanding, and/or more than five Grade B errors outstanding.[1]

---

[1] Refer to Table 26.3 for an explanation of Grade A and Grade B issues.

25.5   BUSINESS CONTINUITY PLANNING

25.5.1   Introduction

Business continuity plans are concerned with ensuring that the firm is able to recover from an emergency such as utility disruptions, software failures and hardware failures – some of the key operational risk events defined in Basel II.

Disaster recovery is the process of regaining access to the data, hardware and software necessary to resume critical business operations after a natural or human-induced disaster. A disaster recovery plan (DRP) should also include plans for coping with the unexpected or sudden loss of key personnel. DRP is part of a larger process known as business continuity planning (BCP).

A "disaster" could be any one or more of the following kinds of events, ranked by increasing severity:

1. One or more of the applications that the firm uses to process its business is lost as a result of either a software or hardware failure. The failure is in one of the firm's own systems, and it is the only firm affected.
2. An external application on which this firm is dependent (such as one provided by an exchange or clearing house system or an information provider's system) is lost as a result of either a software or hardware failure. Other user firms with which the firm trades are also dependent on this application.
3. The firm is the victim of an event such as fire, flood, criminal or terrorist related activity, and has lost access to one of its key buildings. Other neighbouring businesses may also be affected. In locations such as the City of London or Downtown Manhattan, where there is a large concentration of investment firms, there is the likelihood that many of the firm's trading parties and critical suppliers may also be affected.

Since 9/11 much attention has been paid to the most severe event. But let us first look at the less dramatic events that are confined to the loss of an individual firm's applications.

25.5.2   Critical and non-critical systems and standby servers

In section 25.2.2 we examined the benefits of compiling an infrastructure catalogue. As part of this process, it is necessary to make an assessment as to how critical the loss of this application for an extended period would be to the business. Another part of the infrastructure catalogue identifies which servers and other hardware items are concerned with the operation of each application.

Assuming that the applications concerned are client–server applications, then any application that is defined as critical to the running of the business needs to have a standby or DR server allocated to it as well as a production server. In the event that the production server or a software product running on that server ceases to function, then the running of the application will switch from the production server to the **standby server** (also known as the DR server).

The standby server needs to be located at a separate physical location to the production server, so that in the event of a major disaster that restricts access to the building that houses the production server the firm can still gain access to the location of the standby server. Sufficient bandwidth needs to be provided between the two locations so that data may be accessed and entered on the standby server.

Next, the firm needs to determine what level of access it needs to the standby server. The terminology is **cold standby**, **warm standby** and **hot standby**, and these options offer increasing resilience in the case of failure, but of course as resilience increases so does the cost of the service.

Cold standby

A cold standby server is a spare server that is configured similarly to the primary server and is running the same version of the operating system, database and application software, with all the same service packs applied. If the primary server suffers a failure, then the SQL database is restored to the secondary server from the primary's backup files. The backup files may not be totally up to date, for example they may have been made the previous evening, so there may be a large amount of data that needs to be re-entered.

This methodology provides a reliable means to recover the database with minimal loss although there will still be a significant number of manual processes that must be followed in order to get back up and running again, giving a typical downtime of between two hours and one day (a lot depends upon what the client applications are written in, how the client applications connect to the database, how easy it is to switch them to another database name, how many clients are involved, etc.).

Warm standby

To set up recovery using a warm standby server it is necessary to implement a range of automated procedures to maintain same data on the two servers. Typically this involves some form of automatic synchronisation between the databases such as is provided by **log shipping**. Automated log shipping is included in the Enterprise edition of SQL Server.

Log shipping essentially consists of automating and integrating the process of backing up, copying and restoring the database from the primary server to the secondary server. This maintains the secondary server's database as an identical copy of the primary server's database apart from a small time latency of between five and 15 minutes.

While log shipping keeps the databases in synchronisation other procedures are needed for data (such as messages, logins, permissions, DTS packages, SQLServer Agent^{TM} jobs, server configurations, etc.) that are held outside of the database. With a warm standby server and log shipping the aim is to be able to get up and running again with a probable downtime of between 10 minutes and one hour depending upon how easy it is to change the client applications over to another server and how many clients there are.

Hot standby

Hot standby is an approach to maintaining system availability whereby all transactions are routinely written to the production server and the standby server simultaneously. The standby server is therefore ready to take over the processing load instantaneously, should there be any failure in the production system.

When the production server that was lost is up and running again it will need to be updated with the transactions that have only been processed by the standby server. This is usually automated by software programs designed to perform **database replication**.

25.5.3 The business continuity plan

The business continuity plan (BCP) is a plan developed to mitigate different disaster or worst case scenarios. The BCP will contain agreed workarounds and task lists for those supporting the application during a disaster. The goal of BCP processes is to ensure that IT services can be recovered within required, agreed and business sensitive timescales.

It is a comprehensive statement of consistent actions to be taken before, during and after a disaster. The plan should be documented and tested to ensure the continuity of operations and the availability of critical resources in the event of a disaster.

The primary objective of disaster recovery planning is to protect the organisation in the event that all (or part) of its operations and/or computer services are rendered unusable. Preparedness is the key. The planning process should minimise the disruption of operations and ensure some level of organisational stability and an orderly recovery after a disaster.

The steps involved in producing a BCP can be found in Figure 25.4.

Obtain senior management commitment

Management as a whole is responsible for coordinating the disaster recovery plan and ensuring its effectiveness within the organisation. Adequate time and resources must be committed to the development of an effective plan, and the implementation of the plan may require significant financial resources.

Form a planning committee

A planning committee should be appointed to oversee the development and implementation of the plan. The planning committee should include representatives from all functional areas

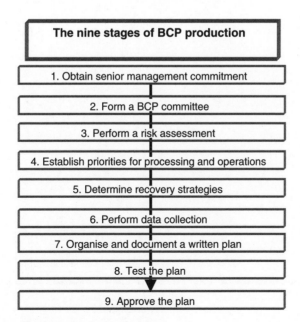

Figure 25.4 Stages of business continuity planning

of the organisation. Key committee members should include the operations manager and the IT manager. The committee also should define the scope of the plan.

Perform a risk assessment and *establish priorities for processing and operations*

The planning committee should prepare a risk analysis and business impact analysis that include a range of possible disasters, including natural, technical and human threats. The planning committee need to consider the likelihood of a range of possible events, the impact of those events on the business and the costs of mitigating them. This risk analysis might be presented in graphical form (see Figure 25.5).

This firm has mapped a number of applications and business services into a risk analysis matrix. Its BCP will therefore concentrate on the items in the top right-hand corner, where it considers that the likelihood of an event is high, and the business impact of that event is also high. It has therefore taken the decision that in the event of a serious disaster where many applications and services are affected, it may have to temporarily suspend its business on the Madrid, Johannesburg and New York Stock Exchanges and its dealings in derivatives. It is not, however, prepared to suspend its business on the London Stock Exchange, or to tolerate the loss of its Reuters services or its main settlement system. It considers that although the loss of its SWIFT connections and its LCH.Clearnet interfaces would be very serious, the likelihood of those events is very low.

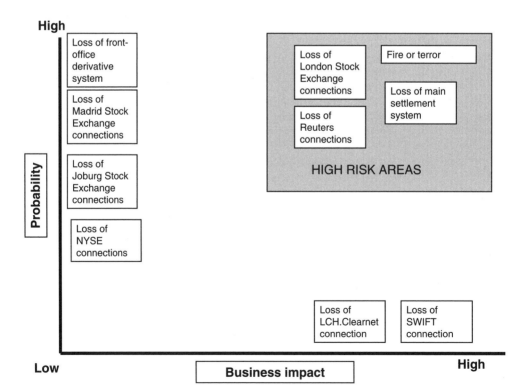

Figure 25.5 BCP risk analysis

Determine recovery strategies

The most practical alternatives for processing in case of a disaster should be researched and evaluated. It is important to consider all aspects of the organisation, such as:

- *Staff*: In the most serious disaster event, there is the possibility that staff members suffer serious, even fatal, personal injury, and procedures need to be put into place to cover this event. Additionally, staff members may be unable to reach either their normal place of work or the backup site.
- *Press relations*: In the event of a serious incident, there may be a high level of interest from press and broadcasters. Resources need to be allocated to deal with this.
- Regulators may take a keen interest in the recovery process, and again resources need to be made available to liaise with them.
- Insurers may bear many of the costs of the use of the DR service, and may wish to be involved to protect their interests.
- Business operations in general, including (*inter alia*) hardware, software, telecommunications facilities, end-user systems, data and physical files and other processing operations, may all need to be operated from a temporary disaster recovery site or sites. These may be provided by any one or more of the following models:
  - Having reciprocal agreements with other firms
  - Subscribing to the services of companies that offer dedicated DR service centres
  - Consortium arrangements
  - Acquiring a dedicated DR site that is private to this firm
  - Combinations of the above.

  When selecting the location of a DR site, bear in mind the following:

- If it is too close to the main site, then it could be overcome by the same factors that affect the main site.
- If it is a site provided by a specialist provider of DR facilities, then that vendor may have a number of clients in the same area as your firm. Is there a danger that they could be overwhelmed and unable to offer the contracted services?

Written agreements with suppliers for the specific recovery alternatives selected should be prepared, including the following special considerations:

- Contract duration
- Termination conditions
- Testing
- Costs
- Special security procedures
- Notification of systems changes
- Hours of operation
- Specific hardware and other equipment required for processing
- Personnel requirements
- Circumstances constituting an emergency
- Process to negotiate extension of service
- Guarantee of compatibility
- Availability
- Non-mainframe resource requirements

- Priorities
- Other contractual issues.

Perform data collection

Recommended data gathering materials and documentation include:

- Critical telephone numbers
- Communications inventory
- Distribution register
- Documentation inventory
- Forms inventory
- Insurance policy inventory
- Computer hardware inventory
- Computer software inventory
- Staff contact details list
- Vendor list
- Notification checklist
- Office supply inventory
- Off-site storage location inventory
- Software and data files backup/retention schedules
- Telephone inventory
- Temporary location specifications
- Other materials and documentation.

It is extremely helpful to develop pre-formatted forms to facilitate the data gathering process.

Organise and document a written plan

An outline of the plan's contents should be prepared to guide the development of the detailed procedures. Top management should review and approve the proposed plan. The outline can ultimately be used for the table of contents after final revision. Other benefits of this approach are that it:

- Helps to organise the detailed procedures
- Identifies all major steps before the writing begins
- Identifies redundant procedures that only need to be written once
- Provides a "road map" for developing the procedures.

A standard format should be developed to facilitate the writing of detailed procedures and the documentation of other information to be included in the plan. This will help ensure that the disaster plan follows a consistent format and allows for ongoing maintenance of the plan. Standardisation is especially important if more than one person is involved in writing the procedures.

The plan should be thoroughly developed, including all detailed procedures to be used before, during and after a disaster. It may not be practical to develop detailed procedures until backup alternatives have been defined.

The procedures should include methods for maintaining and updating the plan to reflect any significant internal, external or systems changes. The procedures should allow for a regular review of the plan by key personnel within the organisation.

The disaster recovery plan should be structured using a team approach. Specific responsibilities should be assigned to the appropriate team for each functional area of the company.

There should be teams responsible for administrative functions, facilities, logistics, user support, computer backup, restoration and other important areas in the organisation. The structure of the contingency organisation may not be the same as the existing organisation chart. The contingency organisation is usually divided into teams responsible for major functional areas such as:

- Staff liaison
- Press liaison
- Regulator liaison
- Administrative functions
- Facilities
- Logistics
- User support
- Computer backup
- Restoration
- Other important areas.

The management team is especially important because it coordinates the recovery process. The team should assess the disaster, activate the recovery plan and contact team managers. The management team also oversees documents and monitors the recovery process. Management team members should be the final decision-makers in setting priorities, policies and procedures.

Each team has specific responsibilities that must be completed to ensure successful execution of the plan. The teams should have an assigned manager and an alternate in case the team manager is not available. Other team members should also have specific assignments where possible.

Develop testing criteria and procedures

It is essential that the plan be thoroughly tested and evaluated on a regular basis (at least annually). Procedures to test the plan should be documented. The tests will provide the organisation with the assurance that all necessary steps are included in the plan. Other reasons for testing include:

- Determining the feasibility and compatibility of backup facilities and procedures
- Identifying areas in the plan that need modification
- Providing training to the team managers and team members
- Demonstrating the ability of the organisation to recover
- Providing motivation for maintaining and updating the disaster recovery plan.

Test the plan

After testing procedures have been completed, an initial test of the plan should be performed by conducting a structured walk-through test. The test will provide additional information regarding any further steps that may need to be included, changes in procedures that are not effective and other appropriate adjustments. The plan should be updated to correct any problems identified during the test. Initially, testing of the plan should be done in sections and after normal business hours to minimise disruption to the overall operations of the organisation.

Types of tests include:

- Checklist tests
- Simulation tests
- Parallel tests
- Full interruption tests.

Approve the plan

Once the disaster recovery plan has been written and tested, the plan should be approved by top management. It is top management's ultimate responsibility that the organisation has a documented and tested plan.

Management is responsible for:

- Establishing policies, procedures and responsibilities for comprehensive contingency planning
- Providing financial resources to implement the plan
- Reviewing and approving the contingency plan annually, documenting such reviews in writing
- Committing the necessary financial resources to make the plan work.

If the organisation receives information processing from service bureaux or other providers of outsourced services, management must also evaluate the adequacy of contingency plans for the supplier and ensure that the supplier's contingency plan is compatible with the firm's own service plan.

25.6   USE OF THE IT INFRASTRUCTURE LIBRARY IN MANAGING IT OPERATIONS

The **Information Technology Infrastructure Library** (**ITIL**) is a set of concepts and techniques that was developed by the United Kingdom government for managing IT infrastructure, development, and operations; and has now become a globally accepted standard for "best practice" in IT management. The examples of best practice that are included within ITIL may be used as a baseline for managing the activities described in Chapters 25, 26 and 27 of this book.

ITIL is published in a series of books which are available in both hard copy and electronic formats, each of which cover an IT management topic. The names ITIL^{TM} and IT Infrastructure Library^{TM} are registered trademarks of the United Kingdom's Office of Government Commerce (OGC). Each volume is designed to be extendable by IT companies. For example, Microsoft is free to add detail to the Service Transition book that is specific to the Windows^{TM} operating system or the MS SQLServer^{TM} database.

ITIL gives a detailed description of a number of important IT practices with comprehensive checklists, tasks and procedures that can be tailored to any IT organisation.

The current version of ITIL is version 3, released in 2007. It consists of five volumes:

- *Service Strategy*: Concerned with defining the set of services provided by the IT department that help achieve business objectives
- *Service Design*: Designing the services with utility and warranty objectives in mind
- *Service Transition*: Moving services into the live production environment
- *Service Operation*: Managing services on an ongoing basis to ensure their utility and warranty objectives are achieved
- *Continual Service Improvement*: Evaluating services and identifying ways to improve their utility and warranty in support of business objectives.

IT practitioners are able to study for the ITIL diploma, which offers a formal qualification in the use of these methodologies.

The Role of the IT Department in Managing Business Change

26.1 INTRODUCTION

The IT department frequently manages, or plays a significant role in, business change activities. These activities vary considerably in terms of the reason why the change is needed as well as the scope, complexity, timeframe and cost of the change. It is helpful to classify business change activities into the following categories, each category having very different characteristics:

- *Externally imposed, mandatory changes*: MiFID in 2007, Y2K in 1999 and European Monetary Union in 1998 are examples of major changes that were imposed in the investment industry by governments and regulators. The characteristics of changes of this type are that:
  - The individual firm *has to* take part. It cannot opt out.
  - There is usually a "drop-dead" date for completion of the change – e.g. 1 November 2007 for MiFID.
  - The changes need to be made by a large number of industry participants at the same time. This adds to risk, because there is a danger that, for example, our firm might be ready but a major counterparty or settlement agent may not be ready.
  - Within the individual firm there may be a large number of individual applications and/or business processes that require amendment or complete replacement. These types of changes rarely affect just a single application, and at the beginning of the change programme it may not be clear which applications are affected or to what extent.
  - Firms often have to base the detail of the changes on interpretation of complex legal documents, whose ramifications and consequences may be the subject of debate, or even initial confusion within the industry.
- *Externally driven changes*: The gradual replacement of the SWIFT MT message series by the MX message series (refer to section 11.1.3) is an example of a change that all SWIFT members will need to make over a period of time if they wish to continue to use SWIFT. However, externally driven changes differ from externally imposed changes in that:
  - The member firm may enjoy several years when it may use an old standard or a new one. For example, while there is a final "drop-dead" date when the MT series will be withdrawn, it will be many years after the MX messages were introduced to SWIFT members.
  - Like the imposed mandatory change, it does affect large numbers of industry participants, but the lack of a single drop-dead date for all of them reduces the inherent risk. However, an element of commercial risk is introduced. For example, if our firm is a settlement agent and it is not ready with its MX messages for several months or years after its competitors, then it may lose market share.
  - At the outset, it should be relatively easy to ascertain which applications will be affected, and how they will be affected.
  - The detail of the changes is usually published by the instigator in comprehensive technical documents that are relatively easy to understand.

- *Internally driven – business opportunities*: For example, the firm wishes to trade new instruments, or new transactions in existing instruments, or otherwise add to the range of services it provides to new clients or existing clients. The characteristics of this type of change may include:
  - Implementation of new applications and business processes to manage the new activities. For example, if the firm wished to trade credit default swaps for the first time then it might build or buy a new front-office system to do so, or it might decide to replace an existing front-office system that processes simpler forms of swaps but does not handle the newer types well.
  - Amendments to the other applications that the front-office systems interact with, and new interfaces to those systems from the new system.

  The business risks involved in this type of change include the following:
  - *Skills deficit*: At the time that the change is instigated, the firm concerned may not yet have staff with a detailed understanding of the new services. If large numbers of firms have taken the decision to provide these new services at the same time, then staff with the right skills may be hard to recruit. Skills deficits can affect both the timeliness and the quality of the end-product.
  - *Commercial risk of project over-run*: In business in general, the largest rewards usually go to the "early adopters", i.e. those firms that are in a position to supply new (to the market as a whole) services first. If such a project over-runs, then the potential customer base may have already been satisfied by competitors and the firm will not benefit from the growth in market share that it expected, which was the justification for the change in the first place.
- *Internally driven – process improvement*: The motivation for this type of change may be any or all of the following:
  - A general need to improve STP, reduce manual intervention and lower costs
  - A specific need to remove an existing problem that is creating operational risk. This problem may have been noticed internally, or by external auditors and/or regulators. If the external bodies have observed the problem then the firm may be under considerable pressure to act quickly.

The scope, complexity, cost and timescales of (and therefore the operational risk inherent in) changes of this sort will vary widely. At the lower end of the scale it might involve just a small number of simple changes to a single application; but at the other end of the scale it might involve the complete replacement of, for example, the main settlement system.

If the main settlement system does need to be replaced, then there are a number of ways of achieving this objective, each of them with their own risk profile. These are the possible options that the firm could adopt (that actual options may be different at the time), sorted by risk – highest risk first:

1. Replace the single settlement system for all business activities on a single day with a number of different settlement systems for different business types.
2. Replace the single settlement system for all business activities on a single day with a new single settlement system for all business types
3. Replace the single settlement system for all business activities over a period of time with a new single settlement system for all business types
4. Replace the single settlement system for all business activities over a period of time with a number of different settlement systems for different business types.

Options 3 and 4 both involve the new system(s) coexisting with the system that they are replacing for a period of time. This may or not be practical due to external or internal constraints. While options 1 and 2 both seem to have a high level of inherent risk, there may still be good business and practical reasons for structuring the change programme in one of those ways. It is not possible to generalise further without a detailed understanding of what the firm is trying to achieve.

In order to manage change effectively, industry, commerce and government have all adopted a number of standard techniques that are described in the other sections of this chapter.

26.2 THE SOFTWARE DEVELOPMENT LIFECYCLE

The **software development lifecycle** (SDLC) is a standardised process of developing infor- mation systems or applications through the completion of defined steps or phases. Synonyms include systems development lifecycle, systems implementation lifecycle and software imple- mentation lifecycle (SILC).

The SLDC recognises that:

1. The further the project is from completing, the higher the risk and uncertainty. Risk and doubt decrease as the project moves closer to fulfilling the project vision.
2. Cost and resource requirements are lower at the beginning of a project, but grow as the project progresses. Once the project moves into the final closing process, cost and resource requirements again taper off dramatically. It is important for a project manager to be able to assess how much resource is actively working on their project (in terms of time or cost) so that this risk can be monitored.
3. Changes are easier and more likely at the early phases of the project lifecycle than at the completion. Changes at the beginning of the project generally cost less and have lower risk than changes at the end of the project. Therefore, stakeholders need to be happy with project deliverables from the early phases or else there is a risk that in the final phases of the project lifecycle additional costs may need to be incurred.

26.2.1 Standardised SDLC approaches

There are a number of standardised versions of the SDLC, but many organisations have adapted their own versions. In the standardised UK version, known as the Systems Life Cycle (SLC), the following names are used for each stage:

1. *Terms of reference*: The management decides what capabilities and objectives they wish the new system to incorporate.
2. *Feasibility study*: Asks whether the managements' concept of their desired new system is actually an achievable, realistic goal – in terms of money, time and end result. Often, it may be decided to simply update an existing system, rather than to completely replace one.
3. *Fact finding and recording*: How is the current system used? Often questionnaires are used here, but also just monitoring (watching) the staff to see how they work is better, as people will often be reluctant to be entirely honest through embarrassment about the parts of the existing system they have trouble with and find difficult if merely asked.
4. *Analysis*: Free from any cost or unrealistic constraints, this stage lets minds run wild as "wonder systems" can be thought up, though all must incorporate everything asked for by the management in the *Terms of reference* section.

5. *Design*: Designers will produce one or more "models" of what they see a system eventually looking like, with ideas from the analysis section either used or discarded. A document will be produced with a description of the system, but nothing is specific: they might say "touchscreen" or "GUI operating system", but not mention any specific brands.

6. *System specification*: Having generically decided on which software packages to use and hardware to incorporate, you now have to be very specific, choosing exact models, brands and suppliers for each software application and hardware device.

7. *Implementation and review*: Set up and install the new system (including writing any bespoke code required), train staff to use it, monitor how it operates for initial problems, and then regularly maintain thereafter. During this stage, any old system that was in use will usually be discarded once the new one has proved it is reliable and as usable.

8. *Use*: Obviously the system needs to be used by somebody, otherwise the above process would be completely useless.

9. *Close*: The last step in a system's lifecycle is its end, which is most often forgotten when the system is designed. The system can be closed, it can be migrated to another (more modern platform) or its data can be migrated into a replacing system.

26.2.2   Customised SDLC approaches – an example

SDLCs may be customised to suit different organisations. The following is an example of a customised SDLC approach that is used by a major vendor of packaged application software to the investment industry. The company supplies large-scale systems to major industry participants, and its SDLC model reflects the large scale of most of its projects, and that it is an external vendor rather than an in-house development team. The company divides its major projects into six stages that are suitable for its business model. Each stage produces a tangible outcome. Unusually, this model combines development, testing and training into a single stage.

The six stages are shown in Table 26.1. As a guideline the company that adapted SDLC in this way expects that on a typical project the breakdowns of time spent, and the mix of technical skills and business skills will be as shown in the table.

This SDLC defines business skills as:

Skills that relate to knowledge required to understand the business environment in which the customer functions, including experience with the application being implemented.

Table 26.1   Customised SDLC stages

	SDLC Stage	Per cent of total hours	Business	Technical
			Per cent of stage hours	
1	Requirements definition	10	80	20
2	Analysis	10	75	25
3	Design	15	30	70
4	Development and testing	50	20	80
5	Implementation	12	40	60
6	Post-implementation	3	80	20
	Total	**100**		

And it defines technical skills as:

> Skills that relate to the use of the computer as a tool for solving the customer's business problem; including knowledge of the capabilities and limitations of the hardware, operating system, database, programming languages, programming techniques and productivity aids.

This SDLC standard also includes a defined list of plans and reports that need to be produced at the end of each stage (see Table 26.2).

In detail, the six stages in this SDLC are as follows.

Stage 1 Requirements definition

Requirements definition: The main aim of this stage is to initiate the project and obtain or assure the customer's commitment to fund the project. The tangible outcomes of this stage include the requirements definition document, which constitutes a formal agreed user request. The requirements definition document includes:

- A first cut data model of data maintained in the current system
- Identification of current problems
- Identification of project objectives – both business and technical
- Identification of project constraints
- Critical success factors
- Definition of vendor and customer responsibilities, relationships and communication channels
- Summary of investment required.

Stage 2 Analysis

The objectives of this stage are to:

- Understand the functionality of the existing system and its inherent problems and the reasons why it no longer meets the users' needs
- Identify the essential business processes and stored data that are to be implemented in the new system
- Identify and evaluate the benefits and risks of alternative design, development, test and implementation options
- Revise the requirements definition and cost estimates if necessary.

Stage 3 Design

The objectives of this stage are to:

- Design the transactions
- Design the database
- Design the user interface
- Design the overnight processes
- Produce the test plan
- Plan for the development phase.

At the end of this stage, there should be no uncertainties about how the project will proceed.

Table 26.2 SDLC deliverables for each stage

	SDLC stage	Output type	Output title	Purpose
1	Requirements definition	Requirements definition document	Requirements definition document	The formal agreed user request
		Plan	Overall project plan	Provides the structure of the project. Provides detail for stage 2 and tentative details (including costs) for the remaining stages
		Plan	Quality plan and risk analysis	Demonstrates to management how the elements of the project plan will be implemented and identifies the risks at each stage
2	Analysis	Plan	Project plan (design)	Shows resource requirements for stage 3 and reflects changes in strategy based on the results of analysis
3	Design	Report	Design stage report	Highlights any deficiencies found during the analysis phase and their remedies. Evaluates any new techniques used during design. Highlights any problems found during the design phase and their remedies
		Plan	Project plan (development)	Detailed plans – including accurate project costs for stage 4
		Plan	Test plans	Separate plans for all the testing that will be done during stage 4
		Plan	Training plan	Timetables for user training courses, etc.
4	Development and testing	Report	Development report	Highlights any divergence from the Project Plan. Highlights how development staff training requirements were met
		Report	Test report	Describes what has been tested and the test results
		Plan	Project plan (implementation)	Shows resource requirements for stage 5 and reflects changes in strategy based on the results of development
5	Implementation	Report	Implementation report	Highlights any problems encountered during implementation and examines the nature of the working relationship with the customer
		Plan	Project plan (post-implementation)	Summarises the activities that vendor and customer expect to carry out after initial implementation. May include a list of further requirements that it was agreed would not be delivered in the initial implementation
6	Post-implementation	Report	Post-implementation report	Summarises the achievements and problems of the projects. Provides feedback for similar projects in the future with this client or future clients

Stage 4 Development and testing

The objectives of this stage are to:

- Produce detailed designs, write and test the programs
- Prove that the software is capable of handling both normal and peak transaction volumes and that is doesn't interfere with other existing software. This will be achieved by integration testing and regression testing.
- Produce the user documentation
- Train the users in the new system
- Demonstrate the system's successful operation to the customer
- Plan for Stage 5 Implementation.

Stage 5 Implementation

The main objectives of this phase are to:

- Convert data from the old system to the new system. This may involve specific tests and "dress rehearsals" of the data conversion process
- Cut over from test/training systems to the production system
- Analyse and correct any problems the users may be experiencing
- Make system operation recommendations based on performance analysis
- Ensure that user and technical documentation is complete and up to date.

Stage 6 Post-implementation

The main objectives of this stage are to:

- Fine tune system parameters in the light of experience
- Provide customer support during the critical period of the first few weeks after implementation
- Commence analysis design and development of any requirements that were deferred from the initial implementation
- Prepare the post-implementation report
- Provide customer follow-up to review the customer's business objectives, win new business and set the baseline for future projects.

26.3 PROJECT MANAGEMENT STANDARDS

There are a number of generally accepted standards for the management and control of projects. Those that are discussed here are the standards of:

- The Project Management Institute
- PRINCE2.

Before we examine these standards in more detail, let us first of all try to define a **project**. Some commonly used definitions (the italics are the author's) include the following:

1. A *temporary* and *one-time endeavour* undertaken to create a unique product or service, which brings about beneficial *change* or added value

2. A set of *inter-related* and *controlled activities* with *start* and *finish dates*, undertaken to achieve a unique **objective** conforming to *specific requirements,* including the *restraints of time, cost and resources.*

The properties of being a *temporary* and *one-time* undertaking contrast with normal operations, which are permanent repetitive functional work carried out to create the same product or service over and over again. Because the objective is to bring about *change* it is necessary to define the reasons for and extent of the change (the *requirements*); the *resources* that are available to make the change and the *costs* of those resources; and the date on which the change is required (the *time* constraint).

As a discipline, project management evolved from different industries such as construction, engineering and defence. Prior to the 1950s, projects were managed on an ad hoc basis using informal techniques and tools. At that time, two mathematical project scheduling models were developed; the "Program Evaluation and Review Technique" or PERT, developed by Booz-Allen & Hamilton as part of the United States Navy's Polaris missile submarine programme; and the "Critical Path Method" (CPM), developed in a joint venture by both DuPont Corporation and Remington Rand Corporation for managing plant maintenance projects. These mathematical techniques quickly spread into many private enterprises.

Project management is the discipline of organising and managing resources (e.g. people) in such a way that the project is completed within defined scope, quality, time and cost constraints.

26.3.1   The Project Management Institute (PMI)

The **Project Management Institute** (**PMI**) was formed in 1999 in the United States to serve the interests of the project management industry. The PMI is now a global body with over 240 000 members in 160 countries. The premise of PMI is that the tools and techniques of project management are common even among the widespread application of projects from the software industry to the construction industry. In 1981, the PMI published the first edition of what is now known as *A Guide to the Project Management Body of Knowledge* (**PMBOK Guide**), containing the standards and guidelines of practice that are widely used throughout the profession.

The Guide is process based, meaning it describes work as being accomplished by processes. Processes overlap and interact throughout a project or its various phases. Processes are described in terms of:

- Inputs (documents, plans, designs, etc.)
- Tools and techniques (mechanisms applied to inputs)
- Outputs (documents, products, etc.).

The Guide recognises 44 processes that fall into five basic process groups and nine knowledge areas that are typical of almost all projects. The five process groups are:

1. Initiating
2. Planning
3. Executing
4. Controlling and monitoring
5. Closing.

The nine knowledge areas are:

1. Project integration management
2. Project scope management
3. Project time management
4. Project cost management
5. Project quality management
6. Project human resource management
7. Project communications management
8. **Project risk** management
9. Project procurement management.

Each of the nine knowledge areas contains the processes that need to be accomplished within its discipline in order to achieve an effective project management programme. Each of these processes also falls into one of the five basic process groups, creating a matrix structure such that every process can be related to one knowledge area and one process group.

Membership of the institute is based upon examination. The institute offers accredited education programmes based on PMBOK in partnership with academic institutions in North America, Europe and Asia, together with a large number of learning tools and publications that are available both to members and non-members.

26.3.2   PRINCE2

Projects in Controlled Environments (PRINCE) covers the management, control and organisation of a project. 'PRINCE2' is a registered trademark of the UKs Office of Government Commerce (OGC). **PRINCE2** is derived from the earlier PRINCE technique, which was initially developed in 1989 by the Central Computer and Telecommunications Agency (CCTA) as a UK government standard for information systems (IT) project management. PRINCE soon became regularly applied outside the IT environment. PRINCE2 was released in 1996 as a generic project management method. PRINCE2 has become increasingly popular and is now the de facto standard for project management in the UK. Its use has spread beyond the UK to more than 50 other countries. The most current revision was released in 2005 by the Office of Government Commerce, and it is currently being revised for publication in 2008/9.

Project planning using PRINCE2 is product based which means the project plans are focused on delivering results and are not simply about planning when the various activities on the project will be done. PRINCE2 defines 45 separate subprocesses and organises these into eight processes as follows:

- Starting up a project (SU)
- Planning (PL)
- Initiating a project (IP)
- Directing a project (DP)
- Controlling a stage (CS)
- Managing product delivery (MP)
- Managing stage boundaries (SB)
- Closing a project (CP).

26.3.3 Starting up a project (SU)

In this process the project team is appointed and a **project brief** (describing, in outline, what the project is attempting to achieve and the business justification for doing it) is prepared. In addition the overall approach to be taken is decided and the next stage of the project is planned. Once this work is done, the project board is asked to authorise the next stage, that of initiating the project.

SU1: Appointing a project board and project manager

The project board is usually chaired by the **project sponsor**. This is normally the senior executive that instigated the change and is responsible to the business for the success of the project. The project sponsor's role includes:

- Championing the project
- Obtaining budgets for the project
- Accepting responsibility for problems escalated from the project manager
- Signing off documents such as the business case and project initiation document.

Due to the problem solving needs of the role the project sponsor often needs to be able to exert pressure within the organisation to overcome resistance to the project. For this reason the project sponsor will ideally be a person with sufficient power and authority within the organisation. Where a project is part of a larger change programme such as MiFID, the project sponsor is often also the overall programme manager.

Other members of the project board will include executives from the various sections of the firm that will either benefit from the project or have a role in delivering it. The **project manager** is also a member of the project board.

The project manager is the individual responsible for delivering the project. The project manager leads and manages the project team, with the authority and responsibility to run the project on a day-to-day basis. This person's roles may include:

- Designing and applying an appropriate project management framework for the project using relevant project standards
- Managing the production of the required deliverables
- Planning and monitoring the project
- Preparing and maintaining the project plan
- Managing project risks, including the development of contingency plans
- Liaising with programme management (if the project is part of a programme such as MiFID) and related projects to ensure that work is neither overlooked nor duplicated
- Preparing reports on overall progress and use of resources, and initiating corrective action where necessary
- Managing change control and any required configuration management
- Liaising with appointed project assurance roles to assure the overall direction and integrity of the project
- Adopting technical and quality strategy
- Identifying and obtaining any support and advice required for the management, planning and control of the project
- Managing project administration
- Conducting end project evaluation to assess how well the project was managed and preparing an end project report

- Preparing a lessons learned report
- Preparing any follow-on action recommendations as required.

In the case of small projects, the roles of project sponsor and project manager are sometimes combined, but for large projects, best practice is to separate the two roles.

SU2: Designing a project management team and SU3: Appointing a project management team

Members of the project management team report to the project manager. Typically the team will include the senior personnel responsible for various parts of the project such as design, development and testing. Team members may include representatives of the IT department, the user departments concerned and also external vendors and consultants if they are involved.

26.3.4   Planning (PL)

PRINCE2 advocates product-based planning, which means that the first task when planning is to identify and analyse products. Once the activities required to create these products are identified, then it is possible to estimate the effort required for each and schedule activities into a plan. There is always risk associated with any work and this must be analysed. Finally, this process suggests how the format of plans can be agreed and ensures that plans are completed to such a format. The planning process is divided into the following stages:

PL1 Designing a plan
PL2 Defining and analysing products
PL3 Identifying activities and dependencies
PL4 Estimating
PL5 Scheduling
PL6 Analysing risks
PL7 Completing a plan.

26.3.5   Initiating a project (IP)

This process builds on the work of the start-up (SU) activity and the project brief is augmented to form a **business case** – the non-technical reason for the project. The logic of the business case is that any time resources such as money or effort are consumed; they should be in support of the business.

An example could be that a software upgrade might improve system performance but the "business case" is that better performance would improve customer satisfaction. At this point the approach taken to ensure quality on the project is agreed together with the overall approach to controlling the project itself (project controls). Project files are also created as is an overall plan for the project. A plan for the next stage of the project is also created. The resultant information can be put before the project board for them to authorise the project itself. The steps in this process are:

IP1 Planning quality – quality assurance is covered in section 26.5
IP2 Planning a project
IP3 Refining the business case and risks
IP4 Setting up project controls
IP5 Setting up project files

IP6 Assembling a **project initiation document** (**PID**) – this is a logical document whose purpose is to bring together the key information needed to start the project on a sound basis, and to convey that information to all concerned with the project. The PID defines all major aspects of a project and assigns responsibilities to members of the project team. It forms the basis for the management of the project and the assessment of overall success.

26.3.6   Directing a project (DP)

These subprocesses dictate how the project board should control the overall project. As mentioned above, the project board can authorise an initiation stage and can also authorise a project. Directing a project also dictates how the project board should authorise a stage plan, including any stage plan that replaces an existing stage plan due to slippage or other unforeseen circumstances. The process also specifies the way in which the board can give ad hoc direction to a project and the way in which a project should be closed down. The individual stages within this process are:

DP1 Authorising initiation
DP2 Authorising a project
DP3 Authorising a stage or exception plan
DP4 Giving Ad hoc direction
DP5 Confirming project closure.

26.3.7   Controlling a stage (CS)

PRINCE2 suggests that projects should be broken down into stages and these subprocesses dictate how each individual stage should be controlled. Most fundamentally this includes the way in which **work packages** (subsets of a project that can be assigned to a specific party for execution) are authorised. It also specifies the way in which progress should be monitored and how the highlights of the progress should be reported to the project board. A means for capturing and assessing project issues is suggested together with the way in which corrective action should be taken. It also lays down under what circumstances, and by what method, project issues should be escalated to the project board.

CS1 Authorising work packages
CS2 Assessing progress
CS3 Capturing project issues
CS4 Examining project issues
CS5 Reviewing stage status
CS6 Reporting highlights
CS7 Taking corrective action
CS8 Escalating project issues
CS9 Receiving completed work package.

26.3.8   Managing product delivery (MP)

This process consists of three subprocesses and these cover the way in which a work package should be accepted, executed and delivered.

MP1 Accepting a work package
MP2 Executing a work package
MP3 Delivering a work package.

26.3.9   Managing stage boundaries (SB)

This process dictates what should be done within a stage. **Managing stage boundaries** (SB) dictates what should be done towards the end of a stage. The fundamental principle of this stage is to ensure that, at the end of each stage, the project stays focused on delivering business benefit. Most obviously, the next stage should be planned and the overall project plan, risk log and business case amended as necessary. The process also covers what should be done for a stage that has gone outside its tolerance levels. Finally, the process dictates how the end of the stage should be reported. There are a number of different software development methodologies that handle stage boundaries in different ways. These are examined in section 26.4.

The stages within this process are as follows:

SB1 Planning a stage
SB2 Updating a project plan
SB3 Updating a project business case
SB4 Updating the risk log
SB5 Reporting stage end
SB6 Producing an exception plan.

26.3.10   Closing a project (CP)

This process covers the things that should be done at the end of a project. The project should be formally decommissioned (and resources freed up for allocation to other activities), follow-on actions should be identified and the project itself be formally evaluated. The stages are as follows:

CP1 Decommissioning a project
CP2 Identifying follow-on actions
CP3 Project evaluation review.

26.3.11   PRINCE2 accreditation for individuals and organisations

Individuals who wish to acquire recognised project management qualifications may sit examinations to become registered PRINCE2 practitioners. Organisations that play a role in the delivery of projects may also choose to have their project management processes assessed.

Such assessment allows organisations that deliver internal projects to identity their strengths, areas for improvement and build an action plan to improve their effectiveness in the use of PRINCE2. This will lead to PRINCE2 being embedded within the organisation and facilitate delivery of the full benefits of using a structured project management method.

For those organisations that provide a project management service, in addition to the above benefits, they will also be able to provide evidence to their clients and prospective clients of their level of maturity in the use of PRINCE2.

26.4   SOFTWARE DEVELOPMENT MODELS

As part of the project planning process, organisations need to select an appropriate **software development model**. There are a number of commonly used software development methodologies that may be employed in a project. Most (but not all) of the differences between the models are concerned with the management of stage boundaries.

The models that are described in detail in this section are:

- Waterfall process models
- Iterative models, including:
  - Prototyping
  - The spiral model
  - The agile model
  - End-user development.

26.4.1   The waterfall model

The **waterfall model** (also known as Royce's model) is a sequential model in which development is seen as flowing steadily downwards (like a waterfall) through the phases of requirements analysis, design, implementation, testing, integration and maintenance (see Figure 26.1).

It maintains that one should move to a phase only when its preceding phase is completed and perfected. The output of each phase becomes the input of the next phase. It assumes that software development is like constructing a building – start with the foundations, then the walls, then the roof, etc. Phases of development in the waterfall model are discrete, and there is no jumping back and forth or overlap between them. However, there are various modified waterfall models that may include slight or major variations upon this process. The waterfall model with backflow (alternatively known as Royce's final model or the implied waterfall model) recognises that issues may be discovered in one phase because of a deficiency in the previous phase, or because since the previous phase was completed there may have been external events that had not been anticipated. The solution to this problem is to go back to the previous phase and rework it before the waterfall continues (see Figure 26.2).

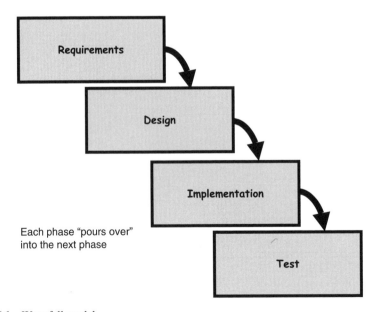

Figure 26.1   Waterfall model

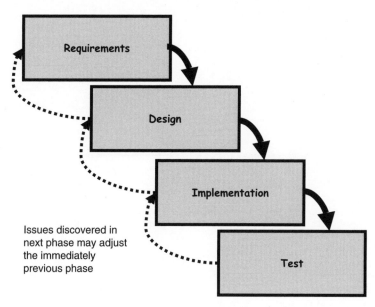

Figure 26.2   Waterfall model with backflow

The **fountain model** recognises that there are opportunities for some phases of the lifecycle to occur at the same time or overlap. The overlap occurs between adjacent phases and change control processes need to be mature to ensure that work is not undertaken on incorrect assumptions (see Figure 26.3).

Pros and cons of the waterfall models

Advantages

1. The staged development cycle enforces discipline: every phase has a defined start and end point, and progress can be conclusively identified (through the use of milestones) by both vendor and client.
2. The emphasis on requirements and design before writing a single line of code ensures minimal wastage of time and effort and reduces the risk of schedule slippage, or of customer expectations not being met.
3. Getting the requirements and design out of the way first also improves quality; it's much easier to catch and correct possible flaws at the design stage than at the testing stage.
4. Because the first two phases end in the production of a formal specification, the waterfall model can aid efficient knowledge transfer when team members are dispersed in different locations.

Criticisms

1. The most prominent criticism revolves around the fact that very often, customers don't really know what they want up-front; rather, what they want emerges out of repeated two-way interactions over the course of the project. For this reason, the waterfall model, with its emphasis on up-front requirements capture and design, is seen as somewhat unrealistic and unsuitable for the complexities of the real world.

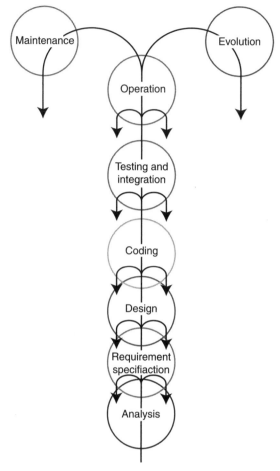

Figure 26.3 Fountain model

2. Given the uncertain nature of customer needs, estimating time and costs with any degree of accuracy (as the model suggests) is often extremely difficult. In general, therefore, the model is recommended for use only in projects which are relatively stable and where customer needs can be clearly identified at an early stage.

3. The model's implicit assumption is that designs can be feasibly translated into real products; this sometimes runs into problems when developers actually begin implementation. Often, designs that look feasible on paper turn out to be expensive or difficult in practice, requiring a redesign and hence destroying the clear distinctions between phases of the traditional waterfall model.

4. Some critics also point out that the model implies a clear division of labour between, say, "designers", "programmers" and "testers"; in reality, such a division of labour in many organisations is neither realistic nor efficient.

26.4.2 Iterative and incremental models

Several **iterative/incremental** models have been developed to overcome the criticisms of the waterfall model. Incremental development is a scheduling and staging strategy in which the various parts of the system are developed at different times or rates, and integrated as they are completed.

Iterative development is a rework scheduling strategy in which time is set aside to revise and improve parts of the system. A typical difference is that the output from an increment is released to users, whereas the output from an iteration is examined for further modification before release.

Common iterative/incremental models include the following:

Prototyping

Prototyping is the process of quickly putting together a working model (a prototype) in order to test various aspects of a design, illustrate ideas or features and gather early user feedback. Prototyping is often treated as an integral part of the system design process, where it is believed to reduce project risk and cost. Often one or more prototypes are made in a process of iterative and incremental development where each prototype is influenced by the performance of previous designs; in this way problems or deficiencies in design can be corrected.

When the prototype is sufficiently refined and meets the functionality, robustness, manufacturability and other design goals, the product is ready for production. The technology used to build the prototypes is not necessarily the same technology that is used to build the production system.

Advantages

- It may provide the proof of concept necessary to attract funding.
- It provides early visibility of the prototype and gives users an idea of what the final system looks like.
- It encourages active participation among users and producer.
- It is cost effective – development costs are reduced.
- It increases system development speed.
- It assists to identify any problems with the efficacy of earlier design, requirements analysis and coding activities.
- It helps to refine the potential risks associated with the delivery of the system being developed.

Criticisms

- Users, once they see the prototype, often have a hard time understanding that the finished design will not be produced for some time.
- Designers often feel compelled to use the patched-together prototype code in the real system, because they are afraid of "wasting time" starting again.
- Prototypes principally help with design decisions and user interface design – however, they cannot tell what the requirements were originally.
- Designers and end users can focus too much on user interface design and too little on producing a system that serves the business process.

26.4.3 The spiral model

This model of development combines the features of the prototyping model and the waterfall model. The **spiral model** is intended for large, expensive and complicated projects.

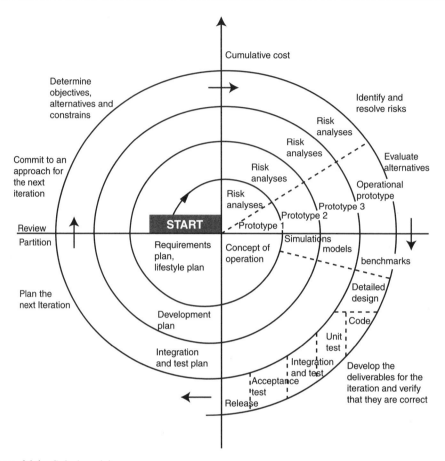

Figure 26.4   Spiral model

The spiral model was defined by Barry Boehm in his 1988 article "A spiral model of software development and enhancement". This model was not the first model to discuss iterative development, but it was the first model to explain why the iteration matters. Graphically, the spiral model is represented by Figure 26.4.

The processes in the spiral model are as follows:

1. The new system requirements are defined in as much detail as possible. This usually involves interviewing a number of users representing all the external or internal users and other aspects of the existing system.
2. A preliminary design is created for the new system.
3. A first prototype of the new system is constructed from the preliminary design. This is usually a scaled-down system, and represents an approximation of the characteristics of the final product.
4. A second prototype is evolved by a fourfold procedure:
   - Evaluating the first prototype in terms of its strengths, weaknesses and risks
   - Defining the requirements of the second prototype
   - Planning and designing the second prototype
   - Constructing and testing the second prototype.

5. At the customer's option, the entire project can be aborted if the risk is deemed too great. Risk factors might involve development cost over-runs, operating cost miscalculation, or any other factor that could, in the customer's judgement, result in a less-than-satisfactory final product.

6. The existing prototype is evaluated in the same manner as was the previous prototype, and, if necessary, another prototype is developed from it according to the fourfold procedure outlined above.

7. The preceding steps are iterated until the customer is satisfied that the refined prototype represents the final product desired.

8. The final system is constructed, based on the refined prototype.

9. The final system is thoroughly evaluated and tested. Routine maintenance is carried out on a continuing basis to prevent large-scale failures and to minimise downtime.

26.4.4   The agile model

The aim of the **agile model** is to minimise risk by developing software in short amounts of time. Software developed during one unit of time is referred to as an iteration, which may last from one to four weeks. Each iteration is an entire software project, including planning, requirements analysis, design, coding, testing and documentation. An iteration may not add enough functionality to warrant releasing the product to market but the goal is to have an *available* release (without bugs) that is capable of being deployed at the end of each iteration. At the end of each iteration, the team re-evaluates project priorities.

The agile model emphasises face-to-face communication over written documents. The method produces very little written documentation relative to other methods. This has resulted in criticism of agile methods as being undisciplined.

The **Agile Manifesto** (http://agilemanifesto.org) is a statement of the principles that underpin agile software development. The major principles in the manifesto are:

- Customer satisfaction by rapid, continuous delivery of useful software
- Working software is delivered frequently (weeks rather than months)
- Working software is the principal measure of progress
- Even late changes in requirements are welcomed
- Close, daily cooperation between business people and developers
- Face-to-face conversation is the best form of communication
- Projects are built around motivated individuals, who should be trusted
- Continuous attention to technical excellence and good design
- Simplicity
- Self-organising teams
- Regular adaptation to changing circumstances.

Advantages

1. The team is able to adapt quickly to changing circumstances.
2. Time periods between releases are measured in weeks not months.
3. All stakeholders collaborate to deliver the solution.

Criticisms

1. There is a lack of formal documentation of both the requirements and the project direction and controls.

2. The ultimate solution may "drift" from the optimal solution. This may be caused by the affect of a dominant personality on the team, or by the fact that the users have poorly formed ideas of their needs.
3. Face-to-face communication can be difficult to implement on large projects, or on projects where the team members are geographically dispersed.

For these reasons, agile software development is not usually recommended for:

• Large-scale projects involving more than 20 developers
• Projects with mainly inexperienced developers
• Projects where the development teams are geographically dispersed
• Life critical or mission critical systems.

Barry Boehm (the inventor of the method) and Richard Turner have suggested that the following factors may be used to choose between adaptive ("agile") and predictive ("plan-driven") methods. The authors suggest that each model has its own "home ground".

Agile home ground

• Low criticality
• Senior developers
• Requirements change very often
• Small number of developers
• Culture that thrives on chaos.

Plan-driven home ground

• High criticality
• Junior developers
• Requirements don't change too often
• Large number of developers
• Culture that demands order.

Note that software that is developed using the agile model also needs to be tested using the same model. Refer to section 26.5.3 for a description of the agile testing method.

26.4.5   End-user development

End-user development (EUD) is a set of activities or techniques that allows individuals who are non-professional developers to create or modify a software object. A typical example of EUD is macro programming in applications such as Microsoft Excel™. End-user development is not limited to programming. Other examples of end-user development include the creation and modification of web pages, wikis, and the use of applications such as Crystal Reports™, which allow users to create online and printed reports based on SQL queries.

Advantages

1. End users may be able to get the results that they require very quickly.
2. End users may be able to employ their specialised business knowledge directly – they know the requirements and can implement them without having to explain them to developers.

Criticisms

1. End-user development often bypasses the organisation's change control procedures. As a result, the precise contents of the configuration may not be documented. This may lead to problems such as:
   - The application is not included in the business continuity plan.
   - When a decision is made to outsource an aspect of processing, this application is not included in the outsourcing arrangements.
   - A change may be made to another software product on which this application relies that destabilises this application.
2. End-user developments that are based on SQL enquiries may result in unacceptable stress on the database unless the enquiries are optimised for performance. End users may not possess the skills to do this.

26.5   REQUIREMENTS GATHERING

The common feature of all major change projects is that the user requirements need to be gathered. Waterfall models insist that the requirements are gathered at the start of the project while iterative/incremental models allow the requirements to be gathered at various points in the development path.

Requirements gathering may be divided into three activities:

1. *Eliciting requirements*: The task of communicating with customers and users to determine what their requirements are
2. *Analysing requirements*: Determining whether the stated requirements are unclear, incomplete, ambiguous, or contradictory and resolving these issues
3. *Recording requirements*: Requirements may be documented in various forms, such as natural-language documents, use cases, user stories, or process specifications.

Eliciting, analysing and recording requirements are time consuming and complex processes. Successful requirements gathering assumes that the analyst (the person doing the gathering) and the stakeholders (the individuals that have the requirements) have good communication skills and the time to devote to the process. It may be a lengthy process, therefore requirements can change as they are being gathered. Both the agile and spiral models reflect these issues in their structure, and both use prototypes. Apart from prototypes, the following are the common processes that are used in requirements gathering. Most analysts will employ a combination of more than one of them in the process.

26.5.1   Stakeholder interviews

This is the traditional method of eliciting requirements. Interviews often pursue the following pattern:

Tell me how you do it now.
Show me how you do it now.
Tell me what needs to be improved.

The problems with relying solely on interviews to gather requirements are that:

- Not all the stakeholders may have been identified.
- Some stakeholders may be dominant personalities that influence the project too much.

- Interviews often reveal requirements that were not part of the original project brief, and sometimes reveal requirements that are contradictory.
- Not all stakeholders will have visualised their requirements prior to the interview.
- Requirements often have cross-functional implications that are unknown to individual stakeholders and often missed or incompletely defined.

26.5.2   Requirement workshops

Requirement workshops are an alternative to a series of individual interviews and, properly managed, can overcome some of the problems of traditional interviews. They are sometimes known as joint requirement development sessions (**JRD**).

These sessions should be carried out in a controlled environment with no distractions. They should have a chairperson to keep the sessions focused and to ensure that the meeting is not dominated by one or two stakeholders to the exclusion of others, as well as a minute-taker to document the discussion. They may use visual aids such as overhead projectors, or diagramming software.

26.5.3   Use cases

Use cases are a means of documenting requirements. Each use case provides one or more *scenarios* that convey how the system should interact with the end user or another system to achieve a specific business goal. Use cases typically avoid technical jargon, preferring instead the language of the end user.

A use case contains a textual description of all of the ways which the intended users could work with the software or system. Use cases do not describe any internal workings of the system, nor do they explain how that system will be implemented. They simply show the steps that a user follows to perform a task.

A use case should:

- Describe a business task to serve a business goal
- Be at an appropriate level of detail
- Be short enough to implement by one software developer in a single *release*.

Consider the following example of a use case statement describing what happens in the early stages when a user goes into a static data repository to inspect the contents of the static data held for a particular security.

The use case statement might begin as follows.

Main path

1. The user requests the application to view security details.
2. The system displays the security details screen.
3. The user types the ISIN code or SEDOL code of the security concerned.
4. The system recognises the security concerned – go to main path section 5; or The system does not recognise the security concerned – go to exception path 1.
5. The system responds by displaying the following details of the security:
   - Security name
   - Security type

Figure 26.5   Use case symbology

- Market where traded
- etc.

Exception path

1. The system displays the message "This security is not in the database".

Use case diagrams

Use cases may be represented diagrammatically. The two main components of a use case diagram are use cases and actors (see Figure 26.5).

The use case described above would be represented as shown in Figure 26.6.

There are a number of software development tools on the market that aid the development of use case requirements documentation. Using these tools, when the user clicks on a use case or actor node, the tool brings up the text description of the use case or actor.

Limitations of use case requirements recording

Use cases are considered good tools for documenting that part of an application that requires human interaction, but they are not well suited to easily capturing non-interaction-based

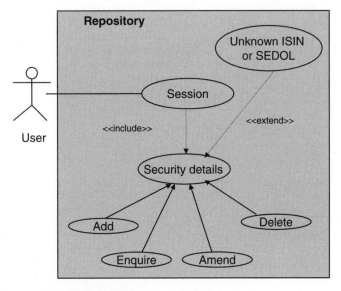

Figure 26.6   Sample use case diagram

requirements of a system (including algorithm or mathematical requirements such as interest accrual or trade computations) or non-functional requirements (such as platform, performance, timing, or safety-critical aspects).

26.6 QUALITY ASSURANCE TESTING

26.6.1 Introduction

Software testing is the process used to measure the quality of developed computer software. Software testing is a value judgement. It is not possible to produce a complex application that is completely free of defects – this would equate to delivering "perfection", which is something that human beings rarely achieve. The number of defects in a complex application can be large; some of them will be critical and some less so. In addition, an individual product may be implemented within a large number of configurations. For example, many applications used in the investment industry run on both SQLServer™ and Unix databases, and even within the confines of one of those operating systems there are a large number of different variables that may be employed by different users. As a result, errors may be found in one configuration variable but not others.

The purpose of testing is, therefore, to gain a level of confidence in the software so that the organisation is confident that the software has an *acceptable* defect rate; where defects do exist they are documented, and there are adequate workrounds available to the users. What constitutes an acceptable defect rate depends on the nature of the software. The level of defects that are acceptable in, say, an arcade game would be completely unacceptable in an application that was used in, say, an operating theatre or in a flight control centre serving a busy airport.

It is necessary, therefore, to grade any problems that may be found during testing. Table 26.3 is an example of a problem grading matrix. Each problem is allocated a severity grade, and the firm that developed the system has a set of rules for deciding how many problems of

Table 26.3 Sample acceptance test problem grades

Grade	Meaning	Implications for putting this release into production
A	An extremely serious problem. An important part of the system does not work as it should, and there are no workarounds available to the users	This release cannot go into production if there are *any* Grade A defects outstanding
B	An *important* part of the system is not working in the way that was intended, but there are workarounds available so that data can be processed in another way	This release can go into production if there are *a very limited number* of Grade B defects outstanding and there is an agreed timeframe for their resolution after live date
C	A *minor* part of the system is not working in the way that was intended, but there are workarounds available so that data can be processed in another way	This release can go into production if there are a *number* of Grade C defects outstanding and there is an agreed timeframe for their resolution after live date
D	Cosmetic error – e.g. a spelling mistake on the headings of an input/enquiry screen or printed report	This release can go into production *despite* the presence of Grade D defects

each grade it will tolerate when it decides whether or not to release the developed software. These rules are normally incorporated into its change control policies (see section 25.4.3 for an example of a change control policy statement).

Software testing axioms:

The following is a list of software testing axioms:

1. It is impossible to test a program completely.
2. Software testing is a risk-based exercise.
3. Testing cannot show that bugs don't exist.
4. The more bugs you find, the more bugs there are.
5. Not all the bugs you find will be fixed.
6. Product specifications are never final.
7. If you find a problem that occurs once, and you can't repeat it, then you can't fix it.

26.6.2   ISO9126

ISO9126 is the international standard for determining software quality. It is divided into four parts which address, respectively, the quality model, external metrics, internal metrics and quality in use metrics. The quality model established in the first part of the standard, ISO9126-1, classifies software quality in a structured set of characteristics and subcharacteristics as follows:

- *Functionality*: A set of attributes that bear on the existence of a set of functions and their specified properties. The functions are those that satisfy stated or implied needs:
  - Suitability
  - Accuracy
  - Interoperability
  - Compliance
  - Security.
- *Reliability*: A set of attributes that bear on the capability of software to maintain its level of performance under stated conditions for a stated period of time:
  - Maturity
  - Recoverability
  - Fault tolerance.
- *Usability*: A set of attributes that bear on the effort needed for use, and on the individual assessment of such use, by a stated or implied set of users:
  - Learnability
  - Understandability
  - Operability.
- *Efficiency*: A set of attributes that bear on the relationship between the level of performance of the software and the amount of resources used, under stated conditions:
  - Time behaviour
  - Resource behaviour.
- *Maintainability*: A set of attributes that bear on the effort needed to make specified modifications:
  - Stability
  - Analysability
  - Changeability
  - Testability.

- *Portability*: A set of attributes that bear on the ability of software to be transferred from one environment to another:
  - – Installability
  - – Replaceability
  - – Adaptability.

26.6.3   Test stages

During the software development lifecycle, applications are usually subject to the following series of tests, usually in this order:

1. **Unit testing** tests the minimal software component, or module. Each unit (basic component) of the software is tested to verify that the detailed design for the unit has been correctly implemented.
2. **Integration testing** exposes defects in the interfaces and interaction between integrated components (modules). Progressively larger groups of tested software components corresponding to elements of the architectural design are integrated and tested until the software works as a system.
3. **Functional testing** tests at any level (class, module, interface, or system) for proper functionality as defined in the specification.
4. **System testing** tests a completely integrated system to verify that it meets its requirements.
5. **Volume testing** or *load testing* tests a software application for a certain data volume. This may be expressed in a number of ways, such as the size of the database, the number of transactions to be processed for a given time period, the length of time that the user has to wait for the results of an enquiry, or length of time that an overnight process should take to complete.
6. **System integration testing** verifies that a system is integrated to any external or third-party systems defined in the system requirements.
7. **User acceptance testing** is conducted by the end user, customer, or client to validate whether or not to accept the product. Acceptance testing may be performed as part of the hand-off process between any two phases of development:
   - *Alpha testing* is simulated or actual operational testing by potential users/customers or an independent test team at the developer's site. Alpha testing is often employed for off-the-shelf software as a form of internal acceptance testing, before the software goes to beta testing.
   - *Beta testing* comes after alpha testing. Versions of the software, known as beta versions, are released to a limited audience outside of the company. The software is released to groups of people so that further testing can ensure the product has few faults.

It should be noted that although both alpha and beta are referred to as testing, it is in fact user immersion. The rigours that are applied are often unsystematic and many of the basic tenets of the testing process are not used. The alpha and beta period provides insight into environmental and utilisation conditions that can impact the software.

Regression testing

After modifying software, either for a change in functionality or to fix defects, a **regression test** reruns previously successful tests on the modified software to ensure that the modifications haven't unintentionally caused a *regression* of previous functionality. Regression testing can be performed at any or all of the above test levels.

26.6.4   Test techniques

Software may be tested by using any or all of the following techniques:

- *Code walkthrough*: A manual testing technique where program logic is traced manually using a small set of test cases to analyse the programmer's logic and assumptions.
- *White box testing*: In white box testing the tester has access to the source code and can write tests specific to the area of change.
- *Black box, concrete box or functional testing*: In black box testing the tester only accesses the software through the same interfaces that the customer or user would, or through automation of similar interfaces, to confirm the functional specification of the program.
- *Grey box testing*: In grey box testing the tester sets up or manipulates the testing environment (through configuration files or seeding of data) to establish a state of the product for testing or verification.
- *Smoke, sanity or skim testing*: A cursory examination of all of the basic components of a software system without reference to the internal workings to ensure that they hang together. Typically, smoke testing is used to verify a software build. The term originates from the electronics industry where the circuits are laid out and power is applied. If anything starts smoking, there is a problem.
- *Agile testing*: Agile software development (described in section 26.4.4) adheres to a test-driven software development model where the unit tests are written first and fail initially until the code is written. The test harness is continuously updated as new failure conditions are discovered and they are integrated with any regression tests that have been developed.

The stages of a test-driven development Cycle are as follows:

- Write the test
- Write the code
- Run the automated tests
- Refactor
- Repeat.

26.6.5   The test cycle

The test cycle usually consists of the following steps:

1. *Requirements analysis*: Testing should begin in the requirements phase of the software development lifecycle. During the design phase, testers work with developers in determining what aspects of a design are testable and under what parameters those tests work.
2. *Test planning*: The planning stage comprises the development of the test strategy, test bed and test plan(s). These, in turn, comprise the following:
   - The test strategy outlines which of the stages (section 26.6.3) will be used and which techniques (section 26.6.4) will be used.
   - The test bed is the definition of the hardware, operating system and database configuration that will be used to perform the testing.

- The test plan allocates resources to the testing, and specifies how issues will be reported, actioned and retested prior to release.
- *Test development*: In this phase the **test scenarios, test cases and test scripts** are written. Consider the following example:

ABC Investment Bank has purchased a new package to process stock loans and repos. The business has told the test team that they intend to process the following transaction types[1]. The list of transaction types forms the test scenario:

1. Stock lent by ABC to a trading party who supplies cash as collateral
2. Stock lent by ABC to a trading party who supplies securities as collateral
3. As (2) with collateral substituted during the lifecycle of the transaction
4. As (1) with margin call payable by party during the life of the transaction
5. Stock borrowed by ABC from a trading party with cash collateral
6. As (5) with collateral substituted during the lifecycle of the transaction
7. As (5) with margin call payable by ABC during the life of the transaction
8. Classic repo – ABC is the borrower of cash
9. Classic repo – ABC is the lender of cash
10. Delivery by value – ABC is the borrower of cash.

For each of the 10 items in the scenario, the test team will prepare a test case – a set of conditions or variables under which a tester will determine if a requirement or use case upon an application is partially or fully satisfied. They will then prepare a test script for each test case. The test script for the first item might include the following level of detail about the transaction that will be entered to test the case:

Test script for Scenario 1

1. Basic trade details:

Trade Date	11 November 2007
Opening leg value date	14 November 2007
Closing leg value date	21 November 2007
Trading party	Merrill Lynch
Price	98%
Haircut	5%
Fee	1 basis point per day
Security	ISIN GB12345678911
Quantity	1 million
Our settlement agent	Euroclear
Their settlement agent	Clearstream

---

2. *Computations*: This part of the script would show, *inter alia*, the results of the computations of the principal amount, accrued interest, fees and charges and the total consideration for both trade legs.
3. *Software objects to be inspected*: This part of the script would list all the reports, enquiries, interfaces and other physical software objects that need to be inspected to prove that this transaction is being correctly processed.

---

[1]Refer to Chapter 12 for an explanation of the transaction types.

4. *Test execution*: Testers execute the software based on the plans and tests and report any errors found to the development team.
5. *Test reporting*: Once testing is completed, testers generate metrics and make final reports on their test effort and whether or not the software tested is ready for release.
6. *Retesting the defects*: Note that not all errors or defects reported need to be fixed by a software development team. Some may be caused by errors in configuring the test bed; others may be as a result of human error in preparing the scenarios or scripts. These types of issues may be rejected by the development team if they deem it appropriate. Some defects can be handled by a workaround in the production environment. Others might be deferred to future releases of the software, or the deficiency might be accepted by the business user.

26.6.6 Test automation

Traditionally, testing of financial sector applications has been performed by test team members manually entering transactions, running background processes such as the sending of settlement instructions, mark-to-market and interest accrual and then reviewing the results of this activity by the inspection of reports, enquiries and interface files created by the application. For a large application, this is a highly labour intensive process that can create bottlenecks. In particular, the resource hungry nature of this way of working makes it extremely difficult to carry out volume tests and regression tests, because of the very large amount of data entry and inspection that is required by these types of tests.

There are now a large number of software tools on the market that can automate some of these activities. Usually, these tools provide record and playback features that allow users to record interactively user actions and replay it any number of times, comparing actual results to those expected. Using these facilities the 10 test case transactions that were developed in the example in section 26.6.5 could become the 10 000 transactions that might be necessary for a volume test of the new stock lending system.

In addition to the tools that provide the "record and playback" facilities there are a number of automation tools available that allow the code to conduct unit tests to determine whether various sections of the code are acting as expected in various circumstances. Test cases describe tests that need to be run on the program to verify that the program runs as expected.

Automated test tools can be expensive to purchase, and can only automate a well-thought-through test script. It is an addition to, not a replacement of, manual testing.

26.6.7 Testing is a part of the change management workflow

In order to execute a test plan, there has to be an agreed methodology for reporting issues, actioning them, retesting them, and either releasing them to the production environment when they pass or reworking the fix if they fail the retest. In addition, the stakeholders will require regular reports of the numbers and severity of issues outstanding. The type of helpdesk management system that was described in section 25.2.1 is usually used for these purposes.

Package and Vendor Selection, Outsourcing and Offshoring

27.1 MAKING THE BUY OR BUILD DECISION

When a new solution is required to resolve a business problem, there is often a decision to be made whether to build it internally or to buy a packaged product. In some conditions it is more cost effective to buy; in others it makes more sense to build the solution in-house.

The overall cost of the solution, whether it is built or bought, should include the cost of delivering the solution to production and the ongoing expenses of the solutions once they become part of business as usual operations. For example, a vendor might build a solution for a very low cost but the ongoing support and maintenance fees may be high. Equally an internal team might be able to deliver a solution relatively cheaply, but the entire team might need to be retained to support the solution in production.

The following are possible reasons to build:

- *Costs*: The cost of an internal development may or may not be lower than either the purchase of a software package, or the fees paid to external developers.
- *Expertise*: Depending on the nature of the product or system being introduced, there may be more expertise within the firm than there is outside the firm.
- *Competitive advantage and intellectual property rights*: If the firm requires an application that will give it some competitive advantage, it might not wish to share the intellectual property with a software vendor that could then sell the application to competitors.
- Resource availability and its affect on the elapsed time to bring the system or product into production.

The possible reasons to buy include the following:

- *Business strategy*: If the new system or product is not a core application, the firm's internal resources may be better spent on core business software.
- *Costs*: If there are package products available that meet the business needs, costs may be lower.
- *Time*: If a packaged application exists, it is likely that it could be implemented in a shorter time frame.
- *Generic solution*: Many parts of the firm's application architecture consist of elements that are needed by all firms in the same sector. For example, all LSE and SWIFT member firms need communications with the LSE and SWIFT, respectively, and all firms in all sectors need to perform bank and depot reconciliations. These bread and butter functions do not usually confer any competitive advantage on a particular firm, and as a result software vendors that specialise in building the necessary applications have evolved. These vendors usually have more skilled resources available in their areas of expertise than an individual securities firm, and are usually able to deliver packaged products for quick delivery.

The build or buy decision is a decision that needs to be answered early in a change project as it is fundamental to the approach of how change is to be delivered. The decision may be self-evident at the outset, in which case the reasons for the decision will be included in the project brief at the beginning of the project. In other cases the build versus buy decision will need research, in which case the project planning phase will include a task to evaluate the alternatives. Until such time as the project steering committee has considered the alternatives it may not be possible to plan the project any further.

27.2   VENDOR AND PACKAGE SELECTION

27.2.1   Introduction

The IT department is often involved in selecting vendors for IT products and services. It is usually solely responsible for selecting suppliers of PC and server hardware, networks and configuration management software. The department usually works alongside the user departments in selecting vendors of:

- Packaged application software such as order management systems, settlement systems and general ledger systems
- Outsourced innovation services such as bespoke software development
- Some outsourced production services such as a settlement/transaction processing service that has a high IT content. Outsourcing is examined in detail in section 27.3.

This section deals with the principles of vendor assessment for these types of products and services where the IT department will be working alongside the users. These activities are projects in their own right, and are normally managed using the project management techniques described in Chapter 26.

27.2.2   The seven stages of vendor selection and assessment

A vendor selection and evaluation project is usually divided into the following stages:

1. Form the project steering board and project team
2. Specify requirements
3. Determine the evaluation criteria
4. Identify companies and packages
5. Send requirements to potential vendors
6. Evaluate vendors and packages
7. Negotiate and place orders.

Form the project board and project team

In essence, this is the same process that was examined in section 26.3. The project team needs to consist of representatives from the relevant user departments and the IT department who have relevant expertise in the package or service being purchased, and who have the time to devote to the vendor selection process. Because this process may be quite time consuming, project team members may need to relinquish some or all of their other routine duties.

Specify requirements

In this context, the requirements are broader than the business requirements that were examined in section 26.5. The list of requirements is usually presented in the form of a **request for proposal (RFP)** that will be sent to a list of potential suppliers in Stage 5. An RFP is a statement of intent to purchase, followed by a list of questions covering all of these issues that can be sent to potential vendors for them to reply to in writing. Some firms use the terms request for quote (RFQ) or invitation to tender (ITT) instead of RFP.

Vendors will need to know the firm's timeline and how the firm will make its decision in order to best match the vendors' capabilities to the firm's needs.

In addition to the functional and performance requirements that are gathered for any new application, the firm also needs to find out from the vendors:

- Whether the operating systems and databases that their packages run under are acceptable to the firm
- How support is obtained
- The costs of licence fees, support and implementation consultancy. Questions need to be framed in such a way that the firm would expect the vendor to provide detailed information about:
  - One-off capital expenditure for the right to use the package or service for a predetermined period
  - One-off capital expenditure for consultancy concerned with essential system enhancements and implementation project activity
  - Annual maintenance and support
  - Whether the amounts quoted include VAT or other local taxes, or whether these amounts are excluded from the quotation
  - Whether the amounts quoted include reimbursement of the vendor's travel and subsistence expenses, or whether these amounts are excluded from the quotation.

Determine the evaluation criteria

In order to make a reasoned selection the most important (e.g. must-do) requirements must be articulated and the criteria must be prioritised and weighted to allow the suitability of the solutions to be ranked. For example, a firm that is considering purchasing a packaged general ledger system may, *inter alia*, have certain requirements concerned with the output from the system (see Table 27.1).

Table 27.1   Sample RFP requirements

Ref. no.	Requirement name	Requirement description
1.1.1	Real-time accounting enquiries	All account balances and account postings must be available for enquiry in real time
1.1.2	Export to Excel	All account balances and account postings must be readily exportable to Excel
1.1.3	Comparison of P&L balances to budget	The system should provide an enquiry that compares the balance of a P&L account to the budgeted P&L account
1.1.4	Comparison of P&L balances to prior period	The system should provide an enquiry that compares the balance of a P&L account to the same balance in the previous month and in the same period in the previous financial year

Table 27.2 Sample FRP questions as presented to vendors

Ref. no.	Requirement name	Requirement description	Supported?	Comments
1.1.1	Real-time accounting enquiries	All account balances and account postings must be available for enquiry in real time		
1.1.2	Export to Excel	All account balances and account postings must be readily exportable to Excel		
1.1.3	Comparison of P&L balances to budget	The system should provide an enquiry that compares the balance of a P&L account to the budgeted P&L account		
1.1.4	Comparison of P&L balances to prior period	The system should provide an enquiry that compares the balance of a P&L account to the same balance in the previous month and in the same period in the previous financial year		

In an RFP, it is common to ask vendors to confirm whether or not their product meets such criteria. The RFP as presented to the vendor then looks like Table 27.2.

The vendor is invited to complete column four according to a pattern. For example, the answer "3" means fully supported, "2" means partially supported, "1" means an enhancement is possible, and "0" means that support cannot be provided for this requirement. The vendor is also asked to insert whatever free text it wishes into column five in support of the claim that it has made in column four.

If the firm has received responses from two vendors with this pattern, then it needs to be able to compare them (see Table 27.3).

The responses can only be meaningfully compared if the firm has decided a weighting for each requirement. Let us assume that the weightings of these four requirements are as shown in Table 27.4.

By multiplying the vendor response by the weighting, it is possible to produce a weighted average score for each vendor (see Table 27.5).

It is clear that, based on these very restricted requirements, vendor two's package has the slight edge over vendor one's package. Some RFP writers advise vendors of what the weightings are in the RFP, others keep the information private from the vendors. The argument in favour of advising the weighting to the vendor is that the customer is seeking a partnership with the successful vendor and wishes in general to be open and frank with it. The argument against is that if vendors know the weightings they will colour their responses – they will tell the prospective customer what it wants to hear.

Table 27.3 Sample RFP answers

Ref. no.	Requirement name	Supported?	
		Vendor one response	Vendor two response
1.1.1	Real-time accounting enquiries	3	3
1.1.2	Export to Excel	3	1
1.1.3	Comparison of P&L balances to budget	2	3
1.1.4	Comparison of P&L balances to prior period	2	3

Table 27.4   RFP weightings

Ref. no.	Requirement name	Weighting
1.1.1	Real-time accounting enquiries	3 – essential
1.1.2	Export to Excel	1 – desirable but not critical
1.1.3	Comparison of P&L balances to budget	2 – required, but not immediately
1.1.4	Comparison of P&L balances to prior period	3 – required, but not immediately

The financial viability of the vendors and their access to skilled project resources must also be evaluated.

Identify companies and packages

Potential vendors may be identified in a number of ways, including:

- The use of internet search engines
- More specialised online directories – for example, if you are looking for a vendor who has consulting expertise or package products concerned with SWIFT connectivity, then the SWIFT Partner Solutions Directory (at www.swift.com) lists several hundred vendors under various searchable geographical and functional categories. Similarly, the London Stock Exchange's website also provides details of a number of vendors that offer connectivity to its trading systems.
- Advertisements and editorial items in trade magazines
- Attendance at exhibitions and conferences
- Word of mouth – what vendors have your counterparties and competitors used? Have any of your project team members worked at other companies who have recently had to do the same type of evaluation? If you are looking for a services connected with a particular stock exchange or clearing house, does the exchange concerned have a list of suitable vendors that isn't shown on its website?

Send requirements to potential vendors

The RFP can then be sent to the vendors identified in the previous stage. If you have identified a very large number of potential vendors, then you might want to consider sending an abbreviated

Table 27.5   RFP scores based on weightings

Ref. no.	Requirement name	Supported?	
		Vendor one weighted score	Vendor two weighted score
1.1.1	Real-time accounting enquiries	$3 * 3 = 9$	$3 * 3 = 9$
1.1.2	Export to Excel	$3 * 1 = 3$	$1 * 1 = 1$
1.1.3	Comparison of P&L balances to budget	$2 * 2 = 4$	$3 * 2 = 6$
1.1.4	Comparison of P&L balances to prior period	$2 * 3 = 6$	$3 * 3 = 9$
Total score		**22**	**24**

version of the RFP at this stage, and using the results of that exercise to form a short-list of vendors to whom you will send the full RFP. The abbreviated form of an RFP is usually referred to as a request for information (RFI).

As well as asking the functional questions you should also ask the vendors to provide you with at least three suitable customer references that you can follow up in stage 6. A suitable reference site is an organisation that is using the same package product or outsourced service in the same industry and geographic region as you intend to use it. If you are selecting a vendor for a bespoke development, then a suitable reference site is a company in the same geographic region as your own for whom the vendor has recently worked on a similar project.

You should also ask the vendor to supply you with a copy of its latest audited accounts, and a draft contract for the service or product to be provided.

Evaluate vendors and packages

In stage 3 you will have already identified the criteria that you are going to use in this stage. Vendors should be evaluated against those criteria using all of the following as evidence of the vendors' ability to deliver and commitment to your company and its project.

Quality of the answers to the RFP questions
- Have all the functional, volume/performance and technical questions you asked been answered in detail, or were the answers woolly and vague? Did the vendor seek clarification from you about any of the questions? Are the answers satisfactory?
- Has the vendor confirmed that it is able to deliver to you on a timely basis?
- Have you now got a clear idea of the level of investment that is needed to purchase this service or package? Is the vendor's quote within your budget?

Product demonstrations
If you are selecting a *packaged application*, then it is essential that you have at least one demonstration of the package – preferably more than one – and that you ensure that the right project team members and other key personnel are able to attend. It is a good idea to ask the vendor to demonstrate using sample transactions or scenarios supplied by your organisation.

If you are selecting a vendor for an *outsourced bespoke development*, then that vendor should be asked to demonstrate something else that it has developed for another company in a similar space.

If you are selecting a vendor for an *outsourced service*, and part of that service involves supplying your company with, say, transaction entry software, then make sure that this software is demonstrated to you at this stage.

Evaluate the vendors' key people
By this time you will have had several meetings with the vendors' key personnel. Ask yourselves the following:

- Do they act in a professional manner? Are they punctual in attending meetings and do they return calls promptly?

- Are you satisfied that they have sufficient domain expertise in the areas that they are working in? Have you met functional and technical experts, or just members of the sales force?

Evaluate the vendors' financial status

A qualified accountant should evaluate the vendors' audited accounts and raise any concerns. If there are any concerns, then raise these with the vendor directly and tactfully and consider their response.

Review the contract

Review the contract to see if the terms of the supply of the service are acceptable. Note that depending upon what type of product or service is being purchased; the contract may not be a single document, but many documents. Appendix 2 describes the common types of documents that apply to various types of purchase.

Take up references from other users

It is essential to take up references from the reference sites that you requested in the RFP. This is especially true if you are commissioning bespoke developments or outsourced services, where there is a limit to what you can learn from product demonstrations; but it is still necessary to take up references when you are purchasing a packaged product.

Be very wary of any vendor who cannot supply you with at least three references that you think are relevant; unless you are purchasing from a start-up company where you may be the first user of the service or product. If this is the case, then the principals of the company should be able to supply you with personal references from previous employers or business associates.

When you take up references, follow these guidelines:

- Visit the reference site – don't just take up references by phone or email.
- Ask questions about the following:
  - *Functional*: Does the product, bespoke development or service that they use do what the vendor said it would do? Does it do what you expected it to do? In what way has it improved the process in your company?
  - *System/service performance*: Does it handle the volumes that you expected it to?
  - *Vendor performance*: Did the vendor deliver on time and within budget? Are helpdesk calls usually resolved satisfactorily and promptly?
- Be reasonable when you make a reference visit – the person who is seeing you is busy and is doing you a favour – don't take up too much of this person's time.

Negotiate and place orders

By now you will have identified the preferred supplier. You now need to negotiate contracts.

Price

The vendor may be prepared to reduce the price that was quoted in the response to the RFP. In return for concessions on price it will usually ask for something in return. Typically, vendors will ask the customer to cooperate in publicity about the latest sale; they will usually ask that you agree to them issuing a press release mentioning your company's name – additionally they may ask for you to cooperate in producing a case study to be published in the trade press.

Contractual terms

The contract may not be a single document, but many documents. Appendix 2 describes the common types of documents that apply to various types of purchase.

27.3   OUTSOURCING AND OFFSHORING

27.3.1   Outsourcing

Definition and concept

Most organisations have never been totally self-sufficient; they have traditionally subcontracted functions such as cleaning and building maintenance, and relied on subcontractors of many kinds to assist them to cope with peak demand. Publishers have traditionally purchased typesetting, printing, and fulfilment services from external firms, and in the securities industry safe custody services have been traditionally provided by custodians, CSDs and ICSDs – virtually no securities firm in the developed world holds securities in the strong room in the course of normal daily operations.

The use of external suppliers for these essential but ancillary services might be termed the baseline stage in the evolution of **outsourcing**. In the 1990s, as organisations began to focus more on cost-saving measures, they started to outsource those functions necessary to run a company but not related specifically to the core business.

One definition of outsourcing is "The delegation of *non-core* operations from internal production to an external entity specialising in the management of that type of operation". Another definition is "The *strategic use* of outside resources to perform activities *traditionally* handled by internal staff and resources" (the italics in these definitions are the author's).

A *non-core operation* may be further defined as any part of the business that doesn't:

- *Generate* recurring income
- *Increase* the value of the business
- *Secure* the income and value of the business.

Outsourcing differs from simple subcontracting in that it usually involves the substantial restructuring of the customers' business activities, often including the transfer of staff from the customer to a specialist company (the provider) with the required core competencies. Management control of and decision making within the outsourced function is either transferred to or shared with the outside supplier. This requires a considerable amount of information exchange, coordination and trust between the two parties. Deciding whether to outsource a particular activity, which supplier to outsource it to, and how to manage the transition is therefore a substantial change programme involving one or more projects and needs to be managed using an appropriate project management methodology. This is particularly true if the programme involves transferring staff to a new employer.

One of the key decisions in an outsourcing programme is deciding which part of the operations are "non-core" and are therefore suitable for outsourcing. For example, XYZ Investment Managers describes itself as a fund manager. It defines its core business as:

- Winning investment mandates from customers such as collective investment schemes, charities, trusts, insurance and pension funds
- Selecting the investment strategies to meet the customers' investment goals
- Executing transactions that align with those goals.

However, once the customers have been signed up, the investment strategies determined and the transactions executed, then XYZ needs to employ operations personnel to settle the transactions, accounting staff to account for them, IT staff to select and manage the systems that play a part in making the investment decisions and process the trades, HR staff to manage the people and building management staff to manage the property, etc.

It is argued that all of these activities are "non-core" operations, and that some or all of them would best be delegated to an outside supplier whose own core competence lies in the management of one or more of these activities. This will leave XYZ's management free to concentrate on its core activities without the distraction of managing the non-core activities.

Almost any non-core activity may be outsourced, some examples are shown in Table 27.6. As far as IT activities are concerned, the table distinguishes between two forms of outsourcing:

- **Innovation outsourcing** is outsourcing the research and development of products, in particular the development of new business applications.
- **Production outsourcing** is outsourcing the maintenance and support of hardware, networks and IT applications that have already been developed

Table 27.6   Examples of outsourced activities

Business area	Department	Activity	Notes
Front office	Investment research	All investment research, or: Economic research for a particular market, e.g. USA; or for a particular sector, e.g. pharmaceuticals	
	Trade execution	All trade execution, or: Trade execution for a particular market, e.g. USA; or for a particular sector, e.g. pharmaceuticals; or for certain types of financial instrument, e.g. FX, derivatives	
Operations	Settlements	All settlement activity, or some of: Settlement activity for a particular geographical market, e.g. USA, Japan Settlement activity for particular financial instruments, e.g. derivatives, FX, equities	Note that when settlement activity is outsourced, the supplier – not the customer – usually takes on the risks of non-payment of debts by the custody services

(Continued)

Table 27.6 Examples of outsourced activities (*Continued*)

Business area	Department	Activity	Notes
	Information technology – "production outsourcing"	All IT activities, or some of: Supply and maintenance of desktop PCs and associated software Supply and maintenance of telecom systems and networks Provision of business continuity (disaster recovery) backup site Supply and maintenance of data servers	
		Maintenance and support of specific (existing) business applications	The customer may choose to outsource the management of all its applications, or just outsource the management of some of them, while developing and supporting the others in-house
	Information technology – "innovation outsourcing"	Development of (specific) new business applications	The customer may choose to outsource the development of all its new applications, or just a single one of them while continuing to develop the others in-house
Administration	HR	All HR activities, or some of: Permanent staff recruitment Temporary staff recruitment Payroll administration Pension and benefit administration	
	Premises	All premises related activities, or some of: Building maintenance Reception services Catering	

What is a non-core operation? A case study

This case study comes from a different industry, but its probably the most dramatic example in recent years of a major business failure where outsourcing played a role.

Railtrack plc

Founded under Conservative legislation that privatised the UK rail network, Railtrack took control of the railway infrastructure in 1995 and was floated on the stock exchange in 1996. From its inception, Railtrack outsourced virtually all of its infrastructure maintenance activities to civil engineering companies.

Fatal accidents at Southall in 1997 and Ladbroke Grove in 1999 called into question the effect that the fragmentation of the railway network had on both safety and maintenance procedures. Regulatory and customer pressure had been increasing, and the company's share price began to fall sharply as investors realised that there were serious faults in the company's ability to tackle and solve its greatest problems. The company's final, very public and humiliating descent into eventual liquidation began, though, with the Hatfield rail crash of 17 October 2000.

Investigations into the causes of the Hatfield crash, where four people were killed and 70 injured, revealed that the most likely cause was "gauge corner cracking" (microscopic cracks in the rails), and that problem was known about before the accident. Replacement rails had been made available, but never installed.

Railtrack had outsourced most maintenance activities to contractors that kept inadequate maintenance records and no coherent and accessible asset register. Often they in turn had subcontracted the activities that Railtrack believed they were performing themselves.

Railtrack did not therefore know how many of the other instances of gauge corner cracking around the network were capable of propagating a similar accident. It then had to impose over 1200 emergency speed restrictions across its network and instigated a nationwide track replacement programme costing over £500 million, and was subject to enforcement action by the Rail Regulator. Regulatory action, disruption and spiralling costs then led to the company being put into administration the following year following an application to the High Court by the then Transport Secretary, Stephen Byers.

This case study raises the following issues that any firm considering outsourcing part of its operations might want to consider:

1. Surely, maintenance of the UK rail network was a Railtrack *core operation* – should it have ever been outsourced in the first place?
2. Railtrack was not exercising management control over the companies that it had outsourced maintenance to. Neither Railtrack itself nor the companies that it had outsourced to were keeping adequate records of what work was being done nor what work needed to be done.

Benefits of outsourcing

Despite the dramatic warnings of the Railtrack case study, many companies have benefited from successful outsourcing arrangements. The benefits of outsourcing are:

- *Specialisation: Providing a higher quality of service.* Activities are usually outsourced by a non-specialist company to a specialist company. The specialist should be in a better position to:
  - Recruit specialist staff as it can provide them with more career opportunities
  - Enable specialist staff to share problems and expertise
  - Leverage the experience gained with working with other customers to the benefit of the new customer
  - Replace outdated technologies and working practices.
- *Specialisation: Enabling cost reduction.* The specialist should be in a better position to:
  - Undertake "joint developments" for all its customers at a lower cost per customer

- Use its bargaining power with key suppliers
- Cover absence of specialist staff without resorting to hiring temporary staff
- Move some operations offshore.
- *Focus on core activities*: The firm that has outsourced its non-core activities is now able to concentrate on the management of its core activities, in particular:
  - Improving customer relationships
  - Improving the quality of their core business activity
  - Extending the range of services offered to its customers – innovation.

Possible disadvantages of outsourcing

Not all outsourcing programmes deliver all the expected benefits. Common issues include:

- *Information security and intellectual property*: Offshoring involves the transfer of intellectual property to the supplier. When an activity is outsourced, sensitive information about customers, staff, investment decisions and positions, the firm's own financial position and its own intellectual property are passed to third parties. The exact nature of the sensitive information that is passed on depends on the type of activity that is being outsourced. Such information can be misused, and in an extreme example could be used fraudulently.
- *Is the decision to outsource reversible?* When an activity is outsourced, the employees that used to carry out the activity either leave the company (often to become employees of the service provider) or are redeployed within the company. If the company wanted to terminate the outsourcing arrangement at some time in the future and bring the function back in-house, then hiring an entire replacement team might be difficult.
- *Work, labour and the economy*: Outsourcing – more specifically offshoring in this context – became a popular political issue during the 2004 US presidential election. The political debate centred on outsourcing's consequences for the domestic workforce. Democratic US presidential candidate John Kerry criticised firms that outsource jobs abroad or that incorporate overseas in tax havens to avoid paying their fair share of US taxes during his 2004 campaign.

  In the UK, offshoring decisions that involve the creation of large numbers of jobs in offshore centres and/or the loss of large numbers of jobs in the domestic economy sometimes generates negative press comment. Some firms are concerned that outsourcing customer focused and visible activities such as call centres may drive customers away. At least one major UK retail bank has run a TV advertising campaign promising customers that all call centre calls are answered by its own employees in the UK.
- *The quality of the service fails to live up to the customer's expectations*: There are a number of reasons why the service that is delivered might fail to live up to the expectations of the management, staff and/or customers of the company that has outsourced its operations. Many of these problems are preventable, and the techniques and procedures to prevent them are discussed in other chapters in this workbook. They include the following:
  - *Outsourcing the wrong activity*: One of the Railtrack problems.
  - *Poor project management*: Managing the transition to outsourcing is a complex project. It needs to be managed using an accepted project management methodology such as PRINCE2 or PMI.
  - *Poor selection of vendor*: The chosen vendor does not, in fact, have the expertise or resources to carry out the functions.

- *Inadequate service level agreement*: The SLA either doesn't cover the real requirements of the service or it defines unrealistically high or low levels of service.
- *Communication*: The SLA has not been properly explained to staff or customers – therefore their expectations are not the same as those of the service provider. They are unsure of what to do when something goes wrong.
- *Inadequately documented systems and working practices*: When an operation is out-sourced, then the systems that are used to support it may or may not change but the working practices always do. There will need to be different procedures for escalating and resolving problems. It is important that the staffs of both companies are provided with comprehensive documentation and training in how to use the systems concerned, how to work with normal and exceptional workflows, and how to escalate and resolve problems.
- *Existing systems and working practices are unsuitable for outsourcing*: In an extreme case, it could prove to be the case that the customer's existing systems and working practices are so company specific and so antiquated that they are basically unsuitable for outsourcing in their current form. In such a case the outsourcing programme should have allowed for the replacement of some systems and workflows before the operation was outsourced. Both parties should have recognised this problem before taking the decision to outsource.
- *Inadequately documented development requirements*: This is a particular problem when commissioning software developments that are to be outsourced to an offshore location for the first time. The customer may have had no experience in this method of working before, and the fact that the users can no longer raise or resolve queries by meeting the developers informally and at short notice may come as a culture shock. For a large outsourced development to be successful there needs to be very clear and precise documentation of requirements, and very clear procedures for raising queries and raising change requests.

How successful is outsourcing?

A number of research companies have surveyed chief information officers in various industries and countries about the success of outsourcing projects. In 2005, the Gartner Group surveyed 200 European companies. Gartner concluded that 55% of those businesses with outsourcing contracts have renegotiated the deal.

One in eight contracts had even been renegotiated within the first 12 months of their operation, Gartner found, while only 23% of companies said they did not expect to renegotiate their contracts.

But only 6% were planning renegotiations to rescue existing deals, which Gartner said confirmed its view that relatively few companies are actively looking to bring outsourced services back in-house.

Half of survey respondents highlighted lack of flexibility as the biggest issue leading to renegotiations. Cost reduction was another key area, with two in five saying they paid too much for their outsourcing.

27.3.2 Insourcing

Definition of insourcing

In this context, **insourcing** (**in**ternal out**sourcing**) occurs where a company sets up an operation to carry out work that would otherwise have been contracted out. Insourcing often involves centralisation of activities that have previously been dispersed across a number of business units and geographical territories. For example, a firm currently has securities settlement operations in every one of its European offices (Amsterdam, London, Frankfurt, Madrid and Paris), each reporting to the local office manager who is also responsible for sales and trading in those centres.

Using the insourcing model, the securities firm would set up a single settlements division reporting to its own manager. The settlements division would centralise all activities in one location. This location could be in one of the cities where there is a sales and trading office or it could be in an offshore location.

The settlements division would treat all the sales offices as customers, in exactly the same way that an outsourced operation would have done. It would charge them a fee for its services, and would expect to recover its costs through this fee.

In other words, the settlement operation has been outsourced, but the provider of the outsourced service is part of the same company as the customer.

Advantages of insourcing over outsourcing

- Centralisation of the activity provides the opportunities to create:
  - Economies of scale
  - A centre of excellence for the activity being insourced.
- The retention of "institutional memory" – i.e. the collective experience, ethos and know-how of the team.
- Goals and vision are shared with the customer business units.
- Continued employee loyalty and Improved career path.

Disadvantages of insourcing over outsourcing

- Unless insourcing is accompanied by offshoring, it presents fewer opportunities for cost saving due to high employment costs in major financial centres.
- Outsourcing offers more opportunities for radical change to systems and working practices. With the insourcing model, there is a danger that the firm carries on doing things in the same way that it has always done them.
- An external outsourcing organisation has the opportunity to learn from other similar engagements, and introduce industry best practice. The opportunities for an insourcing unit to make such changes are far more restricted because of its more limited experience of the industry as a whole.
- Senior management may continue to regard the insourced operation as a cost centre, therefore it may have difficulty getting budget approval for radical developments.

27.3.3 Offshoring

Offshoring is defined as the movement of a business process done at a company in one country to the same or another company in another, different country. Almost always work is moved due to a lower cost of operations in the new location. The reasons why the costs are lower usually include more than one of the following:

- Lower salary rates in the offshore location
- Lower infrastructure costs in the offshore location

- Lower tax rates in the offshore location
- The offshore location may have a weak currency compared to the onshore location
- Possible availability of government grants and other incentives to set up business in the offshore location.

Offshoring is usually – but not always – associated with outsourcing, but it is of course possible to outsource without offshoring and to offshore without outsourcing. Some large banks and other companies have formed wholly-owned subsidiary companies in India and the Philippines to carry out business processes for their parent company – these companies are therefore both insourcing and offshoring.

Classic offshoring

When we hear the term "Offshoring" we usually think of a business process being moved from, say, the UK or the USA to India or the Philippines – several thousand miles and several time zones away. This is classic offshoring, but there are forms of offshoring that have a different model.

Near-shoring

Near-shoring implies relocation of business processes to (typically) lower cost foreign locations, but in close geographical proximity. Some common examples include:

- Shifting United States-based business processes to Canada or Latin America
- Shifting London-based operations either to a lower-cost European country such as Hungary, or to a lower cost part of the UK such as Northern Ireland
- Shifting German-based operations to countries such as the Czech Republic, Poland or Hungary. These countries have a competitive advantage over their counterparts in the "classic" outsourcing countries such as India and the Philippines because German is more widely spoken in these nearshore locations.

Near-shoring is usually more expensive than classic offshoring, so it is usually chosen as an alternative to classic offshoring when any of the following factors become important:

1. There is a shortage of resources in the classic offshoring centres that are able to communicate in the customer's native language.
2. The work involves frequent visits to or by the customer – in such a situation the cost of airfares might erode the classic offshore centre's usual cost advantages.
3. The work being undertaken has such a strong customer focus or regulations-driven reporting element and is tied so intrinsically to the business that it is harder to draw a solid line between them and the rest of the operation.
4. It is not practical to carry out the work in a different time zone

However, the near-shore centres do not, in general, attract a high proportion of "innovation outsourcing" work. This is because new application development usually needs a very large number of man-hours, and the "classic" offshore locations have a significant competitive advantage over the near-shore locations in terms of personnel and premises costs.

Best-shoring

The **best-shoring** concept is that some services need to be delivered in a location close to the customer, while some other services do not. Best-shoring involves tailoring specific customer care needs to locations that are best suited for these functions. It allows the customer to save on the cost of domestically sourcing the work, while at the same time removing the inflexibility of using only one offshore location.

Many of the world's leading consultancy companies, such as IBM, Accenture, as well as many of the large Indian outsourcing companies, have invested in facilities in "Near-shore" locations such as the Czech Republic, Hungary and Northern Ireland, so that they can offer their clients the advantages of best-shoring.

Comparison of each model

Classic offshoring is usually the lowest cost option. In the major offshore centres such as India and the Philippines there are very large numbers of highly skilled personnel available for all kinds of work at very competitive rates. The range of work undertaken is extensive, ranging from production activities such as call centre functions and simple transaction processing to investment research to innovation activities including research and development and large-scale software development and business process re-engineering.

The classic offshoring centres have a considerable competitive advantage in innovation activities because of the very large numbers of people that large development projects often require. There may, however, be problems associated with time zone differences and travel costs, cultural barriers and the classic centres do not always have access to resources that can communicate in European languages other than English.

Near-shoring is usually a higher cost option than classic offshoring. German companies often offshore call centre and customer focused activities to Poland, Hungary or the Czech Republic, where there are pools of resources with German language skills; US companies often offshore to Canada or Mexico and Japanese companies often offshore to China for similar reasons. Northern Ireland (itself of course part of the United Kingdom) sets out to attract call centre and transaction processing work from the rest of the UK.

The advantages that the near-shore centres offer are lower travel costs, fewer or no time zone differences and fewer or no cultural barriers. The types of work that the near-shore centres undertake include call centre functions, work of any kind that requires frequent travel to the customer, and more complex transaction processing – work that perhaps involves a strong customer focus or regulations-driven reporting element. The near-shore centres have not gained a significant share of the innovation outsourcing activities market.

Best-shoring attempts to offer the benefits of both the classic and near-shoring approaches. While it is more expensive than classic offshoring, it is a highly flexible way of outsourcing a wide range of activities, but is, by design, fragmented – the customer may be dealing with service providers in many locations. As a result, this method is only suitable if a large number of functions are to be offshored. Both the customer and the service provider need a management structure capable of handling this fragmentation.

27.3.4 The impact of outsourcing and offshoring on the IT function

A decision to outsource and/or offshore a substantial part of the firm's activities radically changes the role of the IT department. If, for example, the development, testing and support of all new business applications is contracted out then the future role of IT is largely concerned with supplier management which includes:

- Monitoring suppliers' compliance with service level agreements
- Liaising with the supplier
- Negotiating charges for new or changed services
- Monitoring the total value of the deal
- Reviewing the deliverables against overall objectives
- Managing data protection and security issues
- Integrating different applications and services provided by many external vendors.

Contract management is a distinct role in the IT department, but not every IT professional will be well suited to it. Firms need to identify the team that will provide these services and provide any necessary training in good time.

The performance of outsourced services needs to be monitored against objective criteria and problems need to be resolved as they occur. Benchmarking should be used to compare the service quality and value for money achieved through outsourcing with objective standards and best practice in other organisations.

In this scenario, while the IT department is no longer responsible for design, development and the early stages of testing it is still responsible for more tactical or strategic elements such as defining business specifications, change control, programme management and acceptance testing.

Appendix 1
Bond Market Price Calculations

STRAIGHT BOND CALCULATIONS

Simple yield to maturity and gross redemption yield have been developed to value and price these instruments. These measures take into account the pattern of coupon payments, the remaining life to maturity and the capital gain or loss arising over the remaining life of the bond.

Simple yield to maturity

The formula for simple yield to maturity is:

$$\text{Simple yield} = \frac{\text{Coupon rate}}{\text{Clean price}} + \frac{100 - \text{Clean price}}{\text{No. of years to maturity} * \text{Clean price}}$$

For example, given a bond with a 5.5% coupon rate, a current clean price of 98.3% and seven years remaining until maturity, the equation is:

$$\text{Simple yield} = \frac{5.5}{98.3} + \frac{100 - 98.3}{7 * 98.3} = 5.84\%$$

Gross redemption yield

Simple yield to maturity is a good rough and ready guide to bond valuation, but it does not take into account the affect of compound interest. To take this factor into account, the concept of gross redemption yield was developed, and this valuation methodology uses the following equation:

$$P_d = \left[\frac{1}{\left(1 + \frac{1}{2}rm\right)^{N_{tc}/182.5}} \right] \times \left[C/2 + \frac{C/2}{\left(1 + \frac{1}{2}rm\right)} + \cdots + \frac{C/2}{\left(1 + \frac{1}{2}rm\right)^{S-1}} + \frac{M}{\left(1 + \frac{1}{2}rm\right)^{S-1}} \right]$$

$$= \left[\frac{1}{\left(1 + \frac{1}{2}rm\right) N_{tc}/182.5} \right] \times \left[\sum_{t=0}^{S-1} \frac{C/2}{\left(1 + \frac{1}{2}rm\right)^t} + \frac{M}{\left(1 + \frac{1}{2}rm\right)^{S-1}} \right]$$

$$= \left[\frac{1}{\left(1 + \frac{1}{2}rm\right) N_{tc}/182.5} \right] \times \left\{ \frac{C}{rm} \left[\left(1 + \frac{1}{2}rm\right) - \frac{1}{\left(1 + \frac{1}{2}rm\right)^{S-1}} \right] + \frac{M}{\left(1 + \frac{1}{2}rm\right)^{S-1}} \right\}$$

where:

P_d is the dirty price of the bond
rm is the yield to maturity
N_{tc} is the number of days from today to the next coupon date

C is the coupon rate
M is the redemption payment of the bond at maturity (usually face value)
S is the number of coupon payments before redemption.

The simple yield to maturity and gross redemption yield formulae may be applied to straight bonds. They cannot be applied to FRNs because the future values of coupons are not known, so alternative evaluation methods are used for these instruments. Therefore the concepts of **simple margin** and **discounted margin** have been developed.

FRN CALCULATIONS

Simple margin

Simple margin is the average return on an FRN for its life compared to the reference interest rate. It is composed of two elements, the margin (i.e. the difference between the actual coupon rate and the benchmark interest rate), and the capital gain or loss that will be made when the bond matures (i.e. the difference between the cost price and the maturity value of the bond). The formula may be expressed as:

$$\text{Simple margin} = QM + (M - P_d)/100 * T$$

This formula amortises the element of capital gain or loss in a straight line over the remaining period to maturity, rather than at a constantly compounding rate. To achieve this, the discounted margin concept may be used. However, this method relies on a forecast of the benchmark interest rate over the life of the bond.

Discounted margin

This method constantly amortises the capital gains element at a constantly compounding rate. However, it relies on an accurate forecast of the benchmark interest rate over the life of the bond, which can be hard to predict. The formula is:

$$P_d = \left\{ \frac{1}{\left[1 + \frac{1}{2}(re + DM)\right]^{N_{tc}/182.5}} \right\}$$

$$\cdot \left\{ \frac{C}{2} + \sum_{t=1}^{S-1} \frac{(re* + QM) \times 100/2}{\left[1 + \frac{1}{2}(re* + DM)\right]^t} + \frac{M}{\left[1 + \frac{1}{2}(re* + DM)\right]^{S-1}} \right\}$$

where:

P_d is the dirty price of the bond
DM is the discounted margin
re is the current value of the benchmark interest rate
$re*$ is the assumed (forecast) benchmark rate over the remaining life of the bond
N_{tc} is the number of days from today to the next coupon date
QM is the quoted margin
S is the number of coupon payments before redemption.

VALUATION METHODOLOGIES FOR OTHER TYPES OF DEBT INSTRUMENT

None of these methods can be used to value and compare convertible bonds and bonds with warrants attached, because it is necessary to take into account the values of the equities into which the bonds can be converted or the warrants may be used to purchase. Nor are they suitable for index linked securities, where the coupon and/or the redemption value depend upon the inflation rate. It is beyond the scope of this book to provide a comprehensive summary of all the analytical methods that are used for all types of debt instruments, but Appendix 3 suggests some other publications that may be used as reference works.

Appendix 2
Summary of Contractual Documents

This appendix summarises the contractual documents that are likely to be presented to a firm that is considering any or all of the following:

- Purchasing a packaged application
- Outsourcing a software development
- Outsourcing a business process.

In particular, this summary describes any limitations that vendors usually apply to such documents that may impact the level of service they provide, or the cost of the services.

Table A2.1   Summary of contractual documents

Document name	Type of purchase where this document is used	Brief description of document
Software licence	Software package	The document grants the customer the right to use the software package for a given period of time, in return for the payment of a licence fee. Typically, this document may have restrictions about the use of the package. For example: • The user may only use this product in a given location • The licence may expire after a given number of years • The licence may restrict the number of transactions to be processed in a given day, week or month
Software maintenance contract	Software package	The document obliges the vendor to provide support of the package, in return for payment of a maintenance fee. Typically, this document may have limitations about the provision of support. For example: • Support may be restricted to telephone support and not include site visits which are charged separately • Support may either be available 24/7, or it may be restricted to normal business hours/days in the country from where it is provided • Support may be restricted to just problem solving, or it might entitle the user to new releases/upgrades of the package
Development contract	Outsourced development projects/software package	This document commits the vendor to develop software specified by the customer, in return for payment of development fees.

(Continued)

Table A2.1   (*Continued*)

Document name	Type of purchase where this document is used	Brief description of document
		Development fees may be charged on a "time and materials" basis – e.g. $1000 per day, or may be on a fixed price basis – e.g. $250 000 for the complete development. When development fees are charged on a fixed price basis, the scope of the development needs to be agreed at the start, and the contract will cater for variations. Variations are then dealt with by work orders or task orders
Service contract	Outsourced business process	This document describes the work that is to be outsourced to the vendor in return for payment of a services fee by the customer. Typically, this document may have restrictions about the use of the service. For example: • The user may only use this service in a given location • The service usually refers to trading volumes. There may be a minimum charge for the first, say, 1000 transactions per day/week/month, and extra transactions will be charged for on a sliding scale
Service level agreement	Outsourced business process	A service level agreement (SLA) is that part of a service contract in which a certain level of service is agreed upon. Level of service in this context refers to both the quality of the service and the time deadlines for performing the service. It may also specify penalties to be paid by either party if the level of service provided fails to reach the minimum standards in the agreement for an extended period of time
Work order	Outsourced development projects/outsourced business process/software package	In the case of a package, a work order may be used instead of a development contract. In the case of an outsourced development project, work orders are used mainly to vary the scope of the previously agreed development. In the case of an outsourced business process, it is used to request the vendor to carry out work that is outside the scope of the original service contract. It obliges the vendor to carry out the specified work in return for the agreed fee.
Task order	Outsourced development projects/outsourced business process/software package	An alternative to a work order

Table A2.1   (*Continued*)

Document name	Type of purchase where this document is used	Brief description of document
Change request	Outsourced development projects/outsourced business process/software package	An alternative to a work order
Non-disclosure agreement	All	An NDA creates a confidential relationship between the parties to protect any type of trade secret. The RFP that you issue may well contain background information about your current processes that you wish to protect, and equally the vendor will, in its responses, pass confidential information to your firm

Further Reading

Ainley, Michael, Mashayekhi, Ali, Hicks, Robert, Rahman, Arshadur and Ravalia, Ali (2007) *Islamic Finance in the UK: Regulation and Challenges*, Financial Services Authority, London

Choudhry, Moorad (2006) *An Introduction to Bond Markets*, Securities Institute, London

Choudhry, Moorad (2006) *An Introduction to Value at Risk*, Securities Institute, London

Fabozzi, F. and Pollack, I. (2000) *Handbook of Fixed Income Securities*, Dow Jones, New York

Geroulanos, Petros (1999) *An Introduction to Swaps*, Securities Institute, London

Iqbal, Zamir and Mirakhor, Abbas (2006) *An Introduction to Islamic Finance – Theory and Practice*, John Wiley & Sons, Singapore

Simmons, Michael (2002) *Securities Operations*, John Wiley & Sons, Chichester

Steiner, Robert (1996) *Mastering Repo Markets*, FT Pitman Publishing, London

Glossary of Terms

Accounting selection parameters table A data table that contains the rules for selecting which general ledger account to use for a particular posting

Accrual A method of accounting in which each item is entered as it is earned or incurred regardless of when actual payments are received or made

Accrued interest The interest that has accumulated on a transaction since the last interest payment date or start date, up to but not including the current date

ACK/NACK protocol This protocol is used by SWIFT to confirm that messages sent by its members have passed network validation and are therefore good messages (ACK), or have failed validation (NACK)

Affirm The process of affirmation

Affirmation The process where a buy-side firm sends a communication to a sell-side firm indicating their agreement to the details of a confirmation received from the sell-side firm

Agency trade A securities trade where the sell-side firm acts as the agent of its customer, and is remunerated by the payment of commission

Agile manifesto A statement of the principles that underpin agile software development

Agile model A methodology to manage the designing and building of software applications. The aim of this model is to minimise risk by developing software in short amounts of time

Algorithmic trading The placing a buy or sell order of a defined quantity into a quantitative model that automatically generates the timing of orders and the size of orders based on goals specified by the parameters and constraints of the algorithm

Allocation The process where a buy-side firm sends a communication to a sell-side firm advising the sell-side firm of the details of the investors who are parties to a block trade

American style options An option that may be exercised at any time before the expiry date

Application programming interface A source code interface that one computer system provides to support requests for services to be made of it by computer programs running in other systems. It specifies details of how the two independent computer programs can interact

Arbitrage The practice of taking advantage of a price differential between two or more markets

Assets Everything a corporation owns or that is due to it: cash, investments, money due it, materials and inventories, which are called current assets; buildings and machinery, which are known as fixed assets; and patents and goodwill, called intangible assets

Average price   The average price per unit of a position. If the position is long (i.e. positive), then further purchases modify the average price, and sales create P&L but do not modify the average price. If the position is short (i.e. negative) then further sales modify the average price, and purchases create P&L but do not modify the average price

Back testing   The practice of comparing the actual daily trading results to the predicted VaR figure

Bank for International Settlements (BIS)   An international organisation of central banks which exists to "foster cooperation among central banks and other agencies in pursuit of monetary and financial stability". It carries out its work through subcommittees, the secretariats it hosts, and through its annual general meeting of all members. The BIS also provides banking services, but only to central banks, or to international organisations like itself. Based in Basel, Switzerland, the BIS was established by the Hague agreement of 1930

Bargain   See "Trade"

Basel Accord   The set of minimum capital requirements developed by the Basel Committee, originally in 1988

Basel Committee   A committee of central bankers which publishes a set of minimal capital requirements for banks and is known as the Basel Accord

Basel II   The second version of the standards of the Basel Accord, to be implemented by participating countries in 2008

Baseline   A declared summary description of the point in a project, indicating original content and stage reached, as a basis for measuring project performance and estimates to complete

Baseline control   A system of procedures that allows monitoring and control of the emerging project scope against the scope baseline. Also known as "Configuration control"

Basis point   A basis point (often denoted as ‰) is a unit that is equal to 1/100th of 1%, and is used to denote the change in a financial instrument. The basis point is commonly used for calculating changes in interest rates, equity indexes and the yield of a fixed income security. The relationship between percentage changes and basis points can be summarised as follows: 1% change = 100 basis points, and 0.01% = 1 basis point. So, a bond whose yield increases from 5% to 5.5% is said to increase by 50 basis points; or interest rates that have risen 1% are said to have increased by 100 basis points

Basis risk   A form of market risk. The risk that one position has been hedged with another position that behaves in a similar, but not identical, fashion

Bearer securities   Securities for which there is no register or registrar. When the security is first issued on the primary market, the issuer prints certificates representing the entire amount of shares or bonds issued, and these are posted to the investors who have purchased the shares in the primary market

Benchmark interest rate   A reference rate is a rate that determines pay-offs in a financial contract and that is outside the control of the parties to the contract. It is often some form of LIBOR rate, but it can take many forms, such as a consumer price index, a house price index or an unemployment rate. Parties to the contract choose a reference rate that neither party has power to manipulate

Beneficial ownership   A legal term where specific property rights ("use and title") in equity belong to a person even though legal title of the property belongs to another person, the nominal owner.

Best execution   An obligation placed on sell-side firms to get the lowest available price for its customer when the customer is buying, and the highest available price when the customer is selling, taking into account other factors such as speed and accuracy of execution

Best-shoring   The "best-shoring" strategy involves tailoring specific customer care needs to locations that are best suited for these functions. It allows the customer to save on the cost of domestically sourcing the work, while at the same time removing the inflexibility of using only one offshore location

Bid price   The highest price that a prospective buyer is willing to pay for a specific security. The offer, also called the "asking price", is the lowest price acceptable to a prospective seller of the same security. The highest bid and lowest offer are quoted on most major exchanges, and the difference between the two prices is called the "spread"

Bill   A debt instrument issued for a period of less than one year with the purpose of raising capital by borrowing. The Federal government, states, cities, corporations and many other types of institutions sell bonds. Generally, a bond is a promise to repay the principal along with interest (coupons) on a specified date (maturity)

Block trade   The purchase or sale of large quantities of stock. On the New York Stock Exchange trades involving 10 000 or more shares and $200 000 in value are considered block trades. Block trades are often placed by fund managers on behalf of a number of investors, and may need to be allocated to those investors. See "Allocation"

Bond   A debt instrument issued for a period of more than one year with the purpose of raising capital by borrowing. The Federal government, states, cities, corporations and many other types of institutions sell bonds. Generally, a bond is a promise to repay the principal along with interest (coupons) on a specified date (maturity)

Book or trading book   A portfolio of financial instruments held by a brokerage or bank. The financial instruments in the trading book are purchased or sold to facilitate trading for their customers, to profit from spreads between the bid/ask spread, or to hedge against various types of risk. Sometimes this term is used interchangeably with "position"

Business case   The reason, in non-technical terms, why a particular project is to be undertaken

Business continuity management   Review of business continuity, risk analysis and risk management, defining assets, threats, vulnerabilities and countermeasures (protection and recovery), development, testing and maintenance of the IT service continuity plan, IT recovery options and management roles

Business continuity plan   A plan developed to mitigate different disaster or worst case scenarios. The BCP will contain agreed workarounds and task lists for those supporting the application during a disaster. The goal of BCP processes is to ensure that IT services can be recovered within required, agreed and business sensitive timescales

Buy-in notice   Investors and securities firms who fail to deliver securities for an extended period of time may be issued with a buy-in notice. Failure to answer the buy-in notice means the trading party that issued the notice may buy the securities from a third party and cancel the transaction with the original party. If the price has risen, then the selling party has to compensate the buying party any losses

Buy-sellback   A form of a repo where the two legs of the transaction are treated as separate transactions, and the purchaser does not directly pass any coupon payments back to the seller. Instead, the price of the second leg is adjusted by the value of the coupon that the seller did not receive

Buy-side firms   Fund managers that take investment decisions on behalf of investors

CAD   The European Capital Adequacy Directive

Call and notice loans and deposits   Money market loans and deposits with no maturity date agreed on trade date

Call option   See "Option"

Cap   The maximum coupon rate of a floating rate note

Capability maturity model   A description of the common stages that software organisations evolve through as they define, implement, measure, control and improve their software processes

Cash instrument   See "Underlying instrument"

Central counterparty   A central counterparty is a financial institution that acts as an intermediary between security market participants. This reduces the amount of counterparty risk that market participants are exposed to

Central Securities Depository or CSD   An entity holding securities either in certificated or uncertificated (dematerialised) form, to enable book entry transfer of securities. In some cases these organisations also carry out centralised comparison, and transaction processing such as clearing and settlement of securities. The physical securities may be immobilised by the depository, or securities may be dematerialised (so that they exist only as electronic records). International Central Securities Depository (ICSD) is a central securities depository that settles trades in international securities and in various domestic securities, usually through direct or indirect (through local agents) links to local CSDs. ClearStream International (earlier Cedel), Euroclear and SegaInterSettle are considered ICSDs

CFD   An agreement between two parties to exchange the difference between the opening value and the closing value of a particular share. These are generally short-term contracts drawn up by both involved parties. The sell-side firm's exposure to default by its client is controlled by margin requirements and collateral deposits

Change control procedures   A process developed to prevent an item of software or hardware from being amended without auditability and review of the impact by all interested parties

Chart of accounts   The list of accounts used by a general ledger system

Child trade   After a buy-side firm sends its allocation instructions, a single bulk trade executed by a sell-side firm (the parent trade) may need to be broken down into a series of smaller trades – child trades – one for each investor concerned

Chinese walls   Information barriers implemented within firms to separate and isolate persons who make investment decisions from persons who are privy to undisclosed material information which may influence those decisions

Classic offshoring   Offshoring that is neither "near-shoring" nor "best-shoring". In practice this usually implies offshoring to India or the Philippines

Clean price   The price of a bond trade (excluding accrued interest) expressed as a percentage of face value

Clearing house   A financial institution that operates clearing, central counterparty or settlement services

Clearing member   A member of a clearing house that clears only its own trades

Client money   Money belonging to clients which an investment business is holding. It could either be free money or settlement money and in either case it must be kept in a bank account separate from the firm's own money

Cold standby   A standby server that is configured similarly to the primary server and ideally should be running the same version of the operating system and database, and with all the same service packs applied. If the primary server suffers a failure then the SQL database is restored to the secondary server from the primary's backup files

Collar   The range between the cap and the floor of a floating rate note coupon

Collateral   A security or guarantee (usually an asset) pledged for the repayment of a loan

Collateral substitution   The act of returning securities supplied as collateral by a stock borrower to a lender, and replacing them with other securities of a similar value and quality

Commission   The amount charged by a sell-side firm to its customer when executing an agency order

Confirmation   The process where one party to a trade sends the other party a communication that confirms that the order has been executed, and provides details of the resulting trade

Consideration   The total amount paid by an investor when purchasing an investment, or received by an investor when selling. Consideration is the sum of principal amount + accrued interest + commission + fees

Contract for difference   See "CFD"

Convertible bond   A bond that offers the investor the opportunity to surrender the bond in exchange for equity securities at a fixed price per share. The equity securities are usually issued by the same company that issued the bond

Corporate action   Events initiated by a public company that affects the securities (equity or debt) issued by the company; examples include takeovers, stock splits, rights issues and consolidations

Counterparty risk   A form of credit risk. The risk that a trading party cannot meet its obligations to settle trades or make other transaction-related payments (such as swap cash flows) in the future

Coupon   The interest payable on a debt instrument

Coupon date   The interest payment date of a bond

Coupon period   The period of time between the previous coupon date and the next coupon date of a bond issue

Coupon rate   The interest rate of a bond

Credit crunch   An economic condition where investment capital is difficult to obtain. Banks and investors become wary of lending funds to potential borrowers, thereby driving up the price of debt products for borrowers. Credit crunches are usually considered to be an extension of recessions. A credit crunch makes it nearly impossible for organisations and individuals to borrow because lenders are scared of bankruptcies or defaults, which results in higher interest rates. The consequence is a prolonged recession (or slower recovery), which occurs as a result of the shrinking credit supply

Credit default swap   A contract under which two trade parties agree to isolate and separately trade the credit risk of one or more securities or other obligations issued by a third party

Credit limit   The maximum amount of credit that a bank or other lender will extend to a debtor. In the securities industry "debtors" may include clients, counterparties, countries or business sectors. In addition, securities firms usually have limits that they apply to individual traders or trading books

Credit rating   An independent measure of creditworthiness made by a credit rating agency, which affects the interest rate applied to loans

Credit rating agency   A company that assigns credit ratings for issuers of certain types of debt obligations

Credit risk   The risk associated with one party not fulfilling its contractual obligations at a specific future date

CREST   The former name of the Central Securities Depositary for the UK and Ireland. In 2007, CREST changed its name to Euroclear UK and Ireland

Critical path   The series of interdependent project activities, connected end to end, which determines the longest path through the project network and hence the shortest total duration of the project. The critical path may change from time to time as tasks are completed behind or ahead of schedule

Cum-warrant bond   A bond with warrants attached

Currency risk   A form of market risk. The risk to an investment portfolio caused by movements in exchange rates

Custodian bank   A bank, agent, or other organisation responsible for safeguarding a firm's or individual's financial assets. The role of a custodian is to hold in safekeeping assets such as equities and bonds, arrange settlement of any purchases and sales of such securities, collect information on and income from such assets (dividends in the case of equities and interest in the case of bonds), provide information on the underlying companies and their annual general meetings, manage cash transactions, perform foreign exchange transactions where required and provide regular reporting on all their activities to their clients

Customer order priority   An obligation on the firm executing a client order while at the same time executing orders for its own account to execute these orders fairly and in due turn

Customer side trade   One half of an agency trade, the side of the trade that settles with the investor

Data controller   The name of the individual within the firm that is responsible for compliance with the Data Protection Act 1998

Data Protection Act 1998   This act details how personal data should be dealt with to protect its integrity and to protect the rights of the persons concerned

Database replication   The process of creating and managing duplicate versions of a database. Replication not only copies a database but also synchronises a set of replicas so that changes made to one replica are reflected in all the others

Deal   See "Trade"

Debt instrument   Collective name for both bonds and bills

Deliverable   The physical outcome of a task resulting from applying defined processes to a set of inputs. A deliverable is a measurable, tangible, verifiable item produced as part of a project

Delivery by Value (DbV)   A service operated by CSDs for their member firms where the CSD selects the securities to be used in a multi-instrument repo transaction

Delivery date   The date that an investor who held a position in a future at its expiry date has to deliver the underlying instrument, or settle the obligation in cash

Delivery risk   The risk that payment is made for a trade by one party, but the other party fails to fulfil its obligations to deliver securities or make payment in another currency

Delivery versus payment (DvP)   The simultaneous delivery of securities by a seller and payment of sale proceeds by a purchaser of securities on settlement date

Dematerialised securities   Registered securities for which no share certificates are issued. The share register itself is the evidence of ownership

Depot   The account with a settlement agent which is used to record transactions and balances in security quantities

Depot position   Settlement date position + stock borrowed − stock lent

Derivative instrument A financial contract whose value depends upon the value of an underlying instrument or asset (typically a commodity, bond, equity or currency, or a combination of these). Three classes of financial products fall under the heading of derivatives: derivative securities; exchange-traded derivatives; and over-the-counter (OTC) derivatives

Deutsche Borse Group Owner and operator of the Frankfurt Stock Exchange as well as the EUREX futures exchange

Digital certificate An electronic "credit card" that establishes your credentials when doing business or other transactions on the web. It is issued by a certification authority (CA). It contains your name, a serial number, expiration dates, a copy of the certificate holder's public key (used for encrypting messages and digital signatures), the digital signature of the certificate issuing authority so that a recipient can verify that the certificate is real

Direct market access (DMA) The automated process of routing a securities order directly to an execution venue, therefore avoiding intervention by a third party

Dirty price The price of a bond trade (including accrued interest) expressed as a percentage of face value

Disaster recovery The process of regaining access to the data, hardware and software necessary to resume critical business operations after a natural or human-induced disaster. A disaster recovery plan (DRP) should also include plans for coping with the unexpected or sudden loss of key personnel. DRP is part of a larger process known as business continuity planning (BCP)

Discounted margin The average return on an FRN for its life compared to the reference interest rate, calculated at a constantly compounding rate

Diversification Investing in a wide range of assets spread across different countries, industries, etc. so as to mitigate market risk

Dividend A taxable payment declared by a company's board of directors and given to its shareholders out of the company's current or retained earnings. Dividends are usually given as cash (cash dividend), but they can also take the form of stock (stock dividend) or other property. Dividends provide an incentive to own stock in stable companies even if they are not experiencing much growth. Companies are not required to pay dividends. The companies that offer dividends are most often companies that have progressed beyond the growth phase, and no longer benefit sufficiently by reinvesting their profits, so they usually choose to pay them out to their shareholders

Dividend date The date on which a dividend is paid

Double-entry bookkeeping The basis of the standard system used by businesses and other organisations to record financial transactions, where each transaction is recorded in at least two accounts

DvP or DVP See "Delivery versus payment"

Economic and Monetary Union (EMU) On 1 January 1999 the euro became the official currency for 11 participating countries in the European Union (EU). In 2001, Greece also adopted the euro as its official currency. From that date forward, the respective foreign exchange operations, new public debt and all stocks and bonds on all stock exchanges in the participating member areas were quoted or issued in euro. Euro banknotes were first made available three years later

Effective date (of an interest accrual) The date that interest is to be accrued to. Depending on why interest is being accrued this may be the value date of a transaction, today, or the date of a statistical month end

End user development   A set of activities or techniques that allows individuals who are non-professional developers to create or modify a software artifact

Equity   Ownership interest in a corporation in the form of common or preferred stocks or shares

Equity risk   The general market risk of rises or falls of individual share prices or stock market levels in general

Equity swap   A swap where one of the payment streams is based on the return from holding an equity or equity index instead of being based on an interest rate

EURIBOR   EURIBOR (Euro Interbank Offered Rate) is the benchmark rate at which Euro Interbank term deposits within the Eurozone are offered by one prime bank to another prime bank. It is one of the two benchmarks for the money and capital markets in the Eurozone (the other one being Eonia). EURIBOR is sponsored by the European Banking Federation (FBE), which represents the interests of 3000 banks in the 25 member states of the European Union and in Iceland, Norway and Switzerland and by the Financial Markets Association (ACI). The first EURIBOR was published on 30 December 1998

Euroclear   The central securities depositary for France, The Netherlands and Belgium, and owner of CREST CSD in London. Euroclear also provides settlement services for the international bond markets

Euronext   Owner and operator of the Amsterdam, Brussels, Lisbon and Paris Stock Exchanges as well as the LIFFE futures exchange in London

European Economic Area   The 27 countries of the European Union plus Iceland, Norway and Liechtenstein

European style options   An option that may be exercised only at the expiry date of the option, i.e. at a single predefined point in time

European Union   A political and economic community with supranational and intergovernmental dimensions. It is composed of 27 member states: Austria, Belgium, Bulgaria, Cyprus, the Czech Republic, Denmark, Estonia, Finland, France, Germany, Greece, Hungary, Ireland, Italy, Latvia, Lithuania, Luxembourg, Malta, the Netherlands, Poland, Portugal, Romania, Slovakia, Slovenia, Spain, Sweden, and the United Kingdom

Ex-dividend date   A date, usually two working days before record date for a dividend. After the stock exchange closes on the day before the ex-dividend date and before the market opens on the ex-dividend date, the price of all open good-until-cancelled, limit, stop and stop limit orders are automatically reduced by the amount of the dividend, except for orders that the customer indicated "Do Not Reduce". This is because these trades cannot settle until after record date, and the new owners will not receive the dividend concerned

Ex-warrant bond   A cum-warrant bond from which the warrants have been detached

Exercise date   The date on which an option is exercised

Expiry date   For a traded option, the date on which the option expires. For a future, the date when the final price of the future is determined

Face value   The quantity of a bond trade or bond issue. Also known as principal amount

Failed trade   A trade that has not settled by the agreed value date

Fees   Any charges other than commission and accrued interest that are applied to a securities trade

Financial control department   The department of the securities firm that is responsible for managing the financial resources of the business

Financial Services and Markets Act 2000   The Financial Services and Markets Act 2000 (FSMA 2000) introduced a new structure for the regulation of the financial services industry in the United Kingdom, which came into effect from midnight on 30 November 2001. It established a new regulatory regime, empowering the Financial Services Authority (FSA) with broad responsibility for both the prudential and business conduct regulation of firms within the financial services industry

Financial Services Authority (FSA)   The UK regulator for the financial services industry

FIX Protocol   The Financial Interface eXchange (FIX) protocol was initiated in 1992 by a group of institutions and brokers interested in streamlining their trading processes. It is an open message standard controlled by no single entity, which can be structured to match the business requirements of each firm

Fixed income security   See "Debt instrument"

Fixing date   The date on which the benchmark interest rate (such as LIBOR or EURIBOR) for the next coupon period of a bond or swap is published

Floating rate note   A bond whose interest rate is linked to a benchmark interest rate such as LIBOR

Floor   The minimum coupon rate of a floating rate note

Follow the sun model   A method of running a helpdesk where an incident that is reported during one time zone will continue to be worked on and handed over to others around the clock until it is resolved ready for the requestor to sign off and close on their return to the office.

Foreign exchange   The simultaneous buying of one currency and selling of another, either for spot (i.e. immediate) settlement, or for forward settlement (i.e. settlement at a later date)

Forward transaction   A foreign exchange transaction with value date of more than two working days after trade date

Fountain model   A model for software development that is based on the waterfall model

Free of payment (FOP)   A term used in a settlement instruction where the movement of cash and the movement of securities are *not* inextricably linked to one another. In other words, FoP is the opposite of delivery versus payment (DVP)

Functional testing   Tests at any level (class, module, interface, or system) for proper functionality as defined in the specification

Future or futures contract   A legally binding agreement to buy or sell a commodity or financial instrument in a designated future month at a price agreed upon today by the buyer and seller. Futures contracts are standardised according to the quality, quantity and delivery time and location for each commodity. A futures contract differs from an option because an option is the right to buy or sell, while a futures contract is the promise to make a transaction

General clearing member   A futures and options exchange member that is also a member of a clearing house, and which clears trades done by other exchange members, who are known as non-clearing members

General Ledger   The general ledger, sometimes known as the nominal ledger, is the main accounting record of a business which uses the double-entry bookkeeping convention. It will usually include accounts for such items as current assets, fixed assets, liabilities, revenue and expense items, gains and losses

Gharar   Islamic finance term for uncertainty in a contract

Global custodian   A custodian bank that holds securities in multiple jurisdictions around the world, using their own local branches or other local custodian banks in each market

Gross redemption yield   Also known as yield to maturity. The return on the investment on a debt security, taking compound interest into account

Haircut   The difference between the market value of securities lent and the collateral amount required by the lender. For example, if the market value of the securities is £100 000, and the collateral required is £105 000, then the haircut is £5000

Haraam   An Arabic term meaning "forbidden". In Islam it is used to refer to anything that is prohibited by the faith. Its antonym is *halaal*. In the context of Islamic finance it refers to investment in any asset class that is forbidden by Islam

Hedge fund   A pooled investment vehicle that is privately organised and administered by investment management professionals and not widely available to the public. Many hedge funds share a number of characteristics: they hold long and short positions, use derivatives and leverage to enhance returns, pay a performance or incentive fee to their hedge fund managers, have high minimum investment requirements and target absolute (rather than relative) returns

Hedging   The purchase or sale of a commodity, security or other financial instrument for the purpose of offsetting the profit or loss of another security or investment. Thus, any loss on the original investment will be hedged, or offset, by a corresponding profit from the hedging instrument

Helpdesk   A section of the IT department that takes requests from users to deal with system problems and/or out of the ordinary requests, logs them, prioritises them and hands them to the appropriate individuals for action

Hot standby   An approach to maintaining system availability whereby all transactions are routinely written to the production server and the standby server simultaneously. The standby server is therefore ready to take over the processing load instantaneously, should there be any failure in the production system

Hybrid market systems   A stock exchange trading system that uses both an order queue and market makers

IBAN code   A European standard for storing bank account numbers

ICMA   International Capital Markets Association – a Swiss-based organisation with the status of a designated investment exchange in the UK. The ICMA promotes bye-laws, statutes, rules and recommendations for market practices in the bond markets

Illiquid   A financial instrument that is rarely traded is said to be illiquid

Index linked bond   A bond whose interest rate and/or redemption proceeds are linked to an index, such as the Retail Price Index in the United Kingdom

Information commissioner   The UK government agency that is responsible for the operation of the Data Protection Act 1998

Infrastructure catalogue   An inventory of all the applications and hardware used by a business. The infrastructure catalogue is a prerequisite for both helpdesk management and business continuity planning

Initial margin   A margin amount that a member of a clearing house must pay in order to open a position

Initial public offering (IPO)   The first sale of stock by a private company to the public

Innovation outsourcing   Outsourcing the research and development of products, in particular the development of new business applications

Insider dealing   Illegal share dealings by employees of a company where they have used confidential price-sensitive information for their own gain or the gain of their associates.

Insourcing   Insourcing (**internal outsourcing**) occurs where a company sets up an operation to carry out work that would otherwise have been contracted out. It usually implies the centralisation of a service that would have previously been decentralised; and may also imply that the insourced service is now provided offshore

Instrument associations Static data that informs about other instruments into which a complex instrument such as a convertible bond or warrant may be converted into or exercised

Integration testing Testing designed to expose defects in the interfaces and interaction between integrated components (modules)

Intellectual property rights Rights to intangible property that is the product of the human intellect. Intellectual property may be protected by copyright, trademark or patent

Interest rate cap An OTC derivative contract where the buyer receives money at the end of each period in which an interest rate exceeds the agreed strike price

Interest rate collar A combination of an interest rate cap and an interest rate floor

Interest rate floor An OTC derivative contract where the buyer of the floor receives money at the end of each period in which an interest rate is lower than the agreed strike price

Interest rate risk A form of market risk. The risk to a portfolio caused by fluctuating interest rates

International Capital Markets Association (ICMA) A self-regulatory organisation and trade association representing the financial institutions active in the international capital markets worldwide. ICMA provides the TRAX2 central matching engine

International Central Securities Depository or ICSD See "Central Securities Depository or CSD"

International Securities Lending Association or ISLA A trade association established in 1989 to represent the common interests of participants in the securities lending industry

International Standards Organisation or ISO A United Nations sponsored organisation that sets international standards that can be used in any type of business and are accepted around the world as proof that a business can provide assured quality

Internet protocol suite (IP) The set of communications protocols that implement the protocol stack on which the Internet and most commercial networks run

Investment bank Strictly speaking, an investment bank is a financial institution that assists companies and governments and their agencies to raise money by issuing and selling securities in the primary market. Investment banks also act as intermediaries in trading for clients. However, only a few small firms provide only this service. Almost all investment banks are heavily involved in providing additional financial services for clients, such as the trading of derivatives, fixed income, foreign exchange, commodity and equity securities. In this book the term "investment bank" is used to describe an institution that offers some or all of these services

Investment exchange A corporation or mutual organisation which provides facilities for stockbrokers and traders, to trade company stocks and other securities including bonds, derivatives and physical commodities such as precious metals and agricultural products

Investment mandate A contract between an investor and a fund manager that sets out the terms on which the fund manager will act for the investor

Investment Services Directive A European Commission Directive issued in 1993. It specifies that if a firm has been authorised by one member state to provide investment services, this single authorisation enables the firm to provide those same investment services in other member states without further authorisation. The originating state providing authorisation is commonly referred to as the "home" state, whereas other states where investment services are offered are known as "host" states. In 2007, the ISD was superseded by MiFID

IP protocol   The Internet protocol suite is the set of communications protocols that implement the protocol stack on which the Internet runs. It is sometimes called the TCP/IP protocol suite, after the two most important protocols in it: the Transmission Control Protocol (TCP) and the Internet protocol (IP), which were also the first two defined

ISDA   The International Swaps and Derivatives Association

ISDA Master Agreement   A standardised contract (drafted by the ISDA) to enter into derivatives transactions

ISIN code   (International Securities Identification Number): a 12 character, alphanumeric code allocated to each equity and bond that is widely used to identify individual securities in financial messages.

Islamic Financial Services Board (IFSB)   An international standard-setting organisation that promotes and enhances the soundness and stability of the Islamic financial services industry by issuing global prudential standards and guiding principles for the industry, broadly defined to include banking, capital markets and insurance sectors

Islamic window   A department of a conventional bank or other financial institution that only offers Sharia compliant products

ISO9126   The international standard for software testing

Issue   Requests to a helpdesk and defects found during software testing are both often known as "issues".

Issue price   The price that a bond or equity was first issued in the primary offering

Issuer risk   A form of credit risk. The risk that a security issuer may not be able to pay coupon, dividend or maturity proceeds at some time in the future

IT Infrastructure Library^{TM} A set of concepts and techniques developed and supported by the UK government for managing IT infrastructure, development and operations

Iterative/Incremental   A methodology to manage the designing and building of software applications

Joint requirement development sessions   A means of requirement gathering where stakeholders are gathered together in "requirement workshops"

LCH.Clearnet   A recognised clearing house that operates central counterparty services for a number of European markets including the LSE and Euronext.LIFFE

Letter of credit   In the context of stock loans and repos, a document issued by the borrower's bank that essentially acts as an irrevocable guarantee of payment to the lender, should the borrower not be in a position to return the securities

Leverage   The degree to which an investor or business is utilising borrowed money

Liabilities   All the claims against a corporation. Liabilities include accounts, wages and salaries payable; dividends declared payable; accrued taxes payable; and fixed or long-term liabilities, such as mortgage bonds, debentures and bank loans

LIBOR   LIBOR is a benchmark interest rate published by the British Bankers Association (BBA) shortly after 11am each day, London time, and is a filtered average of interbank deposit rates offered by designated contributor banks, for maturities ranging from overnight to one year. The shorter rates, i.e. up to six months, are usually quite reliable and tend to precisely reflect market conditions at measurement time. The actual rate at which banks will lend to one another will, however, continue to vary throughout the day

Liquidity risk   The risk that a firm may be unable to refinance its borrowings as they mature and needs to be renegotiated. For securities firms, this may be because the market for the instruments that it uses for its borrowings becomes too thin to enable efficient and fair trading to take place

Log shipping   A process that allows you to automatically send transaction log backups from a *primary database* on a *primary server* instance to one or more *secondary databases* on separate *secondary server* instances

London Stock Exchange   The largest formal market for securities in the UK; the LSE facilitates deals in equities, bonds and some derivatives such as exchange traded funds and covered warrants

Long position   See "Position"

Lot   Futures and options contracts are denominated in lots. One lot is the minimum quality of the contract that may be traded, and the exchange that lists the contract will specify what precise quantity of the underlying instrument is represented by one lot

Maintenance margin   Margin based on the unrealised losses of a transaction or position

Managing stage boundaries   A key step in a project reflecting the decision point in the continuity of the project as planned, adjusted or stopped. The process involves preparing for the next stage and reviewing the current stage

Margin   The cash or collateral that a holder of a position in securities or in exchange traded derivatives is required to post to cover potential adverse movements in the value of the position

Mark to market   An accounting procedure by which assets are "marked," or recorded at their current market value, which may be higher or lower than their purchase price or book value

Market abuse   An offence introduced by FSMA 2000; judged on what a "regular user" would view as a failure to observe the required standards. The offence includes abuse of information, misleading the market and distortion of the market

Market identifier code   ISO Standard 10383 specifies a universal method of identifying exchanges, trading platforms and regulated or non-regulated markets as sources of prices and related information in order to facilitate automated processing. The market code convention is four alphabetic characters. For example, the code for the London Stock Exchange is XLON

Market maker   A sell-side firm that has accepted the obligation to quote both a buy and a sell price in a financial instrument or commodity, hoping to make a profit on the turn or the bid/offer spread

Market risk   The risk that the value of the investments owned by the investor might decline

Market-side trade   One half of an agency trade, the side of the trade that settles with the market maker of the clearing house appointed by the exchange

Matching engine   A form of trade agreement where both parties input their trade details to the matching engine database, and the matching engine then compares the two trade reports and provides them to both parties in real time

Maturity date   The date when the borrower repays the investors of a bond issue with the face value of the issue

MiFID   The Markets in Financial Instruments Directive (MiFID) introduced a single market and regulatory regime for investment services across the 25 member states of the European Union in 2007

Milestone   A significant event in the project, usually completion of a major deliverable, at a given point in time

Model risk   The risk that models (such as VaR) are applied to tasks for which they are inappropriate or are otherwise implemented incorrectly

Money broker   Traditionally, a firm that acts as intermediary, arranging deals between principals in the FX, money market loan and deposits, debt securities and OTC derivative markets

Money laundering   The process of turning dirty money (money derived from criminal activities) into clean money (money that appears to be legitimate)

Multilateral trading facility   A system that brings together multiple parties that are interested in buying and selling financial instruments and enables them to do so

Near-shoring   A form of offshoring where the business process is relocated to lower cost foreign locations, but these locations are in close geographical proximity to the customer's country of business

Nominal ledger   See "general ledger"

Nominal owner   A person or group that holds title to a security or piece of real estate but is not the true owner

Non-clearing member   A firm that is a member of a futures and options exchange but not its associated clearing house. The non-clearing member relies on general clearing members to clear its trades on the relevant exchanges

Non-disclosure agreement   A legal contract between the parties which outlines confidential materials or knowledge the parties wish to share with one another for certain purposes, but wish to restrict from generalised use. In other words, it is a contract through which the parties agree not to disclose information covered by the agreement. An NDA creates a confidential relationship between the parties to protect any type of trade secret

Normal market size   The quantity of stock that can be purchased without moving the market price. This will vary from security to security, the less liquid that a stock is on a particular market, the smaller the normal market size will be

Nostro   The account with a settlement agent which is used to record transactions and balances in cash amounts

Notional principal   The principal value of a swap or futures deal or position. Because these are off-balance sheet items, their value is said to be "notional"

Novation   The substitution of one party to a contract by another party, in particular novation occurs at the point when the central counterparty assumes the responsibility to settle a trade

Objective   A concise statement (or statements) of what the project is to achieve

OECD   The Organisation for Economic Cooperation and Development (OECD). An international organisation of 30 industrialised countries that accept the principles of representative democracy and a free market economy

Off-balance sheet item   An asset or debt or financing activity not on the company's balance sheet. It could involve a lease or a separate subsidiary or a contingent liability such as a letter of credit. It also includes futures, forwards, swaps and other derivatives

Offer price   The lowest price acceptable to a prospective seller of the same security. The highest bid and lowest offer are quoted on most major exchanges, and the difference between the two prices is called the "spread"

Offshoring   Offshoring is defined as the movement of a business process done at a company in one country to the same or another company in another, different country. Almost always, work is moved due to a lower cost of operations in the new location

Operational risk   The risk of losing money due to mistakes, processing errors or deliberate wrongdoing

Option or options contract A call option gives the buyer (or holder) the right (but *not* the obligation) to purchase the underlying instrument at a specified price on or before a given date. A put option on the other hand gives the buyer (or holder) the right (but *not* the obligation) to sell the underlying instrument at a specified price on or before a given date

Option premium The amount paid in order to purchase an option

Order-driven markets A stock exchange trading system that does not rely on market makers. A member firm who wishes to buy a given stock at a given price submits an order to the system; while at the same time other member firms who wish to sell the same stock submit sell orders to the system

Outsourcing The delegation of non-core operations from internal production to an external entity specialising in the management of that operation

Over-the-counter (OTC) market A decentralised market of securities not listed on an exchange where market participants trade over the telephone, facsimile or electronic network. There is no central exchange providing a trading system

Parent trade After a buy-side firm sends its allocation instructions, a single bulk trade executed by a sell-side firm (the parent trade) may need to be broken down into a series of smaller trades – Child trades – one for each investor concerned

PMBOK Guide *A Guide to the Project Management Body of Knowledge,* published by the Project Management Institute

PMI The Project Management Institute, which had developed a methodology to manage projects of any kind, including those related to software development and implementation

Portfolio In the context of software development, a portfolio is a suite of projects being undertaken by a function. In the context of investment management, a portfolio is a collection of investments held by an institution or a private individual. The term is sometimes also used as an alternative to "book" or "trading book"

Position The net total of all the purchases of a security less all the sales of the same security. When the position is positive it is said to be a long position, when it is negative it is said to be a short position. Sometimes this term is used interchangeably with "book" or "trading book"

Post-trade publication Also known as regulatory trade reporting. In the EEA, broker–dealers have an obligation to report, in real time, all trades executed by them to the National regulator. Similar requirements exist in other jurisdictions

Present value The value on a given date of a future payment or series of future payments, discounted to reflect the time value of money and other factors such as investment risk

Price limit The maximum price that a buyer of securities is prepared to pay for them, or the minimum price that a seller of securities is prepared to receive for them

Primary market The market for new securities issues. In the primary market the security is purchased directly from the issuer

Prime brokerage A bundled package of services offered by investment banks to hedge funds. The business advantage to a hedge fund of using a prime broker is that the prime broker provides a centralised securities clearing facility for the hedge fund, and the hedge fund's collateral requirements are netted across all deals handled by the prime broker. The prime broker benefits by earning fees ("spreads") on financing the client's long and short cash and security positions, and by charging, in some cases, fees for clearing and/or other services

PRINCE2 A methodology to manage projects of any kind, including those related to software development and implementation

Principal amount   The quantity of a bond trade or bond issue. Also known as face value

Principal value   The result of a quantity * price calculation

Principal trade   A securities trade where the sell-side firm sells (or buys) stock to (from) its customer from its own trading book, and its remuneration consists of the spread between the bid and offer prices

Private client stockbroker   A stock exchange member firm that specialises in serving private individuals

Production outsourcing   The maintenance and support of IT applications that have already been developed

Programme   A group of projects that is managed together

Project   A set of inter-related and controlled activities with start and finish dates, undertaken to achieve a unique objective conforming to specific requirements, including the restraints of time, cost and resources

Project brief   A document produced in the early stages of a project that describes, in outline, what the project is attempting to achieve and the business justification for doing it

Project initiation document (PID)   A logical document whose purpose is to bring together the key information needed to start the project on a sound basis, and to convey that information to all concerned with the project

Project management   The discipline of organising and managing resources (e.g. people) in such a way that the project is completed within defined scope, quality, time and cost constraints

Project Management Institute   A professional body formed in 1969 whose objective is to serve the interest of the project management industry. The premise of PMI is that the tools and techniques of project management are common even among the widespread application of projects from the software industry to the construction industry

Project manager   The individual responsible for delivering the project

Project risk   The risk that a business change project is delivered late and/or over budget or has to be abandoned

Project sponsor   Normally, the senior executive that instigated a business change and who is responsible to the business for the success of the project

Prototyping   A form of iterative/incremental software development based in building a model (or prototype) in order to test various aspects of a design, illustrate ideas or features and gather early user feedback

PTM levy   A charge automatically imposed on investors, and collected by their brokers, when they sell or buy shares with an aggregate value in excess of £10 000. The charge is £1, and the money raised goes to the Panel of Takeovers and Mergers

Public offering   See "Initial public offering"

Put option   See "Option"

Quote-driven markets   A stock exchange trading system where some of the exchange's member firms take on the obligation of always making a two-way price in each of the stocks in which they make markets. These firms are therefore known as market makers

Realised P&L   P&L that arises as a result of selling securities

Reconciliation   The process of proving that an organisation's books and records are accurate

Record date   The date on which the share register is frozen for the calculation of the dividend payments to be paid on the next dividend date

Reference rate   See "Benchmark interest rate"

Register   The record of ownership of a company's shares maintained by a registrar

Registrar   An agent employed by a corporation or mutual fund to maintain shareholder records, including purchases, sales and account balances. The registrar is also responsible for the payment of dividends to shareholders and for the management of corporate actions. Also known as transfer agent

Regression testing   After modifying software, either for a change in functionality or to fix defects, a regression test reruns previously successful tests on the modified software to ensure that the modifications haven't unintentionally caused a *regression* of previous functionality

Regulatory news service   A service that transmits regulatory and non-regulatory information published by companies and other securities issuers allowing them to comply with local market transparency legislation

Regulatory trade reporting   Also known as post-trade publication. In the EEA, broker/ dealers have an obligation to report, in real time, all trades executed by them to the national regulator. Similar requirements exist in other jurisdictions

Repo   Repos – sale and repurchase agreements – are transactions where Party A lends money to Party B provided that Party B provides Party A with collateral in the form of government bonds

Repo rate   The interest rate of a repo transaction

Reputational risk   Damage to an organisation through loss of its reputation or standing

Request for proposal (RFP)   An invitation for suppliers, through a bidding process, to bid on a specific product or service. An RFP is usually part of a complex sales process, also known as enterprise sales

Retail service Provider (RSP)   In the context of the London Stock Exchange, an RSP is an automated quoting system similar to a computerised market maker – it is electronically connected to brokers who normally request quotes from several RSPs and trade on the best price

Reverse repo   The repo transaction seen from the point of view of the purchaser of stock/ lender of cash

RFP   See "Request for proposal"

Riba   Islamic finance term for interest or usury

Rights issue   A form of corporate action where the company offers existing shareholders the rights to acquire new shares in the company at a discounted price

Safe custody service   The service provided by a custodian bank

Sale and repurchase agreement   See "Repo"

Secondary market   A market in which an investor purchases a security from another investor rather than the issuer, subsequent to the original issuance in the primary market. Also called aftermarket

Securities   Equities and bonds

SEDOL code   SEDOL stands for Stock Exchange Daily Official List, a list of security identifiers used in the United Kingdom and Ireland for clearing purposes. The codes are assigned by the London Stock Exchange, on request by the security issuer. SEDOLs serve as the ISIN for all securities issued in the United Kingdom and are therefore part of the security's ISIN as well. Although SEDOL was to have been superseded by ISIN, problems with the ISIN system have since forced a reversal of this decision. In particular, a single ISIN is used to identify the shares of a company no matter what exchange it is being traded on, making it impossible to specify a trade on a particular exchange or currency.

For instance, Chrysler trades on 22 different exchanges worldwide, and is priced in five different currencies. An expanded ISIN standard is currently being formulated to address this problem

Sell-side firms   Investment banks and stock exchange firms that execute orders on behalf of investors

Service level agreement   Service level agreement (SLA) is that part of a service contract in which a certain level of service is agreed upon. Level of service in this context refers to both the quality of the service and the time deadlines for performing the service. It may also specify penalties to be paid by either party if the level of service provided fails to reach the minimum standards in the agreement for an extended period of time

SETS   An order-driven trading system operated by the London Stock Exchange

Settle within tolerance   In determining whether instructions match, the settlement agent usually has the ability to "settle within tolerance". That is to say, if the instructions match in every respect apart from a minor difference in the cash consideration, then the agent will settle the trade using the cash figure supplied by the seller

Settlement   The process where the buyer pays the proceeds of the trade and receives legal title to the item it has purchased, while the seller receives the proceeds of the trade and has to deliver the item it has sold to the buyer

Settlement agents   CSDs, ICSDs, clearing houses and custodian banks may be collectively referred to as "settlement agents"

Settlement date   The date that a deal actually does settle, as distinct from value date, which is the date that it should settle

Settlement dated position   The net quantity of an instrument or contract bought or sold that has settled on or before today

Share certificate   A document issued by a registrar that provides evidence of ownership of securities and is sent to the holder of those securities shortly after purchase

Shareholders' equity   Assets less liabilities

Sharia Supervisory Board   A group of Sharia scholars with relevant knowledge of the financial services industry. It is this board that decides what products may be offered to customers by an Islamic bank or a conventional bank that provides an "Islamic window". The board also regulates how those products are to be financed by the institution offering them, and what types of instruments (such as derivatives) may be used to hedge its positions

Short position   See "Position"

Short selling   Selling more securities than are owned, in other words the creation of a short position

Simple margin   The average return on an FRN for its life compared to the reference interest rate, amortised in a straight line over the remaining life of the bond

Simple yield   The return on the investment on a debt security, not taking compound interest into account

SLA   See "Service level agreement"

Software development lifecycle (SDLC)   A standardised process of developing information systems or applications through the completion of defined steps or phases. Synonyms include systems development lifecycle, systems implementation lifecycle and software implementation lifecycle (SILC)

Software development model   A structure imposed on the development of a software product. Synonyms include software life cycle and software process.

Software maintenance   Software maintenance is an ongoing process, and it includes the continuing support of end users, the correction of errors and updates of the software over time

Software testing   The process used to measure the quality of developed computer software. Software testing standards are covered by ISO 9126

Sovereign risk   The risk of default by a government. A form of issuer risk

SPAN   Standard Portfolio Analysis of Risk (SPAN) is a system for calculating margin requirements for futures and options on futures. It was developed by the Chicago Mercantile Exchange in 1988. SPAN is a portfolio margining method that uses grid simulation. It calculates the likely loss in a set of derivative positions (also called a portfolio) and sets this value as the initial margin payable by the firm holding the portfolio. In this manner, SPAN provides for offsets between correlated positions and enhances margining efficiency

Specialist lending intermediary or SLI   A specialist intermediary that provides liquidity to the stock lending and repo markets

Spiral model   An iterative methodology to manage the designing and building of software applications

Spot transaction   A foreign exchange transaction with value date of two working days after trade date

Spread   The difference between the bid and offer prices

SQL   Commonly expanded as Structured Query Language, SQL is a computer language designed for the retrieval and management of data in relational database management systems, database schema creation and modification, and database object access control management

Stamp duty   A UK tax payable by buyers (but not sellers) of most equity shares listed on the UK markets

Standard settlement instructions or SSIs   Static data that provides details of the settlement agents used by both the firm and its clients

Standby server   A spare server that is brought into use when the production server for one or more applications is lost. Also known as the DR server

Static data   Information about the firm, its trading parties and the instruments it trades. Alternatively defined as the store of information that is used to determine the appropriate actions necessary to ensure successful processing of a trade

Static data repository   A system that consolidates the firm's view of static data and feeds it to all the other systems in the configuration

Stock exchange   See "investment exchange"

Stock loan   The process of the lending of securities by one party to another. The terms of the loan will be governed by a "securities lending agreement", which requires that the borrower provide the lender with collateral, in the form of cash, other securities or a letter of credit of value equal to or greater than the loaned securities. As payment for the loan, the parties negotiate a fee, quoted as an annualised percentage of the value of the loaned securities. If the agreed form of collateral is cash, then the fee may be quoted as a "rebate", meaning that the lender will earn all of the interest which accrues on the cash collateral, and will "rebate" an agreed rate of interest to the borrower

Stock record   A system of double-entry bookkeeping that accounts on one side for the ownership of securities and on the other side for the location of the stock

Stock split   A type of corporate action where the total number of shares in issue is increased, and the additional shares are given to existing shareholders in proportion to their existing shareholding free of cost

Stock transfer form   A form submitted to a registrar to change the details of the name on a register

Stop loss   A stop loss order is an order given to a sell-side firm to sell a security if its price falls to a particular level

Straight-through-processing or STP   Working practices and systems that enable transactions to move seamlessly through the processing cycle, without manual intervention or redundant handling

Stress testing   The practice of testing the VaR model against "extreme" market conditions

Strike price   The price at which an option will be exercised

Subprime   Subprime lending is the practice of making loans to borrowers who do not qualify for the best market interest rates because of their deficient credit history. It includes a variety of credit instruments, including subprime mortgages, subprime car loans, and subprime credit cards

Sukuk   (Arabic, "legal instrument, deed, check") The Arabic name for a financial certificate but can be seen as an Islamic equivalent of bond. However, fixed income, interest bearing bonds are not permissible in Islam, hence Sukuks are securities that comply with the Islamic law and its investment principles, which prohibits the charging or paying of interest

Swap   Derivative products that are used to alter the exposure of investment portfolios, or any series of cash flows. The most common kind of swap is an interest rate swap

SWIFT   The Society for Worldwide Interbank Financial Transfers (SWIFT) is an industry-owned utility that operates a secure telecommunications network, and also designs message standards for communications between market players

SWIFT Gateway   A term used to describe software applications that are used to access the SWIFT network, and which have SWIFTNet Link embedded within them

SWIFTAlliance   A SWIFT Gateway product supplied by SWIFT

SWIFTNet Link   A suite of software products, developed by SWIFT that ensures technical interoperability between SWIFT users by providing the minimal functionality required to communicate over these services. It is supplied both to SWIFT member firms directly, and also to software vendors who are able to embed it in their own products.

SWIFTNet PKI   The security component of SWIFTNet Link that uses digital certificates to provide the highest levels of authentication of institutions, end users and servers

System integration testing   Verifying that a system is integrated to any external or third-party systems defined in the system requirements

System testing   Testing a completely integrated system to verify that it meets its requirements

Systematic internaliser   A firm which on a frequent and systematic basis deals on its own account by executing client orders which are outside the "multilateral trading facility" (MTF) or exchanges

Tax sheltered investments   Investments that are managed in such a way as to provide a tax benefit for the investor. For example, in the United Kingdom private individuals may hold some of their investments in an individual savings account (ISA) that frees them from the obligation to pay capital gains tax when those investments are sold; or they may hold some assets in a self invested personal pension plan (SIPP). All contributions to a SIPP are exempt from UK income tax. Similar facilities are offered in other countries; for example, in the

United States a 401(k) plan allows a worker to save for retirement while deferring income taxes on the saved money and earnings until withdrawal

Test case   A set of conditions or variables under which a tester will determine if a requirement or use case upon an application is partially or fully satisfied

Test scenario   A number of similar or linked test cases

Test script   A description of the input data to be entered and the output results to be inspected for a particular test case

Time loans and deposits   Money market loans and deposits with maturity dates agreed on trade date

Timely execution   An obligation on the firm executing an order to select the most opportune time to execute that order

Trade agreement   The processes of trade confirmation, affirmation and allocation

Trade date   The date that a deal is carried out

Trade dated position   The net quantity of an instrument or contract bought or sold up to and including the most recent trade

Trading book   See "Book"

Trading party   Any kind of institution or individual that trades with one firm is a "trading party" of that firm. Trading parties include both counterparties and clients

Transaction risk   A form of currency risk – the risk that particular transactions are adversely affected by exchange rate movements

Transfer agent   See "registrar"

Translation risk   A form of currency risk – the risk that foreign currency assets held on the balance sheet decline due to exchange rate movements

Transmission control protocol   One of the core protocols of the Internet protocol suite. TCP provides reliable, in-order delivery of a stream of bytes, making it suitable for applications like file transfer and email. It is so important in the Internet protocol suite that sometimes the entire suite is referred to as "the TCP/IP protocol suite"

TRAX2   A central matching engine provided by the International Capital Markets Association

Tri-party repo   A repo where a settlement agent acts as the "third party" custodian for the securities held as collateral. Instead of delivering the securities to the buyer, the seller delivers them to the third party which acts as the buyer's custodian

Underlying instrument   An underlying instrument is a security (such as a stock) or other type of financial product (such as a stock index or futures contract) whose value determines the value of a derivative investment or product. For example, if you own a stock option, the stock you have the right to buy or sell according to the terms of that option is the option's underlying instrument. Underlying instruments may also be called underlying products, underlying interest, underlying investment or the cash instrument

Unit testing   Testing of the minimal software component or module

Unrealised P&L   P&L that arises as a result of the mark-to-market process

Use case   A means of documenting requirements. Each use case provides one or more *scenarios* that convey how the system should interact with the end user or another system to achieve a specific business goal. Use cases typically avoid technical jargon, preferring instead the language of the end user

User acceptance testing   Testing conducted by the end user, customer, or client to validate whether or not to accept the product

Value at Risk   Value at Risk (VaR) is an estimate – not a precise measurement – of how the market value of an asset or of a portfolio of assets is likely to decrease over a certain time period (usually over one day or 10 days) under usual conditions. It is typically used by security houses or investment banks to measure the market risk of their asset portfolios (market value at risk), but is actually a very general concept that has broad application

Value date   The date that a deal is expected to settle – i.e. the date that the seller delivers securities and the buyer pays for them

Value dated position   The net quantity of an instrument or contract bought or sold where value date is equal to or earlier than today

VaR   See "Value at Risk"

Variation margin   See Maintenance margin

Version control systems   Software applications that manage multiple revisions of the same unit of information, such as a program or a unit of documentation

Volatility   The relative rate at which the price of a security moves up and down. Volatility is found by calculating the annualised standard deviation of daily change in price. If the price of a stock moves up and down rapidly over short time periods, it has high volatility. If the price almost never changes, it has low volatility

Volatility risk   A form of market risk. The risk in the value of options portfolios due to the unpredictable changes in the volatility of the underlying asset

Volume testing (or load testing)   Testing a software application for a certain data volume

Warm standby   A standby server that is kept synchronised with the production server by processes such as log shipping

Warrant   A security that entitles the holder to buy stock of the company that issued it at a specified price, which is much higher than the stock price at time of issue

Waterfall model   A methodology to manage the designing and building of software applications

Weighted average price   A method of calculating the price of a position, used in a mark-to-market calculation

Wiki   Computer software that allows users to easily create, edit and link web pages. Wikis are often used to create collaborative websites, power community websites, and are increasingly being installed by businesses to provide affordable and effective intranets or for use in knowledge management

Work package   A subset of a project that can be assigned to a specific party for execution

Workflow applications   Systems that manage tasks such as automatic routing, partially automated processing and integration between different functional software applications and hardware systems that contribute to the value-addition process underlying the workflow

XML   A flexible way to create common information formats and share both the format and the data on the World Wide Web, intranets, and elsewhere. XML is a formal recommendation from the World Wide Web Consortium (W3C) similar to the language of today's web pages, the Hypertext Markup Language (HTML)

Yield curve   The relation between the interest rate (or cost of borrowing) and the time to original maturity of the debt for a given borrower in a given currency

Yield to Maturity   See "Gross redemption yield"

Zero coupon bond   A Bond that does not pay regular interest. Instead it is issued at a deep discount to it's final redemption value

Index

Index compiled by Terry Halliday